THE COLONIALS
IN
SOUTH AFRICA
1899 – 1902

*BEING THE SERVICES
OF THE VARIOUS IRREGULAR CORPS
RAISED IN IN SOUTH AFRICA
AND THE CONTINGENTS FROM
AUSTRALIA, CANADA, NEW ZEALAND,
INDIA AND CEYLON
TOGETHER WITH DETAILS OF
THOSE MENTIONED IN DESPATCHES
WITH RELATED HONOURS AND AWARDS.*

JOHN STIRLING
CAPTAIN, 7TH VOLUNTEER BATTALION, THE ROYAL SCOTS

THE NAVAL & MILITARY PRESS LTD
www.naval-military-press.com

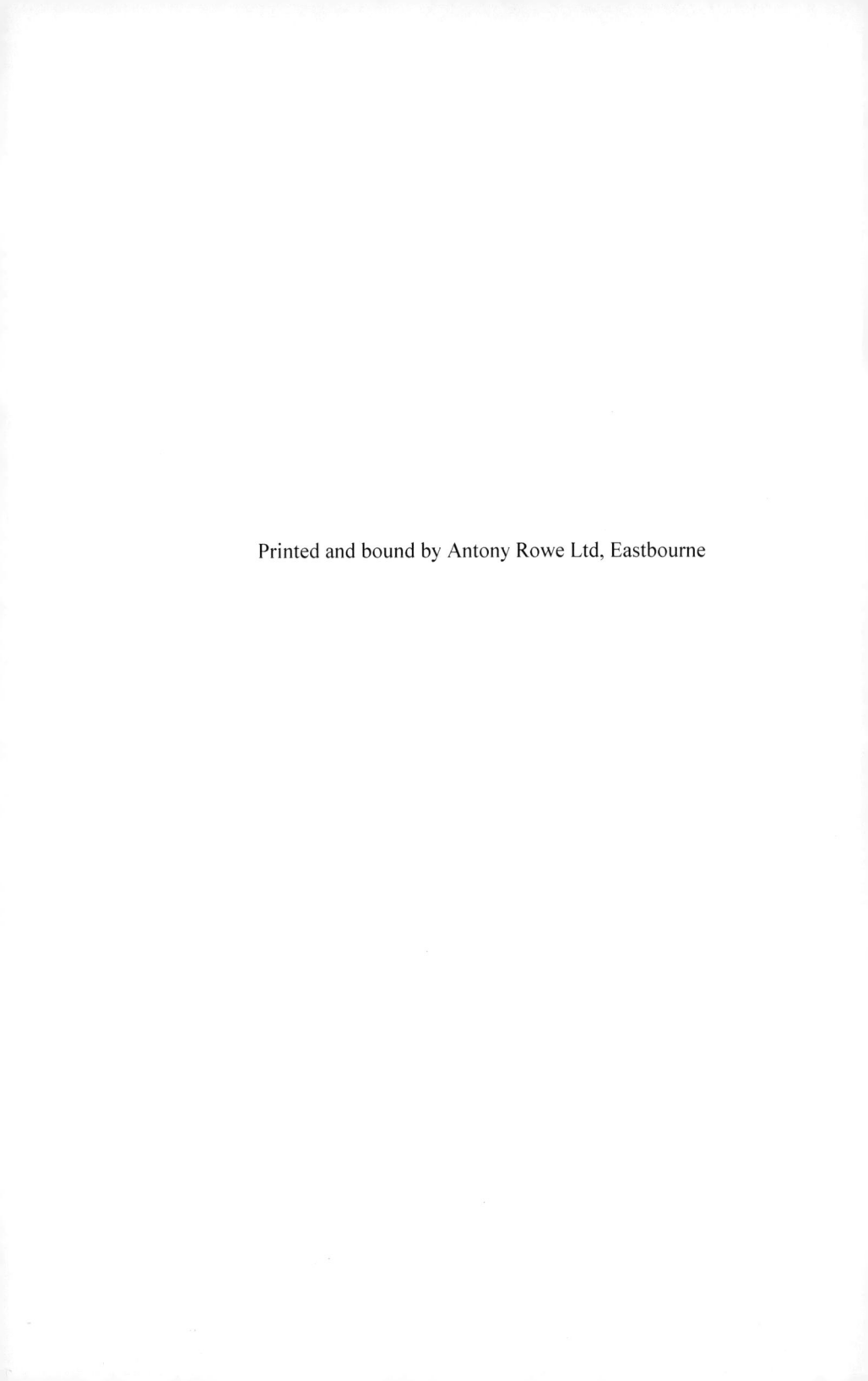

Printed and bound by Antony Rowe Ltd, Eastbourne

THE COLONIALS IN SOUTH AFRICA
1899–1902

*TO THE MEMORY OF
THE FALLEN*

CONTENTS.

	PAGE
INTRODUCTION	ix
CORPS RAISED IN SOUTH AFRICA	1
THE CANADIAN CONTINGENTS	298
LUMSDEN'S HORSE	332
CEYLON MOUNTED INFANTRY	335
NEW ZEALAND CONTINGENTS	337
NEW SOUTH WALES CONTINGENTS	372
VICTORIAN CONTINGENTS	413
QUEENSLAND CONTINGENTS	435
SOUTH AUSTRALIAN CONTINGENTS	451
THE WEST AUSTRALIAN CONTINGENTS	465
TASMANIAN CONTINGENTS	480
THE 4TH REGIMENT IMPERIAL BUSHMEN	490
DOYLE'S SCOUTS	492
COMMONWEALTH TROOPS	493
INTELLIGENCE DEPARTMENT	494
INDEX	495

INTRODUCTION.

WHEN the Author published his 'Our Regiments in South Africa, 1899-1902,' which gave a brief account of the work, in the war, of each regular battalion of infantry, regiment of cavalry, and battery of artillery, he remarked in the Preface that "Some account of the doings of the Colonials should, and may yet, be put together." Some reviewers, especially those interested in the Colonies, encouraged him to carry out the idea thus hinted at, and the present volume is the result of that encouragement.

No attempt has been made to write a detailed account of the work of each corps, but it has been the Author's aim to give a fair idea of the value of the services of each. Where it has been possible to find or get the views of a British regular officer on the worth of such services these views are given, for two reasons — (1) A Colonial corps must realise that such opinions carry infinitely more weight than anything said about them by themselves or by correspondents who were specially interested in their doings; (2) Some regular officers, chiefly among those who did not take part in the campaign, have written and spoken in a way which shows clearly that they

x *Introduction*

have failed to appreciate the importance of the part played by the irregulars. It is well to answer these officers from the mouths of their brethren in the profession of arms.

The book may help to remind some people at home how much we were indebted to the Colonies, including South Africa, for the assistance which they gave. It is proverbially easy to remember what we have given and to forget what we have received. It would be foolish to blink the fact that without the irregulars the war would never have been ended when it was. The mounted troops of the regular army were a mere fraction of what it was found to be necessary to employ. Civilian Britain supplied the Yeomanry, the Colonials provided the remainder of the mounted irregulars.

Colonel Adye, in his evidence before the War Commission, said that the total of the South African irregulars [1] — infantry, mounted, and artillery — was between 50,000 and 60,000, excluding re-engaged men, say 50,000

The contributions from over-sea Colonies were—

Australia 16,415
New Zealand . . . 6,513
Canada, approximately . . 6,500
India and Ceylon, approximately . 500
                                    ——————
                                    79,928

Thus we had in the field about 80,000 men furnished by the Colonies and Dependencies of Britain.

[1] Lord Roberts, in a speech in the House of Lords, said, "No less than 46,858 South African Colonials took part in the war." Of these, 3080 were killed or died of wounds or disease, and 3333 were wounded.

That these great numbers of irregulars were necessary to bring the war to a successful conclusion, and that this class of troops did fine work, even when making attacks as at Elandslaagte or about Dordrecht, or repelling them as at Wagon Hill, Spion Kop, or Eland's River, are facts beyond any possibility of doubt; and one would imagine that with such facts staring him in the face, any Minister responsible for the defence of the Empire would hesitate before embarking on a policy which would diminish the numbers of the auxiliary forces at home; but since the war closed we have seen such a policy seriously adumbrated. South Africa and Manchuria have both taught that numbers are indispensable, and if Britain is ever engaged in a war with an opponent of anything like equal strength, her generals will, as the War Commission pointed out, require numbers far in excess of the regular army and its proper reserve, and they will find that the men who, for some years before such a war, shall have learned to shoot and to drill,—in other words, such men as our average volunteer in his third year,— will be of very slightly less value than those reservists who, it may be, have been civilians for several years. Many officers, who have not commanded anything but regular troops, reiterate the opinion that discipline will be lacking; but those who have been associated with organised volunteers, or irregulars raised for a special campaign, have generally found that discipline —that is, the state of being earnestly anxious to learn and obey — is the quality in which such troops excel.

Introduction

In compiling the records in this volume, use has been made of the despatches and of what proved to be reliable published accounts; but there were many phases of the campaign with which the generals, historians, or correspondents have barely dealt at all. For information as to these, private accounts furnished by officers in the districts have been relied on. The Author has received help from many quarters, but he is specially indebted to **Major Silburn, D.S.O.**, of the Natal Staff, for much information, some of which has not been published before, regarding events in that Colony; to **Major A. Aytoun, D.S.O.**, Argyll and Sutherland Highlanders, at one time on the Queensland Staff, who commanded a Queensland contingent; to **Lieut.-Colonel Montagu Cradock, C.B.**, for assisting with the accounts of the New Zealanders; to **Major John Birkbeck**, 4th Scottish Rifles, for many bits of information as to events in the extreme west of Cape Colony; to **Major Greenhill-Gardyne**, the Gordon Highlanders, for the same as to events in the north and east of the Transvaal; and to many officers of the Australian Contingents, without whose aid it would have been wellnigh impossible to unravel the history of the "Bushmen." Several General officers have kindly furnished notes regarding the component parts of their respective columns, and many officers have checked or revised the accounts of their own corps. To all these, as to the authors and publishers who have given permission to quote, the Author acknowledges his great indebtedness.

The Colonials in South Africa,

1899-1902.

Corps raised in South Africa.

THE IMPERIAL LIGHT HORSE.

APART from the question of seniority,—that is, the relative dates of birth of the various corps,—it is unlikely that any one will be found to deny the outstanding claims of the I.L.H. to the first chapter in a record such as this claims to be. No other corps can point to a prouder history so far as the South African War is concerned; and where many regiments or contingents did splendidly, no other had quite the same opportunities, and none used their chances to finer purpose.

The inception of the I.L.H. took place at Pietermaritzburg in September 1899, when war was a practical certainty. The word "Uitlander" has well-nigh been forgotten, but between 1895 and 1899 it was in every man's mouth. In September and October of the latter year men who had been resident in the Transvaal, but who had retained their allegiance to Britain, were ordered, with their families and dependents, to leave the country. The scenes on the down-journey need not be recalled. Let us hope both sides will forget them. In Natal many of the Uitlanders had congregated, a workless crew, but keen to be of use to their old flag.

In his evidence before the War Commission, Sir Archibald Hunter, after speaking of the Natal Volunteers, said: "Then the other force was the Imperial Light Horse; they were the picked 1200 men out of about 12,000 refugees from Johannesburg; all the British refugees from Johannesburg were well-to-do men; they were all men getting big wages; they were either mine owners or mine managers, or electrical engineers, experts of one sort or another; many of them were men on the Stock Exchange, lawyers, doctors, solicitors, and very few of them were engaged in trade—shopkeepers and suchlike; and they were all men who either in prospecting, or as contractors, or as wood-merchants, or in one form or another, had done a lot of transport-riding to and fro; they were the pick and the cream of the intelligent men who were going out to South Africa, and, naturally, physically they were very fine. The first time I ever saw them was on the first day I arrived at Pietermaritzburg. It was the first day they had ever been on parade as a regiment; up to that time they had only paraded as squadrons under their squadron leaders; it was the first day that Colonel Chisholme had ever had them under his command. Sir Walter Hely Hutchinson drove up on to the ground, as he wanted to see them, and he asked me to go round and look at them. I had not long come from a tour abroad, where I had seen nothing but the picked guards of Sweden, Denmark, Russia, Prussia, and Saxony, and there was nothing I saw on the Continent then, and nothing I have ever seen here, except the Irish Constabulary, that could put a patch on them. You can tell 'men' when you look at them. Every man was a picture of manhood; he was beaming with intelligence. . . . They were a great success, a most undoubted success. They were the finest corps I have ever seen anywhere in my life."

Sir Archibald overstates the strength of the corps. Doubtless he saw 1200 men, but part of these did not belong to the I.L.H. The strength of the first regiment was 502.

From the appendices to the War Commission Report we learn that on 13th October 1899—that is, the day after the declaration of war—the I.L.H., there stated to number about 350, but actually rather stronger, were stationed at Maritzburg; they were, however, taken to the front within the next few days, and were at once put to a severe test. The Boers had not declared war until their forces were concentrated for the invasion of Natal, and before many days they had crossed the passes, and had begun to overrun the northern and western parts of the colony.

The first reference in despatches to the work of the I.L.H. occurs in Sir George White's despatch of 2nd November 1899, describing the battle of Elandslaagte, which was fought on 21st October. The General states that he ordered Major-General French to move out from Ladysmith at 4 A.M. with five squadrons of the I.L.H. and the Natal Field Battery, followed at 6 A.M. by a half-battalion 1st Manchester Regiment and telegraph companies by rail. The enemy were found, and one squadron of the I.L.H., under Major Woolls-Sampson, moved to the north of them, and the battery opened fire, but the enemy replied with artillery and disclosed his position, which was found too strong. Reinforcements were wired for, and arrived in the early afternoon. General White says (para. 17), "As the reinforcements gradually reached him, Major-General French pushed forward again, throwing out one squadron 5th Lancers and four squadrons I.L.H., under Colonel Chisholme, to the right, to clear a ridge of high ground parallel to the enemy's position, from which he considered that an attack could best be developed. This movement was well carried out, the enemy's advance troops being driven back and the ridge gained." After describing the attack by the infantry—the 1st Manchesters, 1st Devons, and 2nd Gordon Highlanders — General White, at para. 23, said "that the Manchesters and Gordons, with the I.L.H. on their right, continued to press forward, losing but few men, until a point was reached about 1200 yards from the enemy's camp." Here the ridge became bare of cover, but the men, well led, crossed the neck in brilliant style, although the losses were heavy. After the enemy's guns were reached a white flag was shown, but when the British stood up the enemy's fire broke out again, and the attack had to be renewed. The Boers now fled in confusion. "The I.L.H. and the 2nd Gordon Highlanders, who encountered the severest resistance during the progress of the attack, suffered the most severely." The losses of the regiment were 1 officer, Colonel Scott-Chisholme, Squadron Sergeant-Major Cuthbert, and 9 men killed, and 9 officers, namely, Major A. Woolls-Sampson, Capts. John E. Orr and C. H. Mullins, Lieuts. M. W. Currie, A. D. Shore, R. W. R. Barnes, W. Lachlan Forbes, Douglas Campbell, and P. H. Normand, and 34 men wounded. Col. Scott-Chisholme was a Roxburghshire man who, as a captain in the 9th Lancers, had gone through the Afghan War, 1879-80, and had then been twice wounded.

It was no small compliment to the I.L.H. that they had been chosen as the reconnoitring force at this the first engagement of Sir George White and General French. Their conduct showed that the confidence reposed in them was not misplaced. The material value of the work which they did could not be more satisfactorily proved than by the wording of the Gazette which conferred the Victoria Cross on Capt. C. H. Mullins and Capt. R. Johnstone, both of the I.L.H. "On 21st October 1899, at Elandslaagte, at a most critical moment, the advance being momentarily checked, these two officers very gallantly rushed forward under this heavy fire and rallied the men, thus enabling the flanking movement, which decided the fate of the day, to be carried out." On this occasion Capt. Mullins was wounded.

On 24th October Sir George White fought at Rietfontein in order to occupy the attention of the enemy and so prevent them falling on General Yule, who had on the death of General Penn-Symons succeeded to the command of the troops in the north of the colony, and finding that after the battle of Talana Hill there was danger of being cut off from Ladysmith, had decided to retreat to that town. The engagement at Rietfontein was successful in obtaining for Yule's force a retreat unharassed by the enemy. The I.L.H., along with the 5th Lancers, did good service in the action in seizing the ridges south of the Modder Spruit, and they thus protected Sir George's right flank.[1]

[1] Sir George White's despatch of 2nd December 1899.

At Lombard's Kop, on the 30th, the regiment was again engaged, this time chiefly in the centre under Colonel Ian Hamilton, whose troops had little to do except to cover the retirement of Grimwood's Brigade on the right.[1] In this action Sir G. White found that he was not strong enough to drive back the enemy, and the result was that his troops were surrounded in Ladysmith.

During the siege of Ladysmith the regiment had very frequently a prominent part to play. Sir George White's despatch of 23rd March 1900 states that on 3rd November Major Karri-Davies, reconnoitring with four squadrons, found a body of the enemy with one gun on Lancer's Hill, and asked for reinforcements to drive them off. Three cavalry regiments and the 21st Battery were sent to his assistance. The battery quickly silenced the gun. "Believing the enemy were evacuating the hill, the two squadrons of the I.L.H. who were facing Lancer's Hill made a gallant but somewhat ill-advised attempt to occupy it, but though they seized and occupied a portion of the hill the enemy was in too great strength for further progress." The enemy being now strongly reinforced our troops withdrew.

On 7th November Cæsar's Camp was subjected to heavy artillery and long-range rifle fire, and the regiment with the 42nd Battery were sent to reinforce the point attacked.

On the 14th the regiment with the Natal Mounted Volunteers, two cavalry regiments, and two batteries, were sent across the Klip River to work round Rifleman's Ridge. The regiment and the Natal Volunteers seized Star Hill, but General Brocklehurst decided that

[1] Sir George White's despatch of 2nd December 1899.

the enemy's position was too strong, and retired his force.

On the night of 7th December Major-General Sir A. Hunter, with 500 Natal Volunteers, which included 100 Border Mounted Rifles under Colonel Royston, and 100 I.L.H. under Lieut.-Colonel A. H. M. Edwards, with a few guides, engineers, and artillerymen, made his famous sortie to capture and destroy the enemy's artillery on Gun Hill. "Sir A. Hunter's arrangements were excellent throughout, and he was gallantly supported by his small force. Gun Hill was taken, a 6-inch creusot and a 4·7 howitzer were destroyed, and a maxim captured and brought into camp." Sir A. Hunter was most highly praised by Sir G. White, and Colonel Royston, Lieut.-Colonel Edwards, and Major Karri-Davies were specially mentioned in the body of the despatch.

Before dawn on 6th January 1900 the Boers commenced their very determined, but fortunately unsuccessful, attempt to carry Ladysmith by storm. The attack was mainly developed on the southern defences, at Cæsar's Camp and Wagon Hill. The usual garrison of Wagon Hill was composed of three companies 1st King's Royal Rifles and a squadron of the I.L.H. On the evening of the 5th a detachment of the Natal Naval Volunteers, with a 3-pounder Hotchkiss gun, had been sent to Wagon Hill. Two naval guns had also been taken to the foot of the hill, and some sailors, Royal Engineers, and men of the 2nd Gordons had accompanied the latter guns. The attack commenced at 2.30 A.M. "It fell directly on the squadron of I.L.H., under Lieut. G. M. Mathias, and the Volunteer Hotchkiss detachment, under Lieut. E. N. W. Walker, who clung most gallantly to their positions and did invaluable service in holding in check till daylight the Boers who had gained a footing on the hill, within a few yards of them. The extreme south-west point of the hill was similarly held by a small mixed party of bluejackets, Royal Engineers, Gordon Highlanders, and Imperial Light Horse, under Lieut. Digby-Jones, R.E. The remainder of the hill was defended by the companies of 1st Bn. King's Royal Rifles." An officer on the Natal Volunteer staff has informed the writer that at one time the Hotchkiss detachment was driven from their gun. Lieutenant Mathias gallantly ran forward and with the assistance of two of his men pulled the gun under cover. It was probably for this act that Lieutenant Mathias was awarded the D.S.O. long afterwards.

The first reinforcements ordered to Wagon Hill were the remainder of the I.L.H. These reached the hill at 5.10 A.M., "and were at once pushed into action. They pressed forward up to and over the western edge of the flat crest of the hill, to within a few yards of the enemy, who held the opposite edge of the crest. They thus afforded a most welcome relief to the small garrison of the hill, but they themselves suffered very severely in occupying and maintaining their position." Other troops arrived, and several attempts were made to clear the hill, but these failed. Never during the whole war did the Boers show finer courage. About mid-day the fighting slackened, but at 1 P.M. "a fresh assault was made with great suddenness on the extreme south-west of the hill, our men giving way for a moment before the sudden outburst of fire and retiring down the opposite slope. Fortunately the Boers did not immediately occupy the crest, and this gave time for Major Miller-Wallnutt of the Gordons, Lieut. Digby-Jones, R.E., Lieut. Fitzgerald, I.L.H., Gunner Sims, Royal Navy, and several N.C.O.'s of the I.L.H., to rally the men. The top was reoccupied just as the three foremost Boers reached it—the leader being shot by Lieut. Digby-Jones, and the two others by No. 459, Trooper H. Albrecht, I.L.H. Had they survived I should have great pleasure in recommending both Lieut. Digby-Jones and Trooper Albrecht for the V.C. I regret to say that both were killed before the conclusion of the action."[1] At 4.45 P.M., during a storm of wind and rain, our troops were again driven from the south-west point of the hill, but they were again rallied and reoccupied it. At 5 P.M. Lieut.-Colonel Park, with three companies of the 1st Battalion Devonshire Regiment, finally cleared the hill by a magnificent bayonet-charge. Sir George White added: "I desire to draw special attention to the gallantry displayed by all ranks of the I.L.H., some of whom were within 100 yards of the enemy for 15 hours, exposed to a deadly fire. Their losses were terribly heavy, but never for one moment did any of them waver or cease to show a fine example of courage and determination to all who came in contact with them." Towards the close of his despatch Sir George, again, said: "Of the Imperial Light Horse, specially raised in Natal at the commencement of the war, I have already expressed my opinion. No praise can be too great for the gallantry and determination which all ranks of this corps have invariably displayed in action." The accounts given by 'The Times' historian

[1] The Victoria Cross was delivered to the representatives of the deceased officer and trooper.

and other writers regarding the attack of 6th January bear out all that Sir George White said as to the unsurpassable conduct of the corps.

The losses of the regiment on 6th January were— Lieutenants W. F. Adams and J. E. Pakeman, and 23 non-commissioned officers and men killed; and Lieut.-Colonel A. H. M. Edwards, Majors Karri-Davies and D. E. Doveton, Captain Codrington, Lieutenants Richardson, P. H. Normand, and D. Campbell, and 27 men wounded. Major Doveton died of his wounds.

Down to the close of the siege the regiment bore its share of the work and the hardships, now, after 6th January, daily increasing.

Five squadrons of the regiment were under Sir George White in the actions before referred to, and in the defence of Ladysmith. One squadron, "A," raised simultaneously with the others, had been ordered to Estcourt, and was on duty there when the others were sent forward to Ladysmith. "A" Squadron took part in General Hildyard's action at Willow Grange on the night of 22nd November 1899. Along with the other mounted troops, the squadron is said in the official account to have behaved "with much coolness and gallantry" when covering a retirement. They lost 1 killed and 3 wounded. Although no great loss was inflicted on the enemy, the action undoubtedly induced him to give up all thought of invading Lower Natal. The squadron was present in all Sir Redvers Buller's operations for the relief of Ladysmith. At Colenso, 15th December 1899, they were hotly engaged on the right, and lost 4 killed and 7 wounded. In the turning movement, viâ Spion Kop, "A" Squadron was in a composite regiment consisting of themselves, a company of King's Royal Rifles Mounted Infantry, and a squadron of Natal Carbineers. It was this regiment which captured a party of about forty Boers at Acton Homes on 18th January 1900. On the 19th Lieut. A. D. Shore of the I.L.H. was dangerously wounded. He had been wounded at Elandslaagte. The squadron had one trooper wounded. Up to the relief of Ladysmith (see South African Light Horse), this composite regiment, under Major Herbert Gough, did very fine work.

About the middle of April 1900 Sir Archibald Hunter with the Fusilier Brigade, the Irish Brigade, and the I.L.H. were brought round by sea from Natal to Cape Colony, and these troops concentrated near Kimberley. The I.L.H., Lieut.-Colonel A. H. M. Edwards commanding, were chosen to accompany Colonel Mahon on his hazardous march to the relief of Mafeking, the other troops of his column being "M" Battery R.H.A., 4 guns, the Kimberley Mounted Corps, and a composite company of infantry made up of four sections of twenty-five selected men each, from each of the regiments in Barton's Fusilier Brigade. The column assembled at Barkly West on 2nd and 3rd May, and set off on its perilous march on the 4th. On the 5th Sir Archibald Hunter attacked the Boers at Rooidam with the object of allowing the column a free road so far, which object was attained; Vryburg was reached on the 9th. Few Boers were seen till the 13th. Colonel Mahon having learned that the enemy was at Koodoesrand Ridge to block his path, moved off to his own left. In the afternoon the Boers, realising what he had done, came up with the right flank near Maritzani and attacked that flank and at the head of the column. The enemy's attack was favoured by the bush; but the troops did well, and the attackers withdrew with a loss of about

20 killed. Colonel Mahon estimated that the enemy numbered 900, with 4 guns. The British loss was approximately 7 killed and 20 wounded, of whom the I.L.H. lost 6 men killed, Major C. H. Mullins and 14 non-commissioned officers and men wounded. Before dawn on the 14th the column again set off, and reached the Molopo, about eighteen miles east of Mafeking, at 5.30 A.M. on the 15th. At daylight touch was gained with Plumer's column, which had come from the north; Mahon crossed the Molopo, and both forces were now combined under him. At 7.30 A.M. on the 16th the column set its face eastwards, towards the little town whose fate had for seven months engrossed the most anxious attention of the empire. At 1.45 P.M. the I.L.H. on the left front became engaged, and it was seen that the enemy were to oppose the relievers. A fiercely-fought action followed, in which the Boers threatened both flanks and rear and heavily shelled the convoy; but again all behaved splendidly, and about four o'clock the enemy began to give way. This corps had Lieutenant Campbell Ross and two men wounded.

Major A. W. A. Pollock, who accompanied the force, in his 'With Seven Generals in the Boer War,' says, at page 252, "Ground was now being gained continuously by the left wing under the clever leadership of Lieut.-Colonel Edwards, whose own corps, the Imperial Light Horse, led the advance with the skill and courage that they have so consistently displayed throughout the war." After describing the general advance, in which the enemy's centre was pierced and his right driven off the ground before darkness set in, Major Pollock says: "Then the Brigadier wisely decided to halt until the moon had risen, and meanwhile sent forward Major

Karri-Davies with six volunteers of the I.L.H. to announce the victory to Baden-Powell, and report that the relief column would enter Mafeking during the night." The troops entered the town at 3.30 A.M. on the 17th. In his report, dated 23rd May 1900, printed among the despatches, Colonel Mahon praised all the troops, but selected the Royal Horse Artillery and Imperial Light Horse for special mention.

The forces of Mahon and Plumer remained at Mafeking until the 28th, when an order was received that Mahon's force was to join General Hunter at Maribogo. At 3 P.M. the column started, and marching south-east joined Sir Archibald Hunter, and afterwards marched viâ Lichtenburg and Potchefstroom to the Central Transvaal, arriving at Krugersdorp on 18th June. At Lichtenburg Colonel Woolls-Sampson had joined the regiment with a welcome draft. Mahon was now ordered to take his column, including the I.L.H., to Irene, east of Pretoria.[1] In his telegram of 5th July Lord Roberts said, "I have recently inspected Mahon's small force, which did such excellent work in the relief of the Mafeking garrison. The Imperial Light Horse, which I purposely brought from Natal to take part in the expedition, are a most soldierly and workmanlike body of men."

In July Mahon's force was, with others, employed in driving back the Boers who were hanging about the country east of Pretoria, and he was afterwards ordered north of the capital for a similar object. On 6th and 7th July there was severe fighting at Witklip, in the Bronkhorst Spruit district, when the I.L.H. lost Captain Curry and Lieutenant Kirk and 7 men killed, and 8 non-commissioned officers and men wounded. In

[1] Lord Roberts' despatch of 10th October 1900, para. 12.

his telegram of 18th July Lord Roberts said: "One squadron of this distinguished corps pressed [by?] a very superior force of the enemy in a gallant attempt to carry off a wounded comrade, to which is attributable the heavy losses it sustained."

About the middle of July Lord Roberts commenced a further advance eastwards from Pretoria. Mahon's troops, which included the I.L.H., were put under General Ian Hamilton, who commanded a strong force, which, starting on 17th July, marched eastwards on the north of the Delagoa Railway. On the 25th Hamilton occupied Balmoral. On the 27th he started to return to Pretoria to operate against a concentration of Boers in the Rustenburg district. Pretoria was left again on 1st August, and the column throughout the month did much heavy marching and some stiff fighting as at Zilikat's Nek, where the Berkshire Regiment distinguished themselves, and bore heavy losses. After taking part in a pursuit of De Wet, then in progress, Hamilton's force returned to Pretoria, which was reached on 28th August. During the four weeks 400 miles had been covered on low rations.

In August Lord Roberts renewed his advance eastward to join General Buller and the Natal Army about Belfast, and on the 30th Mahon left Pretoria for that district. His force now was "M" Battery Royal Horse Artillery, 3rd Corps of Regular Mounted Infantry, Queensland Mounted Infantry, New Zealand Mounted Rifles, 79th Company Imperial Yeomanry, Imperial Light Horse, and Lumsden's Horse.[1]

On 27th August Buller had thoroughly defeated the Boers at Bergendal, near Belfast, and General French had been ordered to seize Barberton, marching *viâ*

[1] Despatch of 10th October 1900, para. 33.

Carolina. On 3rd September, when Mahon arrived at Belfast, he was ordered to join French at Carolina. This he did on the 5th. French now advanced through most difficult country; very high mountains had to be crossed, several times in face of opposition, but a general who made no mistakes was in command, and Barberton was taken on the 13th. The official despatches do not do sufficient justice to the splendid daring of General French, and the marvellously fine work of the troops on this fighting march; but Mr Goldmann, in his most valuable book, 'With General French and the Cavalry' (Macmillan, 1902), gives a fine account of the fighting, and of the wonderful marches by which the troops and their guns and baggage crossed stupendous mountains by mere tracks. The strength of the regiment with Mahon at this time is put down at 26 officers, 367 men, with 444 horses, and Mr Goldmann frequently refers to their outstanding work. After a very short rest in Barberton the mounted troops pushed towards the north-east, and, as mentioned by Lord Roberts, a detachment of the I.L.H. captured, near French Bob on the 21st, 20 prisoners, 200 rifles, and a quantity of ammunition. On 29th September the regiment left General Mahon's force, marched to the railway, and were shortly afterwards entrained for Pretoria.

In his despatch of 15th November 1900, para. 12, Lord Roberts said: "On 18th October Colonel Woolls-Sampson with the Imperial Light Horse joined Barton at Frederickstad, and on the 20th the camp was attacked, and an engagement ensued. The 2nd Royal Scots Fusiliers had one officer and one man killed, and the Imperial Light Horse 12 men wounded." Barton's force had further heavy fighting on the 23rd, 24th, and

25th, which resulted in the thorough defeat of the Boers, who were driven across the Vaal River. The actual losses of the regiment at Frederickstad were 2 men killed and 8 wounded. The regiment remained for the following eight months in the south and southwest of the Transvaal.

Towards the close of 1900 a second regiment of I.L.H. was raised, and it at once took the field in the Eastern Transvaal. The command of the 2nd Regiment was given to Major D. M'Kenzie, and the "second in command" to Major J. R. Royston, both officers of the Natal Volunteers who had greatly distinguished themselves during the siege of Ladysmith and elsewhere.

In December 1900 and January 1901 the 1st Regiment was operating south of the Megaliesberg under Babington. On 31st December Lieutenant D. Maxwell and 1 trooper were wounded at Haartebeest, and on 6th January there was severe fighting at Naauwpoort, in which the regiment lost Captain T. Yockney and Lieutenant A. Ormond and 20 non-commissioned officers and men killed, and Captain and Adjutant B. M. Glossop (5th Dragoon Guards) and 27 men wounded.

On 7th January 1901 Major C. J. Briggs, King's Dragoon Guards, assumed command of the 1st Regiment—a command which he retained until the close of hostilities. Throughout January and February the regiment was constantly in touch with the enemy, and frequently suffered some losses. In March there was some very heavy fighting.

In his despatch of 8th May 1901, para. 11, Lord Kitchener said : " On the 22nd March a strong patrol of the 1st I.L.H., consisting of 200 men and a pom-pom, was attacked near Geduld by General Delarey with

500 men and 2 guns. The enemy, of whom 11 were killed and 13 wounded, were completely defeated. Commandant Venter was found among the dead, and Field - Cornet Wolmarans, who was severely wounded, fell into our hands." The patrol was commanded by Major Briggs. The I.L.H. lost 6 killed, including Lieutenants J. Ralston and A. R. Halling, and Regimental Sergeant - Major Hurst, and 18 wounded, including Captain J. Donaldson, and Lieutenants J. R. Stone and J. H. Dryden.

On the 23rd and 24th General Babington followed up this action and inflicted a severe defeat on the enemy, capturing 140 prisoners, 3 guns, 6 maxims, many waggons, &c. ; 22 dead and 32 wounded Boers were found on the field. Our losses were 2 killed and 7 wounded. Of these the I.L.H. had 4 wounded. In both these affairs the regiment did splendidly, and many mentions were gained. Other Colonials, notably the New Zealanders, also did work which was highly praised.

The 1st Regiment continued to do much trekking and skirmishing in the Western Transvaal under General Babington and other commanders (see despatch of 8th July 1901 and Appendix). On 17th July a strong force of the enemy, well posted, were attacked, 1 officer and 5 men gaining mention on this occasion for great dash and courage. On the 31st of that month Lieutenant L. S. Sanders and 1 man were killed near Lichtenburg.

In the third quarter of 1901 many troops were taken from the Western Transvaal to other districts,— a movement which doubtless had an important bearing on the disaster suffered by Lord Methuen's slender resources in February and March 1902. The 1st

B

Imperial Light Horse were taken to the north-east of the Orange River Colony.

Since taking the field the 2nd I.L.H. had been almost wholly employed in the Eastern Transvaal, where they had done good work under Major-General Smith-Dorrien, Major-General F. W. Kitchener, and other leaders; while Colonel Woolls-Sampson, acting as Intelligence Officer to Colonel Benson, had gained the praises of the Commander-in-Chief.

The 2nd Regiment had fighting on many occasions and sometimes losses. On 25th January 1901, at Twyfelaar, Major Maude and Lieutenant Briscoe were wounded. On 6th February, when Smith-Dorrien's force was fiercely attacked by Botha at Bothwell, Lake Chrissie, the regiment had 2 killed and 4 wounded. The attack was driven off, the enemy leaving 25 dead. During February and March Smith-Dorrien's column was one of those acting under General French when he swept the Eastern Transvaal, driving the enemy to the borders of Zululand, and capturing all his artillery and many prisoners.

In January 1901 many troops were sent from the Transvaal to Cape Colony in consequence of the re-invasion of the Colony by De Wet's men. About the end of January a portion of the 2nd Regiment I.L.H. was railed from the Eastern Transvaal to the south, and in the beginning of February detachments of I.L.H., South African Light Horse, and Nesbitt's Horse came in contact with the enemy about Colesberg. Between 3rd and 23rd February there was almost constant skirmishing, and many stiffly contested rearguard actions. On the 10th Lieutenant D. Farquharson and two men of the I.L.H. were wounded; one of the men died of his wounds. The enemy was driven to the west of the railway on the 16th, and having failed to cross the Lower Orange he turned east again. On the 24th Lord Kitchener was able to wire: "Plumer reports Colonel Owen, with detachments King's Dragoon Guards, Victorians, and Imperial Light Horse, captured De Wet's 15-pr. and pom-pom. Enemy in full retreat and dispersing. He is being vigorously pursued. De Wet's attempt to invade Cape Colony has evidently completely failed." (See also 1st, 2nd, and 3rd New Zealand and 4th Victorians.)

In his despatch of 8th September 1901, para. 6, Lord Kitchener said, "A third mobile column, which will work from Bethlehem (Orange River Colony) as a centre, has just been organised at Harrismith: it will be under the command of Brigadier-General Sir John Dartnell, and will consist of the two regiments of I.L.H. specially equipped with a view to securing increased mobility." In September it became apparent that Botha was about to attempt a reinvasion of Natal; and in the despatch of 8th October, para. 8, after describing certain operations about the Brandwater Basin, east of Bethlehem, in which the I.L.H. took part, Lord Kitchener mentioned that Brigadier-General Dartnell, with the 2nd I.L.H., was ordered to Eshowe on the Zululand Border to assist in keeping the enemy out of Natal. At para. 9 Lord Kitchener said that the 1st I.L.H. remained to act independently from Bethlehem. "This force which was specially organised with a view to mobility has already justified its existence, and some excellent long-distance raids have been undertaken. The most successful of these took place on the night of the 28th September, when after a circuitous march of

38 miles from Bethlehem Lieut.-Colonel Briggs surrounded the town of Reitz at dawn on the 29th. Here he captured 21 prisoners, &c. His return march, however, was much opposed, and several unsuccessful attempts were made at night by parties of Boers, said to be under De Wet, to surround and rush his force." In the despatch of 8th November, para. 6, Lord Kitchener said, "From Bethlehem Lieut.-Colonel Briggs with the 1st I.L.H. has carried out several long-distance raids in all directions, whereby the country round for a radius of 25 miles has been completely cleared." He also mentioned that the 2nd Regiment had returned by march-route from Zululand to Harrismith on 3rd November. A great converging movement was also foreshadowed, and among the troops to be employed the 1st Regiment was to act from Bethlehem and the 2nd from Harrismith. In the despatch of 8th December the results of that movement are given, but the main body of the enemy, which it was hoped to surround, escaped. Lord Kitchener praised highly the way in which the troops bore the very great strain. About the middle of November both regiments were again in a big operation, but few of the enemy were found. On the 24th the 1st and 2nd Regiments "surprised Laurens' commando between Eland's River Bridge and Bethlehem, killing 2 Boers in their attack and capturing 12 prisoners." This success was followed up on the 27th by a combined force of the 1st and 2nd I.L.H. under Lieut.-Colonel M'Kenzie and Lieut.-Colonel Briggs, in which 24 prisoners, 150 horses, and 800 cattle fell into our hands. The despatch of 8th January 1902 describes further operations under General Elliot, in some of which the I.L.H.

took part. When returning to Eland's River Bridge General Dartnell was hotly attacked. "After leaving Bethlehem on the morning of 18th December the latter officer found himself opposed by a large force of Boers under De Wet, who, occupying a position along the Tyger Kloof Spruit, disputed his further advance, whilst he vigorously assailed General Dartnell's flanks and rearguard; sharp fighting was maintained throughout the day. Every successive attack was gallantly repulsed by the two regiments of the I.L.H. until the approach from Bethlehem of the column under Major-General B. Campbell, who had established signalling communication with General Dartnell during the progress of the fight, finally compelled the enemy, about 3 P.M., to beat a hurried retreat" in the direction of the Langberg. In this engagement Surgeon-Captain T. Crean, Captain G. T. Brierley, Captain W. Jardine, Lieutenant J. O'Hara, and 7 men were wounded. It was in this engagement that Surgeon-Captain Crean gained the Victoria Cross. A few days after this, before dawn on the morning of the 25th December, the enemy surprised and captured the camp of a battalion of Yeomanry at Tweefontein, inflicting great loss. As soon as the disaster was known the I.L.H. were ordered to the spot, but the Boers, who had got a good start, were not overtaken. It says a very great deal for the watchfulness and care of the I.L.H. that they were so long in this difficult country, surrounded by a cunning enemy in great strength, but without giving that enemy a chance of doing damage by surprise. The despatch of 8th February 1902 detailed further operations in the same district, which took place about the end of January, in which substantial loss was inflicted on the enemy. During these some great marching was done; the 2nd Battalion Mounted Infantry (Regulars) covered 82 miles in thirty-four hours, the I.L.H. and other troops performing similar feats of endurance. Between 25th and 29th January 1902 there were some casualties about Newmarket, 3 men being killed and Lieutenant Bamford and several men wounded.

The despatches of 8th March and 8th April describe the great combined drives in the north-east of the Orange River Colony, in which a large number of prisoners—over 1500—were captured. The work of the I.L.H. was specially singled out in the account of the Press Association correspondent. They stopped one very determined rush, when the enemy tried, in the darkness, to break through the line at their part. The 1st lost 4 killed. In the drive from the Vaal to Harrismith about 520 prisoners and 1400 horses fell into the hands of the 1st I.L.H.

In the despatch of 1st June 1902 Lord Kitchener details the operations undertaken in the Western Transvaal to clear that district after the disasters suffered by Lord Methuen. Troops were taken from other districts, and the I.L.H. recrossed the Vaal. On 11th April Colonel Kekewich had heavy fighting. Soon after starting in the morning the advance-guard under Von Donop was attacked: the enemy "advanced rapidly to close quarters in very compact formation, the Boers riding knee to knee, and in many places in two ranks, whilst their attack was supported by a heavy fire from skirmishers on both flanks. Many of the men of our advanced screen in forward positions were ridden over by the enemy, who pressed on rapidly to within 700 yards of the main body and

The Imperial Light Horse 23

convoys, keeping up an incessant magazine-rifle fire from their horses as they approached. Here, however, they were checked by Lieut.-Colonel Greenfell's troops, which were at the head of the main body, the Scottish Horse, 5th I.Y., and South African Constabulary dismounting and moving forward steadily on foot to meet the coming charge. This was the crisis of the fight, and it was one which terminated quickly with the complete repulse of the Boers and the death of their Commandant, Potgeiter, who was conspicuous in leading the attack until he fell, only 90 yards in front of our troops. So far, however, it was only a repulse, but the arrival of Lieut.-Colonel Briggs with the I.L.H., detached upon the enemy's right flank from Sir H. Rawlinson's force, turned the repulse into a rout." Colonel Briggs, hearing the heavy firing, of his own initiative took the I.L.H. to the scene of the action. Fifty-one dead and 40 wounded Boers were found on the ground, and in the subsequent pursuit by the 1st I.L.H. and troops of Colonel Kekewich two 15-pounder guns, one pom-pom, some vehicles, ammunition, and 36 unwounded prisoners were captured.

Further successful drives took place in the southwest Transvaal in which the I.L.H. were engaged. Thus from Elandslaagte to the very last stage of the war did this splendid Volunteer Regiment keep steadily at work. Throughout the whole war they had done nobly; no regular troops could have reached a higher standard, and if they were largely men who had a personal stake in the Transvaal, they did all that men could to assist the mother country in the struggle for the maintenance of British sovereignty in South Africa.

Peace was declared on 1st June. On the 17th, both regiments having been brought into Johannesburg marched past Lord Kitchener, who complimented them and some other distinguished Colonial corps also present. The Commander-in-Chief expressed the hope that he would be able to make arrangements for keeping up the I.L.H. as a permanent volunteer corps.

The foregoing account has been read over by Major Sir W. Codrington and other officers of this distinguished regiment, and the casualties, &c., have been duly checked.

The following are the Honours and Mentions gained by the corps :—

Capt. Mullins and Capt. Johnstone, both 1st Regiment, won the Victoria Cross at Elandslaagte under the circumstances set forth in the text, and as mentioned in the text Trooper H. Albrecht (killed) gained the Cross at Wagon Hill. Surgeon-Captain T. J. Crean, 1st I.L.H., also got the Cross for "during the action with De Wet at Tyger Kloof, December 18, 1901, this officer continued to attend to the wounded in the firing line under a heavy fire at only 150 yards range, after he had himself been wounded, and only desisted when he was hit a second time, and, as it was at first thought, mortally wounded."

MENTIONS IN DESPATCHES.

SIR GEORGE WHITE'S DESPATCHES : *2nd December* 1899.—Col. J. J. Scott-Chisholme (killed in action); Majors A. Woolls-Sampson and W. Karri-Davies; Capts. J. E. Orr, C. H. Mullins, J. C. Knapp (killed in action).

23rd March 1900.—Major D. E. Doveton, died of wounds; Surgeon-Major W. T. F. Davies; Capt. C. H. Fowler; Corporals C. Russell, W. Weir; Major (Local Lieut.-Col.) A. H. M. Edwards, 5th Dragoon Guards, commanding I.L.H., twice — one time for gallant behaviour at Gun Hill; Major Karri-Davies for same; Lt. P. D. Fitzgerald, 11th Hussars, attached I.L.H.

GENERAL BULLER'S DESPATCH : *30th March* 1900.—Lce.-Cpl. A. B. Duirs on several occasions carried out dangerous reconnaissances; Capt. H. Bottomley; Lt. G. T. M. Bridges, R.A., attached; Cpls. E. W. Warby, H. Savory; Lce.-Cpl. W. H. Norton; Tprs. H. London, W. Francis, F. H. Metcalfe.

LORD ROBERTS' DESPATCHES : *2nd April* 1901.—Col. F. Rhodes; Lieut.-

The Imperial Light Horse 25

Col. Woolls-Sampson[1]; Majors H. Bottomley,[2] D. E. Doveton (died of wounds), W. Karri-Davies, C. H. Mullins,[2] Surgeon-Major Davies[3]; Capts. Curry (killed), C. H. Fowler[3]; Lts. D. Huntly, Kirk (killed), P. H. Normand[3]; Cpls. C. H. Russell,[4] H. Savory,[4] E. W. Warby,[4] W. A. Weir,[4] W. H. Norton[4]; Tprs. W. Francis,[4] James,[4] Latham,[4] London,[4] Metcalfe.[4] *4th Sept.* 1901.—Cpl. W. F. Loveland.

LORD KITCHENER'S DESPATCHES : *8th May* 1901.—Major C. J. Briggs, 1st King's Dragoon Guards, commanding I.L.H., exhibited marked ability and coolness in the action of 23rd March, and handled his command well on the two following days. Capt. P. H. Normand, D.S.O., Lts. Dryden and Holbrig, since dead, Capts. G. S. Brierley and Donaldson, for excellent services rendered in capture of Delarey's guns and convoy on March 24th. Capt. W. R. Codrington, 11th Hussars, attached, an officer of great promise, has several times done good work when placed in command of detached parties. Tpr. D. Brown, promoted Cpl., carried Sgt. Currie, whose horse had been shot, out of close range under fire on 22nd March. Tpr. Despard, promoted Cpl., although wounded in two places continued to fire until surrounded, same date. Sgt. Osborne[4] went back under heavy fire and took out of action Tpr. Law, who would otherwise have been captured.

8th July 1901.—Lt. D. L. Maxwell,[3] on December 31, at Hartebeestefontein, though wounded, remained with his patrol till he fainted through loss of blood. Sgt. E. A. Belton, for good service in Eastern Transvaal during General French's operations, February, March, and April 1901.

8th August 1901.—Lt. B. F. Webb, recommended for V.C., on July 17th, at Bultfontein, charged Boer position with only twelve men and took it, shooting two Boers himself with his pistol. Cpl. W. G. Hughes, promoted Sgt., Tprs. T. Kelly, M. Symonds, D. Johnston, promoted Cpls., the first men up in charge on a position held by a strong force of the enemy at Doornbult, Western Transvaal, July 17. Tpr. J. B. Rowell, promoted Cpl., in charge of pack-horse with ammunition, and accidentally left behind when patrol retired ; though hotly pursued by enemy, who at one time got within fifty yards of him, and heavily fired on, stuck to his pack-horse and brought it out safely. Tpr. J. P. Smith, at Doornbult, Western Transvaal, July 17, a party retiring and one man being dismounted, he, at great personal risk, returned and took him out of action on his own horse, enemy at time within 400 yards.

8th October 1901.—Cpl. R. Waldeck, 2nd Regt., promoted Sgt., gallantry in action on Oliphant's River, July 30, when troop attacked by very superior numbers.

8th December 1901.—Capts. W. Jardine,[3] J. Donaldson,[3] on Sept. 27, were conspicuous for their coolness and promptitude in fighting in Reitz district. Tpr. R. E. Search, promoted Cpl., in action near Reitz, Sept. 28, seeing enemy making for important position, galloped along across their

---

[1] Awarded C.B.   [2] Awarded C.M.G.
[3] ,,   D.S.O.   [4] ,,   Distinguished Conduct Medal.

front and occupied it against them till reinforced, and then continued to fight though wounded. Cpl. R. F. Matheson, promoted Sgt., Tpr. A. J. Phillips, promoted Cpl., for good capture of three armed Boers, September 22.

8th March 1902.—Capts. G. T. Brierley and W. Jardine, both 1st I.L.H., for good work in holding their position at Langberg, December 18. Tpr. H. D. Osmond, promoted Cpl., for single-handed capture of eight armed Boers in the Langberg, January 11.

1st June 1902.—Lt. B. Nicholson,[1] with Tprs. W. G. Forder, W. A. Allen, E. Eldridge, promoted Cpls., captured eighteen Boers at Yser Spruit, April 15, after a long chase.

23rd June.—1st. Majors W. Karri-Davies, H. A. Rogers ; Lt. S. Tryon ; Regimental Sgt.-Major Harrison,[2] 19th Hussars ; Squadron Sgt.-Majors R. Bombal, T. Sullivan ; Sgts. J. Cranna, T. Curry. 2nd. Lieut.-Col. D. Mackenzie,[3] C.M.G. ; Major D. W. Mackay ; Capt. J. C. Pollock ; Regimental Sgt.-Major Sutherland [2] ; Sgt. H. Miller ; Ptes. C. K. Mackenzie, A. Mansen. Lieut.-Col. J. R. Royston, who had served with the Natal Volunteers, had commanded the 5th and 6th West Australians, and for a time the 2nd I.L.H., was awarded the D.S.O. Col. Woolls-Sampson, C.B., was gazetted to have rank of colonel in the army. Local Lieut.-Col. C. J. Briggs, promoted Brevet Lieut.-Col. Lt. G. M. Mathias, mentioned in the body of Sir George White's despatch regarding the attack on Ladysmith on 6th January 1900, was awarded the D.S.O.

NATAL VOLUNTEERS, POLICE, AND GUIDES.

THE Natal Volunteers are not a creation of yesterday. They were constituted under Ordinance as far back as 1854. In 1873, 300 of the force took part in the Langalibalele Expedition and suffered casualties. The whole force was called out in 1879 to take part in the Zulu War, and at Isandhlwana Lieutenant G. Shepstone and 32 volunteers were killed. In 1896 a new Volunteer Act was passed; members became partially paid and had to undergo ten days' continuous

[1] Awarded D.S.O.   [2] Awarded D.C.M.   [3] Awarded C.B.

training. Colonel William Royston was appointed Commandant, and Lieut.-Colonel Bru-de-Wold Chief Staff Officer. Colonel Royston had taken part in the war service above noted. He had passed through the ranks and knew what his force should be able to do and how they could be best taught. To the unwearied exertions of these two officers, and to the fact that the material was good, must be given the credit for the efficient state in which the force was found when the war broke out,—a state which enabled it to do work which could not have been excelled by regulars.

On 28th September 1899 the whole of the volunteers in the colony were ordered to mobilise, ostensibly for ten days' training, and before the actual declaration of war much good work had been done. In the beginning of October the volunteers and police were distributed as follows :—[1]

Corps and Commanding Officer.	Strength— all ranks.	Station.
Natal Field Artillery (Captain Daniel Taylor)	123 and six 2·5 guns	Ladysmith.
Border Mounted Rifles (Major J. F. Rethman)	286	Ladysmith and Acton Homes.
Natal Carbineers (Lieut.-Col. E. M. Greene)	508	3 squad. Ladysmith. 1 troop Dundee. 1 troop Colenso.
Natal Mounted Rifles (Major R. W. Evans)	220	Ladysmith.
Umvoti Mounted Rifles (Major George Leuchars)	89	Helpmakaar District. 1 troop southern border.
Natal Naval Volunteers (Commander G. Tatum)	123	Ladysmith, 1 R.M.L. 9-pr., 2 Hotchkiss. Estcourt, 15 men, 1 gun. Colenso, 30 men, 2 guns.

---

[1] Appendices to War Commission Report, p. 104, and information supplied by Major P. A. Silburn, D.S.O., Natal Staff.

Corps and Commanding Officer.	Strength—all ranks.	Station.
Durban Light Infantry (Lieut.-Col. T. M'Cubbin)	416	Colenso.
Natal Royal Rifles (Captain A. Williamson)	150	Estcourt.
Natal Bridge Guards (Raised for war)	61	Various Stations.
Natal Volunteer Medical Corps (Major J. Hyslop)	78	Chiefly Ladysmith.
Natal Police	317	Scattered.

A Volunteer Veterinary Corps, under Major Watkins-Pitchford, was raised from veterinary surgeons in the Colony, strength 10, chiefly in Ladysmith. A Hotchkiss gun detachment was in October raised on very short notice at Pietermaritzburg for service in the war, mobilised 21 strong, guns two 3-pounder Hotchkiss drawn by mules, sent to Ladysmith. There was also organised a transport and commissariat corps, Captain G. Geddie, 2 officers, 6 men, and 300 mules; other drivers were enlisted.

As was afterwards stated in despatches, one or other of these bodies was represented in every action fought in the Colony.

On 2nd October the Natal Carbineers were ordered to patrol the Free State Border and observe the passes, and within the next few days the cyclists of the Durban Light Infantry were patrolling from Colenso to Springfield, covering 80 miles on bad roads in twelve hours. Along with the Natal Naval Volunteers the Durban Regiment was employed in building forts near Colenso. The Umvoti Mounted Rifles were watching the drifts lower down the Tugela,—an invaluable service, which they performed for many months; other bodies were on outpost duty.

On 12th October war was declared, the enemy entered Natal, and their movements were reported by the Carbineers. When Major Taunton reported the enemy's movement, the Intelligence Department discredited this, and he had to send a patrol to locate, or rather look into, the hostile laager. On the 17th, No. 1 squadron of the Border M.R., under Captain Royston, was fired on at the foot of the Tintwa Pass; and on the same night Captain Wales, Volunteer Staff, with a troop of Natal M.R., set out to patrol the Waschbank Valley, passing through several parties of Boers and covering 126 miles in forty-eight hours. On the 18th Sir George White asked the Natal M.R. for a bodyguard of 24 non-commissioned officers and men; Captain F. S. Tatham of the Carbineers was chosen as commander. On this date the enemy advanced in force, and the Border M.R. from Acton Homes and the Carbineers from Van Reenen's and other passes had, according to the G.O.C.'s orders, to retire nearer to Ladysmith. On the 20th the Umvoti men reported heavy firing at Dundee. This was, of course, the severe engagement fought by General Penn-Symons in order to drive the enemy off Talana Hill, which commanded his camp. It will be remembered that the general was mortally wounded. His successor, Brigadier-General Yule, finding that he was being threatened by very superior forces, started at 9 P.M. on the 22nd to withdraw his force to Ladysmith. Colonel Dartnell, chief-commissioner of the Natal Police, was on the staff of General Penn-Symons at Talana Hill, and was beside the general when he fell. Two of the police acting as orderlies to Colonel Dartnell were wounded in the engagement. On the 20th No. 4 squadron of the Carbineers captured four Boer scouts.

On the 21st General French and Sir George White fought the battle of Elandslaagte (see Imperial Light Horse). In his despatch of 2nd November 1899, para. 14, Sir George mentioned that before that battle the Natal Field Battery moved out with General French at 4 A.M.; some of the Natal M.R. and Carbineers were also with him. When the enemy were found near the station the battery opened fire, but the position was strong, and the little guns were outranged; reinforcements had therefore to be got. Before the main action commenced one squadron from each of the 5th Lancers, 5th Dragoon Guards, and Natal M.R. were sent out to turn the enemy's right flank and harass his rear. Two squadrons of the Natal M.R. took part in the final pursuit.

On the night of the 21st Sergeant Schroeder and Corporal Jones of the Umvoti M.R. bore the good news of the Elandslaagte victory to General Yule; to reach him they had to pass through large bodies of the enemy. On the 22nd Surgeon Hornabrook, medical officer of the Natal M.R., when seven miles out from Ladysmith, met a Boer patrol of 25 men. Although alone he shouted to the party to surrender, as the Boers had been defeated and they were surrounded. The demand was promptly obeyed, the party giving up their rifles to three of their own number, and the triumphant doctor led his 25 prisoners into Elandslaagte Station. If this tale were not vouched for by the Natal Staff it would probably not be credited.

On the 23rd Colonel Royston got permission to send out Captain Wales and 24 of the Carbineers (Dundee troop), who had themselves arrived in Ladysmith from Dundee on the 22nd. Captain Wales was to endeavour to come into contact with Yule; he found the column at Van Tonder's Pass, to which place it had been led by Colonel Dartnell.

In his despatch of 2nd December 1899 Sir George White mentions that the Natal Mounted Volunteers were with him at Rietfontein on 24th October (see Imperial Light Horse). After the engagement was well developed "the Natal Mounted Volunteers, who had been with the Cavalry, had been recalled, and as the enemy showed some disposition to work round my left flank as if to cut me off from Ladysmith, I sent this force under Colonel Royston to work round the Boer right and cover my left flank, a movement which was most successfully performed." In a report to the Chief-of-Staff Colonel Royston drew attention to the gallant manner in which Major Taunton, Natal Carbineers, afterwards killed, and Major Sangmeister, Border Mounted Rifles, seized a kopje under heavy fire, and bringing a maxim gun into action speedily cleared out the enemy. Also, on the same date, to the gallant behaviour, and devotion to the wounded, under a heavy fire, of Captains Platt and Buntine of the Volunteer Medical Staff. Colonel Royston also detailed gallant acts on the part of Troopers Seed (Police) and C. E. J. Miller, D. A. Shaw, and Rowland Watts (Carbineers). The gun team alluded to lost 2 killed; the other casualties among the volunteers were—Border M.R. 9 wounded, Carbineers 2 killed, 10 wounded, and Natal M.R. 3 wounded.

On the 25th Colonel Royston took out the whole of the Mounted Volunteers to assist Yule, whose force was found eighteen miles out. The roads were beyond description, and the rear of the column had to wade, often beyond their knees, in liquid mud. On the 26th Yule's column entered Ladysmith. On the 27th and two following days most of the Mounted Volunteers were out, and found the enemy gathering in great strength beyond Lombard's Kop.

In describing the battle of Lombard's Kop, 30th October 1899, Sir George said that 200 Natal Mounted Volunteers were sent out on the evening of the 29th to hold Lombard's Kop and Bulwana Mountain; and the remainder of the Mounted Volunteers, with the 5th Lancers and 19th Hussars, moved out with General French at 3 A.M. on the 30th to endeavour to cover the right flank in the main action. The Natal Field Battery formed part of Grimwood's force on the right of the infantry line. It will be remembered that General French could not get much beyond the Pass between Lombard's Kop and Bulwana; while Grimwood's Brigade was heavily pressed on its right, and the whole force had ultimately to retire on Ladysmith. In the same despatch, speaking of Colonel W. Royston, Sir George said—"The services which Colonel Royston and the forces under his command have rendered to the State and Colony have been of the very highest value. In him I have found a bold and successful leader, and an adviser whose experience of the Colony and of the enemy has been of great value to me. Employed on arduous duty from the commencement of the campaign, in touch with the enemy, I have found him prompt and ready for every emergency; he and his force reflect the greatest credit on the colony of Natal." On the 30th the Natal M.R. lost Lieutenant Clapham killed and 3 men wounded.

In the despatch of 23rd March 1900, para. 4, Sir

George stated that on 31st October he sent the 2nd Royal Dublin Fusiliers and the Natal Field Battery to Colenso to assist in defending the bridges on the Tugela; but they were soon forced to retire farther south. When the siege commenced the following were part of the garrison:—

Volunteer Staff, including Medical and Veterinary	11
Natal Carbineers	390
Border Mounted Rifles	260
Natal Mounted Rifles	200
Natal Naval Volunteers	65
Hotchkiss Detachment	20
Natal Police	40
	986

These formed the Volunteer Brigade under Colonel Royston, with Lieut.-Colonel H. T. Bru-de-Wold as Chief Staff Officer. The Naval Volunteers were generally split up throughout the siege, part being on Cæsar's Camp and part at Gordon Post. Between 1st November and the end of February the Natal Mounted Volunteers were frequently engaged. On 2nd November they were, with other troops, out reconnoitring; on the 3rd they were sent to cover the retirement of another force. On this occasion the Carbineers had Major Taunton and Sergeant Mapston killed, and the Border M.R. lost Captain Arnott and 11 men wounded.

Section D of the defences of Ladysmith was placed under Colonel Royston. This included the thorn country north of Cæsar's Camp and the Klip River Flats. Colonel Royston lost no time in building sangars and digging trenches, and soon had his section greatly strengthened. On 9th November the enemy attacked, firing 800 shells into the town; but their attack was driven off. On the 14th the Volunteers were out with Major-General Brocklehurst, and, along with the Imperial Light Horse, seized Star Hill; but it was not held permanently. When Sir Archibald Hunter made his deservedly famous sortie on 7th December to destroy the Boer guns on Gun Hill, his force consisted of 500 Natal Mounted Volunteers, under Colonel Royston, 100 Imperial Light Horse (see that regiment), and a few Royal Engineers, artillerymen, and guides. The storming-parties were 100 Carbineers, Major Addison, and 100 I.L.H., Lieut.-Colonel Edwards. Two big guns were destroyed and one maxim brought back. Colonel Royston was among those specially mentioned in the body of the despatch. Sir George White had the I.L.H. and Volunteers paraded on the following day, and, addressing them, said "that he did not wish to use inflated or exaggerated language, but the men of Sir Archibald Hunter's party were a credit, not only to the colony, but to the Empire. There was a lot of severe fighting to do, but it was a gratification to a General to have the help of such men."

Within the next few days Colonel Royston offered to supply volunteers to blow up Waschbank Bridge, but after the column had been paraded at night those in authority resolved not to send it out. On other occasions Colonel Royston made valuable suggestions, which were acted on.

The town and camps were during the siege constantly under shell-fire, and on 18th December one 6-inch shell bursting in the camp of the Carbineers killed 4 men, wounded 6 men, and destroyed 10 horses. The times were trying, but hard digging, sangar building, and brigade sports kept the men fairly fit.

In the repulse of the great attack of 6th January 1900 the volunteers took a prominent part. The following is the report furnished by Colonel Royston to the Chief of the Staff:—

"I have to report that on Saturday, 6th inst., at about 4.15 A.M., I received information by telephone from headquarters that the enemy were making an attack on Wagon Hill. I at once despatched 80 men of the Natal M.R., under Major Evans, to strengthen the outposts on the Flats, then held by 1 officer and 40 men Natal Police, attached to Volunteers, and 1 officer and 20 men Natal Carbineers. The Town Guard was also directed to stand fast at its post on the left bank of the Klip River. As it had been intimated that a battery of artillery would be placed at my disposal, I directed two squadrons Border M.R., with one maxim, to accompany the guns.

"Major Abadie, at about 5.40 A.M., reported his guns in position near the point where the road to Cæsar's Camp crosses the town rifle-range. On my arrival at the outpost line, at 5 A.M., the enemy were occupying the extreme south-eastern point of Cæsar's Hill, well under cover amongst the rocks and bushes. About 50 men were visible from the Flats, but more appeared to be pushing on from the west in small parties. These men were being fired on from the thorn trees and from sangars below by my men as soon as they appeared in sight. A few minutes after my arrival the enemy advanced north along the top of the hill, firing at a party of 'Gordons' near a sangar about 500 yards to their front. I requested the officer commanding the battery to open fire, which he did with good effect, stopping the enemy's advance, and driving them into the rocks. As there appeared to be only a small party of the 'Gordons' opposed to the enemy at this spot, as far as I could see from below, I directed a squadron of Border M.R., under Lieutenant Royston, to climb the hill and go to their assistance dismounted. This would be about 6 A.M. On my men joining the Gordons the party advanced towards the enemy in the rocks, but were at first driven back by their heavy fire, and the enemy again advanced. The battery again opened fire, and the 'Gordons' and the Border M.R. again advancing, drove the enemy over the point of the hill, and they never again mounted to the crest. At mid-day the enemy had retired about half-way down the southern slope of the hill, but still kept up a heavy fire. Unfortunately, it was impossible to get at these with artillery fire from where the battery was limbered, owing to the danger of hitting our own people on the crest of the hill, and the officer commanding the battery did not consider it advisable, owing to the rough ground to cross, and to exposure to Bulwana, to advance any of his guns as far as our outpost line, from which point the enemy could be reached. Rifle-fire was kept up until the enemy finally got into the bed of the Fourie Spruit, where he could only be reached from the top of Cæsar's Hill. A heavy fire was kept up until dark, when it gradually ceased, and the enemy appeared to be retiring up the Fourie Spruit. My casualties were 4 men killed and 2 officers and 10 men wounded.

"I wish to bring to notice the gallant manner in which the battery of artillery, under Major Abadie, stuck to its ground under the very heavy fire from the 6-inch gun and another long-range gun on

Umbulwana, and also the excellent practice made by the battery.

"I also consider that Lt. Royston, Border M.R., did good service with his men. The behaviour of Capt. Platt and Lt. Hornabrook, Vol. Med. Corps, in attending to the wounded throughout the day under heavy fire, deserves special mention; the last-named officer was wounded, besides having his clothes pierced by a bullet."

A detachment of the Natal Naval Volunteers, with a 3-pounder Hotchkiss, were part of the garrison on Caesar's Camp, and took part in the struggle. On Wagon Hill the Hotchkiss gun, manned by Volunteers under Captain Walker, was very heavily attacked. Case shot was used with some effect, but the gun detachment, having lost 2 killed, were driven back. Captain Walker succeeded in dismantling the breech before leaving.

One of the outposts which were first attacked on the Flats was held by Natal Police; the officer commanding it being absent, the senior non-commissioned officer, Sergeant Woon, although severely wounded in the neck, assumed command, and held the post until reinforced by a squadron of the Natal Mounted Rifles.

Colonel Royston was again most highly praised by Sir George White for his work on the 6th. The Naval Volunteers had 2 killed and several wounded, the Carbineers 4 wounded, the Natal Mounted Rifles had Lieutenant Richardson killed and several other casualties. Captain Wales of the Volunteer staff was killed, and the Police also had a few casualties.

On 18th January Lieut.-Colonel Bru-de-Wold was severely wounded by shrapnel. On the 22nd Troopers Inman and Agnew, Natal Mounted Rifles, volunteered to attempt to blow up railway bridges used by the enemy. These two men made their way through the investing lines, but found the bridges very closely guarded; eventually they succeeded in joining the troops south of the Tugela. On 1st March, the day after Dundonald rode into Ladysmith, Colonel Royston took out 150 Volunteers; he came in contact with the enemy; in this affair 1 officer and 2 men of the Police were wounded.

At the close of his despatch regarding the siege, Sir George White said: "The Natal Volunteers have performed invaluable service; their knowledge of the country has been of the very greatest use to me, and in every action in which they have been engaged they have shown themselves most forward and daring. The Natal Naval Volunteers have proved themselves worthy comrades of the land forces of the colony."

As in the case of the Imperial Light Horse, one portion of the Natal Volunteers took part in the relief of Ladysmith, while another portion was shut up in the town. As soon as the enemy had closed in on Ladysmith, they turned their attention to the force at Colenso: Dublin Fusiliers, Durban Light Infantry, some Natal Naval Volunteers, and the Natal Field Battery. On 3rd November Colonel Cooper, who commanded this force, found it necessary to retire to Estcourt.

Sixty men of the Durban Light Infantry formed part of the personnel of the armoured train which at this time patrolled daily from Estcourt to Colenso. On 15th November a rail was removed or twisted, and the train was attacked; 2 men of the Durban regiment were killed, Captain J. Wyllie and 15 were wounded,

Natal Volunteers, Police, and Guides 39

and 19 were taken prisoners, of whom 8 were wounded, 1 mortally. A squadron of Carbineers and one of Imperial Light Horse came out to the help of the armoured train. These reinforcements drove back the enemy, killing 3. Some of the Durban Light Infantry, Natal Royal Rifles, a squadron of Carbineers, and some of the Police were present in the action at Willow Grange on 22nd and 23rd November under Colonel Martyr (see General Hildyard's Report of 24th November 1899). Four guns of the Natal Artillery were out on reconnaissance work in the same district about this time. On the 27th the Volunteers moved forward to Frere, but when General Buller arrived he sent most of them back to the lines of communication.

On 9th December a detachment of Naval Volunteers, 2 officers and 47 men, joined the Naval Brigade of Captain Jones, R.N., and with him worked the big guns throughout the relief operations. It was soon found that the services of the mounted men would be needed at the front, and a composite regiment was made up, including 1 squadron Imperial Light Horse, 1 squadron Carbineers, some regular Mounted Infantry, and some of the Police. This regiment was, on 15th December, in the battle of Colenso with Lord Dundonald, on the right, at Hlangwane Mountain; the Volunteers were heavily engaged, losing 4 men killed, 2 officers, Lieutenants D. W. M'Kay and R. W. Wilson of the Carbineers, and 6 men wounded. The regiment accompanied Dundonald to Potgieter's Drift, Trichard's Drift, and Acton Homes (see Imperial Light Horse and South African Light Horse). The regiment remained with Dundonald throughout the great struggle to break through the chain of Boer defences. Like the remainder of Dundonald's Brigade they did fine work at Acton Homes on 18th January 1900, where the Carbineer Scouts were the first to discover the enemy; also at the seizure of Cingolo, Monte Cristo, and other important positions (14th to 27th February). In these operations the Volunteers suffered a few casualties.

At the crossing of the Tugela on 17th January Troopers D. Sclanders and F. T. Woods of the Natal Carbineers saved several men from drowning, and Sclanders got the Royal Humane Society's Silver Medal.

When Dundonald rode into Ladysmith on the evening of 28th February, he was accompanied by some Carbineers, Natal Mounted Rifles, Border Mounted Rifles, and Natal Police, the officers being Major D. M'Kenzie, Lieutenants Silburn, M'Kay, Verney, Richards, Ashburnham, and Abraham. None of those present will ever forget this ride, probably the most memorable occasion in the lives of any of them.

To the regret of the whole Volunteer force Colonel Royston was invalided on 16th March. The hardships of the siege had weakened a tough constitution. He was seized by enteric, and died on 6th April. The following sentence extracted from the 'Record' of the Natal Volunteers was penned by one of the officers who served under him: "Called to the command when the hand of a strong man was required to mould an embryo defence force into an efficient fighting machine, the achievements of the Volunteers, whether individually when detached for special duty, or collectively, more than justified the predictions made when he assumed the command, and had he been spared to complete the work he was so peculiarly fitted for, it cannot be denied that the Natal Volunteers would have played an even more important part in the concluding phases of the war than they did."

While General Buller was pounding away along the Tugela some of the Natal Volunteers under Major G. Leuchars were usefully employed about Greytown and the Zululand border. The Umvoti Mounted Rifles, about 80 strong, with 50 Police, were at Greytown and Tugela Ferry from the beginning of the war, and 2 guns of the Natal Field Artillery and 150 Natal Royal Rifles were after 10th January in the Melmoth Field Force operating from Eshowe. The Greytown force did most excellent work; they were practically isolated from 18th November to 13th February, when they were joined by Bethune's Mounted Infantry. During that period the posts and drifts held by the Umvoti Mounted Rifles and Police were repeatedly attacked. On 23rd November a commando 400 strong attacked 100 men holding the drift, but the enemy was driven off. The stubborn defence made by Major Leuchars and his men prevented an invasion from that quarter and had a great moral effect, as was proved by the tenor of despatches from General Burgher to General Joubert which were captured. In this affair Sergeant-Major Ferguson was severely wounded.

After the relief of Ladysmith the Volunteer Brigade was allowed some time to recuperate, and was reorganised. On 3rd April 1900 it consisted of the Natal Carbineers, Natal Mounted Rifles, and Border Mounted Rifles, temporarily under Lieut.-Colonel Brude-Wold. On the 8th Colonel Dartnell was appointed to command the whole of the Natal Volunteers and Police with the rank of Brigadier-General.

In General Buller's movement which commenced on 7th May for turning the Boers out of the Biggarsberg, and so clear Natal, the Volunteers were in the 3rd Mounted Brigade (see South African Light Horse). The Brigade was engaged almost daily between 10th and 19th May. Colonel Bethune co-operated from Greytown, and joined General Buller on 13th May (see Bethune's Mounted Infantry). Bethune's force was composed of 5 squadrons of his own regiment, 1 squadron Umvoti Mounted Rifles, two 12-pounder guns worked by men of the Royal Garrison Artillery, two 7-pounder guns, Natal Field Artillery, 2 Hotchkiss manned by the same corps, and 6 companies of the Imperial Light Infantry, a corps which was raised in the Colony. For seven months this force, or portions of it, had done good work in protecting the north-east of Natal from invasion or raids. On 19th May the Durban Light Infantry and Natal Royal Rifles were ordered to garrison Dundee. When Laing's Nek was turned by General Buller (see South African Light Horse), the Natal Mounted Volunteers were the advanced-guard of General Clery's force, which crossed the Nek itself on 12th June. Dundonald's Brigade had been split up, and the South African Light Horse were part of the turning force.

On 15th June General Buller issued an order recording his high appreciation of the services rendered by Brigadier-General Dartnell and the Natal Volunteers, and he asked the brigadier to release those men who required to go to their homes, and with the remainder to protect Dundee and the eastern portion of the Natal frontier. The latter duty involved much hard and responsible work. Captain Foxon and several men of the Natal Carbineers were wounded on patrol duty about the end of July 1900. During August, September, and October the Natal Mounted Volunteers were employed on the Natal border and in the Vryheid district, and had frequently brushes with parties of the enemy in a difficult piece of country. On 1st October Lieutenant Richardson and 3 men were wounded in a convoy affair.

In his final despatch of 9th November 1900 General Buller said : " I cannot close this report without alluding to the great assistance I have received throughout the war from the colonists in Natal. Colonel (local Brigadier-General) J. G. Dartnell, C.M.G., will no doubt report through the proper channel upon the Natal Volunteers. I can only say that their services were invaluable to the Empire; that they took part in every engagement in Natal, and willingly remained in the field, though at great inconvenience to themselves, until they knew that their services could be spared."

On their return to Maritzburg and Durban the Volunteers got magnificent receptions.

On 21st September 1900 authority had been obtained from Lord Roberts to raise among the Natal Volunteers a composite regiment of 300 mounted men to take over the duties hitherto performed by the Volunteer Brigade, and thus facilitate the return of the remainder of the Brigade to their daily avocations. The Volunteer Composite Regiment was made up as follows :—

	Officers.	Men.
Natal Carbineers	6	125
Natal Mounted Rifles	5	32
Umvoti Mounted Rifles	1	13
Border Mounted Rifles	3	48
Natal Field Artillery	...	19
Natal Royal Rifles	...	8
Durban Light Infantry	...	39
Hotchkiss Gun Detachment	...	6
Volunteer Medical Corps	1	4
	16	294

The regiment, under Lieut.-Colonel Evans, Natal M.R., did much hard and effective work down to the close of the campaign.

In his telegraphic despatch of 15th December 1900 Lord Kitchener mentioned that Colonel Blomfield, between Blood River and Vryheid, had driven the enemy in confusion from Scheeper's Nek, inflicting heavy loss, and he said, " Colonel Blomfield praises the conduct of the Natal Volunteers and Police." Two of the Volunteers were killed. The services of the regiment were particularly valuable during the great operations, February to April 1901, when seven columns under General French swept the Eastern Transvaal and drove the enemy into the south-eastern corner. On 24th April 1901 a party of about 20 Natal Police and 26 Europeans, chiefly civilians, engaged a strong Boer force near Mhalatini in Zululand, and drove them back. There were sharp casualties on either side, the Police losing 5 killed and several wounded. On 28th July 1901, near N'qutu, the enemy made a determined attack on a small column consisting chiefly of the Volunteer Composite Regiment. Major Edwards and several men were killed and several were wounded. The enemy was driven off with much loss.

In September 1901, when Botha made an earnest endeavour to reinvade Natal, the whole of the Natal Volunteers were again called out and were hurried to the front. Botha having been driven out of the southeast of the Transvaal, the Volunteers were discharged again on 14th October 1901, but the Composite Regiment remained in the field.

On 20th February 1902 a patrol of the regiment, consisting of one squadron under Captain Adams, and accompanied by Lieut.-Colonel Evans, officer commanding, and Major Blunt, the staff officer to General Blomfield, made a night raid on a Boer farm near Hlobane, Vryheid district. Only one man of the force was wounded, but these two distinguished officers, who were present practically as onlookers, were killed. Colonel Evans was one of the best known and most popular citizens of Durban.

In March the regiment, under Major Bede-Crompton, was employed blocking the Drakensberg passes while the great drives in the Orange River Colony were going on. About the end of March Natal decided to raise 400 more mounted infantry. This was completed on 17th April, the Durban Light Infantry contributing a mounted contingent, and the new mounted infantry were, along with the old Volunteer Composite Regiment, put under Lieut.-Colonel Bru-de-Wold. They operated about the Buffalo River and the southeast of the Transvaal till peace was declared.

As will be seen from the mentions, General Buller placed very high value on the services of the guides provided to his army by the Natal colonists.

MURRAY'S HORSE AND THE COLONIAL SCOUTS.

Before Ladysmith was invested, the Hon. T. K. Murray, ex-Colonial Secretary, suggested that the Rifle Associations of Natal, which were on a different footing from the Volunteers, should be called out. The authorities did not see their way to adopt this suggestion, but General Wolfe-Murray, commanding the lines of communication, asked Mr Murray to come to Mooi River as soon as he could with the men he could gather. Forty-eight hours afterwards Mr Murray was at the appointed place with 80 well-mounted men, each carrying three days' rations. Within a few days the numbers had increased to 150, and during the first three weeks of November — a most critical period, as the Boers were pushing across the Tugela and the regulars were only arriving—Murray's Horse performed most valuable service, patrolling a very wide district, and probably leading the enemy to believe that lower Natal was better protected than it really was. The regular troops having arrived before the end of November, Murray's Horse was disbanded. The Lieut.-General Commanding in Natal issued the following order : " The services of the Irregular Corps raised by the Honourable T. K. Murray, C.M.G., having been dispensed with owing to the arrival of reinforcements from the Cape, the Lieut.-General Commanding desires to place on record his high admiration for the patriotic spirit with which the men of this corps responded to the call to arms at a critical time, and the efficient manner in which they performed the military duties required of them," &c.

In December 1899 another corps, known as the Colonial Scouts, was raised by the Natal Government ; strength five squadrons, commanded by Colonel F. Addison, M.L.A. They were during part of 1900 chiefly employed in Zululand, and on the border of that country and the Transvaal. The corps did not see much fighting, but their presence in this district was very valuable. The Scouts provided a bodyguard of about 30 men to General Warren. The corps was disbanded in April, but the majority of the volunteers joined other irregular bodies—for example, " G " squadron practically became " F " squadron of Bethune's Mounted Infantry under their old company commander Major Menné, who afterwards raised Menné's Scouts.

Steinaecker's Horse was also at first recruited from men of the Colonial Scouts, in which Steinaecker himself had been a non-commissioned officer.
The Mentions gained by the Natal Volunteers, Police, and Guides were as follows :—

In General Hildyard's report, dated 24th November 1899, as to action at Willow Grange fought on 23rd—"The services of Mr Chapman, who was unfortunately killed, were of the greatest value ; his intimate knowledge of the ground alone made it possible to carry out the operation."

Capt. Jones' report to Rear-Admiral Harris, of 2nd March 1900.—Lt. N. W. Chiazzari, Natal Naval Vols., has been most useful, especially in getting into working order and working the punts across the river, both at Potgieter's and Colenso, by which all the troops crossed.

Sir R. Buller's despatch of 30th March 1900 as to relief operations.—Lt. N. Chiazzari, Natal Naval Vols., was in charge of a detachment who were associated with the Naval Brigade, and took their full share of the good work done by the brigade.

SIR G. WHITE'S DESPATCHES : *2nd December* 1899.—Col. W. Royston, commanding Natal Vol. force, in the terms already mentioned in the text. Col. J. G. Dartnell, Chief Com. Natal Police, "rendered valuable service to the late Lieut.-Gen. Sir W. Penn-Symons and to Brig.-Gen. Yule when the Dundee column fell back on Ladysmith ; his advice and experience were of the highest value, and I found him always ready and willing to help me in any way in his power." Capt. F. S. Tatham, Mounted Rifles. Guides A. B. Allison, T. Loxton, and P. Greathead. Major H. Bru-de-Wold, Senior Staff Officer, Vol. Force ; Capt. H. Platt, Vol. Med. Staff. Civilian Nurses B. Ludlow, S. Patterson, J. Charleson, J. Borlase, S. Lees, R. Shappere, H. Ross, A. Keightly, M. Brice, E. Stowe, D. Belton, I. Stowe, K. Hill, L. Yeatman, S. Otto, E. Early, M. Nicolson, C. Thompson, K. Driser, K. Champion, M. Tentney, R. Davies, S. Ruiter, E. Bromilon. Mr A. Henderson in charge of native guides.

23rd March 1900.—Col. W. Royston, commanding Natal Vol. Force, and in charge of Section D of defences. I can only repeat the high praise which I had the pleasure to bestow on him in my despatch of 2nd December. He commanded Section D in an admirable manner, and with his force, though much reduced in numbers by casualties and disease, continued to the end to perform invaluable service. He is an officer exceptionally suited to his important position as commandant of the Natal Vol. Forces, and I trust he may receive some suitable reward. Col. Royston's gallant behaviour at Gun Hill, 1st December, was noticed in body of despatch. (To the regret of the Colony, Col. Royston succumbed to illness after the relief.) Col. Dartnell possessed an exceptional knowledge of the Colony and of native character. I am greatly obliged to him for the advice and assistance which he has always been ready to afford me, of which I have availed myself freely, and which I have found of the highest value. Capt. F. S. Tatham, Mounted Rifles; Lieut.-Col. E. M. Greene, Carbineers; Majors R. W. Evans, Natal M.R.; F. J. Rethman, Border M.R.; H. T. Bru-de-Wold, C.S.O.; J. Hyslop, P.M.O.; Capt. H. T. Platt, Medical Staff. Guides T. Allison, L. Ashby, H. Thornhill. Condrs. Macfarlane, Bell, Inglethorpe. Storeholder J. Keefe. Foreman Blake. Vols. with Bearer Coy.—J. Taylor, R. H. Coventon, W. Jackson, F. Ellis, P. Smythe.

SIR C. WARREN'S DESPATCH: *1st February* 1900. — Colonial Scouts— Lieut. O. Schwikkard, "A" Squadron, was employed upon a variety of duties; his remarkable knowledge of the ways of the country, and extraordinary power of resource, contributed in a great measure to expedite the progress of the force on many occasions.

SIR R. BULLER'S DESPATCHES: *30th March* 1900.—Carbineers.—Tpr. F. C. Farmer[1] rescued Lieut. Mackay, who was wounded, under very heavy fire at Colenso. Major M'Kenzie, a Colonist of great experience and marked ability as a leader of irregular horse, has rendered excellent service throughout. Naval Vol. Ambulance Corps—Ptes. J. Domingo, F. Clark, G. H. Howard, G. Smith. Mounted Police—Inspectors Fairlie and Abraham.

19th June 1900—Mr (Hon. Major) O. Schwikkard,[2] Ass.-Dir. of Transport, as guide, interpreter, and transport official, was indefatigable, and his services were most useful. The General also expressed his indebtedness to the Hon. T. K. Murray for forming a corps of guides, Mr D. Hunter, Manager of Railways, and Mr W. G. Hamilton, Postmaster-General.

GENERAL BULLER'S FINAL DESPATCH.—Col. T. M'Cubbin, as station commandant at various places. Major Bousfield, Natal Vols., has devoted his local knowledge, his professional skill, and his singular personal influence to making the administration of martial law easy; I owe him a deep debt of gratitude. Capt. Cecil Yonge, Natal Vols., attached to Army Service Corps, and did excellent work. Col. Dartnell was again mentioned as being unwearying in his efforts, while Sir W. Hely Hutchison, G.C.M.G., Governor, Sir A. Hime, Prime Minister, Mr Hunter, C.M.G., manager of the Natal Railways, Mr Shaw, Chief Engineer, Mr Harrison, of the Public Works department, and the Colonial Nurses, were all most highly praised for assistance given. The General also said: "Early in the war a corps of guides was formed in Natal from colonists with local knowledge of the districts in which our forces were operating. These gentlemen rendered the greatest possible assistance. Foremost in every fight, always ready to undertake difficult or dangerous duties, they helped me equally in field operations, with supply, with transport, and in dealing with the Dutch inhabitants. To the Hon. T. K. Murray, C.M.G., at first, and latterly to Mr F. Struben, who were in charge, my principal thanks are due; but I am equally indebted to many others, among whom I must mention Mr F. Knight, the brothers Loxton, the brothers Alison, the brothers Whipp, the brothers Robinson, Mr Foster, Mr Macfarlane, Mr Godson, and Mr Otto

---

[1] Awarded D.C.M.   [2] Awarded C.M.G.

Schwikkard, whose wonderful energy and great knowledge of transport details were invaluable.

The last sentence of General Buller's final despatch is as follows: "Colonists, I cannot close this report without alluding to the great assistance I have received throughout the war from the colonists of Natal. Col. (local Brig.-Gen.) J. G. Dartnell, C.M.G., will no doubt report through the proper channel upon the Natal Vols. I can only say that their services were invaluable to the Empire, that they took part in every engagement in Natal, and willingly remained in the field—though at great inconvenience to themselves—until they knew that their services could be spared."

LORD ROBERTS' DESPATCHES: *2nd April* 1901.—Col. Dartnell, as G.O.C. Natal Colonists, has maintained the best traditions of the regular forces. His name stands very high in the estimation of the colonists, and he possesses the greatest influence over the natives. His advice was of much assistance in the earliest actions of the war, afterwards during the siege of Ladysmith, and finally in the general advance through the Biggarsberg to Laing's Nek, when Natal was cleared of the enemies of the Queen. Col. Dartnell was awarded the "K.C.B." Natal Carabineers—Major D. M'Kenzie.[1] Natal Vol. Med. Corps—Ptes. E. Clark, J. Domingo, G. H. Howard, G. G. Smith. Natal Vols.—Col. W. Royston (dead); Majors Bousfield,[1] H. T. Bru-de-Wold,[1] J. Hyslop,[2] P.M.O. Struben's Scouts—Lieut. R. H. Struben. Umvoti Mounted Rifles—Lieut.-Col. G. Leuchars.

4th September 1901.—Durban Light Infantry—Lieut.-Col. T. M'Cubbin.[1] Murray's Guides—The Hon. T. K. Murray, C.M.G. Natal Guides—A. F. Henderson,[1] W. Knight,[1] T. J. M. Macfarlane,[1] W. M. Struben,[1] A. Allison,[3] M. Allison,[3] G. G. Godson,[3] S. Loxton,[3] T. Loxton,[3] E. P. Robinson,[3] A. Russell,[3] C. S. Whipp,[3] R. T. Whipp.[3] Natal M.R.—Tpr. Redpath.[3]

LORD KITCHENER'S DESPATCHES: *8th August* 1901.—Natal Vol. Composite Regiment—Capt. A. W. Smallie and Lieut. Rundle, for marked good work near Nondweni, Zululand, July 28. Tpr. Banwell for voluntarily taking messages under fire, same occasion.

8th October 1901.—Zululand Police—Sgt. Gumbi, for gallantry and good service in defence of Fort Prospect, September 26.

8th December 1901.—Natal Police—Sgt. Lane, for excellent work in defence of a convoy from Melmoth to Nkandhla, May 29. Sgt. A. J. Smith of the Police, and Tpr. A. W. Evans of the M.R., got the D.C.M.

8th April 1902.—Natal Vols.—Capt. P. A. Silburn.[3]

1st June 1902.—Naval Vol. Composite Regiment—Sgt. Haine; capture of Gen. Emmett, March 15, chiefly due to him.

23rd June 1902.—Natal Police Field Force—Sub-Insp. J. Hamilton; Sgts. Newson, Goode. Natal Vols.—Capt. E. K. Whitehead.[2] Composite Regiment—Lieut.-Cols. R. W. Evans (killed in action), B. Crompton[2]; Capt. F. O. Stiebel; Lieut. J. W. V. Montgomery; Hospital Sgt.-Major A. C. Wearner,[3] Sgt. A. H. Bramwell.

---

[1] Awarded C.M.G.   [2] Awarded D.S.O.   [3] Awarded D.C.M.

50   *The Colonials in South Africa*

SOUTH AFRICAN LIGHT HORSE.

THE S.A.L.H. was raised in Cape Colony in November 1899,[1] and the command was given to Major (local Lieut.-Colonel) the Hon. J. H. G. Byng (10th Hussars). No corps was more fortunate in its leader. Eight complete squadrons were raised by an early date in December. A portion was employed for a short time on the De Aar line, but three squadrons of the regiment were, on formation, taken round to Natal and, with other mounted troops, were employed under Lord Dundonald on the right flank at Colenso on 15th December 1899.[2] Three further squadrons were got ready at Cape Town and sent to Natal, but the other men who had been enrolled were retained in Cape Colony and went to form the nucleus of Roberts' Horse and Kitchener's Horse.

In the orders issued by General Buller on 14th December it was stated, paragraph 7, "The Officer Commanding mounted brigade will move at 4 A.M. with a force of 1000 men and one battery of No. 1 Brigade Division in the direction of Hlangwane Hill; he will cover the right flank of the general movement, and will endeavour to take up a position on Hlangwane Hill, whence he will enfilade the kopje north of the iron bridge. The Officer Commanding mounted troops will also detail two forces of 300 men and 500 men to cover the right and left flanks respectively and protect the baggage." Lord Dundonald and the

[1] Colonel Adye's evidence before the War Commission.
[2] General Buller's despatch of 17th December 1899 and list of troops annexed.

mounted irregulars did attack Hlangwane and made good progress towards its capture. If the General had been able to send adequate infantry support the capture would have been almost certainly assured and the bloodshed of Spion Kop saved, but the entanglement of the guns rendered such support impossible.[1] In his despatch, General Buller said: "I cannot speak too highly of the manner in which the mounted Volunteers behaved." The S.A.L.H. lost 4 men killed, 2 officers—Lieutenants B. Barhurst and J. W. Cock—and 19 men wounded, while 2 officers and 11 men were returned as missing.

When the move to turn the Boer right on the Tugela was commenced, four squadrons of the regiment accompanied Lord Dundonald, marching on the 11th January viâ Springfield and Potgieter's, but a portion remained at Chieveley with General Barton to watch the Boer position at Colenso. In order to keep the enemy engaged there, frequent reconnaissances and demonstrations were made in which the detachment several times had sharp casualties,[2] Captain de Rougemont being killed on 23rd January. On the 11th Lord Dundonald seized the bridge at Springfield over the Little Tugela, and pushing on had, before dusk, secured heights on the right bank of the main river which commanded Potgieter's Drift. Some volunteers from the S.A.L.H. on the 11th swam the Tugela, got into the ferry-boat, and brought it to the right bank.[3] Mr Bennet Burleigh mentions that the party of volunteers were Lieutenant Carlisle, Sergeant Turner, Cor-

[1] Evidence of General Buller and Major-General Barton before War Commission.
[2] Reports by General Barton in White Book "Spion Kop despatches."
[3] See 'London to Ladysmith,' by W. S. Churchill, and 'The Natal Campaign,' by Bennet Burleigh, and 'Times History,' vol. iii.

porals Cox and Barkley, and Troopers Howell, Godden, and Collingwood. For five days the mounted troops did reconnoitring and outpost work. On the 16th they were ordered to march that night to Trichard's Drift. On the 17th they and Warren's troops crossed the river, and on the 18th Lord Dundonald was sent off to the left flank. The Composite Regiment, 1 squadron Imperial Light Horse, 1 company of Mounted Infantry, regulars, and 1 squadron Natal Carbineers, managed to cut off about 40 Boers near Acton Homes, and before dusk these surrendered after the S.A.L.H. had come up in support. On the 20th Lord Dundonald ordered Colonel Byng to seize Bastion Hill. Two squadrons of the regiment were dismounted and ascended the steep ascent, the two others supporting. The Boers fled from the crest, and it was taken with little loss, but the hill, like Spion Kop, was exposed to the enemy's fire, and Major Childe was killed by a shell fragment after the crest had been occupied, and 4 men were wounded. Corporal Tobin was first man up; he stood on the top and waved his hat to let the troops see the hill-top was free of Boers. Next day he was killed. At nightfall 2 companies of the Queen's relieved the regiment. During the following days, until the evacuation of Spion Kop, the regiment held posts on the British line. Between the 19th and 27th the regiment had about 60 casualties.

'The Times' historians have expressed the opinion that if the successes of Lord Dundonald's Irregulars on the 18th, 19th, and 20th had been followed up with energy by the Divisional Commanders, the turning movement viâ Trichard's Drift would have relieved Ladysmith.

During the Vaal Krantz combat, 5th to 8th

February, the mounted troops were mainly on the flanks; but in the earlier part of the fighting which took place between 13th and 27th February, the mounted irregulars, including the S.A.L.H., which had been strengthened by further squadrons from Cape Colony, the whole brigade being under Lord Dundonald, took a most important share of the work. The regular cavalry had now been put into a separate brigade under Colonel Burn-Murdoch, and were left in the Springfield neighbourhood to secure General Buller's left rear. Between 9th and 11th February the army marched back to Chieveley, Lord Dundonald covering the left flank. On the 12th, with the South African Light Horse, the Composite Regiment, Thorneycroft's Mounted Infantry, and the Royal Welsh Fusiliers, he thoroughly reconnoitred and examined Hussar Hill with the view to its being used as a stepping-stone in an attack on the Boer left. The force was ordered to retire in the afternoon, and had a few casualties in the retirement. Lieutenant John Churchill and 7 men of the S.A.L.H. were wounded. On the 14th General Buller decided to occupy Hussar Hill, and the regiment, being the advanced screen, successfully seized the Hill with but slight loss. On the 15th and 16th the fighting was chiefly confined to the artillery. On the 17th the attack on Mount Cingolo was developed. Dundonald's Brigade struck away to the east, through very broken and wooded country, and ascending an almost precipitous face seized the summit, the 2nd Infantry Brigade assisting on their inner flank. The work of the S.A.L.H. was specially commended by some of the correspondents present. The casualties were not serious considering the formidable nature of the task. On the 18th the

2nd Infantry Brigade attacked the summit of Monte Cristo, making a fine advance along the Nek between that mountain and Cingolo. Dundonald's men were again out on the right, and worried the enemy by a flanking fire at long ranges. "The steep crags of Monte Cristo were brilliantly carried after considerable resistance by the West Yorkshire and Queen's Regiments."[1] On the same day the Fusilier Brigade carried another hill. On the 19th heavy guns were got into position on Monte Cristo, and on the 20th it was found that the enemy had left all their positions on the south side of the Tugela. Thorneycroft's Mounted Infantry swam the river, but were driven back. From the 21st to the 27th, when the very strongly fortified positions on Pieter's Hill, Railway Hill, and Terrace Hill were carried, the fighting was mainly done by the infantry and guns. On the 28th Lord Dundonald's Brigade had the honour of being chosen for the direct advance on Ladysmith, and in the evening he galloped into the town with a squadron of the Imperial Light Horse, and one of the Natal Carbineers, and some representatives of his other irregulars.[2]

After the relief, the Natal Field Force had a comparatively easy time until General Buller started on his next great movement with the object of clearing Natal,—a movement admirably conceived, and carried out in a way deserving of the highest praise. On the 2nd of May General Buller received Lord Roberts' instructions to occupy the enemy's attention on the Biggarsberg. On the 7th he set out first towards Elands-

[1] Despatch of 14th March 1900.
[2] The doings of Dundonald's Brigade between 12th and 28th February 1900 are admirably described in Mr Churchill's 'London to Ladysmith.'

laagte to deceive the enemy as to his real direction. General Buller then swept away to the south-east. Lord Dundonald's Brigade, now called the 3rd Mounted Brigade, was chosen to accompany the turning force. On the 13th General Buller arrived at the Helpmakaar road at a point near Uithoek on the left flank of the enemy's position. Here he joined hands with Colonel Bethune, who had been occupying Greytown. The mounted men seized the hill commanding the Pass, and the enemy retired. From this point to Newcastle it was an almost ceaseless pursuit in which the mounted irregulars did splendid work, for which General Buller warmly praised them. The Boers lit grass fires, but Dundonald's men dashed through the smoke, and at times over the burning vegetation, and unweariedly drove the enemy before them. On the 15th the whole force was at Dundee, on the 18th at Newcastle, and the enemy had been driven from his carefully entrenched position on the Biggarsberg at a cost of 7 wounded.

After the occupation of Newcastle General Buller sent a portion of his troops to the Utrecht district, where there was some skirmishing towards the end of May, in which the S.A.L.H. had Lieutenant T. H. Thompson and several men wounded.

The railway having been repaired and supplies got up, General Buller prepared to turn Laing's Nek, and on the 6th June the S.A.L.H. and other troops seized and occupied Van Wyk Mountain. The regiment lost 6 killed and 4 wounded. General Buller said "the occupation was well carried out," although a resolute attack was made on the force under cover of a grass fire. On the 7th an advance was made on Yellowboom. On the 8th the regiment occupied another hill, Spitz

Kop, near Botha's Pass. On the same day the Pass was carried. "The S.A.L.H. got up the Berg to the left of Botha's Pass and pursued for some miles, though they were not able to come up with, a party of the enemy who retired to the westward."[1] On the 10th the advance continued. The regiment was in front and "cleared the enemy off a mountain without difficulty." They found the enemy moving in strength from east to north, and the regiment pushed forward two miles to some kopjes. Three squadrons were closely engaged with the enemy until dusk. Our casualties were 6 killed and 7 wounded, all of the S.A.L.H. Twenty-two of the enemy were found killed. On the 11th the enemy made a stand in a very strong position at Alleman's Nek, but after severe fighting was driven out by the 2nd and 10th Infantry Brigades, Lord Dundonald's men ably assisting against the enemy's left flank.

In his despatch General Buller said "the S.A.L.H. acted as an independent unit, and performed its duties exceedingly well throughout. Lieut.-Colonel Byng proved himself as usual a valuable commander."

During the remainder of June and the month of July the Natal Army was employed in occupying and fortifying posts on the Pretoria-Natal railway and the south-east portion of the Transvaal. In his telegram of 13th July, Lord Roberts mentions that on the night of the 11th the S.A.L.H. by good scouting had prevented the Boers from destroying the railway near Vlaklaagte, and that Lord Dundonald had captured a Boer camp. On 7th August General Buller commenced his advance from the railway to meet Lord Roberts' army near Belfast. On several occasions there was sharp fighting, in which the S.A.L.H. had a most

[1] Despatch of 19th June.

prominent share. On the 23rd August Captain Savory was killed. On the 27th General Buller attacked the immensely strong position held by the Boers stretching across the Delagoa Railway. Bergendal was the point selected for the chief attack, and the 2nd Rifle Brigade deservedly earned the highest praise for their advance and final assault under a very heavy fire. The enemy was thoroughly defeated. On the 29th the S.A.L.H. drove the enemy out of Waterval Boven [1] and captured five waggons. Buller's force now moved north of the railway and after some fighting occupied Lydenburg. Frequently the S.A.L.H. did particularly good service, as near Lydenburg on the 8th and 9th September, and they were often mentioned in the telegrams, as in Lord Roberts' telegram of 3rd October, when he said: "On the 28th Colonel Byng, by a well-managed night-march up the Groodenonein Berg, seized the top of Pilgrim's Hill with the S.A.L.H., forcing the enemy to retire hurriedly." The corps had 3 killed and 6 wounded.

In his final despatch of 9th November 1900, General Buller said in his "Mentions": "Lieut.-Colonel J. H. G. Byng, 10th Hussars, has commanded the S.A.L.H. from its formation in November last. A cavalry officer of the highest qualifications, he has shown singular ability in the command of irregulars. His regiment has done splendid service, and I attribute this in a great measure to Colonel Byng's personal influence. I strongly recommend him for reward and advancement." Many other officers were mentioned. In October the S.A.L.H. were taken to Pretoria, and on the 15th were there inspected and complimented by Lord Roberts.

In the second phase of the war the regiment was

[1] Lord Roberts' telegram of 29th August.

mainly employed in the Orange River Colony. In his despatch of 8th March 1901, Lord Kitchener said that in the beginning of December 1900 Thorneycroft's Mounted Infantry and the S.A.L.H. were railed from Standerton and Volksrust respectively to Bloemfontein, and were sent to occupy a line of posts between Thabanchu and Ladybrand, east of the capital. De Wet was then trying to get into Cape Colony, but was headed by Charles Knox and driven north again. The bulk of the Boers broke through the line above-mentioned and got away to the Senekal district, but in his telegram of 15th December Lord Kitchener was able to say that the S.A.L.H. and Thorneycroft's Mounted Infantry captured one 15-pounder taken at Dewetsdorp, one pom-pom, several waggons of ammunition, 22 prisoners, and some horses and mules. Soon after this the S.A.L.H. and Thorneycroft's Mounted Infantry were, with other troops, railed to Cape Colony to operate against Kritzinger and other leaders. Both regiments took part in many a memorable pursuit. In January 1901 the S.A.L.H. was constantly in touch with the enemy, and on the 16th, in the Murraysburg district of Cape Colony, a detachment acting as advance guard became engaged with a strong force of the enemy. Captain Fitzherbert and 5 men were killed, and Lieutenants H. C. Fleming and Venables and 13 men were wounded. In February De Wet himself with a considerable force got into Cape Colony, but being hotly and constantly pressed by numerous columns, including Thorneycroft's Mounted Infantry and the S.A.L.H., he was driven out again on the 28th February minus 200 prisoners, all his guns, waggons, and ammunition. The S.A.L.H. remained in Cape Colony during March and April and did much hard work. Lieutenant E. H.

Barker was killed at Kaliesfontein on 6th March. Both regiments were brought back to the Orange River Colony, and in May four squadrons of the Light Horse, under Major Gogarty, captured 31 armed burghers with their horses at Luckhoff. On the 21st Lieutenant J. Alexander and 2 men were killed. In his despatch of 8th October Lord Kitchener said that the column of Colonel Byng was brought from the south to the north of the Orange River Colony, and in the Vredefort Road, Reitzburg district, his column and that of Colonel Dawkins captured 81 prisoners in the last fortnight of September 1901. After three days' rest Colonel Byng and his men left Kroonstad on 6th October, and in the next three weeks took other 50 prisoners on the west of the railway. He then moved to the Heilbron district to take part in the great combined movements and drives in the north-east of the Orange River Colony, and until the close of the war the S.A.L.H. and their leader were constantly at the very hardest of work, often trekking for thirty-six hours with scarcely a break.

On 14th November 1901 Byng and Wilson were nearing Heilbron when they were suddenly attacked. The despatch of 8th December says: "The attack, delivered in a resolute manner, was, after two hours' hard fighting, successfully repulsed on all sides by Lieut.-Colonel Byng's rear-guard, which was well and skilfully handled by Lieut.-Colonel Wilson of Kitchener's Fighting Scouts [see that corps]. The enemy retired, leaving 8 dead on the field."

In the despatch of 8th February 1902 Lord Kitchener gives details of certain driving operations, and says: "On the night of 2nd February Colonel Byng, who had remained on Liebenberg's Vlei, to the west of Reitz, learned that a Boer force was rapidly marching north and at no great distance from him. He promptly started in pursuit, and fifteen miles to the east came upon a convoy which was guarded, but not strongly, by a portion of De Wet's commando. The New Zealanders and Queensland Imperial Bushmen at once charged the enemy's rear-guard with the greatest dash and gallantry, whilst the South African Light Horse, rushing the centre with equal bravery, got well home and completed a very gratifying success. The enemy fled in a westerly direction, leaving in our hands one 15-pr. gun, two pom-poms, three waggon-loads of ammunition, 26 prisoners," &c.

Down to the close of the campaign the regiment continued to show the splendid spirit which it had exhibited at Colenso and other hard-fought actions in Natal; and when peace came, the S.A.L.H left the field with a reputation second to that of no corps, regular or irregular, in South Africa.

The Mentions gained by the corps were as follows :—

SIR C. WARREN'S DESPATCH : 1*st* February 1900. — S.A.L.H.—On 20th January a detachment under Major Childe (since killed) did gallant service in capture of Sugar-Loaf Hill. Cpl. Tobin was first man up and was subsequently killed by a shell.

SIR R. BULLER'S DESPATCHES : 30*th* March 1900. — Recommends Cpl. Tobin for D.C.M. Major (local Lieut.-Col.) Hon. J. Byng, 10th Hussars, has commanded S.A.L.H. with marked ability and success and done very good service with them. Capt. H. K. Stewart ; Lieuts. E. Marshall, W. F. Barker, C. Walker-Leigh, R. S. Thorold, G. Marsden, W. P. Pearse, T. H. Carlisle ; Sgt.-Major Mudford (got D.C.M.), East Kent Yeomanry (attached) ; Sgt. R. Turner ; Cpls. W. Cox, G. Barkley ; Tprs. J. Collingwood, C. Godden (since dead), R. Howell.

19*th* June 1900.—Lieut.-Col. Byng. The regiment acted as an independent unit and performed its duties exceedingly well throughout. Lieut.-Col. Byng proved himself as usual a valuable commander. Capt. R. Brooke, 7th Hussars, specially recommended for manner in which he commanded left of line on June 6.

13*th* September 1900. — Major (local Lieut.-Col.) Hon. J. Byng, 10th

Hussars, in the terms already mentioned in the text. Capt. W. H. L. Allgood, King's Royal Rifles, an admirable squadron commander. Capt. A. Solly Flood, South Lancashire Regiment, has rendered excellent service, and been of great value as adjutant. Capt. (local Major) R. G. Brooke, 7th Hussars, has proved himself an excellent second in command. Of the Colonial officers, Capts. S. Tucker, S. Chapin, Grant-Thorold, and Lieut. G. Marsden have done invaluable service throughout the campaign. Non-commissioned officers and men who have rendered continuous good and valuable service: Lce.-Sgt. J. Burrows, A.S.C. Trumpet-Major ; Cpl. F. Filling, 5th Dragoon Guards (acting Sgt.-Major, Colt Gun detachment) ; Lce.-Cpl. P. Melia, Royal Dublin Fusiliers ; Sq. Sgt.-Major C. T. Mudford, East Kent Yeomanry (attached) ; Sq. Sgt.-Majors J. Hopper, G. Mitchell ; Sgts. F. Battershill, A. Sanson, J. Liddell ; Ptes. D. Cochrane, T. Dow. A list is added of those officers and men who, during the twelve months' work, have performed special acts of bravery, or have been selected for, and successfully carried out, arduous reconnaissances or dangerous duties : Lieuts. R. Turner, W. F. Barker, P. H. Goodair, J. S. Churchill, W. L. Edmunds, J. M. O'Brien, R. Johnstone, T. S. Wickham, C. M. Dansey, E. M. Garrard (Colt Gun Detachment) ; Sgts. J. M'Sorley, H. H. Clarke, D. Bennet, C. Green, J. C. White, E. Prowse, C. O. Taylor, C. Baker, W. H. Wesley, H. Tobin, R. C. Alexander, W. J. Cox, T. Marriott, R. Holroyd, J. W. Weekes, J. Dudgeon ; Cpls. F. P. Erdmer, W. M'Arthur, C. H. Wallis, H. Moore, R. Gifford, C. H. Cotterill, J. M'Ewen, J. R. Arrowsmith, W. Hudson ; Lce.-Cpls. F. Murray, J. Kelleher, H. Crane, D. Stewart, J. Howard, T. Braund, E. Constable, C. Flick, J. Banks, G. Earle, W. Desfountain, H. Campbell, F. Stringer, W. Bruyn, V. O'Connor, W. H. Slidolph ; Ptes. F. Crowle, R. Dobson, P. Siegfield, J. Turner, A. Galloway, W. Haylett, W. Heeley, D. M'Coll, C. Van Schade, G. Warren, B. Binks, H. Bickley, D. Blurton, G. Dumsden, W. Gibbon, A. Grant, F. Holmes, T. Kidd, J. Morrison, G. Murgatroyd, P. Murgatroyd, W. Collins, G. Lively, J. Pinch, J. Purkiss, J. M. Brown, E. Brophy, W. Meadows, A. Pirie, W. Thomas, H. T. Smith, S. M. Barnes, H. H. Carroll, O. F. Fielding, J. Gibson, T. V. Hansen, E. H. Campbell, R. M. Smith, R. St John, F. Vallecarde, R. Cook (Bethune's Mounted Infantry, attached with Colt Gun Detachment).

LORD ROBERTS' DESPATCHES : *2nd April* 1901.—Major Childe ; Capts. S. Chapin,[1] S. N. Tucker[1] ; Lieuts. W. F. Barker,[1] G. Marsden,[1] R. Turner,[1] T. S. Wickham[1] ; Sq. Sgt.-Major Hopper[2] ; Sgts. F. L. Battershill,[2] J. Dudgeon,[2] H. Tobin[2] (killed) ; Cpls. A. H. Vallecarde[2] (Colt Gun Detachment), F. P. Erdmer[2] ; Lce.-Cpls. A. J. Miller,[2] F. J. Murray[2] ; Ptes. D. Cochrane,[2] T. Dow.[2]

4th September 1901.—Capt. Allgood (K.R.R.), Capt. H. R. Stewart (late Gordon Highlanders), Cpl. Melia (Dublin Fusiliers).

LORD KITCHENER'S DESPATCHES : *8th July* 1901.—Capt. T. S. Wickham, D.S.O., good leading in night surprise, Metz Farm, Orange River Colony,

---

[1] Awarded D.S.O.   [2] Awarded D.C.M.

May 14. Sgt. C. M'Millan, great gallantry, same occasion, reforming and leading men into buildings after officer fell. Cpl. F. H. Secombe (wounded, promoted Sgt.), first man in. Sgt. A. J. Miller,[1] Bastard's Drift, Orange River Colony, April 15, in command of patrol, coolness in presence of superior forces and skill in extricating men, reported as "constantly brought to my notice for gallantry in action." Mentioned in Army Orders : Tpr. T. Dow, Cpl. J. W. Kendall, at Winter's Kraal, Cape Colony, April 22, under heavy fire at 600 yards, went back to assist a wounded man and brought him out.

8th March 1902.—Capt. and Adjutant W. F. Barker, D.S.O., and Lieut. J. Steele,[2] good service in Col. Byng's capture of laager at Fanny's Home, 2nd February. Tpr. F. Stringer,[1] single-handed capture of a Boer under circumstances of gallantry, 5th February.

23rd June 1902. — Capt. J. M'Sorley ; Lieuts. C. Green, C. M. F. Lilly ; Sq. Sgt.-Majors Holroyd,[1] G. Carpenter, E. H. Tompkins ; Qrmr.-Sgt. H. G. Gilding ; Sgt. M. Farrell ; Cpl. W. Dye ; Ptes. H. H. Bowers, A. Van Schalwyk.

BETHUNE'S MOUNTED INFANTRY.

THIS corps was raised at Durban in October 1899 by Major E. C. Bethune, 16th Lancers, an officer who was to do well throughout the whole war, like several others who undertook the raising and command of irregular corps before the value of these was fully appreciated at home. The regiment was present at General Hildyard's action at Willow Grange on the night of 22nd November 1899, and did good service (see the General's report, dated 24th November). At Colenso, 15th December 1899, the regiment, 500 strong, was present (see General Buller's despatch of 17th December and list of troops appended), but was detailed as portion of the baggage-guard.

When General Buller commenced the movement by which he attempted to turn the right of the Boer

[1] Awarded D.C.M.   [2] Awarded D.S.O.

Bethune's Mounted Infantry 63

positions between himself and Ladysmith (see South African Light Horse), Bethune's M.I. was split up, a squadron being left under General Barton at Frere and Chieveley, in which district they were constantly employed on reconnaissance duties, and had some sharp casualties. The remainder of the corps accompanied their commander to Potgieter's Drift, where they were attached to General Lyttelton's Brigade, and had skirmishing on various occasions. On the 24th January, when the awful combat was going on upon the summit of Spion Kop, General Lyttelton sent the 2nd Scottish Rifles, the 3rd King's Royal Rifles, and Colonel Bethune, with two of his squadrons, to assist. The 3rd King's Royal Rifles seized the Twin Peaks, north-east of the Spion; the Scottish Rifles ascended the latter mountain and were put into the firing-line on the summit, where they did very fine work, but although Colonel Bethune offered to lead his men on to the plateau,[1] they were kept in reserve by General Talbot Coke, probably because the *rôle* of lining the trenches was rather that of the infantry present.

During the Vaal Krantz operations the corps continued to do patrol work, chiefly on General Buller's right and rear. On 11th February Colonel Bethune was ordered to take his men to Greytown,[2] in order to watch the Boers near the Zululand border, and also with the view of ultimately co-operating from Greytown in any movement towards Dundee. The regiment thus missed the fierce fighting which took place near Colenso between 13th and 27th February.

In his despatch of 30th March, General Buller, in

[1] Lieut. Blake Knox's 'Buller's Campaign,' p. 82; also the Spion Kop Despatches.
Lieut. Blake Knox's 'Buller's Campaign,' p. 133.

mentioning Colonel Bethune, said: "He proved himself to be an excellent commander of irregular horse. He has acted with great skill and judgment when in command of a detached force."

It will be remembered that the Natal Army lay chiefly to the north of Ladysmith during March and April. On 7th May General Buller commenced his movement to turn the Boer position on the Biggarsberg (see South African Light Horse). In his despatch of 24th May 1900, para. 10, General Buller said: "While we were at Ladysmith a force under Colonel Bethune had been holding Greytown and the line of the Tugela, that force being five squadrons Bethune's M.I., one squadron Umvoti Mounted Rifles, two 12-pounders, R.G.A., two 7-pounders, Natal Field Artillery, two Hotchkiss, Natal Field Artillery, six companies Imperial Light Infantry. This force I had directed to advance concurrently with our advance on Vermaak's Kraal, and we established connection with it at eleven o'clock (on the 13th). Colonel Bethune's arrangements had been very good. He had seized during the night, with his left, the hills which commanded the southern sides of the pass up which we had to approach. At 11.20 we advanced up the pass." The enemy made a poor defence and fled, pursued by the Colonial mounted troops. Natal was, almost without loss, cleared of the enemy, and Laing's Nek was turned by the battle of Alleman's Nek on 11th June (see South African Light Horse).

Lieutenant J. M. Dalrymple was severely wounded in a skirmish on 10th May near Helpmakaar.

Before Laing's Nek was turned Bethune's M.I. were to suffer a grievous mishap. In his telegram of 21st May 1900 General Buller said that he had detached

Colonel Bethune with about 500 men from Dundee on the 19th, to march to N'qutu, and to rejoin at Newcastle. On the 20th one squadron was ambushed about six miles south of Vryheid, very few escaping. Captain Goff, 3rd Dragoon Guards, Lieutenants Lanham and M'Lachlan, and about 26 non-commissioned officers and men, were killed. Captain Lord de la Warr, Lieutenant De Lasalle, Sergeant-Major Hadler, and about 30 non-commissioned officers and men, were wounded.

Bethune's M.I. was, during the remainder of 1900, mainly employed on patrol work in the south of the Transvaal and in the Utrecht district, with the view of protecting our posts and the railway line, and frequently they had some skirmishing and much very dangerous work. When Vryheid was occupied by General Hildyard on 19th September the strong position of the enemy was turned by the skilful work of Gough's and Bethune's M.I.[1]

In his final despatch of 9th November 1900, General Buller complimented the troops left to protect his rear: "In the area commanded by General Hildyard the mounted work of guarding the communications was performed by Bethune's M.I. and the composite regiment of M.I.;" and he made numerous mentions. Of Colonel Bethune he said: "Raised this regiment and commanded it most efficiently throughout the campaign. I strongly recommend him to your favourable consideration."

About the end of November 1900 Colonel Bethune left the regiment, having been given a command in the Clanwilliam district of Cape Colony, from which, in a few weeks, he was promoted to the command of a cavalry brigade—a compliment to the high order of

[1] Lord Roberts' despatch of 21st September 1900.

the work done in the first stage of the war by himself and his corps.

The corps was, in December 1900, taken to the Lindley district of the Orange River Colony,[1] and Lieutenant-Colonel S. C. H. Monro was appointed to succeed Colonel Bethune. Captain L. M. Boddam and 5 men were wounded on 31st December near Lindley. The regiment was frequently engaged in that district, and in other parts of the Orange River Colony. Captain G. O. Webster was killed in a railway accident at Bethulie on 1st February, and on the 6th 1 man was killed and several wounded. In Lord Kitchener's despatch of 8th May 1901, para. 5, it is mentioned that on 9th April at Dewetsdorp, in the south-east of the Orange River Colony, Lieutenant-Colonel Monro, with a detachment of 150 mounted men and a pom-pom, after two hours' fighting cleverly effected the capture of a Boer convoy and 83 prisoners, including Commandant Bresler and Lieutenant Lindique of the Staats Artillery. Colonel Monro's casualties were 1 man killed and 4 wounded. Private G. E. Duffey was killed; Sergeant-Major Goulding and Private Rosevean died of wounds.

Colonel Monro's column, consisting of Bethune's M.I., about 275 strong, and the 56th, 57th, 58th, and 59th Companies Imperial Yeomanry, with 2 guns of the 39th Battery Royal Field Artillery, was, on 19th May 1901, taken to Cape Colony (see despatch of 8th July), where, down to the close of the war, they were everlastingly pursuing commandos under Kritzinger, Myburg, and other leaders. On 12th September the force was heavily engaged with Commandant Smuts at Stavelberg, in the eastern part of Cape Colony, and

[1] Despatch of 8th March 1901.

lost 7 killed and 6 wounded, the latter including Lieutenant Pollard. On 27th March 1902 Captain Collopy and 4 men were wounded at Mointje's Nek, and a few days later there were further casualties at Maraisburg, Cape Colony.

Like the other troops in Cape Colony, Bethune's M.I. had few opportunities of gaining distinction in the latter phases of the war, but the work of Colonel Monro's column was very often referred to in terms of approval by Lord Kitchener.

The Mentions gained by the corps are as follows :—

SIR R. BULLER'S DESPATCHES : 30th March 1900.—Major (local Lieut.-Col.) E. C. Bethune, 16th Lancers ; Capts. W. E. D. Goff (3rd Dragoon Guards), W. C. C. Erskine ; Lieuts. C. J. Collopy, L. Lanham ; Cpls. F. Howroyd, H. Schott ; Ptes. P. Kilcullen, A. E. Partridge, E. G. Brown, H. Edwards, A. M'Neilage.

9th November 1900.—Lieut.-Col. Bethune (raised and commanded regiment most efficiently) ; Capts. C. J. Collopy, A. E. Capell, Lieuts. Norman Packer and M. Prior have distinguished themselves on more than one occasion ; Capts. F. M. Ford, J. H. A. Annesley (3rd Dragoon Guards), Lieuts. A. A. Slatter and G. Webster performed continuous good work throughout, as also have Regl. Sgt.-Major G. W. Mortiboy[1] (18th Hussars) ; Sq. Sgt.-Majors J. H. Macbeth,[1] H. E. Saunders ; Sgts. A. G. Nichol, A. H. Ball, H. Shackle, F. Howroyd ; Ptes. A. S. Reeves, A. S. Partridge,[1] P. Kilcullen ; Lce.-Cpl. Farquhar.

LORD ROBERTS' DESPATCHES : 2nd April 1901.—Capts. A. E. Capell,[2] Collopy,[2] W. C. C. Erskine, F. C. M. Ford[2] ; Lieuts. Lanham[1] and Prior[2] ; Sgt. F. Howroyd ; Cpl. H. Schott ; Lce.-Cpl. Glassborough ; Tpr. Allen ; Pte. A. S. Partridge[1] ; Sq. Sgt.-Major Murrow.[1]

4th September 1901.—Capt. G. Osborne.

LORD KITCHENER'S DESPATCHES : 8th April 1902.—Lieut. H. H. Shott.[2]

23rd June 1902.—Lieuts. W. A. Pollard,[2] D. Crawford, R. N. B. Needham ; Regl. Sgt.-Major Mortiboy[1] (18th Hussars) ; Trumpet-Major D. E. Densham ; Cpl. F. S. Stallard. Colonel Bethune was awarded the C.B.

---

[1] Awarded D.C.M.   [2] Awarded D.S.O.

THORNEYCROFT'S MOUNTED INFANTRY.

THIS corps, to become famous in the course of the war, was raised at Pietermaritzburg by Major A. W. Thorneycroft of the Royal Scots Fusiliers. Prior to the battle of Colenso, 15th December 1899, they did a good deal of patrol work, and thus had some opportunities of getting into shape. From the start they were, apart from a splendid leader, well supplied with good officers. By the middle of November the corps had reached a strength of 500. Their first engagement was outside Mooi River on 22nd November, under Major-General Barton, when he was endeavouring to clear the enemy from the country between himself and Major-General Hildyard, who, for four days in November 1899, was practically shut up in Estcourt. The corps had two wounded. At Colenso the regiment was heavily engaged, like the rest of Lord Dundonald's Brigade of Irregulars (see South African Light Horse). The regiment was on the extreme right of the British line, and made a fine effort to capture Hlangwane—indeed some of those who were present expressed the opinion that if any substantial support had been sent them, they would have succeeded in their attempt. General Barton explained to the War Commission that, to his regret, this support could not be afforded (see South African Light Horse). The regiment lost 1 officer, Lieutenant C. M. Jenkins, and 4 men killed, and 3 officers, Lieutenants W. Otto, Ponsonby, and Holford (19th Hussars, attached), and 27 men wounded.

In the movement by which General Buller attempted

to turn the Boer right Thorneycroft's M.I. were again with Lord Dundonald. On the 18th and 20th of January 1900 the regiment had not so conspicuous a place as the composite regiment of Mounted Infantry or the South African Light Horse (which see). When Bastion Hill was seized the regiment was on Lord Dundonald's right, keeping in touch with the left of Hildyard's infantry. On the 22nd it was determined that Spion Kop, the great hill, at the angle where the Boer line turned back from the river, must be taken. To allow of the ground being examined the operation was put off till the evening of the 23rd. At first it was arranged to ascend by the south-east face, next Trichard's Drift; but, near dusk on the 23rd, General Woodgate, who was in command of the assaulting force, decided to go by the south-west face. In the brief twilight Colonel Thorneycroft made a hasty reconnaissance, and sketched the outstanding features, trees, kraals, &c. The force employed was the 2nd Battalion Royal Lancaster Regiment, the 2nd Battalion Lancashire Fusiliers, two companies of the 1st Battalion South Lancashire Regiment, and Thorneycroft's M.I., whose strength was 18 officers and 180 men, all dismounted for the task in hand. About 11 P.M. on the 23rd the force moved off, and after the first half-mile Thorneycroft and his men headed the column, the Colonel himself, with Lieutenants Farquhar and Gordon Forbes and Privates Shaw and Macadam, acting as guides. The most perfect silence was maintained. Halts were frequently made in the ascent, which was so difficult that at times the hands had to be used. During the ascent the column opened out into lines, the order being — Thorneycroft's M.I., Lancashire Fusiliers, Royal Lancaster Regiment, and two companies South Lancashire Regiment. At 4 A.M. the last slope was breasted, a Boer sentry challenged, and instantly the picket fired. The leading lines lay down until it was thought the magazines were emptied, then rushed forward with the bayonet; but the picket fled, and the summit was occupied. Steps were immediately taken to make defensive works. In his report, dated 26th January 1900, Spion Kop Despatches, p. 28, Colonel Thorneycroft said: "There was a mist on the hill, and in the darkness and mist it was difficult to get the exact crest line for a good field of fire, and the boulders made it difficult to dig, but we made a rough trench and 'breastwork.' About 4.30 some Boers opened fire; our men replied—then the firing died out for a time. It was found that the trench did not command the ascent, and men were pushed forward to line the crest. The enemy recommenced firing now more heavily. Defensive works were about to be commenced on the crest, about 180 yards in front of the trench, when the mist lifted—this was between 7.30 and 8. The Boers' rifle-fire now became extremely severe, while 3 guns and a Maxim-Nordenfeldt pitched shells on to the plateau with great accuracy from a range of 3000 yards. It was also now discovered that the trench which had been cut was enfiladed at easy range by trenches or natural caves occupied by the enemy. Most of the advanced parties, being also enfiladed, were completely wiped out, but these were constantly reinforced or replaced. Thorneycroft's M.I. had been placed at the left of the trench with parties in advance. When visiting this position about 8 A.M. General Woodgate was mortally wounded. Colonel Blomfield of the Lancashire Fusiliers took command, but he too was wounded. Early in the forenoon, probably about 10 A.M., Colonel Thorneycroft received a message that he was in command of the hill. The messenger was killed as he delivered the order. Over and over again the advance parties were entirely destroyed. No help could be sent to the wounded. Officers and men who were not killed outright kept on firing as long as they could hold a rifle. In his report Colonel Thorneycroft says: "The Boers closed in on the right and centre. Some men of mixed regiments at right end of trench got up and put up their hands; three or four Boers came out and signalled their comrades to advance. I was the only officer in the trench on the left, and I got up and shouted to the leader of the Boers that I was the commandant and that there was no surrender. In order not to get mixed up in any discussion I called on all men to follow me, and retired to some rocks farther back. The Boers opened a heavy fire on us. On reaching the rocks I saw a company of the Middlesex Regiment advancing. I collected them up to the rocks, and ordered all to advance again. This the men did, and we reoccupied the trench and crestline in front. As the companies of the Middlesex arrived I pushed them on to reinforce, and was able to hold the whole line again. The men on the left of our defence, who were detached at some distance from the trench, had held their ground. The Imperial Light Infantry reinforced this part. The Boers then made a desperate endeavour to shell us out of the position, and the fire caused many casualties. The Scottish Rifles came up, and I pushed them up to the right and left flanks as they arrived."

After speaking of the difficulties arising from the

uncertainty as to who was in command on the hill, Colonel Thorneycroft goes on to say: "The heavy fire continued, and the Boers brought a gun and Maxim-Nordenfeldt to bear on us from the east, thus sweeping the plateau from the east, north, and northwest, and enfilading our trenches. The men held on all along the line, notwithstanding the terrific fire which was brought to bear on them as the enemy's guns (which now numbered 5 and 2 Nordenfeldts) were absolutely unmolested. When night began to close in I determined to take some steps, and a consultation was held. The officer commanding Scottish Rifles and Colonel Crofton were both of opinion that the hill was untenable. I entirely agreed with their view, and so I gave the order for the troops to withdraw on to the neck and ridge where the hospital was. It was now quite dark, and we went out to warn all to come in. The enemy still kept up a dropping fire. The regiments formed up near the neck and marched off in formation, the Scottish Rifles forming the rear-guard.[1] I was obliged, owing to want of bearers, to leave a large number of wounded on the field. In forming my decision as to retirement I was influenced by the following — 1. The superiority of the Boer artillery, inasmuch as their guns were placed in such positions as to prevent our artillery-fire being brought to bear on them from the lower slopes near camp, or indeed from any other place.

"2. By my not knowing what steps were being taken to supply me in the morning with guns other than the mountain-battery, which, in my opinion, could not have lived under the long-range fire of the Boer artillery and their close-range rifle-fire.

[1] See also account given under Imperial Light Infantry.

"3. By the total absence of water and provisions.

" 4. By the difficulty of entrenching on the top of the hill, to make trench in any way cover from infantry fire with the few spades at my disposal, the ground being so full of rocks.

" 5. Finally, I did not see how the hill could be held unless the Boer artillery was silenced, and this was impossible. Lieutenant Winston Churchill arrived when the troops had been marched off."

It may be noted that the shells which did greatest damage to the troops on Spion Kop were those fired from the 15-pounders captured by the Boers at Colenso; and we had thus convincing proof of the efficiency of our own "time shrapnel."

It is impossible to do justice to the scene on the hill throughout the day, or to the splendid behaviour of the great mass of the troops. There have been several detailed accounts of the heroic combat published, but none is more realistic than that of Lieutenant L. Oppenheim, of Thorneycroft's Mounted Infantry, published in the 'Nineteenth Century' of 1901.[1] Mr Oppenheim has there given a contribution to the history of the war which is invaluable. Colonel Thorneycroft says little about his own doings, so a quotation from Mr Oppenheim is not out of place. "It was one o'clock. A soldier near to Colonel Thorneycroft in the angle of the entrenchment drew his attention to some movement which was going on on the right of the entrenchment, some fifty yards away. The stretch of wall in between was unoccupied. The soldier said, 'By God, they're surrendering,' and this was what was happening: About forty men of

[1] These quotations are given with the kind permission of 'The Nineteenth Century and After.'

mixed regiments (amongst whom was no man of the Mounted Infantry) were standing up in the entrenchment with their empty arms raised. Their rifles lay at their feet, and their hands were in the air, while coming up the slope towards them were three Boers. Other Boers were following these behind. The three in front turned and beckoned to their comrades to come on, and all were waving small pocket-handkerchiefs. The leader of the Boers was only about thirty yards away from Colonel Thorneycroft. He was a Transvaaler, by name De Kock, and I continue the story of what then happened as he himself described it to a British officer in the Biggarsberg laager in April. 'We had got up, and we should have had the whole hill,' he said; 'the English were about to surrender, and we were all coming up, when a great big, angry, red-faced soldier ran out of the trench on our right and screamed out, "I'm the commandant here; take your men back to hell, sir; there's no surrender!"' and then there was ten minutes *mêlée*. It was just such a trick as the Boers love. Profiting by the shattered *morale* of a small body of men who had lost their officers, the Boers were hoping to start a discussion and gain time for more and more men to creep up into the 'dead' ground behind them. The 'great big soldier' was Colonel Thorneycroft, who, grasping the situation, ran forward to the Boer and then back to his men. . . . Towards sundown the men of the old force were completely exhausted. Since six on the night of the 23rd they had been continuously under arms; they had had absolutely no water and no food. Many of them had been served out with six-pound tins of beef the day before, which they could not carry up the hill, and had, with an improvidence frequently seen, thrown away. Of the lack of water General Woodgate had spoken as early as ten o'clock; a few tins of water had since then been brought up on the backs of mules. Of these more than half had been spilt, for the mules had fallen down the hillside, and the rest was inadequate for the hospital. The intolerable strain of the shell-fire and rifle-fire had told on the stoutest. Amongst the prisoners taken by the Boers from the right of the entrenchment on Spion Kop was an officer. When he arrived in Pretoria on the following day his fellow-captives went out to meet him, anxious to get the news. One asked, 'How's my brother?' His answer was 'Dead.' Another asked, 'How is my brother?' His answer was 'Dead, dead; everybody's dead; the British army is all dead.' And for a month no other answer to every question put to him could an averagely sane and healthy and strong and brave young English officer give to all who spoke to him. Such had been the strain of the 24th of January." The casualties of the corps, according to the lists published at the time, were: killed, 6 officers—Captains the Hon. W. H. Petre and C. S. Knox-Gore, Lieutenants C. G. Greenfell, P. F. Newnham, H. S. M'Corquodale, and the Hon. N. W. Hill-Trevor—and 20 non-commissioned officers and men; wounded, 4 officers—Captain R. A. Bettington, Lieutenants A. W. J. Forster, J. W. B. Baldwin, and N. Howard—and 41 non-commissioned officers and men; missing, 1 officer and 12 non-commissioned officers and men. Nearly all the latter were afterwards returned as killed. This was practically fifty per cent of the strength.

In his despatch of 30th January 1900, para. 6, General

Buller said : " I have not thought it necessary to order any investigation. If at sundown the defence of the summit had been taken regularly in hand, entrenchments laid out, gun emplacements prepared, the dead removed, the wounded collected, and, in fact, the whole place brought under regular military command, and careful arrangements made for the supply of water and food to the scattered fighting line, the hills would have been held, I am sure. (7) But no arrangements were made. General Coke appears to have been ordered away just as he would have been useful, and no one succeeded him ; those on the top were ignorant of the fact that guns were coming up, and generally there was a want of organisation and system that acted most unfavourably on the defence. It is admitted by all that Colonel Thorneycroft acted with the greatest gallantry throughout the day, and really saved the situation. Preparations for the second day's defence should have been organised during the day and have been commenced at nightfall. As this was not done, I think Colonel Thorneycroft exercised a wise discretion. . . . I cannot close these remarks without bearing testimony to the gallant and admirable behaviour of the troops ; the endurance shown by the Lancashire Fusiliers, the Middlesex Regiment, and Thorneycroft's Mounted Infantry was admirable, while the efforts of the 2nd Bn. Scottish Rifles and 3rd Bn. King's Royal Rifles were equally good, and the Royal Lancasters fought gallantly."

It will be remembered that in his covering despatch of 13th February 1900, para. 7, Lord Roberts, in forwarding the despatches as to Spion Kop, said : " The attempt to relieve Ladysmith, described in these despatches, was well devised, and I agree with Sir Redvers

Buller in thinking that it ought to have succeeded. That it failed may in some measure be due to the difficulties of the ground and the commanding positions held by the enemy—probably also to errors of judgment and want of administrative capacity on the part of Sir Charles Warren. But whatever faults Sir C. Warren may have committed, the failure must also be ascribed to the disinclination of the officer in supreme command to assert his authority and see that what he thought best was done, and also to the unwarrantable and needless assumption of responsibility by a subordinate officer." The historian, writing, say, a generation after the war closed, will probably say that the sting in the last sentence lacked the generosity which one likes to associate with the character of a great leader, and it is pardonable to say now that in penning the lines Lord Roberts did injustice to himself. The despatch was dated 13th February 1900, when the Commander-in-Chief was immersed in the great movements for relieving Kimberley, and the day was one of disappointment to himself, as on it he lost the convoy at the Riet river, a loss which was to have no slight effect on his campaign.

The remnant of Thorneycroft's M.I. was with Lord Dundonald protecting the right and rear at Vaal Krantz, and took part in the operations which commenced on 12th February and lasted till the 27th, when Ladysmith was relieved (see South African Light Horse). Thorneycroft's men were the first troops to cross the Tugela on the 20th, and did most valuable scouting work on the 21st.[1] Unfortunately the information which they obtained was not fully utilised.

In his despatch of 30th March 1900, after the relief

[1] 'Times' History, vol. iii.

of Ladysmith was effected, General Buller, in mentioning Colonel Thorneycroft, said: "Raised and commanded Thorneycroft's Mounted Infantry, for which he possessed in a marked degree the necessary qualifications. I have already brought to notice the gallantry and ability he displayed at Spion Kop, 24th January."

Thorneycroft's Mounted Infantry took part in the movement for turning the Boer position on the Biggarsberg and that at Laing's Nek. They suffered slight casualties on various occasions during these operations. In the despatch of 19th June 1900 Colonel Thorneycroft was again mentioned, as was also Captain Mann, killed in action on the 10th. General Buller stated that on the 13th of June he sent back the Telegraph detachment under an escort of 150 men of Thorneycroft's Mounted Infantry under Captain C. F. Minchin. "They were attacked by superior forces south of Gans Vlei, whom they drove off, and the waggons were brought safely back *via* Botha's Pass with the loss of only about seven miles of their line, which they were unable to pick up. I consider that Captain Minchin's dispositions were good." One officer and 2 men gained mention on this occasion.

When General Buller moved north towards Belfast and Lydenburg, the regiment remained with General Clery in the vicinity of the Natal-Pretoria Railway, and had arduous patrol work and often severe fighting, as on 6th September, when 4 men were killed and Captain Molyneux and several men were wounded. General Buller spoke of the great value of their work in his final despatch. In again mentioning the Colonel, General Buller said: "This officer merits the highest commendation I can bestow. His talents both as an organiser and a leader of men are of the highest order."

General Buller's "tenacity" has often been referred to. Here he certainly stuck to his man, and Lord Roberts was to come round so far. In his final despatch of 2nd April 1901, his lordship, referring to Colonel Thorneycroft, said: " Since coming under my immediate command he has gained my confidence as a most gallant and capable leader."

In December 1900 the corps was railed from Standerton to Bloemfontein to strengthen the Thabanchu-Ladybrand line, and if possible to bar De Wet's retreat before the columns of General Charles Knox. De Wet broke through, but lost two guns and some waggons of ammunition [1] (see South African Light Horse). On 16th December Kritzinger and Hertzog, with about 2000 men, entered Cape Colony, and among other troops Colonel Thorneycroft's men were railed to the Colony, where they took part in endless skirmishes and pursuits. On 25th December Lord Kitchener wired that the corps had occupied Britstown unopposed. The Boers retired in the direction of Prieska, and a few days later the corps was reported by the Commander-in-Chief to be pursuing a body of the enemy in the Carnarvon district. In February De Wet himself entered the Colony, but by the splendid exertions of the numerous columns was soon driven out again, having left behind him all his guns and practically all his waggons. The corps took a prominent part in the pursuit between 14th and 24th February, and had casualties on several occasions. During March and April 1901 Thorneycroft's M.I. were operating in the east of the Orange River Colony, at first south of Bloemfontein and afterwards about Brandfort, " surprising and capturing on their farms by night many

[1] Lord Kitchener's despatch of 8th March 1901.

armed Burghers who, having been disbanded from De Wet's commandos, were living at their homes." In April Thorneycroft dispersed a "minor gathering" about Winburg.[1] Thorneycroft's column consisted at this time of the 21st and 22nd squadrons and the 18th Battalion Imperial Yeomanry, 740 men; his own corps, 160; Burmah M.I., 165; 4 guns of the 76th Battery, and 1 pom-pom.

In May and June Thorneycroft's column was employed in the Brandfort-Senekal-Hoopstad district, and made useful captures. On 1st July they were ordered to march to the Basutoland border, and thereafter from Ladybrand through the south-east of the Orange River Colony to Aliwal in Cape Colony, where they arrived about 28th July. They now moved back across the Orange towards Jagersfontein, arriving there about 6th August. On this last march Thorneycroft took 28 prisoners, 1000 horses, and much stock.[2]

In the middle of August it was apparent that there was to be a gathering of Boers in the south-east of the Orange River Colony, a district the regiment had just passed through, so Thorneycroft's column and other troops crossed the railway into the Smithfield-Rouxville district, but "in spite of the close proximity of Colonel Thorneycroft's troops east of Rouxville," Smuts' commando slipped across the Orange into Cape Colony on 4th September.[3] Throughout September the force remained in the same district, and at Florence had sharp fighting, when 3 officers and 5 non-commissioned officers and men of this corps gained mention. Captain Barrett was killed and 3 men wounded at Florence on the 21st.

---

[1] Despatch of 8th May 1901. [2] Despatches of 8th July and 8th August.
[3] Despatch of 8th September.

The corps continued to operate in the Orange River Colony till the conclusion of hostilities, but only on a few occasions were they seriously engaged. In the beginning of April 1902 a portion of the regiment were with Colonel Ternan in the Boshof-Bultfontein district, and a party were in a very mixed patrol under Major Luard, which "was suddenly attacked by a large party of Boers under Commandant Badenhorst, and after an engagement which reflected very little credit upon many of our men the majority of the patrol were captured by the enemy."[1] The party from the corps lost 1 killed and 8 wounded, a larger proportion than the other troops with whom they were associated. It was an unfortunate incident in an otherwise spotless career.

The Mentions gained by the corps were as follows:—

GENERAL BULLER'S DESPATCHES: 30th March 1900.—Lieut.-Col. Thorneycroft in the terms already noted; Capt. (local Major) G. St Aubyn, K.R.R.C., was conspicuous both at Colenso and Spion Kop for great gallantry, has been an excellent second in command. Capts. Hon. J. Petre, Suffolk Hussars (killed), C. H. Knox Gore (killed), E. Molyneux, R. A. Bettington; Lieuts. P. Newnham, I.S.C., H. Sargent, I.S.C., J. H. Baldwin, A. Bensusan, M. G. Farquhar; Colour-Sgt. P. Myall (killed); Cpls. P. Hetherington (killed), E. C. Lithie (killed); Ptes. A. Withers, T. Dolan, J. E. Macadam. Sgt. J. H. Jeffries,[2] conspicuous gallantry on 15th December 1899 at Colenso, and on January 24th at Spion Kop. Sgt. J. Mason,[2] conspicuous gallantry at Spion Kop. Ptes. G. E. Ackland,[2] J. B. Fischer,[2] on February 21st, crossing Tugela River under heavy fire to see if there were barbed wire in the drift.

19th June 1900.—Col. Thorneycroft; Capts. H. Mann (killed), Minchin,[3] I.S.C.; Lieut. Green; Cpl. Teadall; Pte. Macgregor.

9th November.—Col. Thorneycroft in terms already mentioned. Capt. St Aubyn (second in command) is a leader of high ability and courage, much above the average of his rank, and has shown great tact in dealing with Colonial troops. Capt. M. G. Farquhar,[3] who has performed exceptionally good service throughout, only joined for the war, and I recommend him for special consideration. Capt. E. M. J. Molyneux,[3] 12th Bengal Lancers, a

---

[1] Lord Kitchener's despatch of 1st June 1902.
[2] Awarded D.C.M.   [3] Awarded D.S.O.

dashing and capable leader of men, has distinguished himself on several occasions. Capt. E. M. Morris, Devon Regiment, has acted as Adjutant throughout the whole twelve months, and has been distinguished for his power of organisation, his tact and management of men in camp, and his ability and courage in the field. Capt. A. D. Green, Worcestershire Regiment, an excellent officer, has shown great ability as a scout, and has dash, pluck, and good judgment. Capt. C. Minchin, 1st Punjaub Cavalry, an officer of many acquirements, has done specially good service throughout. Lieut. R. Villiers,[1] who joined the regiment as a private, having been in the Ceylon Mounted Infantry, specially good work throughout. Major W. Peyton, 15th Hussars, succeeded Capt. St Aubyn as second in command on July 23rd, when that officer was invalided; with a quick grasp of the situation, he is a leader of high ability, and is also a valuable officer in matters of interior economy. Ptes. A. Neilson[2] and W. Strong are brought specially to notice for gallant conduct.

LORD ROBERTS' DESPATCH: *2nd April* 1901.—Col. Thorneycroft, in terms already mentioned; Capts. Farquhar,[1] C. Hamilton[1]; Lieuts. T. W. Howard,[1] G. S. O. Forbes,[1] W. R. Ponsonby,[1] T. Thompson,[1] R. N. Villiers[1]; Colour-Sgt. Makfeeler[2]; Sgts. J. Mayne,[2] H. Sperling,[2] W. M. Strong[2]; Ptes. F. Glover,[2] W. Lyons,[2] J. M'Kechnie[2]; Saddler W. Fox[2]; Pte. A. Neilson.[2]

LORD KITCHENER'S DESPATCHES: *8th May* 1901.—Pte. G. B. Bromley, near Vlakfontein, Orange River Colony, March 13, on patrol, he in company with Lieut. Rose dismounted and gave his horse to a dismounted man, and covered retirement on foot.

8th October 1901.—Lieut.-Col. C. F. Minchin, D.S.O.; Capts. R. T. Barrett (killed), and T. Thompson, D.S.O., for conspicuous gallantry in attack on Wessel's Commando in September in charging a donga from which enemy was firing heavily; Sgts. H. P. Wheatley, T. P. Jones; Cpl. L. Alderson promoted Sgt.; Ptes. A. H. Horwood and R. J. Dowling promoted Cpls. for marked gallantry in action at Florence, Orange River Colony, in September.

23rd June 1902.—Capts. T. Bruce Steer,[1] W. K. Prettejohn, J. Hendry; Sgt.-Major A. Chadburn,[2] 10th Hussars; Sgts. H. P. Wheatley, L. Alderson, J. P. Jones, F. Hill.

---

[1] Awarded D.S.O. [2] Awarded D.C.M.

IMPERIAL LIGHT INFANTRY.

THIS corps was raised in Natal and was largely recruited from those who had lost their employment through the outbreak of hostilities. The command was given to Lieut.-Colonel Nash (Border Regiment). By the end of December 1899 the regiment was ready for active service, and it was inspected by General Sir C. Warren on 2nd January 1900. When the move by Potgieter's and Trichard's Drifts was projected, this regiment and the Somersetshire Light Infantry were put into General Coke's 10th Brigade, taking the place of the 1st Yorkshire Regiment and the 2nd Warwickshire, both of which had been dropped at Cape Town. The Imperial Light Infantry saw comparatively little training and no fighting until they were thrown into the awful combat on Spion Kop on 24th January 1900 (see Thorneycroft's Mounted Infantry). The Imperial Light Infantry, about 1000 strong, was paraded at 10 P.M. on 23rd January, and, as ordered, they took up positions from which they could reinforce General Woodgate, who commanded the force detailed to capture the hill. Sir C. Warren visited the regiment early on the morning of the 24th, and asked the officers if they had seen anything of a mountain-battery which he was expecting. They had not. He requested that 2 companies be sent forward to a specified point to be ready to escort the battery to the summit. He appeared anxious as to its non-appearance. The companies of Captains Champney and Smith moved out at 6 A.M. and waited as ordered for the battery, but about 9

A.M. a staff-officer told them to reinforce immediately on the summit. The 2 companies advanced and reached the top shortly after 10 A.M.[1] At this hour the enemy's fire was appalling, the hail of bullets and shells being ceaseless, but these untried volunteers are said to have pushed up to the shallow trench and the firing-line beyond it without flinching. They at once commenced to suffer very severe losses. These 2 companies were the first reinforcements to enter the firing-line, and their arrival proved most opportune, some Lancashire companies being very hard pressed at this time and at this part of the position.

About mid-day Colonel Nash was ordered to reinforce on the summit with "every available man." About 2 P.M. he reached the top with his remaining companies, who at once bolted out from the rocks at the head of the ascent and fed the firing-line, pushing forward fearlessly across the open.

Throughout the afternoon and evening the firing was unceasing, and often at very close quarters; after dark it had died away. A field-officer of the Imperial Light Infantry, formerly a regular officer, who was present, has stated to the writer that about 8 P.M. it was whispered a retirement was contemplated, and that about 9 o'clock Colonel Nash intimated that he had got a message to get ready to move off the hill. These hours are uncertain, and might be put somewhat later. The regiment having been collected, fell in and marched off. They had barely gone 200 yards, however, when an officer said to Colonel Nash, "Where are you going?" The latter replied that he had been ordered to take down the regiment. The other officer

[1] Lieutenant Blake Knox's 'Buller's Campaign,' and an account furnished to the writer by an officer of the Imperial Light Infantry.

Imperial Light Infantry

then said, "I am Colonel Hill of the Middlesex; not a man or regiment is to leave the hill." The officers of the Imperial Light Infantry then said to their men that a mistake had been made, and the column "about turned," marched back to the place they had come from, put out pickets, and lay down among the dead and wounded. The worst feature of this very trying experience was the ceaseless crying of the wounded for water: there was none on the hill. During the night a staff-officer informed Colonel Nash that he had better bring down his men before dawn if no fresh troops or orders came up. Between 3 A.M. and 4 A.M. the regiment was again collected and finally left the hill. No Boers had ventured on to the hill up to that time.

From the reports of Colonel Thorneycroft and General Talbot Coke one would gather that all the troops left the hill together, the Scottish Rifles bringing up the rear, but in the darkness the absence of the Imperial Light Infantry from the main body might escape notice. The account given above is confirmed by the terms of a message published in the Spion Kop despatches, p. 32, as follows: "Officer commanding Imperial Light Infantry. Withdraw and at once. 2 A.M. W. J. Bonus, Brigade-Major." No explanation of any kind is given as to this message, although it is appended to a report by General Talbot Coke the text of which gives the impression that the troops were all down the hill before midnight.

The losses of the Imperial Light Infantry, as published at the time, were: killed—2 officers, Lieutenants Rudall and Kynoch-Shand, and 29 non-commissioned officers and men; wounded—3 officers, Captain Coleman, Lieutenants H. R. Brown and Richards, and 110 non-commissioned officers and men; missing—19 men. Most of the latter were afterwards found to have been killed or wounded.

After the army had recrossed the Tugela, General Warren visited the camp of the Imperial Light Infantry and congratulated them on the splendid fight they had made. He specially mentioned by name several men who had distinguished themselves, among them being Private T. Hughes, who, in a duel with some Boers among rocks not 50 yards away, was hit five times.

Coke's Brigade was not engaged at Vaal Krantz in the beginning of February. When General Buller gave up his efforts against the enemy's right and took back his army to the position opposite Colenso, the Imperial Light Infantry were left, with Colonel Burn-Murdoch's cavalry, to protect the left rear of the Natal army, but, before the close of the fourteen days' fighting, all available troops were needed about Colenso. The regiment marched to Chieveley, arriving there on the 22nd at noon. Four companies, under Major Hay, were now ordered to Colenso, where they were to report to General Hart. It was thought that their duties would be the off-loading stores at the railway bridge which was broken. As soon as they had dinners the 4 companies entrained for Colenso, but on arrival there found the army was across the river, very heavy firing going on upon the north side. They crossed in a pont, this operation taking two hours. Major Hay endeavoured to find General Hart's whereabouts while there was still some light; a staff-officer pointed to some hills. After a short sleep and a fatiguing and anxious march, for the enemy's lines were close at hand and the ground broken, Hart's

Brigade was found as reveille was sounding on the 23rd. The 4 companies were put into the Irish Brigade, their companions being the Royal Inniskilling Fusiliers, Connaught Rangers, and Royal Dublin Fusiliers. On the afternoon of the 23rd the Brigade assaulted Hart's Hill, one of the strongest of the many immensely strong positions north of the Tugela. The Imperial Light Infantry were directed by General Hart to move down the river to the right; they then moved up a ravine, turned to the left and assaulted the left of the Boer position on that hill, but a very heavy fire struck them from trenches on the east or opposite side of the ravine, which trenches seemed to be receiving no attention from any one. Major Hay, who was said to have behaved with great gallantry at Spion Kop and on this occasion, fell badly wounded. His men never reached the top of the hill. The Irish regiments in the frontal attack also failed to reach the top. General Buller said the troops failed to carry the top of the hill, but they established themselves in the lower sangars and other positions, "which ensured our ultimate success."[1] The casualties of the brigade were very heavy. There was some confusion about the losses of the Imperial Light Infantry. Lieutenant Blake Knox of the R.A.M.C., who made up the return, says: "The Imperial Light Infantry had Major Hay wounded, and among the men 19 were killed, 105 wounded, and 8 missing—some of these casualties occurring on the 24th," but an officer of the corps says the losses were not so great, and that these figures must have included some men not belonging to them. The 4 companies took part in the

[1] Despatch of 30th March 1900.

further operations which on the 27th were crowned with success, the whole Boer position being captured and the road to Ladysmith opened.

In mentioning Lieut.-Colonel Nash in the despatch of 30th March General Buller said: "Commanded the Imperial Light Infantry. The extremely good work done by the Battalion is due to the excellent manner in which it was commanded by Lt.-Col. Nash." Of course the material must have been very good, otherwise the best of regimental officers could not have got a hastily raised body of untrained men to do this good work with the very limited preparation possible. Seven non-commissioned officers and men were mentioned in the same despatch, 4 of whom got the D.C.M.

After the relief of Ladysmith the regiment was mainly employed in the Greytown district under Colonel Bethune[1] (see Bethune's Mounted Infantry). They performed valuable service until General Buller moved forward to clear the Biggarsberg in May. Col. Bethune's force co-operated with General Buller, and joined him near Helpmakaar about the 14th. From June to October the regiment did garrison duty about Newcastle and Volksrust. In his final despatch General Buller, in referring to the regiment, said: "This battalion, which was raised at a time Natal was short of troops, has done good service. It has latterly been well commanded by Major (local Lieut.-Col.) M. C. Curry, Devonshire Regiment."

During 1901 the Imperial Light Infantry garrisoned various forts and posts on the borders of Natal, and in the south-east corner of the Transvaal. They were disbanded in June, as by that time mounted

[1] General Buller's despatch of 24th May 1900.

troops were what was needed. Many of the men joined mounted corps.

The Mentions gained were as follows :—

SIR C. WARREN'S DESPATCH: 1st *February* 1900, for Spion Kop.—Lieut.-Col. Nash, commanding I.L.I., reports that Cpl. Pack Weldon[1] refused to surrender until compelled to do so; he was killed outside the trenches. Pte. Chambers showed conspicuous bravery under fire when leading men in firing-line; he was killed. Pte. Hughes,[1] wounded five times, wished to return to firing-line, but was prevented by those dressing his wounds.

GENERAL BULLER'S DESPATCHES: 30th *March* 1900.—Again mentions Pack Weldon and Hughes, and states that after being wounded Hughes returned to the firing-line and was wounded on right shoulder, then, firing from left shoulder, he was successively wounded in left arm, throat, wrist, hand, and chest. Pte. R. Hunter,[1] on February 24th in action near Pieter's Hill, whilst under a heavy fire, twice built walls round wounded comrades. Pte. G. Reed in same action, while under heavy fire, carried a wounded man of the Connaught Rangers to shelter of a kraal, and remained with him after other men had retired. Major (local Lieut.-Col.) Nash in terms already given; Qrmr.-Sgt. Hillstead; Pay-Sgt. G. Pirie, R. C. Geddes.

9th *November* 1900.—Major Curry; Capt. C. C. Maynard, 2nd Devons; 2nd Lt. (local Capt.) G. H. Jackson, 1st Border Regiment; Capt. and Adjutant H. Bousfield; 2nd Lt. Gregorie.

LORD ROBERTS' DESPATCH: 2nd *April* 1901.—Capt. Bousfield; 2nd Lt. Gregorie; Cpl. P. M. Weldon[1] (killed); Ptes. Chambers (killed), T. Hughes,[1] Hunter,[1] G. Reed.[1]

CAPE POLICE.

THIS force was so ubiquitous, and its services throughout the whole war were so varied, that to give a connected account of its work is impossible. It must suffice to mention the districts and occasions when these services were of outstanding value. At the commencement of the war the force was distributed

[1] Awarded D.C.M.

as follows[1]: Kimberley district 226, Mafeking 103, scattered over Colony 430.

All through October, November, and December detachments of the Police were doing all the work of regular mounted infantry, and much besides, as when they provided the crews of armoured trains. Towards the end of December there were sundry operations about Dordrecht, in which mixed forces of Cape Mounted Rifles, Police, and Brabant's Horse were employed, and frequently there was sharp fighting (see Cape Mounted Rifles). On the 30th Lieutenant Warren of the Cape Police was killed in one of these actions. On 3rd January 1900 "the Police Camp north of Cyphergat and overlooking Molteno" was attacked in force, and was, indeed, for a time quite isolated. The garrison seems to have been about 140 Police under Inspector Neylan, and 58 Kaffrarian Rifles under Captain R. Maclean. The attack commenced in the early morning, but the defenders held out splendidly till nearly three o'clock in the afternoon, when the Berkshire Mounted Infantry and the 79th Battery R.F.A. drove off the enemy. Major Pollock, in his account of this engagement, notes that Inspector Neylan and Captain Maclean, who came to his assistance, were both satisfied that the site of the camp was badly chosen. "The two put their heads together, and the result was that the camp was left to take care of itself, and the men were judiciously disposed amongst the adjacent rocks, or anywhere that good cover could be found, and a command retained over the approaches to the position. Consequently, although the Boers kept pounding the camp hour after hour with artillery and musketry fire, the very fact

[1] Appendix, War Commission Report.

that their fire was so well directed prevented any mischief being done to the defenders—for the simple reason that not a single man was in the entrenchments! Thus when the enemy, very naturally assuming that their fire had been effectual, advanced to the attack, they were driven back with loss by men who, thanks to smokeless powder, were concealed from their view, and who, having suffered no losses, had not become dismayed by the fire that had been directed upon their supposed position."

Apart from their duties in regular warfare the Police had throughout the campaign to look after the numerous rebels and suspects, very many of whom they captured and brought in during January and February 1900.

When General French was skilfully holding back the Boers about Colesberg in January and February 1900, he had with him 25 Cape Police, with two 9-pounder muzzle-loading guns. As in other districts, their local knowledge was valuable.

When, towards the end of February, General Brabant cleared the north-eastern portion of Cape Colony, some of the Police were with him, and took part in many engagements; while Major Neylan and another detachment were in the advance-guard of Gatacre's force which moved on Bethulie Bridges from Stormberg. The Boers destroyed the railway bridge, but after dark on the 9th Neylan's Cape Police came up, and next morning they and M'Neill's Scouts seized a position commanding the road bridge and held on under very heavy shell and rifle fire until noon, when more troops came up.[1] The little party had prevented the enemy setting off the mines, and on the

[1] 'Times' History, vol. iii. p. 592.

night of the 10th Lieutenant Popham of the Derbyshires and four men removed the mines, and Captain Grant, R.E., cut the wire. Within the next few days Captains Hennessey of the Police and Turner of the Scouts rode to Springfontein on a trolley, surprised and disarmed eight Boers, and next day brought back to Bethulie two engines and forty trucks, a prize of the greatest value.

Before Kimberley was invested several detachments of Cape Police, who had been holding posts on the railway, retired into the town, thus adding about 350 to the strength of the defenders, an addition which was to prove very important. It must suffice here to refer to the sketch of the garrison's work given under the Kimberley Troops, and to the Mentions reprinted at the end of this article from the despatch of Colonel Kekewich.

At Mafeking, also, the Cape Police contributed a very valuable section of the defenders. In his despatch Colonel Baden-Powell stated the total drilled force at 38 officers and 679 men, of whom there were—of Cape Police, Division I., Inspector Marsh, 2 officers and 45 men; Division II., Inspector Brown, 2 officers and 54 men. The defence of Mafeking is dealt with under the Bechuanaland Protectorate Regiment. In the numerous actions and skirmishes, as well as in holding the trenches, the Cape Police with their maxim did excellent work, which was several times mentioned by Colonel Baden-Powell. He also spoke very highly of the individual efforts of several officers and men. In the telegraphic despatch of 13th April 1900 Colonel Baden-Powell, speaking of an attack on the 11th, said: "A small attacking force advanced against Fort Abrams. The garrison under Corporal Webb, Cape

Police, reserved their fire until they were within effective range, and, with assistance from Fort Cronje, repulsed the attack. The enemy left five dead."

From the commencement of the war, or at least the last week of October 1899 to 1st January 1900, a small body of Cape Police under Captain Bates, assisted by Captain Dennison, afterwards of Dennison's Scouts, held the village of Kuruman, situated about 100 miles to the west of the Kimberley-Vryburg railway. The total number of men available to bear arms was 63, and this included half-castes and blacks. The numbers of the assailants varied, running from 300 to over 1000. From 12th to 17th November the place was bombarded, but the enemy failed to effect a lodgment. Frequently the Boers got very close to the trenches and walls of the little forts, but were always driven off with loss up to 1st January, when they brought a second and heavier gun, whose shells smashed the defences and made a surrender inevitable.[1] But too little justice has been done to the defenders of Kuruman: their endurance, watchfulness, and pluck could not have been excelled. They had no artillery, and by rifle fire alone they held the place and kept a considerable body of the enemy employed for two months. They were also a means of getting news to and from Mafeking. About one-half of the force were hit during the siege.

While Lord Roberts was fighting his way to Pretoria, and afterwards to Komati Poort, the Police were struggling with rebels in different parts of Cape Colony. In May and June one detachment, 30 strong, were said to be doing "most excellent work" with Sir C. Warren in West Griqualand (see Duke of Edinburgh's Rifles).

[1] Account in 'A Fight to a Finish.' Longmans, 1904. By Major C. G. Dennison, D.S.O.

In October, November, and December 1900 a body of the Police were in the column of General Settle, which had an immense deal of marching and some very tough fighting in the Orange River Colony. Near Hoopstad, on 23rd October, there was a very severe engagement (see Cape Mounted Rifles), when the Police had 4 killed and 22 wounded. The detachment was complimented by General Settle.

On 14th November Lord Roberts telegraphed: " A Police post near Vryburg, which was attacked on November 10th, succeeded in killing several Boers and capturing 2 wounded prisoners, one of whom is Field-Cornet Du Plessis." The Police had 1 killed and 2 wounded.

In the second phase of the war—that is, after Lord Roberts had handed over his command to Lord Kitchener, November 1900—the Cape Police were still employed in many different districts; and from the date when it was seen the enemy desired to re-invade Cape Colony—that is, early in December 1900—their functions became as important as in the last three months of the previous year. Whenever the invasion became a realised fact, bodies of Cape Police were attached to various columns, and their local knowledge was again of very great value. In January, February, and March 1901 they assisted in the expulsion of De Wet, and did excellent work under Major Berrangé and other leaders. "D" and "I" troops were with Colonel Doran, who was in February endeavouring to keep the Calvinia roads open for convoys: on the 5th and 6th of that month his column had severe fighting. In July and August the Police assisted to keep the native territories on the eastern border of the Colony clear of the enemy. A strong detachment operated during a great part of 1901 in a column under Colonel Gorringe, R.E., and afterwards under other leaders. The despatch of 8th July 1901 shows Gorringe's column to have consisted, in May, of—Cape Defence Force, 263; Cape Police, 212; Tasmanian Imperial Bushmen, 92; 5th Battery, R.F.A., 2 guns, 1 pom-pom. The column did endless skirmishing and very hard marching in pursuit of sundry commandos, chiefly in Central Cape Colony. In August Kritzinger was being driven northwards. "About fifteen miles north-west of Steynsburg he was joined by bands under Erasmus, Wessels, and Pypers. This body was attacked on the 13th near Rooitfontein, twenty miles north-east of Steynsburg, by Lieut.-Colonel Gorringe, who drove the enemy past Venterstad into Orange River Colony."[1] In this fighting the Police had Lieut.-Colonel Neylan, Major Marsh, Captain Wood, and several men wounded.

In the latter part of September the column was engaged in the pursuit of Smuts, who, after his encounter with the 17th Lancers at Tarkastad, made for the south of the Colony. Lord Kitchener said that "the troops under Lieutenant-Colonels Gorringe, Doran, and Scobell responded cheerfully to the great exertions demanded of them." In the Zuurberg Gorringe engaged the enemy, and succeeded in dividing them up. On 3rd October he again attacked them ten miles south of Darlington, when the enemy lost 3 killed and 5 wounded, and were driven north.

During May and following months of 1901 a body of Police were doing column work in the extreme west of Cape Colony, and some were present in a successful engagement against Conroy on 25th June. The detachment with Colonel Doran got credit for a smart

[1] Despatch of 8th September 1901.

piece of work in the west of the Colony on 9th January 1902. At Windhoek, near Van Rhynsdorp, Western Cape Colony, on 26th February, a detachment had severe fighting, in which they lost 2 killed and Captain A. C. Wilson and 5 men wounded.

While these operations were in progress in the south, some of the Police were employed in the Kimberley district and in the Western Transvaal. They had casualties on various occasions. At Zoutlief on 16th September 1901 Lieutenant Moberly was wounded. A body of the Police were in the ill-fated force which accompanied Lord Methuen in the beginning of March 1902, when he was severely defeated by Delarey. In February Major Berrangé with a detachment had been to clear the road to Kuruman, 100 miles west of the Vryburg railway. In the beginning of March Berrangé and Major Paris joined Lord Methuen's column. Lord Methuen's force was wretchedly heterogeneous: he had 900 mounted men from nine different units, 300 infantry from two regiments, and six guns from three batteries; and the force was utterly unworthy, either in composition or numbers, of the leadership of a Lieut.-General. It was quite unfit to move through the heart of a district where the enemy was known to be in very strong force and flushed with the confidence begotten of a recent success, for they had captured a convoy and destroyed a force of about 450 men a fortnight before. The Police, including "Special Police," numbered 233 under Major Berrangé, and were in that part of the force starting from Vryburg under Major Paris on 2nd March. Lord Methuen in his report said on 6th March "there had been some sniping at the rearguard by about 100 of Van Zyl's commando, and seeing some confusion I went back myself, sending at same time for the section of the 38th Battery. I found the men forming the rear screen, which consisted of the 86th Company I.Y., very much out of hand, and lacking both fire-discipline and knowledge how to act. There seemed to be a want of instructed officers and non-commissioned officers." The enemy being accurately shelled, retired and took up a position at Tweebosch in the bed of the Klein Harts River. "Major Berrangé with the Police, the section 4th Battery and the pom-pom, were ordered to move straight on Tweebosch, while Dennison's Scouts, supported by Cullinan's Horse, were to move round the enemy's left flank. The commando retired rapidly, the Police under Major Berrangé working with the greatest quickness. Much praise is due to Major Berrangé for the way in which he handled his men." Shortly after moving off on the morning of the 7th, the rear-guard, consisting of Diamond Fields Horse and Dennison's Scouts, was most fiercely attacked. They were reinforced by other troops, but eventually the screen was broken, and after several hours' hard fighting the enemy captured the infantry and guns. Most of the mounted men took the Boer method of seeking safety in flight and reached the railway. During the fight, and after the screen was broken, Major Paris and Major Berrangé were ordered to occupy a kraal. This they did with some 40 men, and they held out under heavy shell fire and " against repeated attacks" till the main body surrendered. In his telegram of 16th March Lord Kitchener said that in addition to the party of Cape Police in the kraal, " other small parties of Police continued to resist after the panic which had swept the bulk of mounted troops off the ground."

Many of the corps from which Lord Methuen's

column was made up had, previous to this, done lots of hard fighting, and had always done it well. Which corps set the stampede agoing it is impossible to say, but the affair is not a bright spot in the history of the campaign. The infantry and artillery did all that men could do—"held out in a most splendid manner," the despatch said. The Police apparently could not have done more than they did do. Their losses were very heavy, about 60 killed and wounded. General Brabant, in an article contributed to the 'Nineteenth Century' of February 1904, praised Major Berrangé most highly, and said "if his warning and advice had been acted on, Lord Methuen's disaster might not have taken place. Every man of his stood till killed or wounded. He himself had a marvellous escape, his clothes being penetrated by seven bullets."

Down to the end of the war detachments of the Cape Police continued to do most useful service in various localities.

The Honours and Mentions gained by the Cape Police and Cape Special Police during the war were as follows :—

Sgt.-Major A. Young gained the Victoria Cross at Ruiter's Kraal, Cape Colony, on 13th August 1901. "With a handful of men he rushed some kopjes which were held by Commandant Erasmus and 20 Boers, who galloped back to other kopjes held by Boers. Sgt.-Major Young galloped on ahead of his party, and closing with enemy shot one and captured Erasmus, the latter firing three times at point-blank range before being taken prisoner."

In Colonel Kekewich's despatch of 15th February 1900, as to defence of Kimberley, the following were highly praised : Commissioner (local Lieut.-Col.) M. B. Robinson ; Inspectors (local Majors) F. H. Elliot, W. E. Ayliff (wounded 3rd Nov.), S. Lorimer; Sub-Inspectors (local Captains) J. W. Colvin, M. Z. Crozier, S. White (wounded 9th Dec.), Cummings ; Cpl. F. R. Castens ; Ptes. J. Maloney, A. Carr, G. R. Mathieson, S. Brown.

COLONEL BADEN-POWELL'S DESPATCH : 18*th May* 1900, as to Mafeking.—
Inspector Brown commanded detachment of Division II. He and the

splendid lot of men under his command did excellent work throughout, especially in occupation of trenches in the brick-field, where, for over a month, they were within close range of the enemy's fire; Inspector Marsh commanded detachment of Division I. throughout and carried out his duties most efficiently and zealously. Tpr. (local Sgt.-Major) Hodgson acted as Sgt.-Major to Army Service Corps and was of greatest help to Capt. Ryan. Tprs. George Collins and W. F. Green, bringing in wounded man under heavy fire in action of 25th Oct. 1899. Colonel Baden-Powell remarked that "Sgt. Page, champion bait thrower of Port Elizabeth, by using a whipstick and short line, was able to throw dynamite bombs, made up in pottedmeat tins, with accuracy over 100 yards." This is perhaps the first instance of angling qualifications being utilised in war.

LORD ROBERTS' DESPATCHES.—Major Berrangé, got C.M.G., Major J. W. Neylan [1]; Capts. A. Bates, Halse, Pope Hennessy [1]; Lt. Warren; Inspectors Ayliff, Brown, F. H. Elliot; Sub-Inspectors Crozier, Cummings; Sgt.-Major Fuller; Sgts. Abrams,[2] Jenkins; Cpls. R. B. Christie, H. M. B. Currie [2] (local Lt.); Tpr. Lloyd; Pte. Richards; Lieut.-Colonel Robinson, got C.M.G.; Capt. W. M. Schenk; Tpr. A. H. Blake.[2]

LORD KITCHENER'S DESPATCHES : 8*th March* 1901.—Cpl. J. Mulligan.

8*th July* 1901.—Pte. Stouffer, gallant conduct near Kenhardt, C.C., 17th May.

8*th Dec.* 1901.—Major C. M. Marsh, Capts. E. Woon, F. Harvey, Lt. W. P. Harley, conspicuous gallantry with Gorringe's column. Lt. G. B. Gash, bringing in man from exposed position, 200 yards from enemy's trenches, Vryburg, 16th Sept. Sgt.-Major R. G. Stirling,[2] Ptes. G. De B. Lewis, J. A. Ives, helping Lt. Gash; Lce.-Cpl. Schley, Pte. Clarkson, gallantry Gorringe's column; C. Vanderwest Huizen, accurately locating enemy at great personal risk. Pte. J. Growden, galloped 600 yards under heavy fire to warn officer he was mistaking enemy for own men.

8*th April* 1902.—Lieut.-Colonel R. Macleod.

23*rd June* 1902.—Lieut.-Colonel Neylan, D.S.O.; Major J. N. Brown [1]; Capts. J. F. White, W. Crawford; Lt. Davidson; Sgt. Carson; Cpl. Van der Merwe; Lce.-Cpl. A. C. Weirich. Sgt. J. H. Evans (District Police) got the D.C.M.

---

[1] Awarded D.S.O.   [2] Awarded D.C.M.

CAPE MOUNTED RIFLES.

(CAPE PERMANENT FORCES.)

THIS fine corps is the regular military force of Cape Colony. They were at one time in the pay of the Imperial Government, but since 1870 the Colony has borne the expense. The men engage for five years, and are regular soldiers.[1] On 13th October 1899 the corps numbered 924, all ranks, with a full supply of horses and eight guns; they saw service in many districts, but it was perhaps in the Queenstown-Dordrecht country, in December 1899 and January 1900, that their services to the Empire were of greatest, nay, inestimable value.

Major Pollock, in his 'With Seven Generals in the Boer War,' mentions that on his arrival at Queenstown, about 6th November 1899, the garrison was a Naval Brigade with two 12-pounders, four companies of the Berkshire Regiment and their mounted infantry company, sundry detachments of Cape Mounted Rifles, Cape Police, and Volunteers. The C.M.R. had also their battery of six 7-pounder muzzle-loading screw guns as well as a battery of maxims. "A couple of days after my arrival it was my good fortune to witness the detraining of a detachment of the C.M.R., who formed a most valuable addition to our little force. I never saw a more workmanlike body of men. Smart, active fellows, in the prime of life and evidently in a

[1] General Sir E. Y. Brabant, in an article in the 'Monthly Review,' sketched the history of the Cape Mounted Rifles. In another article in the 'Nineteenth Century' he used the expression, "They are grandly trained soldiers."

most satisfactory military condition. The discipline seemed to be excellent, and the men the most willing workers that it is possible to imagine. . . . The Cape Mounted Rifleman is a first-rate fighting man and a downright good soldier all round. The corps has but one fault, so far as I could judge, and this is that the officers are in many cases far too old." The history of the corps throughout the war proved that Major Pollock's praise was well bestowed. The British regular officer has a weakness for young officers, but in a campaign with an enemy so wily as the South African Dutchman it was fortunate that a corps should have a large proportion of officers who had lived long enough to acquire a little of the serpent's wisdom. More than one British officer has remarked to the writer that for all the qualities which make for the most perfect efficiency in a fighting unit, discipline, intelligence, endurance, pluck, and skill in all the tasks of a soldier, they had never seen anything to beat the C.M.R.

Early in November the corps watched the passes about Barkly East. On 22nd November the C.M.R. and their guns and maxims went to Putter's Kraal. In a few days General Gatacre sent some of the C.M.R. and Brabant's Horse to Penhoek, east of the Queenstown-Stormberg railway. Neither of these corps was in the actual engagement at Stormberg on 10th December. It will be remembered that in General Gatacre's despatch of 19th January 1900, regarding his defeat, he said: "160 Brabant's Horse and 235 C.M.R. with four 2·5-inch guns should have started from Penhoek, but did not arrive at Molteno owing to the failure of the telegraph clerk to transmit the message handed to him at midnight on the 8th." The presence of the Penhoek force would have been very valuable, particularly if they had attacked from the east or Boer rear. Brabant's Horse, 160, arrived near Molteno on the afternoon of the 10th and scouted back some distance towards Stormberg on the line of the British retreat. The C.M.R., having their guns, could not travel so fast.

After Stormberg there was no big engagement in the eastern portion of Cape Colony, but the mounted troops in that district had many skirmishes and some hard-fought little actions. On 24th December the C.M.R. occupied Dordrecht, and there was frequently fighting in that neighbourhood, as on the 30th when a party under Lieutenant Milford of the Frontier Mounted Rifles were cut off and had their horses all shot. The detachment held their ground splendidly, inflicting considerable loss on the enemy, until they were rescued next morning by Captain de Montmorency, V.C., with some of his own scouts and Brabant's Horse and 115 men of the C.M.R. On 31st December Dordrecht was evacuated, the C.M.R. falling back on a position at Bird River.

In Lord Roberts' first despatch, that of 6th February 1900, he said: " A subject which from the first attracted my special attention was the development and organisation of the Colonial forces, of which I was inclined to think that sufficient use had not been made. I, therefore, arranged for one mounted corps to be raised by Colonel Brabant, to whom, with the approval of the High Commissioner, the rank of Brigadier-General has been given. Inclusive of this corps it is intended to place a body of Colonial mounted troops, about 3000 strong, under Brigr.-Genl. Brabant's command, on Lieut.-Genl. Gatacre's right flank for the purpose of guarding the eastern portion of the colony and pushing back the enemy from the neighbourhood of Stormberg. The headquarters of this Colonial force will be at Dordrecht, where it will be in readiness to operate northward towards Jamestown."

On 7th February there was some fighting in which Brabant's Horse drove back the Boers, suffering a few casualties. In the despatch of 28th February 1900 Lord Roberts said: "On the eastern frontier Brigr.-Genl. Brabant moved forward on the evening of the 16th February, and after continuous fighting on the 17th stormed the Boer position near Dordrecht." Brabant's force included the 79th Battery R.F.A., Cape Mounted Rifles, Brabant's Horse, Kaffrarian Rifles, Queenstown Volunteers, and a portion of the 1st Royal Scots. Brabant lost little time and kept the enemy moving, and while Lord Roberts was driving the force in front of him across the Orange Free State, Brabant pushed his opponents northwards through Labuschagne's Nek to Jamestown, and thereafter cleared them out of all the positions in the Aliwal North district of the Colony, but not without some determined fighting, as on 5th March when the C.M.R. had 7 killed and 9 wounded, and on the 11th when 2 men were killed and Lieutenant Taplin and 9 men were wounded. On 2nd April Colonel Dalgety left that town to occupy Wepener and to command Jammersberg Drift and bridge over the Caledon River. Colonel Dalgety arrived at Wepener on the night of the 4th, and on the 5th the troops under his command were one company Royal Scots Mounted Infantry; C.M.R., 427; 1st and 2nd Brabant's Horse, 804; the Kaffrarian Rifles, 393; Driscoll's Scouts, 58; with a few Royal Engineers and the Artillery Detachment — 93 — of the C.M.R., with two 15-pounders, two naval guns, two 2·5 guns, and one Hotchkiss. A position, about six miles in circumference, was taken up. On the 6th it was seen Wepener was to be isolated, and defensive works were pushed on. On the morning of the 9th the enemy opened with artillery. In his report Colonel Dalgety said: "The weakest part of the position was on the extreme left rear, which was held by the Cape Mounted Rifles, and it was here that the heaviest casualties took place, the C.M.R. losing 21 killed and 75 wounded, out of a total of 33 killed and 133 wounded." Colonel Dalgety gives an account in his report of the fierce attacks made by the enemy, especially on the position occupied by the C.M.R. He said that "it was found to be impossible to contract our lines or to give up any portion of the position held, so that I had no reserve available for relief, and consequently for sixteen days and nights the whole force was constantly in the trenches, and in the case of the Royal Scots, C.M.R., and Scouts, they had nothing but cold food and water during the whole sixteen days, while for three days the trenches were flooded by rain. I cannot speak too highly of the behaviour of the whole force during all this time; all did their work cheerfully and well, although the continued strain was telling on all ranks." He brought forward the names of a number of officers, non-commissioned officers, and men of this corps.[1] Wepener was relieved on the 24th April. During the siege Major Springer, Lieutenant Taplin, and Sergeant-Major Court, and about 20 non-commissioned officers and men were killed; 7 officers and about 70 non-commissioned officers and men wounded.

[1] Report of Colonel Dalgety, dated 29th April 1900.

There are few more gallant pieces of work recorded in the history of the war than the splendid defence of Wepener, and the Cape Colony soldiers and volunteers will always be able to point to these as gold-letter days in their records.

Brabant's Colonial Division moved north from the Wepener district in May and operated at first on the extreme right flank of the British advance, being out on the right of General Rundle after Thabanchu was passed. The division was afterwards split up, and a portion came to the west or Senekal part of Rundle's line. They frequently had most onerous work and stiff fighting, but the despatches barely do justice either to their operations or to those of the VIIIth Division. All through June and July there was constant skirmishing and some very severe marching, with the view of containing the Boers until Sir Archibald Hunter got Prinsloo and about 4000 of his men surrounded in the Brandwater Basin, where they surrendered on 30th July. When Sir Archibald Hunter entered Fouriesburg on 26th July he found to his surprise that Driscoll's Scouts of the Colonial Division were there before him "after a forced march from Commando Nek of 25 miles."

On 16th July De Wet with about 1600 men broke out of the Brandwater Basin, and Broadwood with the 2nd Cavalry Brigade went in pursuit. Other troops joined him, and De Wet then made for the Reitzburg Hills, south of the Vaal, where he remained for about three weeks. On the 27th July the Colonial Division was taken from Rundle's district and marched *viâ* Kroonstad to the Rhenoster River to watch the drifts there. On the night of the 6th August De Wet with his force crossed the Vaal, and the Colonial

Division followed, and joining Lord Methuen, who had been posted on the north of the river, they accompanied that General in the chase to the Megaliesberg, where De Wet escaped through Olifant's Nek, from which, by some mistake, the blocking force had just been removed. The Colonial Division now accompanied Lord Methuen to Zeerust, in the north-west of the Transvaal.[1] On the 25th August the division along with the 3rd Cavalry Brigade started on their return journey to the Orange River Colony, Colonel Dalgety of the C.M.R. being in command of the force. They met with much opposition between Zeerust and Krugersdorp. The losses of the division on this march were 10 men killed and 5 officers and 20 men wounded. About the middle of September the division was concentrated at Rhenoster, in the Orange River Colony.

In October part of the Cape Police and Cape Mounted Rifles were in a column under Major-General Settle operating about Hoopstad, and on the 7th Lieutenant Orley Humphry and one man were wounded at Rhenoster. On the 19th the C.M.R. had Sergeant-Majors Pearce and Kennedy wounded. On the 23rd Settle was closely engaged by a Boer force of about 650 strong. "The Cape Police and Cape Mounted Rifles bore the brunt of the fighting, covering the baggage of the column, 73 waggons, and were heavily engaged for two hours before the Boers were driven off. The Cape Police were forced to abandon their two maxims, having first rendered them useless, owing to the horses being shot and darkness setting in. Our casualties were 7 men killed, 12 wounded, and 17

[1] Lord Robert's despatch of 10th October 1900, para. 28.

missing."[1] Of these the Police had 4 killed and 8 wounded, and the C.M.R. 3 killed. Lieutenant W. Rolfe of the Rifles died at Kimberley on 13th November of wounds received. Settle's column arrived at Boshof on 30th October, then moved south and crossed the Orange River Colony to the Bloemfontein Railway in November. On the way his mounted men assisted Sir C. Parsons to relieve Koffyfontein, which had been invested.

A portion of the Cape Police and Cape Mounted Rifles were taken to Cape Colony to pursue Kritzinger and other leaders who had managed to cross the river.

Stories of ammunition about to be landed at Lambert's Bay, and the very apparent resolution of commandos to push into the extreme south-west of Cape Colony, caused Lord Kitchener to send various columns to that district, among whom went the C.M.R. Some fighting was seen, and on 1st March 1901 Captain J. F. Purcell of the C.M.R., and Lieutenant Grant of Brabant's Horse, were mentioned for coolness and skill displayed in handling their men in action near Lambert's Bay. In April a portion of the C.M.R. were engaged near Philippolis, when Lieutenant D. A. H. Bowers gained mention for presence of mind and boldness in carrying out the relief of some troops who were hardly pressed.

The next notice of the work of the corps to be found in despatches is in the despatch of 8th July 1901, where it is stated that on 20th May Lieutenant-Colonel Scobell, whose column consisted of one squadron 9th Lancers, 200 men of the C.M.R., and 3 guns

[1] Despatch of 15th November, para. 10.

belonging to the corps, surprised Malan's commando west of Cradock, killing 4 men and capturing 40 horses and many saddles and rifles. Scobell and other leaders now went in pursuit of some commandos in the Zuurberg, but although some losses were inflicted the main bodies generally escaped, sometimes to do damage, as when on 2nd June they captured Jamestown after a defence by the Town Guard which was the reverse of heroic. Colonel Scobell was more successful than any other leader in Cape Colony, but few officers have the gifts of resourcefulness and lightning-like decision which he proved himself to have while still a Major in the Scots Greys. "On the 6th of June Colonel Scobell's column caught a commando asleep at 3 A.M. Lieutenant-Colonel Lukin with a squadron of C.M.R. rushed the laager in the dark, killing 6 Boers and capturing 25 prisoners and all the saddles of the commando." Lieutenant-Colonel Lukin was mentioned for his gallant leading.

The despatch of 8th August detailed another success by Scobell. The columns had been driving the enemy north of Richmond, and his force surprised Lategan's laager, taking 10 prisoners and 105 horses and saddles. On the 22nd July at Tweefontein the Rifles had about 6 wounded, and on 8th August Captain J. F. Purcell was wounded. In his next despatch of 8th September Lord Kitchener again expressed himself as greatly pleased with the column. "On 5th September Lieutenant-Colonel Scobell was able to achieve a brilliant success near Petersburg, 40 miles west of Cradock, where he surrounded and captured the whole of Lotter's commando and a party of Boers under Breedt. 14 of the enemy were killed and 105 captured (46 of whom were wounded). The prisoners included Commandant Lotter and Field-Cornets J. Kruger, W. Kruger, and Schoeman, and amongst the dead were two notorious rebels named Voster. 200 horses and 29,000 rounds of ammunition and all the vehicles and supplies of the enemy fell into our hands. Colonel Scobell, who deserves the greatest credit in connection with this affair, had brought to my notice the exceptional gallantry displayed during the engagement by Captain Lord Douglas Compton, 2nd Lieutenants Wynn and Neilson, all of the 9th Lancers, and Captain Purcell and Lieutenant Bowers, Cape Mounted Rifles. Our casualties were ten men killed and 8 wounded, the latter including Lieutenant Burgess, Cape Mounted Rifles." The Rifles had 2 men killed and 3 wounded. In September and ensuing months the pursuit of small bodies of the enemy was carried on with untiring energy, and Lord Kitchener praised Colonel Scobell's column along with three others for responding cheerfully to every call. In the despatch of 8th November it is stated that Lieutenant-Colonel Lukin surprised a laager six miles south-west of New Bethesda at dawn on 21st October, killing 1 and taking 14 prisoners.

Down to the close of the campaign the C.M.R. continued to operate in Cape Colony, for a time in the extreme west, always doing conscientious work of the highest order. No corps, whether regular or volunteer, could point to a better record. The number of Mentions gained was not very large, because the commanders had an extremely high standard of what was needed to get that honour.

The following extract from General Colvile's work of the IXth Division is given, not so much to show what Sergeant Bettington did, but as an example of the dangerous work constantly undertaken by men of the Colonial corps. At the time he speaks of General Colvile was fighting his way from Lindley to Heilbron, and was cut off from the main army. "As we had been less pressed on our left flank than on any other side, I thought the best chance of getting this through was to send it to the railway, and told Gleichen to give it to one of his men; but the natives all said that we were too closely surrounded, and were afraid to go alone. Sergeant Bettington, however, of the Cape Mounted Rifles, who was attached to the Intelligence Department, volunteered to take it, and started off with a Kaffir who pretended to know the road. We learnt afterwards that, having passed safely through the Boer lines, he bolted with his escort's horse and rifles, and left Sergeant Bettington to make his way for twenty-eight miles on foot as best he might. For the sake of those readers who do not know Sergeant Bettington, I may say that the message was safely delivered; those who do know him will never have had any doubt about it. He had first turned up at Modder River Camp—how or why I do not know— and varied the monotony of those dull days by his habit of appearing unexpectedly outside our outpost line after a stroll through the Boer lines. After a time our sentries got accustomed to him, and did not shoot at him any more. When the reports that 'a man in the uniform of the Cape Mounted Rifles was discovered,' &c., ceased to come in, I am ashamed to say that I forgot all about him till, on the morning we attacked Cronje's laager at Paardeberg, a figure which I recognised ran past me at early dawn. It happened that we were then in doubt as to whether a certain trench on the river bank was held by the Boers or not, and on seeing him I at once said, 'Why, here is the very man to find out,' and calling him back asked if he would do so. 'All right, sir,' said Bettington, with the cheerful smile which any chance of extra danger always brought on to his face, and started off at the double. My Intelligence Officer was with me at the time, and said nothing; but the next time I saw Sergeant Bettington he was in charge of 'Gleichen's Horse.'" The other messengers sent out by General Colvile failed to get through. To carry out successfully tasks such as those Sergeant Bettington undertook required a combination of qualities that one could scarcely expect to find in the British regular. To the fearlessness, coolness, and physical fitness which the regular generally has, there had to be added a profound knowledge of the Boer and the Black, and of the country they lived in; and, above all, the ever-ranging eye, a product of the veldt, bred or educated up to distances at which the home-trained vision is useless.

The Mentions gained by the C.M.R. are as follows :—

Lieut.-Col. Dalgety's Report as to Wepener, 29th April 1900.—Capt. Lukin commanded artillery and did most excellent work, putting one of enemy's guns out of action. Capt. Cantwell, after Major Sprenger was killed and Major Waring wounded, on the 9th and 11th respectively, commanded in advanced schanzen. Capt. and Quartermaster Phillips, when 2 officers were killed and 5 wounded, took command of 50 men, and held a most important position. Capt. Grant, Field-Adjutant, did the work of half a dozen men. Sgt. Roberts, Ptes. Rawlings and Robarts, and Trumpeter Washington brought in wounded comrades under heavy fire.

LORD ROBERTS' DESPATCHES: *2nd April* 1901. — Lieut.-Col. E. H. Dalgety; Major C. F. Sprenger (killed); Capts. Cantwell, C. L. J. Goldsworthy, Grant,[1] Lukin [1]; Lieut. Roy [1]; Sgt.-Major Robson [2]; Sgt. Roberts [2]; Cpl. Bettington [2]; Ptes. Rawlings, Robarts, Washington.[2]

4th September 1901.—Sgt.-Major G. P. Roberts.[2] Artillery Troop—Gunner Anderson.[2]

LORD KITCHENER'S DESPATCHES: *8th May* 1901.—Capt. J. F. Purcell,[1] coolness and skill at Lambert's Bay.

---

[1] Awarded D.S.O. [2] Awarded D.C.M.

8th July 1901.—Lieut. D. A. H. Bowers, boldness in relief of troops near Philippolis; Lieut.-Col. Lukin,[1] gallant leading in night-attack on laager; Pte. White,[2] on 9th May, Molteno district, signaller with a patrol engaged with superior numbers, caught and took back a horse to one man, and took up another on his own—both acts under fire.

8th October 1901.—Capt. J. F. Purcell; Lieut. Bowers, marked gallantry, capture of Lotter's commando; Pte. Haines,[2] conspicuous gallantry, same occasion.

8th December 1901.—Sgt. A. Allen; A. C. Archibald (Archdeacon); Cpl. W. Reder, coolness, courage, and gallantry while with Col. Scobell.

23rd June 1902.—Major Hook; Sgt. G. H. Randolph; Cpl. R. Stopford.

Colonel Dalgety got the C.B.; Surgeon Lieut.-Col. Hartley, V.C.; and Lieut.-Col. Lukin the C.M.G.

KAFFRARIAN RIFLES.

(CAPE COLONY VOLUNTEERS.)

IN the reports by General Forestier-Walker of 18th October 1899 and subsequent dates, given in the Appendices to the War Commission Report, the Kaffrarian Rifles, strength 385, were stated to be embodied at that date, and to be the garrison of East London. They were soon taken farther north, and when active operations under General Gatacre commenced the corps was given a post of honour. The officer commanding the corps was Major H. W. Cuming. On 21st November General Gatacre visited Sterkstroom, where the bulk of the Kaffrarian Rifles were stationed, also Bushman's Hoek, where a mounted company was posted, both these places being considered important points. Major Pollock, in his 'With Seven Generals,' says: "The General paid some well-deserved compliments to that excellent corps, and thereby pleased

[1] Awarded D.S.O. [2] Awarded D.C.M.

them greatly. Really, the Kaffrarians had done plenty of hard work during the past three weeks, and they had, moreover, been exposed to no inconsiderable danger, holding the post of honour at the head of the Division, and, until Thursday, being wholly unsupported by any other troops nearer than Queenstown." The Kaffrarian Rifles did not take part in the Stormberg expedition. All through December and January they continued to hold Bushman's Hoek and other posts, and to patrol their district—work which they did so well that the wily enemy never caught them napping. Fighting frequently took place in the neighbourhood, and when the enemy in great force, probably 2000 to 3000, attacked the camp of the Cape Police on 3rd January 1900, a mounted company, about 60 of the Kaffrarian Rifles under Captain Maclean, reinforced the Police in time to take part in the very excellent defence (see Cape Police).

The corps, now 600 strong, were in the Colonial Division, under Brigadier-General Brabant, and took part in his rapid and very successful operations in February, which regained possession of the Dordrecht-Jamestown and Aliwal North districts and drove the enemy out of many strong positions in the north-east of Cape Colony (see Cape Mounted Rifles). On 5th March, at Dordrecht, this corps lost 1 killed and ·7 wounded, and on the 11th, at Aliwal North, they had 1 man killed and Captain E. Muller severely wounded. A portion of the Kaffrarian Rifles, about four squadrons, took part, under Colonel Dalgety, in the splendid defence of Wepener in April, and one squadron was in the relieving force under Brabant. During the siege they had 1 man killed and Lieutenant Lister and about 12 men wounded. The corps afterwards took part in the other work of the Colonial Division, which has been already briefly sketched under the Cape Mounted Rifles. They were several times sharply engaged in the Orange River Colony and Transvaal in 1900, particularly on the march from Zeerust to Krugersdorp in the latter half of August 1900. At Quaggafontein, on 31st August, the Kaffrarian Rifles lost 6 non-commissioned officers and men killed, and Capts. P. Farrar, Rose-Innes, J. M. Fairweather, J. Donovan, and R. H. Price, Lieutenant Beswick, and about 18 non-commissioned officers and men wounded.

Before Lord Roberts left South Africa the Colonial Division was broken up, and in October 1900 many members of the corps were allowed to return to their homes. On their arrival at East London, on 3rd November, the Kaffrarian Rifles got a magnificent reception. To their credit an immense proportion expressed a desire to take the field again immediately after 1st January 1901. The corps was soon well filled up, and going north again joined a column under the command of Colonel Crewe of the Border Horse. This column took part in General C. Knox's operations in the Orange River Colony against De Wet in January 1901. In his despatch of 8th March 1901, paragraph 9, Lord Kitchener mentioned that the Boer leaders were, towards the end of January, concentrating in the Doornberg, north-east of Winburg. Knox and Bruce Hamilton were ordered against this body, but De Wet on 27th January broke up his laager and marched south with great rapidity. Knox followed, and the columns of Pilcher and Crewe fought a very hotly contested action with De Wet's rear-guard at the Tabaksberg on the 29th. In this action the Kaffrarian Rifles bore the bulk of the casualties, their losses being 5 killed and about 20 wounded, including Lieutenant Weber. The troops of Knox and Bruce Hamilton were entrained for Bethulie and then moved rapidly west to Philippolis, but they were unable to prevent the enemy's force from crossing the Orange. Knox and Bruce Hamilton crossed at Sand Drift,—a most difficult undertaking, as the river was in flood. They now joined in the pursuit, in which the corps suffered a few casualties. De Wet having been driven out of Cape Colony, Crewe's column moved from Orange River Bridge on 4th March 1901, and crossed to Bloemfontein *via* Koffyfontein and Petrusburg. Near the latter place they had an engagement with Brand's commando. On this march the column took 5 prisoners, 21 waggons with teams, and 2000 horses. After this the column was again taken to Cape Colony and commenced a series of pursuits and skirmishes which was to go on for another fifteen months. The despatch of 8th July 1901, appendix, shows that Colonel Crewe's column at that time consisted of the Kaffrarian Rifles, strength 301, with 374 horses and two machine-guns; the Queenstown Volunteer Rifles, 78 men and 137 horses; 44th Battery R.F.A., two guns, one pom-pom. Casualties were suffered on various occasions, as on December 15, near Jamestown, when Captain Fairweather and a party of his men surprised a laager. In rushing the Boers Captain Fairweather was wounded for the third time in the campaign. A Dundee man, located when the war began at Port Elizabeth, he put off his civilian's clothes and took to fighting as the proverbial duck takes to water. Sandhurst could not have turned out a better adjutant.

The corps continued to operate in the east of Cape Colony until peace was declared.

The Mentions gained by the corps were:—

In Colonel Dalgety's Report as to Wepener, 29th April 1900.—Capt. Farrar was invaluable in obtaining supplies from Wepener on 6th, 7th, and 8th.

LORD ROBERTS' DESPATCH : *2nd April* 1901.—Lieut.-Col. H. D. Cuming ; Major R. H. Price ; Capts. G. Farrar,[1] J. P. Farrar,[1] E. H. Muller ; Sgt.-Major R. Anderson ; Signalling-Sgt. C. W. Jones[2] ; Tprs. J. D. R. Macfarlane (dead), J. Rupert (killed).

LORD KITCHENER'S DESPATCHES : *8th March* 1901.—Major R. H. Price ; Capt. and Adjutant J. Fairweather, D.S.O. ; Sgt. S. R. Hains, promoted 2nd Lieut.

8th March 1902.—Capt. and Adjutant Fairweather, for very good service at Patriot's Klip, Cape Colony, 15th December 1901.

Col. Cuming got C.B. ; Major Price got C.M.G. Major Price (now Lieut.-Col.) was again mentioned in Lord Kitchener's final despatch.

BRABANT'S HORSE.

THIS corps was raised and took the field in the Queenstown-Dordrecht district. Major Pollock in his volume frequently refers to them in appreciative terms. On 28th November he visited their camp and saw them at drill and musketry. "The progress already made quite astonished me. . . . Poor De Montmorency [3] was then adjutant, and judging by the results, both he and his predecessor, Collins of the Berkshire, had a great deal to be proud of. The shooting on the range was very good." These facts are noted to show how quickly the volunteer and irregular troops got into fighting trim. The regiment was very soon sent to hold various posts, and when General Gatacre went out to

---

[1] Got D.S.O.   [2] Got D.C.M.
[3] The late Captain the Hon. Raymond H. L. J. de Montmorency, V.C., 21st Lancers, born February 1867, killed at Schoeman's Kop, near Stormberg, February 1900.

attack Stormberg, on the night of 9th December, 160 of Brabant's were intended to join the attacking force from Penhoek, but it will be remembered the telegram was not delivered (see Cape Mounted Rifles). The detachment under De Montmorency did arrive at Molteno on the afternoon of the 10th, and scouted back on the line of the British retreat.

On 22nd and 23rd December De Montmorency and his men had skirmishes near Dordrecht, in which they got the better of the enemy, who had the stronger force. About this time Captain De Montmorency raised his body of scouts, all picked men, who did some very fine work. On the 28th, with some of his own scouts and some of Brabant's Horse, he was out near Dordrecht, but little was to be seen of the enemy. On the 30th, however, there was quite a stiff little fight, in which a party of the Frontier Mounted Rifles was cut off and only rescued the following day (see Cape Mounted Rifles). Captain Flanagan's company of Brabant's was said to have done very well. The corps did an immense amount of patrol work throughout January, and Captain Flanagan's company were the first troops in the Queenstown district to gain touch with the VIth Division, then approaching the Stormberg country from Cape Town *viâ* Thebus.

As already stated (see Cape Mounted Rifles), Lord Roberts had in January announced the appointment of Brigadier-General Brabant as Commander of the Colonial Division, which included the two regiments of this corps, and under that general they did excellent work in the clearing of the north-east of Cape Colony. In the fighting about Dordrecht, in the second half of February 1900, the corps took a very prominent part and were several times very heavily engaged. In Lord

Roberts' telegram of 18th February he mentioned that Brabant "had attacked Boer position on 16th. He gradually closed in on laager during the day. Fighting lasted from 9 A.M. till dusk. At midnight Capt. Flanagan, 1st Brabant's Horse, attacked and took laager at the point of the bayonet, capturing the stores." Captain Crallen and Lieutenant Chandler and 4 non-commissioned officers and men were killed, and 5 non-commissioned officers and men wounded. On 5th March there was again severe fighting near Dordrecht, in which the Cape Mounted Rifles bore the heaviest share of the losses. At Aliwal North, on the 11th, Brabant's Horse had 3 killed and 6 wounded.

A second regiment having been raised in December, Lieut.-Colonel H. M. Grenfell, 1st Life Guards, was appointed to command it, and when Colonel Dalgety was besieged in Wepener (see Cape Mounted Rifles), the first and a portion of the second regiment were with him, their strength being respectively 345 and 459. One squadron of Brabant's Horse took part in the relief of Wepener. During the siege Lieutenant Thurston and 4 men were killed, and 5 officers—Surgeon-Captain Perkins, Lieutenants W. E. Holford, Turner, and Duncan, and Quartermaster Williams—and about 30 men were wounded.

In the advance northwards, and in the operations preparatory to the surrounding of Prinsloo, the corps was very frequently engaged. In the Hammonia district they had an immense amount of difficult scouting, and several times, in the latter half of May and in June, they had encounters with superior forces and rather heavy losses. On 29th June Lieutenant J. S. Orr was severely wounded, and other casualties were suffered in an action in which the enemy had to be driven across the Zand River. On 3rd July Lieutenant and Adjutant A. F. C. Williams was shot through the lung. On the 6th to 8th July at the capture of Bethlehem, on the 16th near Witnek, and on the 23rd, 24th at Slabbert's Nek, Brabant's Horse were in the forefront and gained distinction, but, as a matter of course, had to pay the price. 'The Times' historian points out that it was some "adventurous scouts" of Brabant's Horse who, by discovering on the night of the 23rd a commanding summit to be unoccupied, enabled Clements to seize the ridge at daybreak—the corps being entrusted with this task.

The 1st Regiment of the corps, now commanded by Major Henderson, 8th Hussars, accompanied Dalgety to the Reitzburg district, and thence in August across the Vaal in the pursuit of De Wet (see Cape Mounted Rifles). In his despatch of 1st September 1900 Lord Roberts said that "the enemy managed to derail another supply train south of Klip River (Johannesburg district) early this morning. Two men were killed, 1 wounded, and 35 taken prisoners. The engine was blown up, and thirteen trucks were burned. A party of Brabant's Horse on duty at Klip River Bridge followed the enemy as soon as the report of the accident reached them, drove them into the neighbouring hills, and recovered all the prisoners."

The 2nd Regiment was ordered to the eastern Transvaal in August, to take part under General Hutton in the movement from Belfast to the Portuguese border, crossing some of the most difficult country in South Africa. In November they were operating about Frederickstad in the Central Transvaal with General Barton. They had skirmishing very frequently, and on 11th December had 1 man killed and 3 wounded. A detachment of Brabant's Horse remained in the Orange River Colony in August. On the 27th of that month Sergeant-Major Rutters of the 2nd Regiment was killed, and Corporal Abernethy was wounded at Winburg. During the last quarter of 1900 a portion of the corps was with Bruce Hamilton in the Orange River Colony. In the despatch of 8th March 1901, dealing with the events for the preceding four months, Lord Kitchener said that when, in November, it became apparent that De Wet was to attempt to invade Cape Colony, he (Lord Kitchener) railed certain forces from the Transvaal to the south of the Orange River Colony; these included the 2nd Regiment of Brabant's Horse. In his telegraphic despatch of 15th December 1900 Lord Kitchener said, "During the recent operations in the Zastron district, a party of Brabant's Horse became detached, and being surrounded in a defile had to surrender." The casualty list showed 3 men killed, 11 wounded, and 106 missing. The mishap was unfortunate, coming after so much good sound work; but at that time numerous small columns and patrols were then pursuing the enemy, who was in great strength in the south-east of the Orange River Colony, while to keep touch with him forces had to be greatly scattered, and there was always a chance of any little detachment being cut off. About 18th to 24th December the 2nd Brabant's had much fighting about Steynsburg, Cape Colony—the object being to prevent the Boers working south. On 28th December the 2nd Regiment had Captain Cholmondley and 5 men wounded. When it was seen that Kritzinger and Smuts, about 16th December, had effected an entrance into Cape Colony with about 2000 men, more troops were railed from the Transvaal to Naauwpoort, and in this second batch were the 1st Brabant's Horse.[1]

In February 1901 a portion of Brabant's Horse was operating in the south-west of Cape Colony, and Lieutenant J. M. Grant gained mention near Lambert's Bay on 1st March. Near Jansenville on 20th March 2 men were killed and 6 wounded in an action when Colonel Scobell and Colonel Colenbrander inflicted a severe defeat on Scheepers and Malan. About this time there was fighting daily, and casualties came often. The despatch of 8th July 1901 shows that two squadrons of Brabant's Horse were in May and June, along with a squadron of the 9th Lancers and three companies of Imperial Yeomanry, operating in the Cradock and Richmond districts, chiefly against Malan's commando. On 28th June the 1st corps were heavily engaged near Richmond, and had 2 officers, Captain M. Bowker and Lieutenant J. R. Thompson, and 6 men wounded. On 18th July Captain W. J. S. Rundle and several men were wounded. During the remainder of the war Brabant's Horse were employed in Cape Colony, traversing almost every part of it. On 5th February 1902 they were in the sharp fight at Uitspanfontein near Beaufort West, when they had about half a dozen casualties. During the last year the work was harder than ever, and there was seldom the satisfaction of a fight, except when the enemy was confident that he had a successful trap laid.

The Mentions gained by the corps were as follows :—

In his despatch of 2nd April 1901 Lord Roberts referred to Brigadier-General Brabant, and said, "Has been in chief command of the Colonial troops from the Cape Colony, which, amongst other distinguished actions,

---

[1] Despatch of 8th March 1901, para. 3.

furnished the contingent which, under Lieut.-Col. Dalgety, so gallantly defended Wepener. Colonel Brabant is a fine leader of men; he represents the true Imperial feeling in the Cape; and, aided by his fellow-colonists, has furnished an object-lesson in loyalty and devotion to the Crown."

In Colonel Dalgety's Report as to Wepener, 29th April 1900, "Lieut.-Col. Grenfell, commanding 2nd Brabant's Horse, my second-in-command, rendered most valuable assistance. Pte. Anderson,[1] assisted in bringing in wounded comrades under heavy fire."

LORD ROBERTS' DESPATCH : *2nd April* 1901.—Lieut.-Col. H. M. Grenfell (1st Life Guards), Capts. H. R. Cholmondley,[2] J. S. G. Douglas,[2] Hon. L. Ogilvie,[2] Surg.-Capt. R. C. Perkins,[2] Lts. E. S. Stephenson[2] (appointed to Gloucestershire Regiment), A. F. C. Williams (Adjutant),[2] Sgt. Campbell, Cpl. Dutton,[1] Tpr. P. E. J. Kornell.[1]

LORD KITCHENER'S DESPATCH : *8th May* 1901.—Lieut. J. M. Grant, for coolness and skill handling men in action near Lambert's Bay.

THE BORDER HORSE.

THE Border Horse was raised in the Eastern portion of Cape Colony in February 1900, their commander being Colonel Crewe, and when General Brabant was driving the Boers from about Dordrecht, 200 of the corps joined Major Maxwell at Labuschagne's Nek on 5th March. On the 4th Maxwell's Colonials had established themselves on a mountain 1500 feet high on the east of the Nek, but the troops in front of the position had been held up, and indeed withdrawn. 'The Times' History, vol. iii. p. 491, mentions that the two squadrons of the Border Horse, when they arrived on the 5th, "proceeded to storm the Boer schanzes. By noon the whole Boer force was in full retreat towards Aliwal North," to which place Brabant and Maxwell followed. On the 5th the Border Horse lost 2 killed

[1] Awarded D.C.M. [2] Awarded D.S.O.

and several wounded. Their casualties were not so severe as the Cape Mounted Rifles or Frontier Mounted Rifles.

The Border Horse were stationed at Aliwal North in April 1900, and were reviewed there by General Brabant, under whom they were to act in the operations for the relief of Wepener (see Cape Mounted Rifles). In the advance to Wepener they were in the forefront, and several times had sharp fighting with casualties. Their work was highly spoken of by those who witnessed it.

After Wepener was relieved the Border Horse was a component part of the Colonial Division under General Brabant (see Cape Mounted Rifles), and in the advance to the Brandwater Basin the whole of the Division often had fighting. The scouting and patrol work was constant, hard, and, from the nature of the country, very dangerous, and casualties were frequent. Of the work and the losses the Border Horse had their full share, but they had the satisfaction of helping to hem in Prinsloo and his 4000 men. Lieutenant L. G. Longmore was severely wounded near Hammonia towards the end of May, and on same occasion 3 men were killed and several wounded.

At Doornhoek, on 26th August 1900, the corps was heavily engaged, and had Major M. W. Robertson severely wounded and about 20 other casualties. Towards the close of 1900 the Border Horse were with Colonel Crewe in the Winburg district (see Kaffrarian Rifles), and at Tabaksberg, on 29th January 1901, they had 10 casualties, including Captain Cameron wounded. They took part in further fighting about Winburg towards the end of February. Under Colonel Crewe a portion of the corps were engaged in the pursuit of De Wet in

Cape Colony, and the very arduous work by which he was driven back across the river and through the central district of the Orange River Colony in February and March 1901. Sergeant-Major Cruden and 1 man were wounded at Petrusburg in that district on 9th March. Throughout the remainder of the year the Border Horse operated chiefly in Cape Colony under various column commanders, and saw much fighting.

The Mentions gained by the corps were as follows :—

LORD ROBERTS' DESPATCHES : *2nd April* 1901.—Majors C. P. Crewe, M. W. Robertson, Regl. Sgt.-Major E. Burgess,[1] Tpr. H. E. Rutherford.

LORD KITCHENER'S DESPATCHES : *8th March* 1901.—Lt. M. G. (or J.) Foxcroft, Coy. Sgt.-Major Johnston promoted 2nd Lt., Lce.-Cpl. A. J. Shout promoted Sgt.

8th July 1901.—Cpl. J. Stevens,[1] promoted Sgt., in Cape Colony, April 23rd, held a kraal alone and covered retirement of party ; in every engagement has behaved most gallantly.

Colonel Crewe got the C.B. and Major Robertson C.M.G. Pte. G. Doyle the D.C.M. in April 1901.

MONTMORENCY'S SCOUTS.

THIS corps, strength 100, was raised by Captain the Hon. R. De Montmorency, V.C., 21st Lancers, in December 1899. Their work during the next three months was constantly referred to in terms of praise by Major Pollock and other writers on the operations in Central Cape Colony. In the last fortnight of December and in January they did particularly well.

The corps lost their gallant leader in a skirmish near Stormberg on 23rd February 1900. It is said that he

[1] Awarded D.C.M.

fired eleven shots after being mortally wounded. On the same occasion Lieutenant-Colonel Hoskier, a Middlesex artillery volunteer officer, was killed, and several men were killed and wounded. Captain M'Neill, of the Seaforth Highlanders, who had been aide-de-camp to General Gatacre, succeeded to the command of the scouts on Montmorency's death. After the British had crossed the Orange River in March, Captain Turner along with Captain Hennessy of the Police carried out a most gallant and fruitful piece of work (see Cape Police).

When the Boers had been driven from the neighbourhood of the Orange, the corps took part in the operations for the relief of Wepener. They were in the advance to the Transvaal, and were among the first troops to gallop into Pretoria. After Pretoria was occupied, Montmorency's Scouts were split up. In July a detachment served in the column of Lieutenant-General Ian Hamilton, which did much hard work marching and fighting, both east and west of Pretoria, during July, August, and September 1900.[1]

The Mentions gained were :—

LORD ROBERTS' DESPATCH : *2nd April* 1901.—Capts. A. M'Neill, H. G. Turner,[2] Cpl. C. Roberts,[3] Scout J. Murray.[3]

---

[1] K.O.S.B. in South Africa, p. 106.
[2] Awarded D.S.O.   [3] Awarded D.C.M.

FRONTIER MOUNTED RIFLES.

(CAPE COLONY VOLUNTEERS.)

THE reports by General Forestier Walker showed that in October 1899 this corps, strength 229, was embodied and was stationed at Barkly East, Cathcart, Molteno, and Indwe. When General Gatacre arrived they gave him great assistance, their local knowledge being invaluable. For some months their work was much akin to that of the Cape Mounted Rifles, the Kaffrarian Rifles, and Brabant's Horse. In several of the actions in the Dordrecht district the Frontier Mounted Rifles took a prominent share, and always did well. At Dordrecht, on 5th March, there was a severe engagement in which this regiment had 3 killed and 7 wounded.

When the Colony was invaded for a second time in November and December 1900, the Frontier Mounted Rifles again got opportunities of being of great use, and for the remainder of the campaign did much hard and valuable service.

The Mentions gained by the corps were as follows:—

LORD ROBERTS' DESPATCH : *2nd April* 1901.—Lts. De Cergat, Gordon-Turner, A. Milford,[1] H. Whittaker.

---

[1] Awarded D.S.O.

DRISCOLL'S SCOUTS.

THIS corps was raised, on a modest basis as regards numbers, about the time Lord Roberts landed at Cape Town. Their leader, Captain Driscoll, was a British resident in Burma, who made his way to the front, and whether his motives were love to do something for the mother country, ambition, or mere love of adventure, he most certainly did work of the highest value throughout more than two years' hard campaigning.

The corps took part in General Brabant's operations in February and March 1900 for clearing the north-eastern portion of Cape Colony (see Cape Mounted Rifles); and when Colonel Dalgety occupied and defended Wepener, 3 officers and 52 men of Driscoll's Scouts were with him. During the siege Lieutenant Weiner and about a dozen non-commissioned officers and men were wounded. After Wepener was relieved the corps was attached to the Colonial Division under General Brabant, and were in the advance through the east of the Orange River Colony to the line Senekal to Hammonia; the right or eastern end of that line being largely left to the keeping of the Colonial Division during June and July 1900, when the operations for surrounding the enemy were in progress. The corps were present at the severe engagement fought by General Rundle at Biddulphsberg on 29th May. They had several casualties in this action and in the fighting during June and July before Prinsloo's force was surrounded.

In a telegram dated 12th July the 'Daily Telegraph' correspondent said: " Captain Driscoll, leader of the

Scouts bearing his name, captured four armed Boers single-handed and brought them prisoners into camp. This was a splendidly plucky feat. Driscoll's Scouts are rendering General Rundle most valuable service." Another correspondent mentioned that at the time Captain Driscoll was quite alone. He had been taking coffee at the door of a store, when he saw four armed Boers go round the house. In a second he had "covered" them, and they agreed to hand over their arms. He then marched them to his men some miles away.

Sir Archibald Hunter, in his despatch of 4th August 1900 regarding the surrender of Prinsloo, said, para. 26: "The following day, the 26th, I entered Fouriesburg with my mounted troops, and found that the town had already been occupied by a portion of Sir Leslie Rundle's Division, headed by Driscoll's Scouts, after a forced march from Commando Nek of twenty-five miles." The corps were very highly thought of by Sir Leslie Rundle, and he kept them as scouts for his division when the bulk of the Colonials were taken north to the Transvaal on the trail of De Wet.

The corps were for a time under Major-General Hector MacDonald in the Bethlehem district, and in October they were attached to a column based on Harrismith under Brigadier-General Campbell. Under these leaders they did a great deal of marching and skirmishing.[1] In November and December they were with Bruce Hamilton, under whom they had constant hard work, which they performed to the general's satisfaction. He frequently complimented them.

In the second phase of the war the corps was greatly augmented in numbers; having done well and made a

[1] Despatch of Lord Roberts of 10th October 1900.

name, it got recruits. The despatch of 8th July 1901 shows that the strength in May was 422 men and 489 horses. At that time, and for some months previous, they had been operating in the Orange River Colony both east and west of the railway, along the Vaal river, and in the south of the Transvaal. Early in February they were engaged near Ladybrand, and had some casualties. On the 24th they lost 2 killed and 6 wounded, and on the 26th had further losses in the Winburg district. On 4th March Lieutenant Moss was severely wounded near Jagersfontein in the south of the Orange River Colony. On the 2nd a party of 50 had been sent to join a column. They were surrounded by 300 Boers, but about 35 got into a kraal, which they held for twenty-four hours until relieved. On 16th March Lieutenant MacMinn and several men were wounded. Driscoll's Scouts were for a considerable time in the column of Colonel Western, who was frequently credited in the despatches with useful captures made chiefly in the neighbourhood of the Vaal. Near Parys, on 19th April 1901, Lieutenant Norman Breslin was severely wounded. In August Western's column was taken to Cape Colony, and operated for a short time against Myburg about Jamestown. In September the corps was taken to the south-east of the Orange River Colony, where for about four months they operated under General Knox, Colonel Rochfort, and Colonel Western. In the despatch of 8th January 1902 Lord Kitchener remarked that Colonel Rochfort's troops, under Lieut.-Colonel Western and De Moulin and Major Driscoll, were moved to the west of the railway in pursuit of straggling bands of the enemy.

In the despatch of 8th February 1902 Lord Kitchener said: "On the 26th January Major Driscoll, whose column had called at Petrusburg to obtain supplies there, learned that on the previous evening Nieuwhoudt's commando had been seen in the vicinity of Makaw's Drift on the Modder. He at once started in pursuit, and crossing at the drift, came up with the Boer force, which was in movement on the Boshof road about eight miles to the north of the river. A short engagement ensued, in which Major Driscoll was successful in capturing 17 prisoners, including 2 field-cornets, 12 waggons, 69 riding-horses." Driscoll was then sent to the extreme south-west of the Orange River Colony. The despatch of 8th March 1902 mentions that in February Western and Driscoll's troops moved north towards Boshof; Driscoll's Scouts had an engagement on the way at Simon's Vallei, capturing 6 prisoners, 180 horses, mules, some cattle, waggons, and ammunition.

The enemy having been very aggressive in the south-west of the Transvaal in February and the first half of March, Driscoll's Scouts, acting as one of Colonel Rochfort's columns, were taken to the valley of the Vaal. About 11th April they crossed the river, and paid some surprise visits to various likely resorts of the enemy. A forced march on the 15th resulted in a successful surprise near Schweizer Reneke, when 57 prisoners were taken, including two of De Wet's staff. Other efforts also met with success. After this Driscoll's Scouts took part in the final great drives in the Western Transvaal under General Ian Hamilton, which Lord Kitchener said were extremely successful.

The following Mentions were gained by the corps:—

LORD ROBERTS' DESPATCH : *2nd April* 1901.—Capt. D. P. Driscoll.
LORD KITCHENER'S DESPATCHES : *8th May* 1901.—Lieut. Breslin, in command of a post near Kroonstad, attacked by Boers on 27th February 1901,

held out from morning till midnight. Sgt. Pogson for assisting on same occasion.

8th August 1901.—Qrmr. R. J. M'Kinnery, at Maatjesspruit, July 7th, rallied a troop without an officer; materially checked enemy, who were pressing rear-guard.

LORD KITCHENER'S FINAL DESPATCH.—Major D. P. Driscoll,[1] Capt. C. F. Smith,[1] Lieut. K. Sartorius, Regl. Sgt.-Major F. J. Kirkwell,[2] Sq. Sgt.-Majors J. Ellis, W. Morgan, J. Hunt, and Sgt. S. P. Pontas.

CAPE TOWN HIGHLANDERS.

(CAPE COLONY VOLUNTEERS.)

THE reports of General Forestier Walker in October 1899 show that this corps, strength 458, was then under arms and forming part of the garrison of Cape Town. Throughout the campaign they did much useful service, but were employed chiefly in garrison duty and in guarding the Cape to Kimberley railway. It has to be borne in mind that at the commencement of the campaign neither the Cape Government nor the British generals encouraged the idea of employing the Cape Colony Volunteers at the front. The view taken was to keep them on the railways or about their own towns; some corps, indeed, do not seem to have been even embodied. The consequence of this discouraging policy was, as has been pointed out in 'The Times' History, that an immense number of the best men in the Colony Volunteer forces joined the South African Light Horse, Roberts' Horse, Kitchener's Horse, and other irregular regiments. For example, the Army List of December 1900 showed that 4 officers from the Cape Town Highlanders, 5 from the Duke of Edin-

[1] Awarded D.S.O. [2] Awarded D.C.M.

burgh's Volunteers, and 1 from the Cape Garrison Artillery, were serving in Kitchener's Horse alone.

As a corps the most prominent appearance of the Cape Town Highlanders in despatches was in connection with a mishap for which, however, they were in no way to blame. It will be remembered that in October 1900 the enemy, having been beaten in the Transvaal, made a great effort all over the Orange River Colony, attacking or sneaking into various towns. In Lord Roberts' despatch of 15th November 1900, after referring to the attempts on Jagersfontein, Fauresmith, and Philippolis, he said: "Again at Jacobsdal on 25th October the treacherous part played by some of the inhabitants in admitting the Boers into their houses during the night led to the temporary occupation of that town. The Boers opened fire at daybreak on the garrison, and 14 men were killed and 13 wounded, nearly all belonging to the Cape Town Highlanders and Cape Artillery. On the news reaching the Modder River Post, troops were at once detached to Jacobsdal and drove the Boers off. The houses of the treacherous inhabitants were destroyed; in three of them were found large stores of soft-nosed bullets. In this engagement the Boer commandant, Boshman, was killed." Many of the defenders were shot at close range in their tents or as they were rushing out. Unfortunately the tents were on the market square, practically surrounded by houses to which the enemy had got access and from which they were able to fire in comparative safety. As the attack commenced at 4.30 A.M. and continued till 2.30 P.M., it was most creditable to the garrison, numbering in all under 60, that they did not surrender. Eight dead Boers were found. The relieving force was a very small party of Cape Police, Cape Town Highlanders, and Cape Garrison Artillery, about 50 in all. As the Boers were nearly 300 strong, they evidently took the relieving party for the advanced guard of a stronger body.

Throughout 1901 detachments of the Cape Town Highlanders were garrisoning Ookiep and other places in Namaqualand, and although the enemy made sundry attempts none of these places fell into his hands. In his telegram of 21st April 1902 Lord Kitchener said: "In west bulk of enemy's force is round Ookiep, which has been attacked unsuccessfully. Reinforcements have arrived now." The defenders of Ookiep were afterwards congratulated on what was a most creditable stand. They held out against repeated attacks from 3rd April to 4th May. Lord Kitchener said in his despatch of 1st June, "No details of the defence of the town have as yet been received, but General French is of opinion that Colonel Shelton and his men offered a gallant and determined resistance to the many unsuccessful attempts made to capture the position." The garrison consisted chiefly of the Namaqualand Town Guard, small detachments of the 5th Royal Warwickshire Militia Regiment, of the Cape Garrison Artillery, the Namaqualand Border Scouts, and a few Volunteers.

The Mentions gained by the corps were as follows:—

LORD ROBERTS' DESPATCHES: 31*st March* 1900.—Capt. H. Watermeyer, who acted as aide-de-camp to Lord Roberts.

2nd April 1901.—Capt. Watermeyer,[1] for performing various duties loyally and well. Pte. T. Moore,[2] since killed.

LORD KITCHENER'S DESPATCH: 23*rd June* 1902.—Lieut.-Col. W. Standford[1]; Capts. W. A. Hare, J. D. Dell; Qrmr.-Sgt. W. Clark[2]; Company Sgt.-Major P. Hardy; Sgt. C. Penthill.

[1] Awarded D.S.O.   [2] Awarded D.C.M.

CAPE GARRISON ARTILLERY.

THIS corps was embodied in October 1899, the strength then being 373. Throughout the war they did much good work. During 1900 they were chiefly employed on the western railway and west of the line. A section was for some months operating under Sir C. Warren and other leaders against the Griqualand rebels. The corps assisted in garrisoning various important posts. Some were in Jacobsdal when that town was attacked on 25th October 1900 (see Cape Town Highlanders), and some were in the relieving force. In his telegram of 31st August 1900 Lord Roberts deals with an attack on Kraaipan station, in which he remarks: "Sergt. Southrood, Cape Garrison Artillery, behaved with great gallantry."

In 1901 detachments of this corps garrisoned, along with the Cape Town Highlanders and various locally raised troops, the towns in the extreme west of Cape Colony and sundry posts right up to the border of German South-West Africa, which were successfully held against repeated attacks.

A detachment was part of the little garrison of Ookiep.

Lieutenant J. C. Campbell of the C.G.A. was, when serving with an armoured train, unfortunately killed in an accident north of Pretoria on 8th May 1902.

The Mentions gained by the corps were—

LORD ROBERTS' DESPATCH : *2nd April* 1901.—Driver Rodger.[1]

LORD KITCHENER'S DESPATCH : *23rd June* 1902. — Lieut.-Col. T. E. Lawton[2]; Capt. J. Sampson; Company Sgt.-Major W. G. Duncan; Sgts. W. Lewis, R.G.A., F. C. Honey, W. Carruthers,[1] W. Vye.[1]

---

[1] Awarded D.C.M. [2] Awarded D.S.O.

DUKE OF EDINBURGH'S OWN VOLUNTEER RIFLES.

(CAPE COLONY VOLUNTEERS.)

IN October 1899 the corps was embodied, and, according to General Forestier Walker's Distribution State of the 26th, 498 were in Cape Town and 98 were at Fraserburg guarding the railway. Later on the corps, recruited up to 1000 strong, was on the line between Cape Town and De Aar. Afterwards it got an opportunity of moving to the front, where it did excellent work. As has already been stated under the Cape Town Highlanders, a great many officers and men from all the Cape Colony Volunteer battalions joined the different irregular regiments, because it was seen that this was the surest method of getting quickly to the front. In November 1900 five officers of the Duke of Edinburgh's Volunteers were serving with Kitchener's Horse.

Early in 1900 a detachment of the Duke of Edinburgh's Volunteers were taken by sea to Walfish Bay in consequence of its having been reported that a force of Boers were working through the sparsely inhabited parts of German South-West Africa to attack the British port. The projected attack did not come off. All through the campaign much unostentatious but responsible work of this kind was cheerfully undertaken by the Cape Colony Volunteer battalions. When Sir Charles Warren was appointed Military Governor of Cape Colony, north of the Orange River, on 26th April 1900, that district was in a most disturbed state, the rebel Dutch aided by some Boers having the ascendancy. Sir Charles Warren had consequently to undertake numerous operations in order to regain control over this very wide district. This was absolutely necessary if the safety of the Kimberley line was to be maintained. In his despatch of 29th June 1900 Sir Charles stated that on 21st May he occupied Douglas, and that his next objectives were Campbell and Griquatown. He began to concentrate at Faber's Put on 27th May, but his advance was delayed by his having to wait for a convoy, which came in on the night of the 29th. His force then consisted of four and a half companies Duke of Edinburgh's Volunteers, the 23rd and 24th companies Imperial Yeomanry, a small detachment of Paget's Horse, four guns "E" battery Royal Canadian Artillery, and a small body called Warren's Scouts. Before dawn on the 30th the camp was attacked by the enemy from three sides. Creeping up through bush, they occupied some gardens and other positions in the darkness, from which they stampeded the horses by fire at close range, and also poured a very heavy fire into the camp. Fortunately the troops were astir when this fire broke out. It was after reveille, but daylight did not come till after six o'clock. The advanced pickets held their ground well; indeed, the whole of the troops behaved splendidly. Two companies of the Volunteers moved out on the eastern side and drove back the enemy; another company in reserve acted, in the words of Sir Charles Warren, "with all the steadiness of seasoned troops." After about an hour of fighting the attack was repulsed, the enemy having lost heavily; indeed, their loss was so severe that the rebellion suddenly collapsed. The losses of the Duke of Edinburgh's Volunteers were Col-

Duke of Edinburgh's Own Volunteer Rifles 137

onel Spence, Sergeant Orchard, and Private Cheverly killed, and four men wounded. Colonel Spence was killed while sitting up to direct the fire of his men. As to him Sir Charles said, "I regret very much the loss of Colonel Spence, a most gallant and efficient commanding officer." Sir Charles also mentioned Major Lewis, Captains G. Twycross and W. Simpkins, Lieutenants W. Prince and B. J. Thorne, and Sergeant-Major Pearson in charge of the maxim.

In 1901, and until the close of the war, the regiment was chiefly employed in the west of Cape Colony, about Griquatown and Daniel's Kuil; and although very frequently engaged and suffering some losses, they seem always to have done well, often in difficult circumstances, as when they had to take convoys or to guard posts very far from the railway and the main force of the army. While in Griqualand, throughout part of 1901 and 1902, the corps had to observe great watchfulness, and be ever ready for surprises. The enemy did not leave the posts—such as Griquatown and Daniel's Kuil—unworried, and casualties were frequent. A portion of the regiment was in the Port Nolloth-Ookiep district in 1902 when the enemy developed considerable activity in that neighbourhood. One detachment of twenty, which held a kopje near Arrenons, made an excellent defence when attacked on 15th April by a strong force.

In addition to the names already given as in Sir C. Warren's despatch, the regiment gained the following Mentions :—

LORD ROBERTS' DESPATCH : *2nd April* 1901.—Major J. Lewis, awarded C.M.G. Capt. W. V. Simkins ; Capt. Prince.
LORD KITCHENER'S DESPATCHES : *8th March* 1901.—Lieut. Cullum.[1]

---
[1] Awarded D.S.O.

8th July 1901.—Lieut. G. C. Cullum, for his defence of Daniel's Kuil in January 1901, when by his forethought and organisation he kept off very superior numbers.

8th August 1901.—Capt. G. S. Pearson, for prompt action and enterprise in capture of Boer laager in Griqualand West, 2nd August.

23rd June 1902.—Capt. W. F. Gregory, Lieut. Charrington, Qrmr.-Sgt. T. H. Bassett,[1] Coy. Sgt.-Major W. Cotton, Sgt. H. H. Saby, Lce.-Cpl. A. N. M'Leod. Major Lewis was awarded the C.M.G.

CAPE MEDICAL STAFF CORPS.

THIS corps was mobilised in October 1899, and performed most valuable work throughout the campaign. In November 1899 "A" Company of the Cape M.S.C. acted as Bearer Company to Lord Methuen at Belmont, Graspan, Modder River, and in December at Magersfontein. It will be remembered that the Royal Army Medical Corps were scarcely able to meet the great pressure on their department, particularly after Lord Roberts commenced his advance into the Orange River Colony. In these circumstances, the Cape Medical Staff had full opportunity of proving the worth of their previous training, and exhibited a very high ideal of what the services of such a corps should be. In Sir C. Warren's engagement at Faber's Put on 30th May 1900, the corps had Sergeants Blizzard and Rosscan wounded.

The Mentions gained were :—

LORD METHUEN'S DESPATCH AS TO MAGERSFONTEIN.—Cape Med. Corps—Pte. A. Bettington, C.M.R., attached, helped to remove a wounded Highlander from the front under a heavy fire.

---

[1] Awarded D.C.M.

LORD ROBERTS' DESPATCH, PAARDEBERG OPERATIONS.—Capt. J. J. Brownlee,[1] Sgt. A. Bettington.
GENERAL WARREN'S DESPATCH AS TO ACTION AT FABER'S PUT: 30th May 1900.—Major Cox, commanding Cape Field Hospital.
LORD ROBERTS' DESPATCH: 2nd April 1901.—Surg. Lieut.-Col. C. B. Hartley, V.C., awarded C.M.G.; Staff-Sgt. Wunschow; Ptes. M. Cheese,[2] S. Nathan.[2]
LORD KITCHENER'S DESPATCH: 23rd June 1902.—Qrmr. and Hon. Major W. Dawson.

PRINCE ALFRED'S VOLUNTEER GUARD.

(CAPE COLONY VOLUNTEERS.)

THE reports of General Forestier Walker in October 1899 show that this corps was embodied at that time, and had a battery of artillery, strength 116, and a battalion of infantry, 339, afterwards increased to 500.

The battery remained for a considerable time about Cape Town and the line between that and the Orange River, the infantry at the same time being the garrison of Port Elizabeth, and afterwards guarding the railway. The greater portion of the corps were mounted in January, when it was seen that mounted men were required. In the latter half of February 1900 the mounted squadrons of the corps were employed, under Major-General Clements, about Arundel, and did good work, particularly on the 20th, when they assisted to repel an attack in force, and on the 24th. On the latter date the two squadrons were sent out to reconnoitre towards Kuilfontein—a position which the enemy had been occupying in great strength. Suddenly they were fired on from both flanks and front, and had to take refuge in a gully which they

[1] Awarded D.S.O.   [2] Awarded D.C.M.

held for three hours, but from which they had eventually to retire owing to the enemy placing a gun so that it enfiladed the shelter. The officer in command, Captain Lascelles of the Australian Regiment, ordered a retirement, which was well carried out with a loss of 2 men mortally wounded and 6 taken prisoners. General Clements issued an order as follows: "The G.O.C. noticed with much satisfaction yesterday the courageous manner in which the Cape Colony Mounted Volunteers held the enemy in front of Kuilfontein farm, and retired under a very heavy fire in good order, covering the retreat of their comrades who were without horses."[1] On the 27th it was found that the Boers had retired, and General Clements' force, including Prince Alfred's Guards, moved forward.

In April a portion of the corps were employed about Bethulie, and on 25th April Private King was killed on patrol duty. A mounted detachment of the corps joined the main army at Brandfort about 4th May, and then took part in the advance towards Pretoria, generally acting as part of General Tucker's mounted screen. On 15th May Lord Roberts telegraphed as follows from Kroonstad: "Two officers and 6 men of Prince Alfred's Guards were out foraging yesterday a few miles from Kroonstad. They had visited a farm flying the white flag, the owner of which surrendered himself, his arms, and his ammunition. They then approached another farm from which was also flying the white flag. When within 40 yards of the enclosure they were fired upon by 15 or 16 Boers concealed behind the farm wall. Pte. A. E. Goldsmidt and Pte. James Coltherd were killed. Lieut. E. B. Walton received a slight flesh wound in the thigh,

[1] Major Reay's 'With the Australian Regiments.'

and Lieut. W. B. Everton, Cpl. W. B. Sagar, and Lance-Cpl. E. George were taken prisoner. The owner of the farm states that the Boers threatened to shoot him when he protested against their making improper use of the white flag."

A detachment of Prince Alfred's Guards also took part in the operations for surrounding Prinsloo, and a detachment 93 strong formed part of the escort to a large convoy which, under the command of Colonel Brookfield, was, on 25th June 1900, sent out from Kroonstad to General Paget, who was near Lindley. The convoy was fiercely attacked, but got through after heavy fighting. This squadron was also engaged on 3rd July 1900 in General Paget's sharp action at Baken Kop or Leeuw Kop, an account of which will be found in 'The Honourable Artillery Company in South Africa,' page 65 (see 4th South Australians). They were also in the pursuit of the Boers who crossed to the north of the Vaal. In August and September 1900 a portion of Prince Alfred's Guards were employed in the Johannesburg and Krugersdorp districts. In Lord Roberts' telegram of 20th October he spoke of an attack on some Boers near the railway, and said—"Much credit is due to Lieut. Walton and Prince Alfred's Own Volunteer Guards for their steadiness, 14 of them keeping off 100 Boers. Colonel Bullock, who was in command, specially mentions also Sergeant Holmes, who brought up his party from Honing Spruit, placing the Boers between the cross fire."

In the second phase of the war the corps was chiefly employed in Cape Colony, but one detachment long remained in the Kroonstad district. About the last days of December 1900 a party of about 60 of the corps were in a train which was derailed in Cape

Colony. They promptly got out, and fired till their ammunition was exhausted; 2 were killed and about 5 wounded. On 17th March 1901, near Strydenburg, 2 men were killed, and Lieutenant E. V. Morgan wounded. In May and June a detachment of the mounted infantry was about Kopjes Station, in the Orange River Colony, where Captain Leeds and 2 men were wounded on 20th May 1901. Lord Kitchener's despatch of 8th July 1901 shows that 200 of the corps were, in May and onwards, in the column of Colonel Crabbe, which did an immense amount of work in the operations for clearing Cape Colony (see Marshall's Horse). Both they and Marshall's Horse had casualties on many occasions. Captain Walton and several men were wounded about 17th to 21st July. In August this body assisted to drive Kritzinger out of Cape Colony; and in September, while still under Colonel Crabbe, they did good work at the defeat of Van der Merwe on 9th September. A few days later they had further fighting, when Captain E. B. Walton was again, for the third time, wounded. On the 27th Captain A. J. Annison and 1 man were killed and several wounded.

The battery of the corps continued to do useful work throughout the campaign, and in 1901 was at Kimberley, Warrenton, Koffyfontein, and other places in the Orange River Colony and Cape Colony. They returned to Cape Town in January 1902.

The Mentions gained were—

As already noted, Lieut., afterwards Capt., Walton was specially mentioned in Lord Roberts' telegram of 20th October 1900.

LORD ROBERTS' DESPATCH: *2nd April* 1901. — Capt. F. W. Leeds and Lieut. E. C. Olerenshaw.

LORD KITCHENER'S DESPATCH: *23rd June* 1902.—Battery Sgt.-Major M. Mullins, Artillery (awarded D.C.M.)

CITY OF GRAHAMSTOWN VOLUNTEERS, UITENHAGE VOLUNTEERS, AND MARSHALL'S HORSE (CAPE COLONY VOLUNTEERS).

MARSHALL's Horse was mainly composed of the mounted portions of the two corps first mentioned. In the despatches and in unofficial accounts the corps are mixed up, and sometimes are called Grahamstown Volunteers, sometimes Marshall's Horse.

In October 1899 the City Volunteers, strength 244, were the garrison of Grahamstown, and after doing useful work there and on the railway, they were taken to the scene of more active operations. Their numbers were shortly increased to 500. In pursuance of his declared policy to make use of the volunteers of the Colony at the front, Lord Roberts had a proportion of these corps mounted, and they were to do much most excellent work throughout the campaign. These mounted squadrons formed part of his army which, in February and March 1900, advanced from Modder River to Bloemfontein, and on the way they saw a great deal of fighting. In the despatch of 15th March 1900 Lord Roberts said that during the advance on Bloemfontein—that is, after the surrender of Cronje at Paardeberg—he had reorganised the mounted infantry, and the 1st City of Grahamstown Volunteers were said to have been put into the 4th Brigade of Mounted Infantry, commanded by Colonel C. P. Ridley. On 7th March the battle of Poplar's Grove was fought. The cavalry and mounted infantry did most of the work on that occasion, and suffered practically all the casualties; these included Lieutenant Frieslich of this corps, killed. The strength of the corps when it arrived at Bloemfontein was 12 officers, 245 men, and 231 horses.

Prior to Lord Roberts commencing his advance on Pretoria it was necessary to clear the enemy from their stronghold at Thabanchu, and a powerful force was put under General Ian Hamilton for the purpose of carrying out this object. It included Colonel Ridley's Brigade of Mounted Infantry, which again embraced the 5th Corps of Mounted Infantry, under Colonel Dawson, made up of the 5th Battalion Regular Mounted Infantry, Roberts' Horse, Marshall's Horse, the Ceylon Mounted Infantry, and a pom-pom. An excellent account of the work of Ian Hamilton's army is furnished by Mr Winston Churchill in his 'Ian Hamilton's March.'

On 25th April the enemy had to be cleared out of a very strong position at Israel's Poort. The frontal attack was entrusted to the Canadian Regiment of Infantry and Marshall's Horse, who had to lie for over four hours at about 800 yards from the enemy while the remainder of the mounted infantry were working round on the left. After heavy fighting the position was carried. In his telegram of the 27th April Lord Roberts said that among the casualties were no less than 7 officers of the Grahamstown Volunteers. Captain Gethin was killed, and Major Marshall, Lieutenants Murray, Winnery, Rawal, Barry, Hull, and 4 non-commissioned officers and men were wounded. In his telegraphic despatch of 27th April Lord Roberts said that the Royal Canadian Regiment and Marshall's Horse did particularly well.

All through May, during the advance to Pretoria, Ian Hamilton's force, which was first the army of the right flank and afterwards crossed the centre and became the army of the left flank, was constantly and most obstinately opposed, but every one, from the General downwards, did unsurpassably well. For the army of the centre it was practically a walk-over, the fighting being almost wholly on the flanks. Marshall's Horse frequently took a prominent share of the work. On 5th June at Schippen's Farm, for example, they had 1 killed and 5 wounded. They were engaged at Doornkop, south-west of Johannesburg, on 29th May, and in the battle of Diamond Hill, east of Pretoria, on 11th, 12th, and 13th June, and had slight casualties in both actions.

After Diamond Hill a large force was put under Sir A. Hunter to clear the north-east of the Orange River Colony (see also Roberts' Horse). Ridley's Mounted Infantry was part of the force, and Marshall's Horse were engaged at Heidelberg on 23rd June and were left there as part of the garrison. In his telegram of 22nd July Lord Roberts mentioned that a post on the railway east of Heidelberg had been attacked, and that General Hart had started from Heidelberg to succour the defenders. Part of Hart's force was 140 of Marshall's Horse. The attack was driven off before Hart arrived.

When De Wet broke out of the Brandwater Basin on 15th-16th July, Broadwood's Cavalry and Ridley's Mounted Infantry dashed off in pursuit, and Marshall's Horse and other troops under Hart were brought down the railway to co-operate. About Rhenoster Marshall's Horse had sharp fighting and some casualties.

For a time De Wet skulked in the Reitzburg Hills, but on the night of 6th August broke out across the Vaal. Ridley's force took part in the pursuit, and

Marshall's Horse was at times engaged with De Wet's rear-guard. De Wet escaped through Olifant's Nek to the north of the Megaliesberg about 15th August. At the request of Lord Roberts, Lord Kitchener with the bulk of Ridley's Mounted Infantry and other troops pressed on to the relief of Hore at Eland's River (see Rhodesian Regiment). In the latter part of August and during September Marshall's Horse was employed about Krugersdorp and in the Gatsrand, and frequently had fighting and rather heavy casualties. In October, November, and December they were with Barton in the Frederickstad district, and on 18th October a foraging party got into a nasty place when Marshall's Horse lost 2 killed and 4 wounded. The corps took part in the very severe fighting which Barton's force had between 20th and 25th October, which resulted in the total defeat of the force opposed to him. Marshall's Horse had Lieutenant Mullins and 2 men wounded.

When at the end of 1900 and beginning of 1901 the enemy reinvaded Cape Colony, the greater part of Marshall's Horse, like most of the Cape raised corps, were brought south to protect their own colony and for long did good service in the columns of Colonel Crabbe and other leaders. They were constantly in action and often had casualties. Lieutenant Cliff Turpin was killed and 6 men were wounded on 24th March 1901 in the Zuurberg Mountains when on patrol duty. In July and August they assisted to drive Kritzinger from the Colony. On 9th September Colonel Crabbe completely defeated the commando of Vandermerwe, that leader being killed and 37 of his men captured. Marshall's Horse, under Major Corbett, and Prince Alfred's Guards did a great part of the

City of Grahamstown Volunteers, &c.

fighting, and did it well. Marshall's Horse had 3 men killed and Lieutenant Tyler and 1 man wounded.

Part of the corps remained throughout most of 1901 in the Transvaal; about 30 were in the column of Brigadier-General Cunningham, afterwards of Brigadier-General Dixon, which operated about the Gatsrand and Megaliesberg (see war record of 1st Battalion Derbyshire Regiment). This detachment had 1 man killed and 1 man wounded at Modderfontein on 31st January, and 1 man killed and 1 wounded at Randfontein on 8th February, and had other casualties. A portion of the corps were also in the Kroonstad district in April, May, and June 1901.

In 1902 the corps was in the west of Cape Colony, where fighting was continuous and the marching very severe. On 24th March at Rhenoster Valley a detachment of Marshall's Horse was badly cut up, losing 7 men killed and 1 officer, Lieutenant A. P. L. Gabbatt, and 7 men wounded.

The Mentions gained by the corps, which were unaccountably few considering the acknowledged value of their work, were as follows:—

LORD ROBERTS' DESPATCH: *April* 1901.—Major G. Marshall, awarded C.M.G.

LORD KITCHENER'S DESPATCH: *1st June* 1902.—Tpr. A. Lloyd, promoted Cpl., in Cradock district, Cape Colony, March 24th, when advanced scout with one other man who was dangerously wounded, picked him up and carried him into cover, though himself wounded in the side and twice again wounded whilst carrying him in.

QUEENSTOWN RIFLE VOLUNTEERS.

(CAPE COLONY VOLUNTEERS.)

IN the reports by General Sir Forestier Walker, dated 17th and 26th October 1899, the Queenstown Rifle Volunteers, strength 245, were stated to be part of the garrison of that town, and they were then mobilised and under arms. After General Gatacre arrived the corps, slightly increased in strength, were under his command and did useful service, freeing the regular troops for action at the front. By-and-by the authorities came to think more highly of the various Colony Volunteer Battalions, and when Brabant was clearing the Dordrecht-Jamestown district in February and March 1900 (see Cape Mounted Rifles), the Queenstown Volunteers formed part of his force. They were not with Colonel Dalgety in Wepener in April, but under General Brabant took part in the operations for the relief of the brave garrison: thereafter they formed part of the Colonial Division in the advance northwards (see Cape Mounted Rifles and Brabant's Horse). The corps seems to have always done well.

After Prinsloo had surrendered, the Queenstown Volunteers continued to operate in the Orange River Colony, and in August General Kelly-Kenny issued the following Order, which speaks for itself: "The Lieutenant-General commanding the Line of Communications wishes the following incident to be made known throughout his command. Colonel Ridley, Imperial Yeomanry, with about 240 men mostly

Colonial Troops—Queenstown Volunteers—while engaged in a reconnaissance north-east of Winburg on August 23rd was cut off and surrounded by 1500 of the enemy with three guns. Ridley and his little force, notwithstanding two days' shelling and rifle fire, and three nights' sniping, held their position until relieved. The enemy twice demanded his surrender without avail. His loss was 30 killed and wounded. The Lieutenant-General brings this gallant defence to the notice of his command with the view of showing how a few determined men, skilfully commanded, can hold their own even in an unprepared position, much more so in positions carefully entrenched such as ours." Lord Roberts in his telegram of 26th August also referred to the engagement with satisfaction, and praised the defence. Three of the Queenstown Rifle Volunteers were killed and 14 wounded, including Lieutenant C. Smith. In his despatch of 10th October 1900, paragraph 43, Lord Roberts mentioned that "on the 27th August a Boer force, 1400 strong, under Olivier, attacked Winburg. They were repulsed by Bruce Hamilton, 29 prisoners being taken, including Olivier and his three sons, who were captured by a small detachment of the Queenstown Rifle Volunteers." Nothing could be more creditable than these two references.

Towards the close of 1900 and in 1901 a company, mounted, of the Queenstown Rifle Volunteers was in Colonel Crewe's column which operated in the Orange River Colony and afterwards in Cape Colony. The company were present in the severe fighting about Tabaksberg towards the end of January 1901 (see Kaffrarian Rifles). They then took part in the weary pursuit of De Wet, and the endless chasing and fighting which resulted in his being driven from Cape Colony.

The Mentions gained by the corps were as follows :—

LORD ROBERTS' DESPATCH : *2nd April* 1901.—Majors J. W. Bell[1] and H. L. Haliwell,[1] Capt. H. G. Bell, Lts. Collins and Robins (killed), Sgts. Arnott [2] and Temlett,[2] Cpls. F. Hayes [2] and W. W. Richards, Ptes. H. N. B. Helms,[2] W. M. Sladdin,[2] P. G. Stillwell,[2] T. N. Niland,[2] C. Currie,[2] D. Barton,[2] G. Bourchier.[2]

RIMINGTON'S GUIDES AND DAMANT'S HORSE.

RIMINGTON'S Guides were raised in South Africa at the outbreak of the war by Major M. F. Rimington, 6th (Inniskilling) Dragoons, who had been on special service in South Africa prior to the commencement of hostilities. As far as numbers go they were not strong, but for quality, officers and men could not be surpassed. The corps was fortunate in that it produced its own author—one can scarcely say historian,—for Mr March-Phillipps gives in his 'With Rimington' not so much a formal record of work as an exquisite series of pictures, showing in every line insight into men in all fields— —warlike or peaceful—great power of observation, and a graphic force and directness that are a treasure. His first letter is dated 18th November 1899, from Orange River Camp, just before Lord Methuen set out from that starting-point. In it he says : "It is lucky for our corps that it has in its leader a man after its own heart ; a man who, though an imperial officer, cares

[1] Awarded C.M.G.   [2] Awarded D.C.M.

very little for discipline or etiquette for their own sakes, who does not automatically assert the authority of his office, but talks face to face with his men, and asserts rather the authority of his own will and force of character. They are much more ready to knock under to the man than they would be to the mere officer. In his case they feel that the leader by office and the leader by nature are united, and that is just what they want."

At that time the corps numbered about 150, but as even then many were detached to act as guides with different units, only about 100 remained with their leader.

In November 1899 the corps showed their grit and confidence by undertaking an expedition to Prieska, which had the effect of temporarily stifling the rebellious spirit in that district.[1] Prior to the battle of Belmont, 23rd November, much patrol and reconnaissance work was done. The corps were present at that battle on the extreme right; at Enslin or Graspan on the 25th, again on the right; at Modder River on the 28th, on the left, being among the first troops to cross the river; at Magersfontein on the 10th and 11th December, again on the left. All of these were mainly infantry battles, but the few mounted men at Lord Methuen's disposal had very hard work scouting before each engagement and watching the flanks and otherwise helping during the fighting.

After Magersfontein the main body of the Guides, about 175 strong, with their leader was taken south to the Colesberg district to assist General French, a section under Lieutenant Chester-Master being left at Modder River Camp to act as eyes to Lord Methuen.

[1] 'The Times' History, vol. iii. p. 115.

General French was not long in discovering the worth of Major Rimington and his detachment. On 1st January 1900 the Berkshire Regiment attacked and captured a hill—part of the Colesberg defences; a body of the enemy—about 1000 strong—in the afternoon made a counter-attack on the British right at Jasfontein, attempting also to outflank it, but this was frustrated by the Carbineers and Major Rimington's men.[1] Rimington with his detachment, a squadron of cavalry and a company of New Zealand M.R., was afterwards sent to Kleinfontein, an isolated position, in touch with the enemy, which they held successfully. General French mentioned Major Rimington in his despatch as to the Colesberg operations.

Rimington and his men were brought up to Modder River early in February 1900 to assist in Lord Roberts' big movements. The corps was distributed among the various columns. The company which had been at Colesberg and their leader accompanied General French in the cavalry rush to Kimberley; some of the Guides claim they were the first men in. Chester-Master's section did not start with French, but made up to him at the drift on the Modder; however, they were left behind to guide the Mounted Infantry and 6th Division. Fortunately they used their eyes as soldiers should, and discovered a train of waggons trekking eastwards —Cronje bolting from Magersfontein,—and Chester-Master lost not a moment in sending to hurry up the Mounted Infantry, and in reporting to Lord Kitchener, who sent him through to Kimberley with orders for General French (see Roberts' Horse).

On the march to Bloemfontein and at the fighting at Paardeberg, Poplar Grove, and Driefontein, the

[1] General French's despatch of 2nd February 1900.

Rimington's Guides and Damant's Horse 153

corps was able to be of good service, as will be seen from the mentions gained. Among many other pieces of fine work accomplished, Rimington and about 60 of his men, pushing to the very front as usual, were able to afford assistance to Major Scobell of the Greys when the latter with a weak squadron seized a hill commanding Bloemfontein on the night of 12th March.

A portion of the corps was in Broadwood's mishap at Sannah's Post, and lost several killed and wounded (see Roberts' Horse). The Guides were on the right rear, and assisted to keep back Piet de Wet's attack from the north. Had they been in advance of the convoy, no doubt the disaster would never have taken place. As it was, their services were valuable.

The corps was in the advance to Pretoria. At the capture of Brandfort (see 1st New Zealand Mounted Rifles) and on other occasions their services were very valuable. At Kroonstad they were attached to Ian Hamilton (acting as his bodyguard). They were present at the battle of Doornkop (29th May), in which the 1st Gordons did so splendidly. Mr March-Phillipp's account of that battle is a most valuable contribution to the history of the war.

After the occupation of Pretoria the corps was sent east, and was present at Diamond Hill, 11th and 12th June 1900 (see also Canadian Mounted Rifles, p. 309).

When the operations to clear the north-east of the Orange River Colony were begun, the greater part of the corps was part of Sir Archibald Hunter's force; and when De Wet and about 1500 men broke out of the Brandwater Basin on the night of 15th July, Sir Archibald Hunter sent Broadwood with the 2nd Cavalry Brigade and some Imperial Yeomanry in pursuit, so that Rimington's Guides and Lovat's Scouts had now to do an immense deal of scouting, and the work of both corps was frequently praised. In closing his despatch as to the surrounding and capture of Prinsloo's force, Sir Archibald Hunter said: "Rimington's Guides.—Major Rimington has gathered a body of men whose virtues are like his own. They can ride, see, fight, and shoot straight. They are in the forefront where there is danger. They have never disappointed me, let alone failed me."

A detachment, 27 strong, was with Colonel Brookfield when on 25th June 1900 he left Kroonstad with a big convoy for General Paget. The convoy was heavily attacked (see 4th South Australians), but got through successfully.

A portion of the corps remained in the Transvaal during July, and had fighting and casualties east of Pretoria. During the latter half of 1900 the bulk of Rimington's Guides were in the Orange River Colony doing hard work under Generals Hunter and Bruce Hamilton, and other leaders. During November their daring and skill were constantly referred to by correspondents.

On 16th January 1901 Major Rimington left the Guides to take another command. On taking leave of the corps Major Rimington gave them every praise for good work and bravery. "You are absolutely the finest class of men I could have had under me. I could not have wished for better, and every general under whom you have served has the highest opinion of you." By his men the commander had been always implicitly trusted, generally beloved, and sometimes feared. Of no leader in the campaign has a finer word-portrait been painted than that of "Mike" Rimington by Mr March-Phillipps.

Rimington's Guides and Damant's Horse

Rimington's Guides seem to have been paid off in January 1901, but they were resuscitated as Damant's Horse under one of their old leaders, Major Damant. In February 1901 the corps, still called officially Rimington's Guides, were along with General Bruce Hamilton's 21st Brigade in Cape Colony, helping to drive out De Wet. On 24th February they had several casualties at Strydenburg, including Captain T. Harvey, mortally wounded. Soon after this Major Damant was put in command of a small column, including his own corps, which took part in the operations of Charles Knox and Bruce Hamilton between April and September 1901. In the despatch of 8th October Major Damant "of Rimington's Guides" was mentioned "for very able command of a column in south of Orange River Colony, a most gallant and exceptionally good officer."

In September the column was taken to Heilbron. "On the 13th October Major Damant engaged 300 Boers near Naude's Drift, on the Wilge River, and two days later encountered a commando 500 strong, under Commandants Ross and Hattingh, which he drove towards the Bothasberg. Among the prisoners taken on this occasion was Adjutant Theron. On the 25th Major Damant returned to Frankfort, bringing in with him 19 prisoners" and much stock. At another place Lord Kitchener said, "Some minor night raids by Major Damant's corps have resulted in the capture of 12 other prisoners." In these affairs they escaped with comparatively few casualties, because their work was most skilfully carried through.

The despatch of 8th December 1901 contains the following passage, very flattering to the work of both the leaders mentioned: "Since the fifteenth of November successful operations have been carried out by Colonel Rimington and Major Damant, operating from Frankfort, along the valley of the Vaal. Frequent captures have been made by these officers, who have exhibited marked ability in adapting themselves to the peculiar methods of Boer warfare. It would be tedious, indeed, to give in detail the many minor successes which have rewarded their energy and ingenuity. The most important capture effected by Colonel Rimington was that of Commandant Buys, who fell into his hands after being wounded in a skirmish with a detachment of the Railway Pioneer Regiment, to whose assistance Colonel Rimington had gone."

In the despatch of 8th January 1902, after referring to De Wet's successful rushing of the camp of a Yeomanry battalion at Tweefontein, in the Harrismith district, in the early morning of 25th December 1901, Lord Kitchener said: "Another very determined attack was also made upon Lieutenant-Colonel Damant's column in the vicinity of Tafel Kop, between Frankfort and Vrede. On the evening of the 19th December, this column, together with Colonel Rimington's troops, who had also moved from Heilbron to Frankfort, marched from the latter town towards Tafel Kop to cover the extension of the blockhouse line in that direction. They moved throughout the night by two parallel roads, some three miles apart, and to the north of the proposed line of blockhouses, and, after circling round Tafel Kop, were at daybreak in the vicinity of Bacchante Farm. Here a resolute attack was suddenly made by some 800 Boers, under General Wessels, upon Colonel Damant's advanced guard, who were deceived by the khaki disguise of the enemy, and their clever imitation of the formation usual with regular mounted troops. To complete the deception the enemy even fired volleys, as they approached Colonel Damant's men, in the general direction of some Boers who were escaping across the front of the two forces. This clever ruse enabled them to get sufficiently close to Colonel Damant's troops to anticipate them by a few yards in the occupation of the crest of a kopje which commanded the whole field, including the guns and the main body of our troops. Lieutenant-Colonel Damant's men displayed the utmost gallantry, holding on to their inferior position so as to save the two guns which accompanied the advanced guard, and every officer and man, except four, of the leading troops was shot down before reinforcements, which were pushed forward from the main body and from Colonel Rimington's column directly firing commenced, could arrive upon the scene. The appearance of these reinforcements compelled the Boers to relinquish their attack, and they fled over the Wilge River, pursued for some miles by Colonel Rimington's troops. Since the date of this affair the troops of Colonels Rimington and Damant have continued to operate in the neighbourhood of Tafel Kop, where I am reinforcing them by two of the newly formed battalions of Royal Artillery Mounted Rifles, and by the Canadian Scouts under Major Ross." In his telegram of the 21st December Lord Kitchener said that the losses of the column were 2 officers and 20 men killed, and 3 officers and 17 men wounded. These turned out to be rather greater; the 39th Battery—one section—had 6 killed and 8 wounded. The losses of Damant's Horse were severe, but nothing like those of the 91st Company Imperial Yeomanry, which had 32 hit out of

40, and, in the words of Lord Kitchener, "sacrificed itself almost to a man to save Damant's guns." Lieutenant-Colonel Damant was wounded in four places, Lieutenant Shand (Cameron Highlanders, attached Damant's Horse) was killed, Lieutenant C. H. A. Wilson was wounded, 5 men were killed and 10 wounded.

In the despatch of 8th February 1902 it was stated that "in the north of the Orange River Colony columns under Lieut.-Colonels Keir and Wilson, together with Damant's Horse, have acted vigorously wherever opportunity offered against the enemy's bands." The corps took part in many driving operations in this district, and when it was seen, after Lord Methuen's defeat, that the Western Transvaal was insufficiently supplied with troops, the columns of Keir, Wilson, and Damant marched through Vrede to Volksrust to entrain for Klerksdorp. They were at once again put into the field, and took part in the last big operations under General Ian Hamilton, which destroyed the power of Delarey in the Western Transvaal. In the drive of 23rd and 24th March 80 miles were covered in twenty-four hours. In this operation the corps had 2 killed. On the 31st March the Boers made a most determined attack on the column of Colonel Cookson near Boschbult, and a fight as fierce as, and on a bigger scale than, that at Tafel Kop took place. Damant's Horse again did well, as will be seen from the Mentions. Their losses were Lieutenant J. J. Roach and 4 men killed and Lieutenant Harold Creed and 17 men wounded.

It may be thought that too much space has been given to these two corps, but their services were of outstanding value during more than two years' fighting.

The Honours and Mentions gained were :—

Cpl. J. J. Clements, Rimington's Guides, gained the Victoria Cross "on 24th February 1900, near Strijdenburg; when dangerously wounded through the lungs and called upon to surrender, he threw himself into the midst of a party of five Boers, shooting three of them with his revolver, and thereby causing the whole party to surrender to himself and two unwounded men of Rimington's Guides."

The Mentions gained by Rimington's Guides were :—

GENERAL FRENCH'S DESPATCH : *2nd February* 1900.—Major M. F. Rimington, employed in command of a corps of Guides, has rendered me much assistance since he has been attached to this command.

LORD ROBERTS' DESPATCHES : *31st March* 1900.—Major Rimington ; Lieuts. R. Chester-Master (King's Royal Rifle Corps), and W. F. Murray [1] ; Cpl. Kirton [2] ; Guides E. Christian and H. E. Jackson.

2nd April 1901.—Lieut.-Col. Rimington, 6th Dragoons, "has rendered very exceptional service with a specially raised corps of scouts. He had an intimate knowledge of the whole of the Orange River Colony, and no hardship was too severe or peril too serious to deter him from pushing his reconnaissances far to the front or flanks of the force to which he was attached" (awarded C.B.) ; Captain Brown ; Lieut. W. F. Murray,[1] Sgt. A. O. Vaughan,[2] Cpl. W. Kirton,[2] Tprs. Hardnek, Murchie,[2] Nelson, Patten ; Guide H. E. Jackson.[2]

4th September 1901.—Capt. C. H. Rankin,[1] 7th Hussars ; Cpl. J. Spence.

LORD KITCHENER'S DESPATCHES : *8th March* 1901.—Lieut. Harvey ; Cpl. Clements, Pte. Wilson (promoted Cpl.)

8th October 1901.—Major J. H. Damant,[1] for very able command of a column in south of Orange River Colony, a most gallant and exceptionally good officer. Cpl. J. Spence, of the Guides, also got the D.C.M.

WITH DAMANT'S HORSE.

LORD KITCHENER'S DESPATCHES : *8th March* 1902.—Lieut. Clive Wilson,[1] marked gallantry ; Tpr. J. E. Spreckley, good service ; Sgt. Carson, gallantry—all in action of 20th December 1901. "The following are some of the men who charged with Major Webb, took the ridge and held it, thereby, in a great measure, saving the guns : Sgt. J. Carson, Cpl. T. Duff (killed), Tprs. A. Forsyth (killed), R. Dunham."

1st June 1902.—Capt. Williams Scott [1] ; Sgt.-Major J. Byrne ; Sgts. W. Roberts, A. R. Lake, H. E. G. Noble, J. C. Cullinan, for good service at Boschbult, 31st March ; Tpr. R. Morrisy (promoted Cpl.), for gallantry, same action.

23rd June 1902.—Brevet-Col. M. F. Rimington, C.B., 6th Dragoons, is a

---

[1] Awarded D.S.O. [2] Awarded D.C.M.

leader of mounted troops who is particularly well qualified for the conduct of special and independent raids or enterprises ; his knowledge of the theatre of operations, his energy and his soldierly instincts, have enabled him to render exceptional services ; Reg. Sgt.-Major A. Jenkins ; Qrmr.-Sgt. De Landre ; Squad. Sgt.-Major Roberts[1]; Sgt. E. H. G. Noble; Cpl. A. R. Lake. Col. Damant was awarded the C.B. as well as the D.S.O.

ROBERTS' HORSE.

IN the despatch of 6th February 1900 Lord Roberts, after referring to the organisation of the Colonial Division under Brigadier-General Brabant (see Cape Mounted Rifles), said : " Two other regiments, designated, at the particular request of the members, Roberts' Horse and Kitchener's Horse, have also been formed, chiefly from men who have found their way to South Africa from various parts of the world." These corps were at first intended to be called "The second and third regiments of the South African Light Horse," but the names were changed as a compliment to the new Commander-in-Chief and his chief of the staff.

Appended to the despatch of 16th February, written after Lord Roberts had commenced his great movement for the relief of Kimberley and the advance on Bloemfontein, there is a list of the troops taking part in the movement, and among these is Roberts' Horse, set down at a strength of 550. Before this the corps had been doing some work on the western railway, and a detachment had taken part in an expedition to Prieska, but the regiment was attached to General French's

[1] Awarded D.C.M.

Cavalry Division before it set out for Kimberley. They joined General French at Ramdam before midnight on 11th February, and at 2 A.M. on the 12th started off with the cavalry division to seize the fords on the Riet. French did not carry the whole of his mounted infantry with him in his rush to Kimberley: he had to leave strong bodies on the 13th and 14th to keep touch with the infantry divisions who were following. On the 15th part of Roberts' Horse was in the Mounted Infantry Brigade under Colonel Hannay when Cronje was discovered to have left Magersfontein and to be trekking through the gap which, on 15th February, existed between the cavalry heading for Kimberley and the main army. As it was, the gallant Hannay's Mounted Infantry, although but very recently raised and mounted, did splendid work from the time Cronje was discovered until he was surrounded at Paardeberg. Mr Goldmann, in his 'With General French and the Cavalry,' gives a fine description of the rush to Kimberley, the heading of Cronje, and the many engagements on the way to Bloemfontein. At page 77, speaking of the seizing of the drifts on the Riet, he tells how General French manœuvred so as to deceive the enemy as to the point of crossing: "Finding that his bait had taken, General French at once made for Dekiel's Drift with the first Brigade, the mounted infantry, and Roberts' Horse. The banks of the river were very steep and difficult, but by following the track a fordable place was discovered. Some Boers, seeing the cavalry make a dash for the ford, also had a race for it, and attempted to dispute the passage, but, out-manœuvred by a boldly handled party of Roberts' Horse, came up too late to offer more than a show of resistance. Captain Majendie of the Rifle Brigade, attached to Roberts' Horse, was the only man killed, and but two were hit."[1] One man of Roberts' Horse was killed. On the 15th Lieutenant Gray was wounded near Kimberley. On the 16th some of the corps were in the fighting round Kimberley. On the 18th a portion of the corps were assisting Brigadier-General Gordon to the north of Paardeberg. Gordon had left Kimberley that morning about twenty-four hours after Broadwood's Brigade, which, it may be remembered, headed Cronje on the 17th. On the 19th Roberts' Horse did good work in seizing Koedoesrand Drift and the hills south of it, and part of them were at the taking of Kitchener's Hill next day. This was an important position two miles south of the Boer laager, which, if held by the enemy, made it possible for them to send help to Cronje. The regiment had casualties several times between the 15th and 28th February, including Lieutenant Grant wounded. This officer died in Kimberley shortly afterwards. During that period they had suffered severe hardships: the work had been incessant, and the rations for officers, men, and horses most scanty.

In the despatch of 15th March it was noted that Roberts' Horse had, about 2nd March, been put into the brigade of mounted infantry under Lieut.-Colonel Alderson, along with the first and second regiments of regular mounted infantry, the New Zealand Mounted Rifles, and Rimington's Guides. At the seizing of the positions commanding Bloemfontein on the evening of 12th March Roberts' Horse had again a prominent place. On their arrival at Bloemfontein the strength of the regiment was 35 officers, 358 men, and 387 horses.

[1] See also 'The War Record of the Inniskilling Dragoons,' p. 39.

After the occupation of the capital Alderson's Mounted Infantry, including Roberts' Horse, accompanied Major-General Broadwood on an expedition to Ladybrand. Broadwood, thinking the enemy was in too great force beyond Thabanchu to allow of his small body remaining long so far from a base, decided to retire on Sannah's Post. On 30th March he fought a rear-guard action. On the 31st his camp was shelled from the east or rear at daybreak, and he decided to push on to the west. In his report he said: "Roberts' Horse and 'U' Battery moved off on opposite sides of the baggage column, which was clearing rapidly out of the shell-fire, and before they had cleared the column came to a deep spruit about 2000 yards west of the bivouac. This spruit was occupied by about 600 of the enemy, who seized five guns of the battery and the convoy, and opened a heavy fire on Roberts' Horse and the main body of the cavalry which was following: these retired out of fire." "Q" Battery wheeled into action about 1200 yards from the spruit, and the Durham Mounted Infantry formed up on its flank. This checked any intention of the enemy to come out of the spruit. General Broadwood ordered the Household Cavalry and 10th Hussars to move to the south, crossing Koorn Spruit above the Boers, and to press down the gully on their right flank. The cavalry got across, but do not seem to have made any determined attempt to press or enfilade the Boers. To Alderson's Mounted Infantry, including Roberts' Horse, was allotted the post of honour—that of rear-guard—and to the splendid stand which they made was due the fact that any of the guns were saved. When Alderson was finally ordered to retire he was holding his position with comparatively little difficulty. A regular officer who saw their work that day has told the writer that nothing could have been finer than the conduct of Roberts' Horse throughout the trying hours after the first outburst of fire from the spruit. "Q" Battery had to leave two guns, for which no horses were available; indeed the guns saved were only got out by hand and with the greatest difficulty. Lieutenant Maxwell, D.S.O., 18th Bengal Lancers; Sergeant J. C. Collins; Troopers T. Murphy and V. D. Todd, all of Roberts' Horse, were mentioned by Brigadier-General Broadwood. Lieutenant Maxwell got the Victoria Cross for heroic efforts made in the saving of the guns, and the others got the D.C.M. In his telegraphic despatches of 1st and 2nd April Lord Roberts mentions that Roberts' Horse and some regular mounted infantry covered the retirement of the guns, first from the proximity of the spruit and again from the position taken up by "Q" Battery.

The approximate losses of the regiment were Lieutenant Crowler and about 30 men killed, Major A. W. Pack Beresford, Captain H. C. Smith, Captain P. D. Bray, Lieutenant Darley, Lieutenant Kirkwood, and Lieutenant and Quartermaster Hawkins, and about 50 men wounded. About 70 were made prisoners.

Notwithstanding the losses at Sannah's Post the corps was soon in action again, taking part in the operations under Generals French and Rundle for clearing the south-east of the Orange River Colony and effecting the relief of Wepener. On 23rd April, at Kariefontein near Leeuwkop, they were sharply engaged and had some casualties. Several correspondents spoke of the regiment as doing their work exceedingly well and taking a prominent share in the attack on a strong position. On 1st May Lord Roberts inspected the corps and complimented them on the good work which they had done.

Roberts' Horse were with Ridley and Ian Hamilton in the next advance from Bloemfontein to Pretoria. The regiment was now in the 5th Mounted Infantry Corps under Lieut.-Colonel Dawson, along with the 5th Mounted Infantry Regulars and Marshall's Horse. Frequently during the advance Roberts' Horse was heavily engaged and suffered sharp losses. The regiment was in action to the south of Pretoria before the occupation; at Diamond Hill, 11th-12th June; and in other fighting immediately after that battle. They took part in the initial operations for the surrounding of Prinsloo, and again had sharp fighting near Heidelberg on the north side of the Vaal on 23rd June. The day was a disastrous one for the officers of the corps. Captain Whitaker was mortally wounded, Captain M. Browne and Lieutenants C. L. Learmonth and Rix King were wounded, while there were about 20 casualties in other ranks. Broadwood's Cavalry Brigade and Ridley's Mounted Infantry were detached by Sir Archibald Hunter to pursue De Wet when he broke out of the Brandwater Basin, and between 16th and 20th July Roberts' Horse were frequently engaged with the Boer rear-guard, having Lieutenant J. C. Collins wounded, and about half-a-dozen other casualties. On the 24th, at Stinkhoutboom, 150 of the corps boldly pursued and captured some waggons, but the detachment was in turn attacked, and only managed to withdraw their booty by the prompt assistance of Kitchener's Horse. They took part in the pursuit after De Wet and his men had broken across the Vaal on the night of 6th August, and thereafter they operated in the Krugersdorp district under Ridley and Clements. The regiment was present in Pretoria as representing the South African forces at the ceremony of proclaiming the annexation on 25th October 1900.

In November the regiment was with Hart in the Gatsrand, and frequently had fighting, as on 23rd and 24th November, when they had one killed and two wounded. Their good work at this period was referred to by the General. After Clements' mishap at Nooitgedacht, 13th December 1900, a large force was employed to clear the country west of Krugersdorp. Roberts' Horse took part in these operations under Brigadier-General Cunningham, and was engaged at Olifant's Nek on 22nd January 1901, and in the action at Middelfontein, 23rd January. During February and March they were often in action, and on 17th March Lieutenant F. C. Montgomery was killed near Lichtenburg, in the Western Transvaal. On the 18th, Lieutenant A. F. Todd and some men were wounded.

In the second phase of the war—that is, after Lord Roberts had handed over his command to Lord Kitchener—the regiment had one signal opportunity of gaining distinction. In the despatch of 8th May 1901, Lord Kitchener, dealing with operations in the Western Transvaal, said : " A night march across the hills south of Kaffir's Kraal resulted in the surprise of the Boer camp at dawn of the 14th April, the laager being rushed by the men of Roberts' and Kitchener's Horse under Lieutenant-Colonel Sir Henry Rawlinson. The enemy, numbering some five or six hundred, fled in haste, pursued by our troops. The enemy's losses included 6 killed, 10 wounded, 23 prisoners, 1 12-pounder gun, 1 pom-pom, 2 ammunition waggons," and an immense amount of ammunition. " Our casualties were 3 men wounded." To have accomplished so telling a victory with such a light casualty list reflected the greatest credit on Sir Henry Rawlinson and the officers and men of the two regiments.

Roberts' Horse continued to do good work in the Western Transvaal under Sir Henry Rawlinson and other leaders. For a time they were in the column of Colonel Hickie (see despatch of 8th July 1901). On 8th and 9th July, Roberts' Horse had 6 wounded, and Kitchener's Horse 3 wounded. They were afterwards employed in the Eastern Transvaal under General Bruce Hamilton, and took part in some of his very successful movements by which large numbers of prisoners were taken. To the close of the war they maintained the splendid reputation which they had gained in the first six weeks of their service.

The Honours and Mentions gained by the regiment were as follows :—

"Lieut. F. A. Maxwell, 18th Bengal Lancers, attached Roberts' Horse, gained the Victoria Cross. Lieut. Maxwell was one of three officers not belonging to 'Q' Battery, R.H.A., specially mentioned by Lord Roberts as having shown greatest gallantry and disregard of danger in carrying out the self-imposed duty of saving the guns of that battery during the affair at Koorn Spruit (Sannah's Post), March 31, 1900. This officer went out on five different occasions and assisted to bring in two guns and three limbers, one of which he, Capt. Humphreys, and some gunners dragged in by hand. He also went out with Capt. Humphreys and Lieut. Stirling to try to get the last gun in, and remained there till the attempt was abandoned. During a previous campaign—Chitral Expedition, 1895—Lieut. Maxwell displayed gallantry in the removal of the body of Lieut.-Col. F. D. Battye, Corps of Guides, under fire, for which, although recommended, he received no reward."

Mentions were gained as follows :—

LORD ROBERTS' DESPATCH: 31st *March* 1900, for advance to Bloemfontein.—Col. H. L. Dawson, 9th Bengal Lancers, attached, awarded C.B.;

Capt. A. W. Pack Beresford, Royal Artillery; Tprs. L. Chadwick[1] and C. H. Worrod. For Sannah's Post, the names already quoted.

LORD ROBERTS' FINAL DESPATCHES.—Capts. E. R. King,[2] F. C. Vignolles, and J. S. J. Baumgartner; Sgt.-Major (Lieut.) Montgomery[2]; Lieuts. R. Singer, C. Ross[2]; Doctor Leslie[2]; Farrier-Sgt. Robinaus; Cpls. A. Hayne, R. Thurston,[1] E. D. Patterson[1]; Tprs. L. H. T. Apel, J. M'K. Chadwick,[1] G. Cullen,[1] P. Fitzherbert, T. Jones, H. Hilton, T. Murphy,[1] V. D. Todd.[1]

LORD KITCHENER'S DESPATCH: 8th March 1902.—Brevet-Major H. C. Smith, Royal Dublin Fusrs., for conspicuous good service in General Bruce Hamilton's operations in Ermelo district, December 1901 and January 1902. Sgt. Brown, for great dash and energy on occasion of capture of Boers, Ermelo, December 11 and 13. Sgt. J. C. Collins and Trumpr. O'Hara got the D.C.M. Tpr. Chadwick got one of the four scarves knitted by Queen Victoria, he having been selected as the South African representative. Gallant conduct in the field was the primary consideration in the awarding of these scarves.

KITCHENER'S HORSE.

THIS corps was raised at the same time as Roberts' Horse, to which reference is made. Both regiments were employed in the operations undertaken by Lord Roberts in February 1900 for the relief of Kimberley and in his advance to Bloemfontein; but one squadron of Kitchener's Horse was left on the lines of communication, and was utilised as part of the force with which Lord Kitchener and General Settle put down the rebellion in the Prieska district, March and April (see Orpen's Horse).

On 9th February the Mounted Infantry Division, under Colonel Hannay, Argyll and Sutherland Highlanders, left Orange River station. After some fight-

[1] Awarded D.C.M. [2] Awarded D.S.O.

ing, the Division on the 12th reached Ramdam, where Lord Roberts was concentrating his army; but the bulk of Kitchener's Horse had preceded the rest of the Mounted Infantry, and had joined General French before midnight on the 11th. At 2 A.M. on the 12th they set out with French for Dekiel's Drift, on the Riet. On the 13th, General French, who had crossed the Riet River on the 12th, left a squadron of Kitchener's Horse at Blaauwbosch Pan, about eight miles north-east of Dekiel's Drift, on the Riet, in order to protect the wells until the infantry, who were following, should arrive. Unfortunately the infantry took a different course, and instead of them a large force of Boers turned up, who attacked the squadron and compelled their surrender after they had made a very creditable defence in a farmhouse for two days. Lieutenants Carstens and Buchanan were killed in action about this time. Another squadron was part of the slender escort of the convoy which was lost on the Riet on the 13th. The convoy is said to have been seven miles long, and the escort, left to see it over a most difficult drift with Boers all round, was 300 strong. The escort was not captured. Notwithstanding this bad luck, the corps did excellent work before Bloemfontein was reached. About one half of the regiment was with Colonel Hannay when Cronje was discovered to be trekking across the front of the VIth Division on 15th February, and they took part in the pursuit and the other operations which led to his capture. On 7th March they were engaged at Poplar Grove. Five officers and five non-commissioned officers and men gained mention in the despatch of 31st March for good work on the way to Bloemfontein. According to the official statement, the strength of the corps when it entered Bloemfontein on 13th March was 26 officers, 402 men, 270 horses, and 2 maxims.

About the beginning of March Kitchener's Horse had been, along with the 6th and 8th Regiments of Regular Mounted Infantry, the City Imperial Volunteers Mounted Infantry, Nesbitt's Horse, and the New South Wales Mounted Infantry, put into the 2nd Brigade of Mounted Infantry under Colonel P. W. J. Le Gallais, 8th Hussars,—a splendid officer, who led his brigade to victory on many occasions, but who afterwards fell at Bothaville, 6th November 1900, in the moment of success. The regiment fought with Le Gallais and General Tucker at the battle of Karee Siding on 29th March 1900, and they were attached to Ian Hamilton's force, which, towards the end of April, set out first to clear Thabanchu and thereafter take part in the northern advance, during which the regiment, along with the 2nd Mounted Infantry Regulars and Lovat's Scouts, was in the 6th corps under Colonel Legge, who was afterwards killed at Nooitgedacht.

Mr Churchill, in his 'Ian Hamilton's March,' relates that on 26th April Kitchener's Horse and a company of regular mounted infantry were told to hold a kopje near Thabanchu for the night, but about dusk they were ordered to retire. This the Boers endeavoured to prevent, attacking the force with great determination : however, the attack was driven off, and the little body got into camp during the night. Captain F. J. Warren was severely wounded, 1 man killed, and several wounded. On the 30th, at the battle of Houtnek, the regiment, with great boldness and skill, seized Thoba Mountain, and it was during the enemy's attempt to regain this commanding position that a party of about 12 Gordon Highlanders and 13 of Kitchener's Horse under Captain Towse of the Gordons made the famous stand and bayonet charge. The incident is admirably described in 'Ian Hamilton's March' by Mr Churchill, who was a spectator. Captain Towse, blinded, alas! by a bullet in the hour of triumph, got the V.C. Lieutenants Parker and Munro and 5 men of Kitchener's Horse were killed, and Captains Ritchie and Cheyne and 8 men were wounded at Houtnek. In his telegram of 2nd May Lord Roberts remarked: "Kitchener's Horse is spoken of in terms of praise." On 4th May Ian Hamilton was again engaged, "and succeeded in preventing a junction of two Boer forces by a well-executed movement of some of the Household Cavalry, 12th Lancers, and Kitchener's Horse, who charged a body of the enemy and inflicted serious loss. They fled leaving their dead on the field, and their wounded to be attended by our doctors" (see Lord Roberts' telegram of 2nd May). In this affair Lieutenant Patrick Cameron was mortally wounded. The 'Standard' correspondent drew attention to the good work of the regiment at the crossing of the Zand River on 10th May.

The regiment was present at Ian Hamilton's other actions on the way to Pretoria and at Diamond Hill (11th and 12th June). They started as a portion of Hunter's force designed to surround Prinsloo, but like Roberts' Horse were detached to pursue De Wet. On 24th July the regiment lost 9 men wounded at Stinkhoutboom, but about the same date they captured 5 of De Wet's waggons.[1] When De Wet left the Reitzburg Hills Kitchener's Horse again crossed to the north of the Vaal and operated under Ridley,

[1] 'War Record of Cameron Highlanders,' p. 85.

Hart, Clements, and other commanders in the district west of Johannesburg and Pretoria. In the despatch of 10th October 1900 Lord Roberts mentioned that "De Lisle's corps of mounted infantry was withdrawn from Clements' column and moved by rail on 17th September to Rhenoster, where it was joined by 250 men of Kitchener's Horse from Kroonstad." The work of De Lisle's men is briefly sketched under the 1st and 2nd New South Wales Mounted Infantry. This portion of Kitchener's Horse took part in the pursuit of De Wet on the south side of the Vaal and other operations under General C. Knox in the Kroonstad district during September, October, and November, and were present on 27th October when 2 guns were captured at Rensburg, and in the very successful action of Bothaville on 6th November when 6 guns, a pom-pom, a maxim, and 130 prisoners were taken.

Another portion of the corps was employed in the Eastern Transvaal, and frequently had odd casualties about Brugspruit in September and the first half of October. They took part in French's march from the Delagoa Railway to Heidelberg in October 1900,—a march which only a great leader could have brought off successfully, having regard to the strength of the enemy in the district at the time. The fighting was continuous and the strain on all most severe. In Lieut.-Colonel Watkin-Yardley's 'With the Inniskilling Dragoons,' page 217, speaking of the arrival of the force at Heidelberg, he says: "Lieut. Elphick, with his troop of Kitchener's Horse, which had requested to be attached to the Inniskillings at Machadodorp, and fought gallantly with us throughout the march, also left the column." On this march the troop lost Sergeant Hunter killed, 2 wounded, and 2 missing.

A detachment which had remained in the Gatsrand and Krugersdorp district on the north side of the Vaal operated throughout September with Clements and Ridley, and had sharp fighting under General Hart on 23rd and 24th November 1900, when they lost 2 men killed.

This portion of the regiment was with General Clements when he was attacked and met with disaster at Nooitgedacht in the Megaliesberg on 13th December 1900. It will be remembered that a high hill commanding the camp, and which was garrisoned by 4 companies of the 2nd Battalion Northumberland Fusiliers, was assaulted by the enemy in great force and was captured. Kitchener's Horse and the 2nd Battalion Mounted Infantry were on the west or left front of the camp; the enemy attacked upon this side in the most determined manner, and although some pickets were captured or wiped out entirely, the attack on the west was driven off, the enemy losing very heavily in his endeavour to push into the camp from that direction. When, however, it was seen that the high hill commanding the camp had been captured by the enemy, the General decided to retire. With difficulty General Clements got away his guns and most of his ammunition, but the camp was left standing and some stores were lost. The losses of Kitchener's Horse were severe: Lieutenant Skene and 8 men were killed, and Captain Stevenson and about 12 men wounded and about 40 taken prisoners. Some of the latter were wounded. Several mentions were gained by the corps on this occasion, and those who were present praised very highly the conduct of

Kitchener's Horse and their old comrades the 2nd Battalion Regular Mounted Infantry, also the 2nd Battalion King's Own Yorkshire Light Infantry. The regiment, sadly reduced in numbers, operated in the second phase of the war chiefly in the Western Transvaal, and had a few casualties on various occasions. A reference in the despatch of 8th May 1901 to a very valuable bit of work by men of Roberts' Horse and Kitchener's Horse has already been quoted under the former corps. Both regiments were for a time in a column under Colonel Hickie (despatch of 8th July 1901), and continued to do good work in the Transvaal. On 8th and 9th July both Roberts' and Kitchener's Horse were sharply engaged and suffered casualties. They were, during the next few months, constantly in touch with the enemy, and often suffered losses, as on 4th November 1901, when Kitchener's Horse had 5 men wounded at Vaalbank.

The Mentions gained by the corps were as follows :—

LORD ROBERTS' DESPATCH : 31*st March* 1900.—Major N. Legge, D.S.O. (20th Hussars); Capts. W. N. Congreve, V.C. (Rifle Brigade), H. J. MacAndrew [1] (5th Bengal Lancers); Capt. and Adj. G. H. M. Richey [1]; Lieut. J. E. Jackson [1]; Squadron Qrmr.-Sgt. D. P. Bree; Tprs. T. Maldrett, T. Huckle, A. Miller, A. Lewis.

FINAL DESPATCHES. — Major F. J. Warren; Capts. G. H. M. Richey,[1] W. Vaughan; Lieuts. Clayton, J. E. Jackson,[1] Skene; Squadron Qrmr.-Sgt. Bree [2]; Sgts. Drannette, Brunette, Coopers,[2] G. Dawes,[2] W. White, W. O'Shaughnessy,[2] G. Hoitzel; Cpl. G. Hill [2]; Tprs. O. S. Purchase,[2] Suckle.

LORD KITCHENER'S DESPATCHES : 8*th March* 1901.—Lieuts. L. A. Myburg and G. Dobree [1]; Cpl. G. Pitt; Tprs. H. Anderson, C. Brown.

8*th July* 1901. — Pte. G. Davidson, promoted Cpl.; as a scout he has shown exceptional skill and nerve. With Private Wilson, Victorian Rifles, and alone, voluntarily took most important messages through Boer lines.

8*th December* 1901.—Lieuts. M. Chinnery and J. Monro, gallant leading under heavy fire and capturing prisoners. Tprs. G. H. Brown and G. Swift, for gallantly sticking to retreating enemy, Barnard's Kop, 14th October 1901.

---

[1] Awarded D.S.O.   [2] Awarded D.C.M.

NESBITT'S HORSE.

THIS corps, about 300 strong, was raised in the eastern portion of Cape Colony in December 1899 by Colonel Nesbitt, "a veteran South African campaigner."[1] As in the case of many other Colonial bodies, the strength varied greatly in the course of the campaign, being at one time about 5 squadrons, but probably not much more than a squadron was in the field when peace came.

Part of the corps accompanied Lord Roberts in the great fighting march from Modder River to Bloemfontein, being in the 2nd Brigade of Mounted Infantry, at first under Ridley, afterwards under Le Gallais (see Kitchener's Horse), and they were generally attached to the VIIth Division under General Tucker. On arriving at Bloemfontein the strength of the corps was officially stated at 8 officers, 119 men, and 136 horses. Very few corps were so well supplied with horses, a fact which tends to prove the good mastership of the South African Colonials. Nesbitt's Horse were with Le Gallais and Tucker in the stiffly contested battle at Karee Siding on 29th March, Le Gallais' men taking a very important share in the work. The Boers were driven from their position, and the road towards Brandfort was opened.

When Lord Roberts moved north from Bloemfontein, Nesbitt's Horse were with the City Imperial Volunteers Mounted Infantry and Lumsden's Horse in the mounted infantry corps which did the scouting work on the front and flanks of the central divisions

[1] 'The Times' History, vol. iii. p. 94.

of the army, being more particularly attached to Tucker's VIIth Division. During the whole advance from Bloemfontein to Pretoria they had work which was hard, continuous, and most responsible, and several times had sharp fighting, as at the Vet River on 3rd May, when they suffered some casualties. After Johannesburg was reached the mounted infantry of the VIIth Division were split up: neither that Division nor Nesbitt's Horse were present at the battle of Diamond Hill.

It will be remembered that when Lord Roberts was advancing to Bloemfontein disaffection broke out to the west of the De Aar line (see Orpen's Horse). Among other troops employed on the Lower Orange and about Prieska was one squadron of Nesbitt's Horse which did much hard patrol work. They operated during part of March and April 1900 under Lord Kitchener and General Settle, and were present with Colonel Adye in a sharp fight in the Kheis district, Griqualand West, on 28th May 1900, when Lieutenant Venables and 1 man were wounded. The total British losses in Adye's action were about 7 killed and 20 wounded, and that of the enemy was heavier, 20 of them being taken prisoners. This squadron of Nesbitt's remained in the Prieska district for over one year.

After Pretoria was occupied, the detachment which had accompanied Lord Roberts northwards was taken south of the Vaal in consequence of De Wet having attacked the railway, and they afterwards did duty in the Orange River Colony and in Cape Colony. In his despatch of 15th November 1900, Lord Roberts mentioned that when the enemy moved south in force in October, Philippolis in the south of the Orange

River Colony, was attacked almost daily between 18th and 24th October. The Magistrate with 11 police and 18 British residents skilfully entrenched a kopje having a water-supply, and held out till relieved on the 24th. The enemy at first numbered about 100, but other commandos coming up, their force was increased to 600. On hearing of the investment of the place, the commandant at Colesberg sent on the 20th October Lieutenant Hannah and 34 of Nesbitt's Horse to relieve or assist the garrison,—surely a dangerously small force for the object. Lieutenant Hannah approached Philippolis on the 21st and posted pickets. These were heavily attacked early on the 22nd and were practically annihilated, but he and 6 men succeeded in joining the garrison. The party of Nesbitt's Horse lost 9 men killed and 12 wounded.

During the second phase of the war Nesbitt's Horse was employed in Cape Colony. They were frequently engaged, and took part in many pursuits. On 14th December a small post near Colesberg, garrisoned by 14 of the corps, was attacked. Lieutenant Kelyl and several men were severely wounded. Lieutenant Hannah was severely wounded on 12th May, and on 9th August Captain Noel Nesbitt was severely wounded at Maraisburg. For a great part of 1901 a portion of the corps was in the western district doing column work under Colonel Capper and Major Jeudwine, and their fine scouting often prevented loss [1] (see Border Scouts). Another portion worked in the central district of the colony. The corps remained in the field to the very end, and when Commandant Malan was defeated in Central Cape Colony three

[1] 'A Militia Unit in the Field,' War Record of 6th Battalion Lancashire Fusiliers.

days before peace was declared, he himself being wounded and captured, the successful British force was composed of the Jansenville district mounted troops, Nesbitt's Horse, and some other local troops, Lovat's Scouts helping indirectly.

The Mentions gained by the corps were:—

LORD ROBERTS' DESPATCH : 31*st March* 1900.—Major W. L. Currie.

LORD ROBERTS' FINAL DESPATCHES.—Lieut.-Col. R. A. Nesbitt, Major Currie, Capt. C. W. Nesbitt,[1] Tprs. F. Hill, Hiscock,[2] and L. F. Brown. Col. Nesbitt got the C.B., Major Currie the C.M.G.

LORD KITCHENER'S DESPATCH : 8*th December* 1901—Lieut. S. A. Callaghan, by coolness and good dispositions repulsed enemy's attack at Ganna Hoek, Cape Colony, 21st September. Tpr. R. Nel, in same action by coolness and courage under close fire rendered most valuable service; wounded in three places but continued to fight.

Lieut. Harvey was on 25th October 1900, at Pretoria, presented by Lord Roberts with the Royal Humane Society award for gallantry in saving a man from drowning.

EASTERN PROVINCE HORSE.

DURING February 1900 this corps, which was raised in the eastern portion of Cape Colony, did very good work in the Colesberg district as part of the mounted troops under Colonel Page Henderson, particularly between the 20th and the 24th when Clements' force had much fighting round Arundel. On the 24th he endeavoured to push back the Boers who were threatening to cut him off from Naauwpoort. Little progress was made, but on the 27th the enemy was found to have retired. The plight of Cronje was having effect on the Boers under Delarey and Grobler in the

[1] Awarded D.S.O.   [2] Awarded D.C.M.

colony. On the 24th the Eastern Province Horse had 3 killed and several wounded. On the 28th Clements' force commenced their advance first on Colesberg and thereafter into the Orange River Colony. The corps was taken north to Bloemfontein, and when Sir H. E. Colvile was about to set out with the Highland Brigade from Bloemfontein towards Winburg and Heilbron, the Eastern Province Horse, one squadron, under Captain Higson, was sent to Colvile as his complement of mounted troops. Sir Henry has been blamed for not recovering Broadwood's guns at Sannah's Post, and for not rescuing the Irish Yeomanry at Lindley at the end of May,—in the first case, without a shadow of justification, the writer thinks; in the second, with perhaps a very little. But General Colvile's critics and judges never seemed to take into account how the difficulties of the task set to him had been incalculably increased by the non-provision of a reasonable mounted force. A week after the Eastern Province Horse joined Colvile they were taken away again to escort a convoy to the XIth Division, of which Colvile's Brigade formed no part. After that they were employed on cattle gathering, and when they got back to Colvile their horses were utterly unfit to do the scouting necessary for an infantry brigade in most difficult country, and with the enemy in strong force all round. On 2nd May, when the advance had barely commenced, Colvile wrote to the Chief of the Staff: "About 50 of the E.P.H. are dismounted owing to their last week's work with the XIth Division. Their blankets and kit have not yet arrived."

About 15th May Lieutenant Bowker and 12 men of the E.P.H. were sent on a mission some distance from the brigade and were captured. Some drafts, however, shortly arrived, making up the corps to 107 mounted men, but these were still utterly inadequate to scout in front of and on the flanks of a column which was always, at least, three and a quarter miles long. About the 24th 1 man was killed and Lieutenant Bertram and 3 men were wounded in endeavouring to ascertain the strength of the enemy who were then opposing the advance. On the 26th, in the action at Blaauwberg, the corps was heavily pressed at different times. Speaking of this, General Colvile said: "The Eastern Province Horse, whose scouting was very bold, suffered much more heavily in proportion, losing 4 men killed and 8 wounded and 6 horses, nearly all in the first fusillade";[1] and again, "This movement was greatly helped by Lieutenant Kirkwood and the remainder of the E.P.H., who made a wide sweep round the hill." When the Boers retreated their string of waggons could be seen filing out of their laager two and a half miles away, but Generals Colvile and MacDonald could do nothing, owing to the want of mounted men and horse artillery. "The E.P.H. horses were by this time reduced to 80; of these 55 were on the flanks."

At Roodepoort, on 28th May, there was again heavy fighting. At page 197 of his work General Colvile says: "The day had been a trying one, and with less trustworthy troops might have ended badly for us, but the Highlanders, who had always been ready to go ahead against any odds, had by this time picked up a good many wrinkles from their enemies, and were as clever as the Boers in making the best use of ground. The excellent practice of the two batteries had enabled us to clear Roodepoort with hardly any loss, and later

[1] 'The Work of IXth Division,' Arnold, London, p. 169.

the naval guns had kept those of the enemy at a distance, while the Field Battery had removed the pressure on the Seaforth and materially helped the Argyll and Sutherland to hold their own. The Eastern Province Horse, by this time reduced to 35 mounted men, had enabled us to seize the advanced position." At Roodepoort the tiny mounted force had Sergeant Deynedale and Troopers Lee, Corbett, and Wright killed, and 3 corporals and 3 troopers wounded. On 29th May, the day on which Colvile had been ordered by Lord Roberts to be at Heilbron, he occupied that town.

After General Colvile left the force the Eastern Province Horse remained with the Highland Brigade under General MacDonald at Heilbron till July, and then assisted in the operations for surrounding Prinsloo in the Brandwater Basin.[1] When De Wet broke across the Vaal in August, the Eastern Province Horse followed to the north side of the river and were employed in the Krugersdorp district during September and October. On several occasions they had severe fighting. On 18th September 1 corporal and 2 men were killed, and shortly before that three others of the little band had been wounded.

The corps remained in the field throughout 1901, but got no opportunities of gaining distinction such as fell to them in May 1900.

The Mentions gained by the corps were :—

LORD ROBERTS' DESPATCHES : *2nd April* 1901.—Lieut. E. H. Higson, Lce.-Cpl. Abrahamson, Tprs. Collett and Ruddlesdin, Sgt. P. T. Sherriff (17th Lancers).
4th September 1901.—Tpr. T. Adams (afterwards Rand Rifles) and Tpr. Honman.

---

[1] Lord Roberts' despatch of 10th October 1900, para. 6.

WARWICK'S SCOUTS.

THIS was a small body raised by Captain J. A. Warwick early in 1900, primarily for the class of work indicated by their name. They saw service in many parts of the seat of war. After the relief of Kimberley they operated with Lord Methuen in the Boshof and Warrenton districts of the Orange River Colony. They accompanied that General eastwards towards Lindley, and saw some fighting there at the end of May and in June. Along with the remainder of Lord Methuen's column they were railed from Kroonstad to Krugersdorp in the Transvaal on 12th July, and advanced with him in a pursuit of De Wet northwards to Olifant's Nek, where there was some fighting in which Warwick's Scouts had two casualties. After this the corps saw endless marching and skirmishing in the Western Transvaal. On 16th February 1901, when operating with Lord Methuen, Captain Warwick was seriously wounded in the severe engagement at Hartebeestfontein.

The Mentions gained by the corps were as follows :—

LORD ROBERTS' DESPATCH : *2nd April* 1901.—Capt. J. A. Warwick,[1] Lt. H. Macandrew,[1] Tprs. Bentley, W. G. Froude, Irving. (Froude and Irving were subsequently designated as Imperial Yeomanry Scouts.)

---

[1] Awarded D.S.O.

FRENCH'S SCOUTS.

THIS corps was formed towards the close of 1899. Its greatest strength was about three squadrons, but it afterwards fell much in numbers. The corps was commanded by Captain Bettelheim, and was composed of men selected for knowledge of the country and its ways.

French's Scouts did fine work throughout two years' campaigning, generally in the districts in which the great cavalry leader after whom they were called was operating, but the whole of the corps were not always with General French; as, for example, while he was relieving Kimberley part of the Scouts went with him, but another portion was left in the Colesberg district with General Clements, under whom they fought and suffered some losses in February 1900.

When the advance from Bloemfontein to Pretoria was undertaken French's Scouts accompanied the cavalry, operating on the left flank. They were present at Diamond Hill, 11th to 13th June, where they had several casualties. After that they undertook many very daring reconnaissances north and east of Pretoria. In July 1900 the corps was in the forefront of the advance along the Delagoa line, and afterwards in the movements to Barberton in September (see Imperial Light Horse) and to Heidelberg in October. Having operated for a time in the central district, they took part in the great sweeping movement in the first quarter of 1901 to the eastern border of the Transvaal. During all these months of constant fighting their losses had been wonderfully few when the extremely dangerous nature of their tasks is borne in mind, but the evil day was to come. The corps had been taken back to Cape Colony, and near Bethesda, on 12th August 1901, they lost Sergeant Stacey killed, and the commander, Captain Bettelheim, Lieutenant C. de V. Duff, Sergeant-Major Chiazzari, and several men wounded.

The Mentions gained by the corps were :—

LORD ROBERTS' DESPATCHES : 31*st March* 1900, for relief of Kimberley and advance to Bloemfontein.—Sgt. A. K. Green [1] and Pte. W. S. Penny.[1]

2*nd April* 1901.—Capt. Bettelheim ; Sgt. (now Lieut.) A. K. Green [1]; Pte. W. S. Penny.[1]

LORD KITCHENER'S DESPATCH : 8*th July* 1901.—Lieut. F. Maxwell, for coolness and courage with which he extricated a patrol on 16th June. Sgt.-Major Chiazzari, at Kalabashfontein, 10th June, rendered most valuable service by holding a ridge with a small party ; mentioned in Army Orders.

LOCH'S HORSE.

THIS corps was raised by Lord Loch in February 1900. It might be said that having been largely recruited in England it was not a Colonial force, but in the official army lists Loch's Horse was always included among the South African Irregulars.

After the occupation of Bloemfontein Loch's Horse, strength about 220, was stationed in the line of outposts beyond Glen Siding. They shared in the advance from Bloemfontein to the Transvaal as part of the 8th Corps of Mounted Infantry commanded by Colonel Ross of the Durham Light Infantry, the Brigadier being Colonel Henry. The 8th Corps were

[1] Awarded D.C.M.

part of the advance guard or screen to the centre of Lord Roberts' army, and had a lot of scouting and skirmishing in the northward march. Colonel Henry's men, including the 1st and 2nd Victorian Mounted Rifles, South Australians, Tasmanians, Lumsden's Horse, Loch's Horse, and the 4th Mounted Infantry Regulars, were among the first to cross the Vaal, and had very stiff fighting before the infantry got up, particularly at the mines in the neighbourhood of Vereeniging, about Elandsfontein, and outside Pretoria. Their work was highly praised by the Generals and by the correspondents. A good account of the work of Colonel Ross's corps is to be found in the 'Oxfordshire Light Infantry in South Africa,' Eyre & Spottiswoode, 1901.

After the occupation of Pretoria Loch's Horse were chiefly employed about Springs and Irene, and in the neighbourhood of the Vaal; later they were moved a little farther south, and the remainder of their campaigning was chiefly done between Kroonstad and the Vaal, but in December 1900 they joined the column of Colonel De Lisle, and with him went to the extreme south-west of Cape Colony. De Lisle's column gained much credit for their work in the Piquetberg-Calvinia district in January and February 1901, when Hertzog was driven out of the district.

The Mentions gained by the corps were :—

LORD ROBERTS' DESPATCH : *2nd April* 1901.—Capt. J. H. Hodgson (Lieut.-Col. retired); Lieut. S. E. Craig;[1] Cpl. Picton ; Tpr. Blades.[2]

---

[1] Awarded D.S.O.   [2] Awarded D.C.M.

THE KIMBERLEY TROOPS.

AT the commencement of the war there were in existence and stationed at Kimberley the following volunteers [1]:—

Diamond Fields Horse, strength 178
Diamond Fields Artillery, ,, 97 and 6 guns
Kimberley Regiment, ,, 352
Kimberley Town Guard, ,, 1303

These were afterwards increased in numbers, and the Kimberley Light Horse and Kimberley Mounted Corps were organised.

These various corps were so constantly mixed up, and partook so largely of the same work, that it will be well to deal with them under one heading. The first and greatest debt under which they laid the Empire was their share in the defence of Kimberley. The town was one of the three which the Boers had shown themselves very desirous of occupying; its name was familiar all over the world as the place where the great diamond mines were located. Mr Rhodes had gone to his residence there before the war broke out, and it was, for South Africa, a large town. From a census taken during the siege the population was roughly 48,000—18,000 of whom were Europeans, the remainder blacks. The above total includes 22,000 women and children.

When the siege commenced there was in the gar-

[1] See Appendix to War Commission Report.

rison half a battalion, 444 all ranks, of the 1st Battalion Loyal North Lancashire Regiment. The only other regular troops in the garrison were the 23rd Company, 93 all ranks, Royal Garrison Artillery, with six 7-pounder R.M.L. guns; 1 section, 1 officer, and 50 men of the 7th Field Company Royal Engineers; 5 non-commissioned officers and men of the Army Service Corps; and 1 officer and 5 non-commissioned officers and men of the Royal Army Medical Corps. In his report, dated 15th February 1900, Colonel Kekewich said: "Every effort was made to increase the numbers of this volunteer force, and to provide horses for the mounted portion thereof. . . . The Right Honourable C. J. Rhodes, and also the De Beers Consolidated Mines, Limited, came most generously to my assistance in the matter of providing horses and mules." By 26th November the strength of the Town Guard, which was to perform valuable service, had been increased to 130 officers and 2520 non-commissioned officers and men.

Hostilities commenced near Kraaipan on 12th October when the armoured train was taken. By the evening of 22nd October the various detachments of the Cape Police, who had been stationed along the railway from Vryburg southwards, had retired on Kimberley. In his evidence before the War Commission Colonel Kekewich referred in somewhat ungenerous terms to the retirement of these detachments, but there seems to be no doubt whatever that the Police did the right thing. Had they endeavoured to hold the posts at, say, Vryburg or Fourteen Streams, each lot in turn would have been cut off and captured, and Colonel Kekewich would have had 350 fewer fighting-men in

Kimberley.[1] On 19th October Major H. S. Turner of the Black Watch, who was a son-in-law of one of the directors of De Beers, was appointed to command the mounted troops, and with splendid energy he set to raising and training the Kimberley Light Horse, which, by 26th November, numbered 360. On 24th October there was a fight at Macfarlane's Siding in which considerable loss was inflicted on the enemy.

On 3rd November the Boers made an attempt to drive off the cattle, but were themselves repulsed, and on the same day the Kimberley Light Horse and Police had an engagement on the west of the town in which the enemy were again driven back. On the 4th the surrender of Kimberley was demanded and refused. On the 16th Major Scott Turner took out detachments of Diamond Fields Horse, Light Horse, and Police, and drove the enemy back towards Alexandersfontein. In this affair Captain Bodley of the Diamond Fields Horse was wounded. After this there were very many skirmishes and sorties in which the mounted men did most of the fighting; while the infantry, including the Town Guard, held the trenches and defensive works. In the making of these works coloured labour, largely provided by the De Beers Company, was mainly employed. Very soon the defences were so strong that the Boers were afraid to face an assault. Indeed, all through the siege the defenders did most of the active or attacking work, the enemy relying mainly on artillery and long-range rifle-fire. Of course the little guns in the town were hopelessly outranged, and it was not

[1] Since the above was written the author has seen an article by General E. Y. Brabant in the 'Nineteenth Century' for February 1904 on the War Commission Report. General Brabant has no doubt whatever that in retiring on Kimberley the Police did rightly, and differs very strongly from the opinions expressed by Colonel Kekewich.

until the De Beers workshops had, on 19th January 1900, turned out "Long Cecil," under the superintendence of the gifted Mr Labram, that the British had a gun worthy of modern warfare. "Long Cecil" was a 4·1 breech-loading weapon, and threw a 30-pound shell. The manufacture of this powerful gun was commenced about Christmas, and it was completed in a marvellously short time.[1]

On 25th November Major Scott Turner with the mounted troops made a reconnaissance, and succeeded in surprising the enemy at Schmidt's Drift Road. He inflicted some loss and captured 29 prisoners, his own casualties being—Cape Police 2 killed, Captain Rush and 6 men wounded; Kimberley Light Horse 3 killed, Captain Bowen and 13 men wounded; Diamond Fields Artillery, Captain Hickson and 2 men wounded. Major Scott Turner's horse was killed, and he was slightly hit on the shoulder.

On the 28th a demonstration was made towards "Wimbledon Rifle Range." "Major Scott Turner, with mounted troops, attacked enemy's right flank, capturing laager and three works; enemy in fourth work offered stubborn resistance, when Turner was killed; we captured many shells and destroyed other stores."[2] Our other casualties on this occasion included—Cape Police, 2 men killed, 8 wounded; D.F.H., 3 men killed, Captain S. P. Waldeck and 8 wounded;

[1] In the article already referred to General Brabant has pointed out that it was extraordinary that Colonel Kekewich, when questioned about his artillery, took no notice of this great feat performed by the servants of the De Beers Company. It has also to be borne in mind that when, soon after the commencement of the siege, it was seen there was no adequate supply of shells for even the smaller guns, the De Beers Company set to work, and by 21st November were turning out shells with fuses complete at the rate of about 50 per diem.

[2] Colonel Kekewich's telegram.

Kimberley Light Horse, about 13 killed and the same number wounded, including Lieutenant H. S. Watson. Major Scott Turner was an officer of outstanding ability, and worthy of the very distinguished regiment to which he belonged. Although an infantry officer, he had proved himself unsurpassable in the raising, training, and leading of mounted men. On the 29th Colonel Kekewich issued an order in which he praised most highly the services of the deceased officer.

Major Peakman, a colonial officer, was appointed to succeed Major Scott Turner in the command of the Kimberley Light Horse. Major Peakman had been slightly wounded early in November.

In his report, para. 34, Colonel Kekewich said: " My general plan for the defence of Kimberley was based on the principle of always keeping the enemy on the move and constantly in fear of attack from an unexpected quarter. . . . It will be observed that portions of the mounted corps were employed on every occasion. The work which fell on the detachment (mounted) of the Loyal North Lancashire Regiment, Cape Police, Diamond Fields Horse, and Kimberley Light Horse, and the Diamond Fields Artillery was in consequence very arduous: not only did the corps mentioned respond cheerfully, but nothing can exceed the bravery and dash with which these troops attacked the enemy on several occasions in his entrenched positions."

Down to the day of the relief the tension remained very high, and the Kimberley troops had to be ever on the alert and always ready for fighting. They had many little engagements not mentioned in the report of Colonel Kekewich; indeed one feels that that report was scarcely worthy of the occasion.

According to the casualty list "during the siege," published on 24th April 1900, the colonial forces had the following losses; but this list is clearly supplementary to the losses already noted on the occasion of the sorties in November:—

> Diamond Fields Artillery—Sergt.-Major Moss killed and 11 men wounded.
> Diamond Fields Horse—14 killed; Capts. Bodley and Waldeck, Lieut. Smith, Sergt.-Major Macdonald, and 10 non-commissioned officers and men wounded.
> Cape Police—12 killed; Major Ayliff and Capts. White and Rush, and 27 non-commissioned officers and men wounded.

The historian of the defence of Kimberley will require to deal with the disagreeable subject of the alleged friction between Cecil Rhodes and Colonel Kekewich. From the evidence of the latter before the War Commission it is clear that friction did exist. Men of very different minds have sometimes had difficulty in appreciating one another. Than Rhodes no man of the day was more highly endowed with the gift of being able to stir others to almost any degree of effort. He has been called the Napoleon of South Africa. Flattering, in a sense, that characterisation may be, but it was inadequate. His energy, the grandeur and wealth of his conceptions, were worthy of the great Emperor; but he had qualities the latter had not, chief of which was the ever-present desire, not, we believe, the outcome of ambition alone, to treat with friendly consideration, with far more than the stinted measure of conventional justice, those of a subject or of a veiledly hostile race. The measure of Rhodes' greatness will never be correctly taken if we overlook his ascendancy over the despised black man or the respect in which he was held by great numbers of the non-British colonials. Colonel Kekewich is of a very different stamp. He does not appear to be greatly endowed with the gift of inspiring enthusiasm, although his other military qualities are of a very high order. Referring to Rhodes in a report regarding the defence, Colonel Kekewich said: "Took a special interest in the raising of the Kimberley Light Horse, and worked most zealously in providing horses for all the mounted troops in Kimberley. To him, therefore, is in a large measure due the credit for the rapidity with which the mobility of my mounted corps was obtained." And it is due to Colonel Kekewich to say that he has been just enough to deny the allegation that he had ever said or hinted that Rhodes threatened to bring about surrender if relief did not come quickly. Lord Roberts had apparently gathered that this threat had been uttered. It is possible that Colonel Kekewich carried to excess some of the theories held as gospel truths by many regular officers. One would gather this from what he told the War Commission. In face of the splendid work which he himself saw done by the commanders of the Imperial Light Horse, Kimberley and other Colonial mounted troops, and what he knew to have been done by men like Brabant, Dalgety, Colenbrander, Woolls-Sampson, Spreckley, Peakman, and others, he said in his written memorandum: "I think that to get the best value out of all irregular corps it is very important that regular officers should command, and that the staff and at least one non-commissioned officer per squadron should be regulars."

As Sir Edward Brabant has pointed out, it is perhaps unfortunate that there was no South African or Australian Colonial on the Commission, who could by a little cross-questioning have brought out points which, in justice to the Colonials, the Commissioners should have had before them.

After the relief of the town the Kimberley and Diamond Fields mounted troops were amalgamated under the title "Kimberley Mounted Corps." According to the despatch of 21st May 1900, para. 24 and *note*, the K.M.C. were at this time 600 strong.

The corps, under Lieut.-Colonel Peakman, who had commanded the mounted troops since Major Scott Turner's death, operated with Lord Methuen in the Boshof district. On 5th April Lord Methuen was successful in surrounding a detachment under Villebois de Marueil. The kopje on which the enemy had taken up a position was, after shell and rifle fire, assaulted with the bayonet. The enemy lost 7 killed, 11 wounded, and 51 unwounded prisoners. In his report of 6th April Lord Methuen spoke in terms of praise of the way the troops worked, and mentioned Lieut.-Colonel Peakman.

The corps continued with Lord Methuen chiefly about Boshof during April, and frequently had skirmishing. At the end of that month they moved west to join Colonel Mahon's column, which was to start from Barkly West on 4th May for the relief of Mafeking. The work of Mahon's column has already been touched on under the Imperial Light Horse. In Major Pollock's account of the relief, he said: "Finally, just to give one more instance of the fine spirit that animated this gallant little force, it should be mentioned that Lieutenant Watson of the Kimberley Mounted Corps, who was on sick leave at Cape Town, heard of the march to Mafeking, hurried back to the front, and having ridden absolutely alone all the way from Barkly West, joined the column on Sunday, just in time for the fight (near Kraaipan), having covered 220 miles in five days. With such officers and men a commander may safely face pretty long odds." In that fight Captain Maxwell of the K.M.C. and 4 men were wounded.

On the 16th May was fought the stiff engagement outside Mafeking. The Boers attacked Mahon's flanks and rear. Speaking of the latter attack, Major Pollock said : " But the brigadier had complete confidence in Lieut.-Colonel Peakman, who had command of the rearguard, and right well did this gallant officer fulfil the trust committed to him. A considerable number of mounted Boers galloping down by the village of Saani gained the bed of the Molopo river, and from there sought to assail the rear-guard, but so accurate was the fire of the party of Kimberley Mounted Corps that the enemy was not only checked, but was also unable to retire" until after nightfall. Lieut.-Colonel Peakman was praised by Major Pollock for the cleverness with which he chose the ground, " yet the trial, in spite of the excellent cover, was no light one," the Boer shells pitching all over Peakman's position. Captain C. P. Fisher and several men of the corps were wounded.

Mahon's column marched from Mafeking to Potchefstroom, and there most of the K.M.C. left the column, which continued its march to Krugersdorp. A portion of the K.M.C. operated for a time with Baden-Powell in the Mafeking-Zeerust district (see Lord Roberts' despatch of 14th August 1900, para. 33).

In his brief despatch regarding the relief of Mafeking, dated 23rd May 1900, Colonel Mahon mentioned that on 5th May, the day after leaving Barkly West, he detached Captain Rickman with one squadron of the K.M.C. to join Sir Archibald Hunter, who was then driving the enemy from the border near Warrenton, and whose force marched into the Transvaal and was joined by Mahon at Lichtenburg on 6th June.

In July and onwards part of the K.M.C. were employed in the Krugersdorp-Potchefstroom district. On the occasion of a train being derailed near Bank Station about 20 non-commissioned officers and men were captured, and about the same time one man was killed and Lieutenants Drew and Watson and some men were wounded. On 25th July Klerksdorp, where a squadron was stationed, seems to have been surrendered by Captain Lambart without any serious defence being made (see 'The Times' History, vol. iv. p. 362). On 7th August and for some days thereafter a portion of the corps was in contact with De Wet's forces when these broke across the Vaal. At this time a portion of the corps was employed about the Kimberley - Mafeking line, and a squadron was with Lord Erroll in the Western Transvaal in August and September.

In October, November, and December 1900 the Diamond Fields Horse was in the column of Major-General Settle which assisted to clear the western portion of the Orange River Colony (see Cape Police). On 28th November the D.F.H. were in a sharp skirmish near Luckhoff.

When it was seen that Hertzog and other leaders were penetrating to the south-west of Cape Colony the corps was put into Colonel Bethune's column, which, in January and February 1901, assisted to drive these commandos out of Cape Colony. In March, April, and May the D.F.H. were in central Cape Colony, where they were frequently in action under Major Berrangé and other commanders. On 1st May

Lieutenant Matthews was severely wounded near Cradock.

From May 1900 to May 1901 a section of the Diamond Fields Artillery was in the garrison of Boshof which successfully held that town and repelled many attacks. The main portion of the garrison was the 4th Scottish Rifles (Militia), and a good account of their work is to be found in Colonel Courtenay's record of that battalion.

Captain Robertson of the Kimberley Light Horse was appointed Assistant Resident Magistrate at Koffyfontein, a small mining town in the south-west of the Orange River Colony. In the beginning of October 1900 there was a recrudescence of Boer activity in the district. Robertson found himself the only military man in the town, but he armed some fifty miners. On 12th October Commandant Viser demanded the surrender of the place, which was refused. On the 16th Robertson withdrew from the town and occupied a position at the mines which he entrenched. On the 21st the enemy attacked but did not press home. On the 23rd Robertson raided a farm-house occupied by the enemy, and a fierce hand-to-hand struggle took place. One man on each side was killed and two Boers were captured. On the 25th Hertzog demanded surrender and next day attacked fiercely, but the enemy was driven off. On 3rd November the gallant garrison was relieved by Sir C. Parsons. Lord Roberts complimented Captain Robertson and his men.

Among the numerous columns at work during the second phase of the war was one known as the Kimberley Column, which for some months was composed as follows: 74th Squadron Imperial Yeomanry, 125; Kimberley Light Horse, 94; Dennison's Scouts, 81;

The Kimberley Troops

Royal Welsh Fusiliers, 20; Volunteer Company of the Northumberland Fusiliers, 102; 3rd Leinsters, 100; 2nd Royal Scots Fusiliers, 38; 2 guns of the 38th Battery R.F.A.; and 13 men of the Diamond Fields Artillery with a maxim. During 1901 this column under Major Paris long operated in the west of the Orange River Colony, and was also at work in the south-west of the Transvaal. On 2nd August 1901 Captain G. C. Cory Smith, of the K.L.H., was wounded at Zwartputs, and there were several other casualties on this occasion.

In 1902 the Diamond Fields Horse and Artillery still kept the field and were in many engagements. Major Paris's column was part of Lord Methuen's force in his disastrous engagement of 7th March 1902 (see Cape Police). In his report Lord Methuen said that the column before being reinforced at Vryburg consisted of the 86th Imperial Yeomanry, 110 men; Diamond Fields Horse, 92; Dennison's Scouts, 58; Ashburner's Light Horse, 126; 2 guns 38th Battery; 1 pom-pom of the Diamond Fields Artillery. In the fighting on the 7th the Kimberley troops suffered very severely, the Diamond Fields Horse having about 20 casualties and the Artillery detachment had several killed and wounded.

In May some of the Kimberley troops were operating in the Douglas district, west of the railway. On the 21st Lieutenant R. J. Stone and one man of the Light Horse were wounded.

The Mentions gained by the Kimberley troops were as follows:—

COLONIAL ORDNANCE DEPARTMENT.

Capt. C. L. Ricketts,[1] proved himself most valuable officer.

---

[1] Awarded D.S.O.

DIAMOND FIELDS ARTILLERY.

COLONEL KEKEWICH'S REPORT: 15th February 1900.—Capt. (local Major) May, invariably handled his guns with much coolness under fire, is a most deserving and efficient officer. Surgeon-Lieut. A. J. Ortlepp, attached, rendered considerable assistance to wounded in the field.

LORD ROBERTS' DESPATCH: 2nd April 1901.—Major T. J. May, who afterwards got the C.M.G., Surgeon-Lieut. Ortlepp, Gunner F. D. Payne.

LORD KITCHENER'S DESPATCHES: 8th October 1901.—Lieut. A. Kidd, for excellent work in difficult situation near Griquatown, 24th August. 23rd June 1902.—Capt. C. C. Sheckleton.

DIAMOND FIELDS HORSE.

COLONEL KEKEWICH'S REPORT.—Major T. H. Rodger, is a resourceful and excellent officer, always ready and cool under fire; Sgt. A. B. Nicholetts, on several occasions undertook duties which involved great personal risk; he carried despatches to our troops engaged on 28th November.

LORD ROBERTS' DESPATCH: 2nd April.—Major Rodger,[1] and Sgt. Nicholetts.

LORD KITCHENER'S DESPATCH: 8th October 1901.—Tpr. J. Evans,[2] on 12th February a cattle guard of four men being surprised by enemy kept them off single-handed, sent off remaining man and saved whole herd and killed two Boers.

KIMBERLEY REGIMENT.

COLONEL KEKEWICH'S REPORT.—Lieut.-Col. R. A. Finlayson, commanded his regiment and a section of defence with marked success; Major A. O. Black, commanded a section of defence and rendered good service; Capt. and Adj. E. T. Humphrys, performed his duties with great zeal and tact. Surgeon-Major J. A. J. Smith,[1] attached, rendered most valuable assistance to wounded in the field. Sgt. S. H. MacCullum, is deserving of mention for good work.

LORD ROBERTS' DESPATCHES: 2nd April 1901.—Lieut.-Col. Finlayson, awarded C.M.G.; Sgt. MacCullum.[2]

4th September 1901.—Capt. Humphrys.

LORD KITCHENER'S DESPATCH: 8th July 1901.—Lce.-Cpl. G. R. Mason, in action at Koffyfontein, on 3rd June, a man being wounded in an exposed position Mason went to his help and remained with him under fire until an ambulance fetched him.

LORD KITCHENER'S FINAL DESPATCH.—Major A. O. Black, Capt. Sheckleton, Sgt.-Instructor D. K. Macfarlane.

KIMBERLEY LIGHT HORSE AND MOUNTED CORPS.

COLONEL KEKEWICH'S REPORT.—Major (local Lieut.-Col.) T. C. Peakman was associated in early days of siege with organisation of Town Guard; his experience and local knowledge were of great assistance to me; subse-

---

[1] Awarded D.S.O.   [2] Awarded D.C.M.

quently he commanded a squadron of Light Horse, and on death of Lieut.-Col. Turner was selected by me for command of all mounted corps ; he has shown much courage under fire, and is a most deserving and excellent officer ; wounded November 18th. Major R. G. Scott, V.C., is an officer of tried experience and gallantry, has on all occasions exhibited the best qualities of an officer. Capt. H. T. Ap-Bowen, commanded a squadron with much success, and has on several occasions shown great gallantry in action ; very severely wounded, November 25th. Capt. H. Mahoney, performed distinguished service ; wounded November 25th. Capt. J. A. Smith, as Quartermaster, performed much hard work in connection with equipping irregular forces under great difficulties. Capt. J. W. Robertson, performed the duties of Paymaster and also acted as galloper to Lieut.-Col. Turner in a most efficient manner. Capt. W. E. Rickman, handled his men with great coolness ; his conduct on many occasions has been most distinguished. Capt. G. E. Heberden,[1] medical officer, frequently accompanied mounted troops in sorties and reconnaissances, and rendered most valuable service in attending to wounded. Lieut. C. A. Hawker, performed excellent service ; wounded November 22nd. Lieut. W. Newdigate, did much good work with his squadron ; has also executed valuable survey work in connection with defence. Lieut. D. B. Fenn, proved himself an invaluable officer ; he supplied much valuable information before the outbreak of the war, and has done real good work with the mounted troops from the first day Imperial troops arrived in Kimberley. Lieut. G. Harris, Kimberley Light Horse, good service and conspicuous gallantry. Lieut. R. Chatfield, an excellent officer, has shown conspicuous gallantry. Sgt.-Major W. H. Oatley, Cpl. H. Harris, Tpr. A. H. Armstrong, are deserving of mention for good work.

LORD ROBERTS' DESPATCHES : *2nd April* 1901.—Majors Peakman, who got the C.M.G., R. G. Scott, V.C.,[1] Capt. W. E. Rickman,[1] Sgt.-Major Oatley,[2] Cpl. H. Harris, Tpr. A. H. Armstrong.

4th September 1901.—Capt. Ap-Bowen.[1]

1st March 1902.—Capt. F. J. Frost, Troop Sgt.-Major C. J. Greetham (Lieut. Johannesburg Mounted Rifles).

LORD KITCHENER'S DESPATCH : *23rd June* 1902.—Capt. H. P. Browne, Tpr. J. T. Halkett.

KIMBERLEY AND BEACONSFIELD TOWN GUARDS.

Major J. R. Fraser, late Loyal North Lancashire Regiment, retired, at first as Staff-officer and later as C.O., did excellent work, and has shown great energy and resource. Capt. C. A. Blackbeard did much good work in connection with interior economy of the Guard and keeping order in Beaconsfield. Capt. W. Nelson, valuable services in collection of information and procuring enemy's cattle for food of garrison. Lieut.-Col. D. Harris, V.D., arrived when Town Guard was being raised, threw himself most heartily into work, and was of greatest assistance ; much praise is due to

---

[1] Awarded D.S.O.   [2] Awarded D.C.M.

him for his good work in looking after comforts and interests of Town Guard in works and redoubts, which entailed much hard work and fatigue. Capt. S. Richards, good work as Staff-officer. Capt. B. E. A. O'Meara performed duties of garrison-adjutant and quartermaster with much zeal and energy; rendered valuable services. Capt. T. Tyson performed duties of assistant military censor to my complete satisfaction. Capt. W. Pickering, rendering much valuable assistance from date of my arrival, and during a portion of siege commanded a section of defence with success. Capt. T. L. Angel did good work in command of Cyclist Corps. Lieut. E. F. Paynham, assistant to the Intelligence Officer, rendered very great assistance in dealing with correspondence of a confidential nature. The following officers also did good work:—Capts. F. Mandy, J. R. Grimmer, W. S. Elkin, H. Pim, J. Adams, C. E. Hertog, J. Morton, C. Tabuteau, E. H. Moseley, G. White, W. H. Faulkner, A. Blum, H. Rugg, J. Armstrong; Lieuts. C. D. Lucas, H. Tabuteau, J. J. Coghlan, T. Callen, W. G. Wright, J. A. Carr, J. Brander-Dunbar, S. O'. Molony. Sgt.-Major J. P. Russell, late R.E., as warrant officer, did much valuable work in connection with superintendence of native labour employed on construction of defence works. Sgt. J. Russell, Cyclist Corps, is deserving of mention for good work.

LORD ROBERTS' DESPATCHES: *2nd April* 1901.—Lieut.-Col. D. Harris, V.D., who got the C.M.G., Capts. T. L. Angel,[1] F. Mandy, B. E. A. O'Meara,[1] W. Pickering,[1] S. Richards[1]; Lieuts. C. D. Lucas,[1] E. F. Paynham,[1] Sgt.-Major J. P. Russell,[2] Sgt. J. Russell.

4th September 1901.—Major J. R. Fraser, Capt. W. Nelson, Capt. L. R. Grimmer, Lieut. J. Brander-Dunbar (Captain, 3rd Cameron Highlanders).

WINDSORTON TOWN GUARD.

Lieut. W. A. Williams.

THE RHODESIAN REGIMENT AND RHODESIAN VOLUNTEERS.

IN July 1899 Colonel Baden-Powell was sent out to Rhodesia to raise two regiments, in order to protect the borders of that country and of the Bechuanaland Protectorate in the event of war. Recruiting began on

[1] Awarded D.S.O.   [2] Awarded D.C.M.

10th August, and the two regiments, namely, the Rhodesian, under Colonel Plumer, and the Protectorate, Colonel Hore, were raised, trained, and equipped before war broke out. Colonel Baden-Powell had about twenty regular officers to assist him in his task. In September Baden-Powell took down to Mafeking the Bechuanaland Regiment. He left Colonel Plumer with the Rhodesian Regiment, and some of the British South Africa Police, &c., to watch the northern and north-western borders of the Transvaal, and if possible to keep the railway from Bulawayo to Mafeking open. Colonel Plumer and his regiment went to Tuli, where about 100 British South Africa Police were already posted. Between 11th October and 25th November the Tuli force was very frequently engaged, a Boer force of about 1700 being opposed to them. On 22nd October there was sharp fighting at the drifts on the Crocodile River, in which Captain Blackburn was mortally wounded, Sergeant-Major Young and 3 men were killed, and several were wounded. About the middle of December it was ascertained that the Boer force had retired towards the south, and Colonel Plumer then moved west towards the railway, which had been broken by the enemy. Colonel Nicholson, of the British South Africa Police, with 350 men of the Police and Rhodesian Volunteers, had taken up positions on the railway, the most southern being Palapye, about 200 miles from Mafeking. On 14th January 1900 Colonel Plumer got to Gaberones, 100 miles farther down the line. Ten miles south of that place the Boers held a strong position, and Plumer's men did a lot of fighting before the enemy cleared out of their position on 25th February 1900. On 12th February Captain French and 6 men were killed, and Major Straker and Lieutenant-Colonel H. F. White and about 20 men were wounded. On 6th March Lobatsi, 60 miles from Mafeking, was reached by Plumer. On 15th March the Boers attacked Plumer's force. Lieutenant Tyler was killed and several men were wounded. Lieutenant Chapman, whose horse fell close to the enemy, was captured. After more fighting Sefetili, 30 miles northwest of Mafeking, was reached, and a message sent into Baden-Powell was duly replied to. Colonel Plumer and his little force had done, and continued to do, all that men could do to keep the enemy off the town. On 26th March they made an incursion into the Transvaal to within twelve miles of Zeerust, and on the 31st they reconnoitred to within six miles of Mafeking. On this date the enemy was found in strength, and the British mounted troops lost heavily. Colonel Plumer was wounded on the arm. The Rhodesian Regiment had Captain F. Crewe and Lieutenant Milligan and 6 men killed, and Major Weston Jarvis, Captain Maclaren, and Captain Holt, and 30 men wounded. Lieutenant F. Smitheman, who had distinguished himself as a scout in Matabeleland, penetrated the lines of the investing force, got into Mafeking on 4th April, and rejoined Plumer on the 8th. "By his influence he induced"[1] many natives to break out, and between his visit and the relief 1200 natives came out, and so saved the garrison's food-supplies. On 1st May 100 men of the British South Africa Police from Mashonaland joined Plumer. On the 12th he received a message that Colonel Mahon would be on the Molopo on 15th May, and on the 14th he was joined by a most welcome reinforcement of over 100 Queensland Mounted Infantry, dismounted, and a Canadian battery

[1] Colonel Plumer's evidence before War Commission.

of 4 guns. On the same day Plumer, with about 800 men and 8 guns, set out, and succeeded in joining hands with Mahon on the Molopo on the 15th. On the 16th was fought the engagement already touched upon under the Imperial Light Horse, and Mafeking was entered on the 17th before dawn.[1] Lieutenants Harland and Lloyd and several men of the regiment were killed, and Major Bird and Lieutenant A. J. Forbes and 20 men were wounded in the fighting outside Mafeking. Out of thirteen Imperial officers serving with the regiment four had been killed, five wounded, and one captured, up to 18th May; while one volunteer officer had been killed and two wounded.

On the 17th the Boers were driven from the confines of the town, and on the 20th Plumer occupied Zeerust, and afterwards Ottoshoop and Polfontein.[2] Baden-Powell and Plumer now moved farther east, and Rustenburg was occupied on 10th June.

After the relief of Mafeking the Rhodesian Regiment was much split up: the greater portion accompanied General Plumer to the Rustenburg district, but detachments were left at different posts. In Lord Roberts' telegram of 8th August 1900 he said that he feared that Colonel Hore's force at Eland's River (between Rustenburg and Zeerust) had been captured. He also said that the garrison consisted of about 140 Australian Bushmen, 80 of the Rhodesian Regiment, and 80 Rhodesian Volunteers. Mr Green, in his 'Story of the Australian Bushmen,' Sydney, 1903, gives what appears to be the best account yet published of the Eland's River defence. He arrived there on 16th

---

[1] These dates, &c., are taken from Colonel Plumer's evidence before the War Commission.

[2] Lord Roberts' despatch of 14th August 1900.

July. Even then the Boers were in strong force in the neighbourhood, and Colonel Hore kept his men busy on entrenchments, but the garrison could scarcely be got to believe that this was necessary work. On the 19th Major Tunbridge and a squadron of the 3rd Queensland Mounted Infantry brought in a convoy. The intention was that he should go on with it to Rustenburg, but Hore deemed this inadvisable. Patrols were kept moving out, and there was often fighting, as on the 21st and 23rd. On the 22nd there was a severe engagement at Koster's River, between Eland's River and Rustenburg (see 1st New South Wales Bushmen). On 3rd August Hore learned that there was a concentration of Boers, over 2000, in his immediate neighbourhood. On the 4th the enemy commenced the attack by opening a heavy fire on parties who were taking the horses to water. Mr Green states that the garrison was now as follows :—

Queensland Mounted Infantry, Major Tunbridge	140
New South Wales Bushmen, Captain Thomas	100
Rhodesian Regiment and Volunteers, Protectorate Regiment, Captain Butters and Lieutenant Myburg	150
Victorian Bushmen, Captain Ham (3rd Contingent)	50
A few British South Africa Police were also present. Total about 500.	

The garrison possessed one 7-pounder gun and two maxims; the enemy had nine modern guns.

On the 4th no less than 1500 shells fell within the perimeter of the defence, and the casualties were 32, of whom 5 were killed. On the night of the 4th and every night afterwards the men worked hard at the trenches, deepening those already made, and providing head cover from waggons which had been smashed.

No part of the camp was secure from shell-fire, and the hospital was several times struck. On the 5th Carrington's force approached so near that they could be plainly seen, but his effort to break through seems to have been almost contemptible, and Mr Green states that he actually retreated seventeen miles that night, to the amazement of his own officers and men. On the 6th an attempted relief was commenced by Baden-Powell: he got within twenty miles but turned, because he had heard the garrison had surrendered. According to Mr Green's account, and his version is well supported, there was bungling all round, and Lord Roberts was anything but satisfied with his lieutenants. After the 6th shell and rifle fire continued, but were not so heavy as on the 4th. Some incidents of how snipers stalked snipers were almost amusing. One Boer, who had done much firing but could not for some time be located, was at last found in a tree and duly brought to the ground. About the 8th Delarey sent in what was a very gentlemanly letter, asking surrender: he said he had driven back Carrington, which was true. Hore declined to surrender, and asked his opponent to keep his shells off the hospital, a request which was attended to. Fighting continued till the 15th. On that morning there was no reply to the defender's fire. A force could that day be seen in the distance, but could not be identified as friend or enemy. On the 16th, at 3 A.M., some West Australians, the advance scouts of Lord Kitchener's Division, rode in. Lord Kitchener came in at 7 A.M. He remarked: "You have had a hot time, but have made a wonderful defence." The severity of the fire may be guessed from the fact that out of 1540 animals in camp, 1379 were lost. Owing to the good trenches, the casualties among the troops were slight in comparison. About 10 men were killed and 43 wounded, of whom 8 died. The Rhodesian Regiment lost 4 killed and 2 wounded, the Volunteers 2 killed and 2 wounded, and the British South Africa Police 2 killed and 2 wounded. Lord Roberts said: "The gallant defence of this post was most creditable to Colonel Hore and the troops under his command." Lieutenant Sandilands, of the Cameron Highlanders, who was with his own mounted infantry in the relieving force, wrote in the 'War Record of the 79th': "To my mind the defence of the garrison at Eland's River was quite one of the finest things in the whole war," and he goes on to give some details, and says every one will agree that it was a defence of which the Colonies "may well be proud."

After the relief Lord Kitchener split up his force, sending part of it on to Mafeking with Lord Methuen, who took the garrison with him.

In regard to the attempts at relief, Major-General Carrington, who had landed at Beira to command the brigade of Australian Bushmen which disembarked there, had crossed Rhodesia and entered the Transvaal from the north-west border. General Carrington had been compelled to split up the Rhodesian Field Force, and to despatch portions of it across the north-west of the Transvaal to reinfore Generals Baden-Powell and Plumer. He had thus had to weaken the portion at his own disposal in August, but he was still in command of a fairly strong force—about 1000 men and a 15-pounder battery manned by New Zealanders,—and no one seemed to have any doubt that he would be able to push through to Rustenburg if necessary. He had left Zeerust on 3rd August to go to Eland's

Rhodesian Regiment and Rhodesian Volunteers 207

River, and it is said that on the way he received a message from Hore that the enemy were very threatening. But Carrington did not push through, as he was expected to do, at all costs. After an engagement which cannot be described as severe, and after reconnoitring to within a few miles of Hore's camp, he retired, not only to Zeerust, but actually to Mafeking.[1]

Perhaps General Carrington's information was that the enemy's strength in the district was overwhelming, and certainly two correspondents who were with him did wire that his force was too weak. But that does not seem to have been the opinion of Lord Roberts, who on 14th August, after he had learned of Carrington's retreat, wired: "Carrington has been ordered to proceed at once to Zeerust."

On 6th August Baden-Powell approached Eland's River from Rustenburg, "but," in the words of the despatch, "though firing was going on, its sound became more distant; and concluding that Lieutenant-Colonel Hore's force had either been captured by the enemy or relieved by Carrington, he retired to Rustenburg."[2] Want of supplies prevented another attempt being made from the Rustenburg direction.[2] Between 7th and 14th August Lord Kitchener, with several columns, was pursuing De Wet from the Vaal towards the Megaliesberg. On the 13th August a messenger reached Mafeking: he had been sent on the 10th by Hore with a request for assistance. Lord Roberts at once directed Lord Kitchener to press on to Hore's

---

[1] Press Association telegram, and Lord Roberts' despatch of 10th October, para. 26. The despatch does not even mention that Carrington was engaged.

[2] Lord Roberts' despatch of 10th October 1900, para. 26.

relief; and, as already stated, this was effected on 16th August.

The Eland's River garrison having, as already stated, marched to Mafeking with Lord Methuen, was, after some weeks' rest there, railed viâ De Aar and Bloemfontein to Pretoria, where it was inspected and congratulated by Lord Roberts on 1st October.

The bulk of the Rhodesian Regiment was, during July, August, and September, operating to the east of Rustenburg and to the north of Pretoria. In Lord Roberts' telegram of 22nd August, he said that Paget reported from Haman's Kraal that Baden-Powell was engaged with Commandant Grobler's rear-guard all the previous day. Grobler was driven back on the east of the Pienaar's River. During the fight, Baden-Powell's and the enemy's advance guards galloped into each other. The Rhodesians suffered severely, Lieutenant-Colonel Spreckley, commanding Rhodesian Volunteers, and 4 men being killed, and Lieutenant Irvine and 6 men wounded. In the despatch it was stated that, as a result of this fighting, 100 British prisoners were rescued and 25 Boers captured. Colonel Spreckley was a splendid type of the colonial officer, and had done grand work in the Matabele Wars.

Soon after this, about the end of September, the year for which the Rhodesian men were engaged expired, and they were disbanded.[1] Neither the regiment nor the Rhodesian Volunteers seem to have suffered any casualties in action after 22nd August 1900.

In his evidence, already quoted, General Plumer remarked: "In connection with engineer services I should like to record the excellent work done by the engineer troop of the South Rhodesian Volunteers who

[1] Evidence of Colonel Plumer before War Commission, p. 339.

came and repaired the railway. They were all railway employees, and it was owing to their work that the railway from Bulawayo, on which so much depended, was so rapidly repaired." They also manned the armoured trains.

The Mentions gained were as follows :—

LORD ROBERTS' FINAL DESPATCHES.—Col. Beale (B.S.A. Company); Col. Spreckley (killed); Major A. Weston Jarvis (got C.M.G.); Capts. G. Glyn,[1] F. Smithermann[1]; Lieut. A. Myburgh, Rhodesian Regiment; Capt. G. Hook[1]; Sgt.-Major J. Lough,[2] South Rhodesian Volunteers; Tprs. C. Bentley,[2] G. F. Burton or Parton,[2] Rhodesian Regiment; Tpr. C. Duner[2]; Sgt.-Major Webb,[2] South Rhodesian Volunteers; Lieut. Duly,[1] Rhodesian Volunteers, commanding cyclists.

LORD KITCHENER'S DESPATCH : 8*th May* 1901.—Capt. and Local Lieut.-Col. Grey's fine leading has much contributed to the success of the operations (March 1901); he at all times displays marked ability as a leader of men. At the time to which this entry refers, Lieut.-Col. Grey was commanding some New Zealand troops in the Western Transvaal; he had at one time been an officer in the Inniskilling Dragoons, and his old regiment were very proud of his success on 23rd March (see War Record of the Inniskillings).

THE BECHUANALAND PROTECTORATE REGIMENT.

THE raising of the Rhodesian Regiment and of the Bechuanaland Protectorate Regiment has already been touched upon under the first-named corps. When in September 1899 Colonel Baden-Powell determined to himself command the garrison of Mafeking, he took with him the Protectorate Regiment, which was then about a month old. According to his report on the siege, the garrison of the town was composed of the regiment under Colonel Hore, total strength 469;

[1] Awarded D.S.O.   [2] Awarded D.C.M.

British South Africa Police (Colonel Walford), 91; Cape Police (Inspectors Marsh and Browne), 103; Bechuanaland Rifles (Volunteers), 81; Town Guard, untrained, 296—total, 44 officers, 975 men. The total white population of the place was about 1000, and the natives usually resident numbered 6000; but before hostilities commenced, about 1000 more came in, and had to be fed. On the other hand, before the siege ended, about 1500 natives had been persuaded to break through with the view of economising food. Some natives were enrolled to assist in protecting their own stadt, as cattle-guards, &c., and they were largely employed on the construction of defensive works. The town was 1000 yards square, and its best features, from the defenders' point of view, were that it was not commanded by hills, that the trenches had a good field for fire, and the ground outside of these being for a long distance very flat, full advantage could be taken of the low trajectory of the Lee-Metford rifle. "The perimeter of the works at first was approximately seven miles; latterly it extended to a little over ten miles." It is difficult to understand how such a small force could hold such an immense area. The artillery of the garrison was commanded by Major Panzera of the B.S.A. Police, and was worked by men of that force and of the Cape Police. They had four 7-pounder muzzle-loading guns, one 1-pounder Hotchkiss, one 2-inch Nordenfeldt, seven ·303 maxims; and there were added during the siege an old ship's gun, found about the place, and a 16-pounder muzzle-loading howitzer, which was made in the railway workshop. The powder, shells, and fuses used by the garrison were also manufactured in that workshop. Opposed to this slender and poorly equipped garrison, the enemy had at first 8000 men, with ten guns, under Cronje. After he had become tired or disheartened, he went south towards Kimberley and Magersfontein, leaving Snyman with about 3500 men and six guns, one of which was a new 94-pounder Creusot. The latter gun fired 1497 rounds between 13th October 1899 and 17th May 1900.

The principal engagements during the siege, as mentioned in the report of 18th May 1900, were as follows:—

Action of 14th October, before the investment was complete, fought about six miles north of town. Patrols having found the enemy advancing along the railway, an armoured train with a Hotchkiss, a maxim, and 15 of the B.S.A. Police, were sent out. It became heavily engaged with Boers who had 2 guns. Captain FitzClarence, with a squadron of the Protectorate Regiment, attacked, the train being on his left. Another troop under Lord C. Bentinck, with a 7-pounder, reinforced, and after four hours' fighting the enemy was driven off. The armoured train put one of the Boer guns out of action before it had fired a shot, and drove the other gun from the field. When Captain Fitz-Clarence withdrew the enemy made no attempt to follow him. The Boers lost 53 killed, including 4 field-cornets, and many wounded. The British loss was 3 men killed, 2 officers (Lieutenant Lord C. C. Bentinck, 9th Lancers, attached, and Lieutenant Brady) and 13 men wounded, all of Protectorate Regiment, and 1 cyclist taken prisoner. Colonel Baden-Powell said: "In this, their first engagement, the Protectorate Regiment showed a spirit and dash worthy of highly trained troops, and were most ably led by Captain FitzClarence and Lord C. Bentinck.

This smartly fought little engagement had a great and lasting moral effect on the enemy."

Enemy's attack on the stadt, 25th October 1899. The Boers commenced shelling from east and south with seven guns at 6.30 A.M., and continued till noon. At noon about 3000 advanced to attack, firing heavily from long range inwards. The garrison reserved their fire till the attackers were close, then opened with maxims and rifles. This, and a flanking fire from natives in the stadt, was enough, and the attempted assault spluttered out. The Boer loss was not known, but their ambulances were seen picking up a number of casualties. There was only one of the garrison wounded.

Night attack on Boer trenches, 27th October 1899. The attacking force was Captain FitzClarence's squadron, supported by a party of Cape Police. At 9.30 P.M. the attackers moved out in silence. "The night was dark but still. The squadron attained its position on the left rear of the enemy's trench without being challenged or fired at. Captain FitzClarence then wheeled up his men, and, with a cheer, charged into the main and subsidiary trenches and cleared both with the bayonet. The enemy's rearward trenches opened a heavy fire, to which the Cape Police replied from a flank in order to draw the fire on to themselves, and so allow Captain FitzClarence's squadron to return unmolested. The whole operations were carried out exactly in accordance with instructions, and were a complete success." Parties of the enemy in the darkness and confusion fired into one another. Their losses were stated at 100 killed and wounded. The British loss was 6 killed, 9 wounded, including Captain Fitz-Clarence and Lieutenant Swinburne, and 2 captured.

Action at Cannon Kopje, 31st October 1899. The enemy commenced the engagement with a heavy concentrated fire on the kopje, one of the enemy's guns taking the work in reverse. No reply could be made by artillery or maxims, which had to be stowed underground for protection. After half-an-hour's shelling the enemy advanced to the attack. Our people then manned their parapets and got the maxims up. A 7-pounder was "run out under cover of houses, near south corner of town." Under Lieutenant Murchison this gun opened fire on the enemy's flank, and their advance was stopped. The garrison lost Captain the Hon. Douglas Marsham, Captain Charles A. K. Pechell, and 6 non-commissioned officers and men killed, and 3 wounded The casualties among the rank and file fell chiefly on Colonel Walford's B.S.A. Police, by whom the work was defended. The defenders were congratulated by Colonel Baden-Powell. The enemy were said to have lost heavily. In a skirmish on the 3rd November Captain Goodyear was wounded.

Surprise attack on enemy's western laager, 7th November 1899. At 2.30 A.M. Major Godley paraded his force. Two 7-pounders, one Hotchkiss, one squadron Protectorate Regiment (dismounted), 60, under Captain Vernon, one troop, 30, Bechuanaland Rifles, Captain Cowan. Captain Vernon's squadron led the attack. At 4.15 A.M. the guns opened on laager at 1800 yards. The surprise was complete, and the enemy bolted in all directions, but were soon strongly reinforced, and Major Godley had to withdraw. This he did successfully under very heavy fire. The Hotchkiss upset and broke limber-hook, but Gunners Cowan and Gordon "very pluckily stood up and repaired damage" under heavy artillery and rifle fire. Major Godley and 4 men were wounded. Again the Boers lost heavily.

Action at Game Tree Hill, 26th December 1899. "Two squadrons Protectorate Regiment, supported by armoured train and Bechuanaland Rifles, were ordered to attack enemy's works from left flank under Major Godley, while three guns and a maxim prepared the way from the right front of the work. On pressing home the attack a heavy fire killed or wounded most of the officers and leading troops. These succeeded in gaining the parapet, but the work was found to have been strongly roofed in and so closed as to be impregnable." The British losses were this time very serious. Captain R. J. Vernon, Captain H. C. Sandford, Lieutenant H. P. Paton, and 21 non-commissioned officers and men were killed, Captain FitzClarence and 22 men wounded, and 3 missing. Colonel Baden-Powell said—"If blame for this reverse falls on any one it should fall on myself, as everybody concerned did their part of the work thoroughly well and exactly in accordance with the orders I had issued. Both officers and men worked with splendid courage and spirit."

During February 1900 there was fighting on various occasions, and on the 12th of that month Captain Girdwood was mortally wounded.

Boers' attack, 12th May 1900. The enemy evidently determined to make a final attempt to capture the town before the relief column could come up. At " 4 A.M. on the 12th they opened a very heavy long-range musketry fire on the town from the east, north-east, and south-east. . . . I therefore wired to the southwest outposts to be on the outlook." The Colonel's judgment was, as usual, correct. "At about 4.30 300 Boers made a rush through the western outposts and got into the stadt; this they then set fire to. I ordered the western defenders to close in so as to prevent any supports coming in after the leading body, and sent the reserve squadron there to assist. They succeeded in driving off an attack of about 500 without difficulty." The upshot was that those who got in got divided into three parties. "The first surrendered, the second was driven out with loss by three squadrons Protectorate Regiment under Major Godley, and the third, in the B.S.A. Police fort, after a vain attempt to break out in the evening, surrendered. We captured this day 108 prisoners, among whom was Commandant Eloff, Kruger's grandson. We also found 10 killed and 19 wounded Boers, and their ambulance picked up 30 men killed and wounded. Our losses were 4 killed, 10 wounded," including Captain Singleton and Lieutenant Bridges. "Our men, although weak with want of food and exercise, worked with splendid pluck and energy for the fourteen hours of fighting, and instances of gallantry in action were very numerous."

During the action between the relief column and the enemy on the 16th, part of the garrison demonstrated in the enemy's rear. On the morning of the 17th, after the head of the relief column was in, Colonel Walford was sent out against the laager on the east. Some Boers were killed, and they were prevented removing a gun, many waggons, camp equipment, &c. Thus to the very last the little garrison behaved with that splendid courage, energy, and fighting skill which they had exhibited from their first encounters onwards.

The Empire may hold together many decades without any body of her sons doing for her a finer piece of work than "the defence of Mafeking." It has become the custom to smile, if not to sneer, at the Mafeking celebrations. Seldom has the Empire had greater cause for joy, and not a cap too many was thrown in the air or a shout too many or too loud given. When we fail to rise to enthusiasm on such an occasion we shall have become unable to do the deeds that can arouse it.

The Protectorate Regiment saw some fighting in the Transvaal, but anything they did is pale in colour after "the defence." They were disbanded before the close of 1900.

The Regiment gained the following Honours and Mentions:—

Capt. FitzClarence (Royal Fusiliers), twice wounded, gained the V.C. for great courage and fearlessness on 14th and 27th October and 26th December 1899. On 27th October Capt. FitzClarence was the first man into the trenches, and accounted for four of the enemy with his sword. Sgt. H. R. Martineau gained the Cross on 26th December 1899. He picked up Cpl. Le Camp and took him back 150 yards under very heavy fire. In doing this he was wounded, but continued to assist his comrade, and received two additional wounds. Tpr. H. E. Ramsden, on 26th December 1899, also gained the Cross. He picked up his brother and carried him 700 yards under heavy fire.

COLONEL BADEN-POWELL'S DESPATCH.—Lieut.-Col. Hore, Staffordshire Regiment; Major Godley, Dublin Fusiliers; Capt. Marsh, Royal West Kent; Capt. Vernon, K.R.R.C.; Capt. FitzClarence, Lieut. C. Bentinck, 9th Lancers; Lieuts. Holden,[1] Greenfield, and Feltham.

LORD ROBERTS' DESPATCH.—Lieuts. G. Bridges,[1] J. A. P. Feltham,[1] Greenfield, Mossum or Moorsom, Waller; Sgt. J. W. S. Lowe,[2] Cpl. Metcalfe[2]; Tprs. Bryant, Calderwood, Johnson,[2] Parsons, Stevens[2]; Gunner Mulholland.[2] Sgt. Lowe and Gunner Mulholland actually belonged to the Mafeking Railway Volunteer Corps.

[1] Awarded D.S.O.   [2] Awarded D.C.M.

BECHUANALAND RIFLE VOLUNTEERS.

THIS corps was, at the beginning of the war, stationed about Mafeking. A company, 81 strong, under Captain Cowan, formed a valuable part of the garrison.

In the actions of 7th November and 26th December (see Bechuanaland Protectorate Regiment) the Rifles took a prominent part, and their work was several times highly praised by Colonel Baden-Powell. In his despatch Captain Cowan was mentioned. He had his corps in such a "condition of efficiency as enabled me to employ them in all respects as regular troops. He was at all times ready, and zealous in the performance of any duty assigned to him."

After the relief of Mafeking the corps was employed, not only in Bechuanaland, but also in Cape Colony and all over the Western Transvaal. In 1901 a squadron was in Lord Methuen's column, which did much good work in the south-west of the Transvaal (see despatches of 8th July 1901 and other dates). They took a prominent part in many engagements down to the close of the campaign, and frequently had a share of the casualties. At Zandfontein, 2nd-3rd September 1901, 1 man was killed and Lieutenant T. E. P. More and 1 man were wounded. On 4th October 4 men were killed near Zeerust, and on the 18th 2 men were killed at Rhenosterfontein. Captain Cooke was severely wounded on 2nd January 1902, and the corps had casualties at Trenafontein on the 21st. The corps gained distinction at Rhenosterfontein on 5th September 1901, and at Kleinfontein, near Zeerust, on 24th October 1901. In each of these engagements the enemy exhibited very great determination and boldness, and only with difficulty were they driven off. On the latter date they left over 40 dead on the ground.

In January, February, and March 1902 the Bechuanaland Rifle Volunteers were generally with or under Lord Methuen. A detachment was in the force which escorted the convoy captured near Klerksdorp on 25th February 1902. On this occasion the Rifles had 5 killed and about the same number wounded.

It will be remembered that the Western Transvaal had been dangerously denuded of troops while the great driving operations were in progress in the eastern part of that country and in the Orange River Colony, hence Lord Methuen was unable to cope with Delarey and other leaders, strengthened as they were by commandos driven from elsewhere. (See Cape Police.)

When the forces in the Western Transvaal had been strengthened, the Bechuanaland Rifles took part in the last great drives which, under the direction of General Ian Hamilton, finally broke Delarey's power. At Rooival on 11th April there was a well-fought engagement, when the Rifles had about 9 casualties. Thus, from the commencement of the war to its close, Major Cowan's little body did work of outstanding value, and all through the two years and nine months maintained the splendid degree of efficiency which they had shown when the siege of Mafeking commenced.

The Mentions gained by the corps were as follows :—

COLONEL BADEN-POWELL'S DESPATCH.—Capt. Cowan (see above); Sgt. Lionel Cook,[1] for clever and plucky scouting and gallantry in action.
LORD ROBERTS' DESPATCH.—Capt. Cowan and Sgt. Rowlands.[1]
LORD KITCHENER'S DESPATCHES : 8*th October* 1901.—Capt. Cowan[2];

---

[1] Awarded D.C.M.   [2] Awarded D.S.O.

Sgt.-Major Watts ; Sgt. Shipman ; Tpr. Austin (promoted Cpl.), gallantry at Rhenosterfontein, 5th September 1901 ; Lce.-Cpl. Sutherland (promoted Cpl.), in same action retained two prisoners under fire of 30 Boers.

8th November.—Sgt. Rowlands, for marked gallantry in collecting men and carrying messages under heavy fire, Col. Von Donop's action at Kleinfontein, 24th October 1901 (twice previously mentioned).

8th March 1902.—Lieut. Shipman, at Jackalsfontein, 8th February, attacked a laager with his troop and held them till reinforcements arrived.

23rd June 1902.—Major B. W. Cowan[1]; Lieuts. T. Christie, S. Hall ; Sgts. A. W. Shipman,[2] R. Galbraith, G. Gordon ; Cpls. B. Roy, and H. B. Wall.

BRITISH SOUTH AFRICA POLICE.

IN the earlier stages of the war this fine force did particularly valuable work. When war was declared their strength was 1106 of all ranks,—a most useful body of trained horsemen, good shots, and wily to the last degree. The bulk of the regiment was employed on the Rhodesian border and in the relief of Mafeking, while a detachment, 10 officers and 81 men, were in the town when the investment commenced, and formed an important part of the garrison. When Colonel Plumer with the Rhodesian Regiment reached Tuli, near the northern border of the Transvaal, on 11th October, 100 men of the B.S.A. Police were already there with 3 guns and 2 ·450 maxims; another detachment being on the railway north of Gaberones under Colonel Nicholson, the Commandant of the Police. Both these bodies took part in endless skirmishes and had to watch a very extended front. In the Boer attack on Plumer at Lobatsi, 14th March,

[1] Awarded D.S.O.   [2] Awarded D.C.M.

Captain Mowbray and 1 man of the Police were wounded. The work of Colonel Plumer's force generally is dealt with under the Rhodesian Regiment, and that of the Mafeking garrison under the Protectorate Regiment. In his evidence before the War Commission Colonel Plumer said that it was largely due to the initiative and energy of Colonel Nicholson that such an ample supply of stores had been accumulated in Rhodesia before the war broke out and the southern line was cut. He also referred to the work of the Police, and said their shooting was better than that of any other troops he had commanded.

Thanks to the daring of a native runner, Reuter was able to send off a telegram from Magalapye on 19th November which said: "Our third engagement of importance, which will rank perhaps among the most gallant and brilliant of the engagements of this war, was the defence of Cannon Kopje on Tuesday, 31st October, by the officers and men of the B.S.A. Police under Colonel Walford. Upon this isolated position the 96-pr. and 4 field-guns were brought to bear, and under cover of their fire the enemy made a most determined attempt to carry the fort by storm. The B.S.A. Police lost 2 officers, 2 N.C.O.'s, and 4 men killed, and about 6 wounded."

In Colonel Baden-Powell's despatch on the defence of Mafeking, dated 18th May 1900, he referred at length to the action at Cannon Kopje, mentioning the names of the killed and wounded. The officers killed were Captain the Hon. Douglas Henry Marsham and Captain C. A. Kerr Pechell. The casualties were not altogether among the Police; some of the Protectorate Regiment were killed and wounded. In his mention of Colonel Walford, B.S.A. Police, at the close of the report, Colonel Baden-Powell said : " Commanded the southern defences with his detachment of B.S.A. Police throughout the siege with conspicuous success. Always cool and quick to see what was wanted, his services were most valuable."

Regarding Major Panzera of the B.S.A. Police Colonel Baden-Powell said : " As commanding artillery, showed himself a smart and practical gunner, endowed with the greatest zeal, coupled with personal gallantry in action. The great success gained by our little guns, even when opposed to the modern armament of the enemy, was largely due to Panzera's handling of them."

When the Australian Bushmen landed at Beira, on Portuguese territory, in May and June 1900, they were met at the Rhodesian border by detachments of B.S.A. Police, some of whom, often mounted on tricycles, accompanied each body of Australians across Rhodesia.

In 1901 and 1902, down to the close of the war, the B.S.A. Police did good work on the Rhodesian border and in the western and northern districts of the Transvaal, and their services were of great value when some native chiefs took their followers into the field. The lesson which the Police gave put an end to all further thoughts of interference on the part of the coloured man. The corps had casualties on many occasions during 1901 and 1902, as at Trenafontein on 21st January 1902, when they had 2 killed and 5 wounded. A detachment were with the escort to a convoy which was captured near Klerksdorp on 25th February 1902. At that time another body under Colonel Walford was employed in keeping open the road to Kuruman, 100 miles west of the Vryburg railway. This detachment, or part of it, was with Lord Methuen when he was defeated by Delarey on 7th March. The B.S.A. Police had several casualties in that action. (See Cape Police.)

In addition to those already given the Mentions gained by the corps were :—

COL. BADEN-POWELL.—Capts. A. Williams and Scholfield ; Lieut. Daniells.

LORD ROBERTS' DESPATCHES.—Col. Walford [1] ; Lieut.-Cols. W. Bodle, got C.M.G., and H. White [1] ; Capts. F. L. Bowden,[1] Greener,[1] Hoël Llewellyn,[1] P. W. Williams,[1] W. Ashby [1] ; Surg.-Major Holmden [1] ; Sgts. G. O. Delegh, R. C. Murray ; Cpls. J. H. Houite, H. Gearey.[2]

LORD KITCHENER'S DESPATCHES : *8th May* 1901.—From Col. Manners Wood's despatch on native attack on patrol from Fort Darwin, Rhodesia, Lieut.-Col. Flint desires to bring to notice the gallant conduct of Capt. C. H. Gibson,[1] who commanded, and to whom every credit is due for the defeat inflicted on Mapendera's Impis. Sgt. T. Barclay,[2] during native rising near Fort Darwin, and force obliged to withdraw, was the last to retire, and by his coolness and good shooting kept the natives off. Capt. Gibson says he cannot speak too highly of him, both on this occasion and during rising in 1896.

23rd June 1902.—Major Everett ; Capts. S. W. J. Scholfield, Drury ; Sgt. C. L. St Hill ; Farrier-Sgt. Scholes. Sgt. French and Cpl. P. Darnley also got the D.C.M.

DENNISON'S SCOUTS.

THIS corps was raised at Vryburg by Captain, afterwards Major, G. C. Dennison, D.S.O., in September 1900.

The despatch of 8th July 1901 shows that prior to that date the corps, about 80 strong, was part of the column working from Kimberley, chiefly in the west of the Orange River Colony. In the first months of 1901 they saw a good deal of fighting

[1] Awarded D.S.O.   [2] Awarded D.C.M.

about Koffyfontein. In the despatch of 8th August 1901 Lord Kitchener said: "Major Paris, R.M.A., with the Kimberley column, left Warrenton on 19th July, and after an engagement with 150 of the enemy, who were gallantly driven from a strong position by Dennison's Scouts, effected a junction on the 24th with Colonel Henry near Aaronslaagte. Operating from Palmietpan on the 25th July with 230 mounted men, 2 guns, and a pom-pom and 30 infantry, carried in carts, Major Paris again found the enemy in some strength at Wolvepan under Commandants Badenhorst and Erasmus and Field-Cornet van Aswezan. He attacked on 3 sides, maintained a running fight, in which the 74th Squadron Imperial Yeomanry, the Kimberley Light Horse, and Dennison's Scouts seem to have been well handled, and finally forced the enemy to beat a very hasty retreat. Seven dead burghers were left upon the field" and Van Aswezan was captured, Major Paris's casualties being 1 man killed and 2 wounded. After this Major Paris returned to Warrenton and was employed in the South-West Transvaal and Griqualand. In January he was frequently engaged, and on the 5th he effected the capture of a convoy of 40 waggons and much stock.

Dennison's Scouts were still with Major Paris when he joined Lord Methuen in the beginning of March, and were in the column when it was defeated on 7th March (see Cape Police). Dennison Scouts, commanded at the time by Captain Brown, were part of the rear screen, and held on till ridden down. They suffered severely, losing 6 killed out of a strength of 58.

In his 'A Fight to a Finish,' Longmans, 1904, the commander of Dennison's Scouts describes what he saw of the campaign, including his experiences as a prisoner—he was captured at Kuruman (see Cape Police), —but the value of the book is greatly affected by the entire absence of dates.

The Mentions gained by the corps were :—

LORD KITCHENER'S DESPATCHES : 8th *March* 1901.—Capt. G. C. Dennison.[1] 23rd *June* 1902.—Sgt.-Major W. J. Hagan.

ASHBURNER'S LIGHT HORSE AND CULLINAN'S HORSE.

THESE corps were employed in the Warrenton-Vryburg-Kuruman district, and in the south-west of the Transvaal during the last sixteen months of the war, and both saw much hard work and a lot of fighting. Both corps suffered casualties on many occasions. They had the ill-fortune to be part of the column of Major Paris, and under Lord Methuen, when that General was defeated by Delarey on 7th March 1902 (see Cape Police and Kimberley troops). The approximate losses were—Ashburner's Horse, 12 killed and over that number wounded out of a strength of 126 ; Cullinan's Horse, 4 killed and 4 wounded out of a strength of 64. In Lord Kitchener's despatch of 23rd June 1902, the latter corps got two Mentions,—Lieutenant J. Macbeth, Sergeant A. J. Marshall.

[1] Awarded D.S.O.

THE COMMANDER-IN-CHIEF'S BODYGUARD.

About 15th January 1900 Lord Roberts announced the intention to form a bodyguard from picked Colonials, to be commanded by Major Laing, an officer who had served in the 91st and 93rd regiments (Argyll and Sutherland Highlanders), and had settled in South Africa. In the Matabele Rebellion he had again taken to soldiering, and had done work of a very high order.

In his telegraphic despatch as to his entry into Kroonstad on 12th May 1900, Lord Roberts said, "The procession entering the town was headed by my bodyguard, all of them Colonials."

In November 1900 Lord Roberts issued an order empowering Major Laing to raise a fighting regiment, 570 strong, with 2 guns, 2 pom-poms, and 2 machine-guns, to be called "The Bodyguard." So great was Laing's popularity that he almost at once got over 1000 recruits. The corps took the field in the Orange River Colony. Unfortunately, the first reference to them in a despatch was in connection with a grievous mishap which took place on 3rd January 1901. In his telegram of 6th January Lord Kitchener said: "From reports of some wounded who have arrived at Heilbron, it appears that a detachment of Bodyguard 120 strong, belonging to General Charles Knox's force, came in contact with a superior number of the enemy near Lindley. I regret to say that Lt.-Colonel Laing, 2 officers, and 15 men were killed, 2 officers and 20 men wounded. No details have been received from General Knox of this action." The other officers killed were

Lieutenants King and F. C. Vonschade. Captain A. Butters died of his wounds. Lieutenants F. H. Skyes, J. Simpson, S. Lewis, W. G. Perrin, and D. W. Robertson were wounded. The fighting was of the most severe character, and the casualties in the rank and file turned out even larger than the numbers stated by Lord Kitchener.

In February and March the corps were several times engaged in the Orange River Colony, Lieutenant L. H. Harding being mortally wounded.

In April, May, and June, the Bodyguard, 1000 strong, under Colonel Chesney, was in a column which operated in the Eastern Transvaal under Brigadier-General Bullock, and in July under Brigadier-General Spens. An account of the work of the column is given in Lieutenant Moeller's 'Two Years at the Front.' They had no very serious fighting while the Bodyguard was in the column, but towards the end of July they had skirmishes in which Captain O'Flaherty and 1 man were killed and several wounded. Not long after this the corps was disbanded, many of the officers and men joining other regiments.

THE RAILWAY PIONEER REGIMENT.

ABOUT 18th December 1899 recruiting for this corps was opened at Cape Town; and before Lord Roberts commenced his advance from Bloemfontein to Pretoria the first regiment was organised, its work being to assist in protecting the railways and to repair bridges, culverts, and lines when broken. Without outside assistance the corps of Royal Engineers could not have faced the enormous amount of work naturally falling to their department. From the Railway Pioneer Regiment they received very valuable help. On the other hand, the Railway Pioneers were leavened by officers and non-commissioned officers of the Royal Engineers, who are always so efficient that they can infect all those who serve with them with *esprit de corps* in a marvellously short space of time. Of such value was the work of the Railway Pioneer Regiment that before the close of the war a fourth battalion had been organised. The battalions were employed chiefly on the Cape-Pretoria railway, but they were also on the Krugersdorp line, and sometimes operated as a fighting force a considerable distance from railways. The regiment also did admirable service on the armoured trains which did so much to make railway traffic possible during the guerilla stages.

In his evidence before the War Commission, vol. i. p. 445, Lord Roberts said: "An enormous amount of reconstruction was carried out by the Railway Pioneer Regiment and the Railway Companies Royal Engineers. The Pioneer Regiment consisted almost entirely of civilian refugees, mostly mechanics from Johannesburg, and it rendered excellent service. To its aid and that of the Royal Engineer officers and men we were indebted for the fact that the railways very seldom lost touch with the fighting portion of the army, and that we were able to seize Johannesburg and Pretoria, distant about 1000 miles from our base upon the coast, and 260 miles from Bloemfontein, our advanced depot, with such rapidity that the enemy were unable to concentrate their resources and offer a strongly organised resistance."

When the 4th Derbyshire Regiment was attacked at Roodewal, Kroonstad district, on 7th June 1900, a detachment about 70 strong of the Railway Pioneer Regiment was present and in the fighting, which ended in the capture of the post. They lost Captain Gale and 4 men killed and about 16 wounded.

In the published despatches there is one from Major-General Charles E. Knox to Lieutenant-General Kelly-Kenny forwarding a report by Lieutenant-Colonel Capper, R.E., commanding Railway Pioneers at Virginia, Kroonstad district, Orange River Colony, as to an attack delivered by the commandos of Muller and Boerman at daybreak on 14th June 1900. The enemy was "said to be about 800 strong, with one or two pom-poms, a maxim, and, I think, one field-gun, but this is uncertain. We had to hold rather an extended position, our left being in trenches on very broken ground and in thick scrub which there was no time to clear. The enemy got into this scrub and gave some trouble by sniping. The garrison consisted of four companies 3rd Battalion Royal Lancasters under Colonel North, about 250 fit for duty, and four companies Railway Pioneer Regiment under Major Seymour, about 300 fit for duty, together with 25 men Royal Irish (Rifles) Mounted Infantry under Lieut. Davenport, 16 fit for duty. The attack was most pressed on our left, and was held most steadily by No. 3 company Railway Pioneer Regiment, under Lieut. Mitchell of that regiment : fighting was continued on all sides until about 11 A.M., when it quieted down, and the enemy had practically retired by the time a body of 170 Yeomanry, under Lt. Crane, arrived from the south at about noon. . . . The troops behaved very well and steadily. The Railway Pioneer Regiment in the advanced trenches, on the left especially, were most cool and collected, engaging the enemy at very close quarters. They were for part of the morning surrounded by the enemy in the scrub, but never lost their heads, and the enemy were ultimately driven out of the scrub by the advance through it of a line of reserve Railway Pioneer Regiment aided by half a company of militia." The losses of the regiment were Major Seymour and Lieutenant Clements and 5 non-commissioned officers and men killed; Lieutenant Mitchell and 2 non-commissioned officers and men wounded. Colonel Capper added that he could not "speak too highly of Lieut. Mitchell, a young officer who was wounded in both thighs about 6 A.M. in going from one trench to another to encourage the men, and remaining throughout the day in the most exposed trench, keeping his men, 22 in number, scattered in several small trenches, calm, ordering them not to waste ammunition, &c. I attribute to his example, and the very steady conduct of the men of his company in the advanced trenches, who suffered severely—one holding three men had one killed, and one holding five men had two killed,—the fact that our losses were so comparatively small. I especially deplore the loss of Major Seymour, whose loss will not only be felt by us as a regiment but by the whole of South Africa. He was killed while advancing with the extended line through the bush to clear out the snipers." Six dead Boers were found, four of them within 40 yards of Mitchell's trenches.

The regiment continued to do most excellent work, chiefly on the lines of communication between Bloemfontein and Pretoria, and their posts had constantly to be on the alert. In his telegram of 26th November 1900 Lord Roberts said: " Barton reports that Brakpan was attacked at 3 A.M. on the 24th, and was defended against a fierce attack by 7 of the Railway Pioneer Regiment and 10 mounted infantry. Our men behaved splendidly, and drove off the enemy, who left 3 dead. A Transvaal flag was captured."

On 27th March 1901 the 1st Battalion had 1 man killed and Captain Mitchell, mentioned above, severely wounded near Boksburg.

In a telegraphic despatch of 21st November 1901 Lord Kitchener stated that Commandant Buys had been captured, after attacking a patrol of about 100 of the Railway Pioneer Regiment on the Vaal near Villiersdorp; and in the telegram of 23rd November he stated: " Further report of Major Fisher's engagement near Villiersdorp, 20th November, shows that during the night of 19th patrols sent from his post at Rietfontein, slightly in advance of South African Constabulary, on Kalkspruit, to seize ridge overlooking Landsdrift, found enemy in possession. At dawn Major Fisher moved forward towards ridge, and was attacked both from north and south, but gradually took up a position giving good cover to his small force. At 9 A.M. his horses near south end of position stampeded, and in confusion enemy effected a lodgment. Major Fisher and Captain Langmore were both dangerously wounded, and the small parties taken in detail by the enemy, about 300 strong, were all forced to surrender by 10 A.M. Colonel Rimington's column came up about 11 A.M., but enemy, except small rearguard, had gone off, releasing prisoners. Rimington's

The Railway Pioneer Regiment

men captured Commandant Buys, who was wounded." The casualties of the Railway Pioneer Regiment were about 6 killed and 6 wounded. Captain A. B. Inglis was returned as severely wounded in addition to the officers named above. The regiment continued its good work, chiefly on the railways, down to the close of the war. Captain H. C. Thorold (Leicester Regiment, attached) was killed at Rietfontein on 18th February 1902.

The Mentions gained were as follows :—

LIEUT.-GENERAL KELLY-KENNY'S DESPATCH.—Lieut. Mitchell deserves special recognition. Previous to the attack on post, during the action, and since, Lieut.-Col. Capper has been untiring in his duties.

LORD ROBERTS' DESPATCHES ; *2nd April* 1901.—Majors G. H. Goodwin, awarded C.M.G., N. Wilson,[1] Capt. W. E. O. Mitchell,[1] Qrmr.-Sgt. W. Cartledge, Co. Sgt.-Major S. Beaton,[2] Sgt. (now Capt.) C. E. Marchant,[2] Cpls. T. M'Meekan,[2] G. M. Smythe,[2] Ptes. S. Stafford,[2] W. Ure.[2]

4th September 1901.—Cpls. W. J. Thomas,[2] R. Mackie, S. Richards, J. R. Shipley, J. W. Roach, Lce.-Cpl. C. Goulding, Ptes. J. Holmes, W. Doons, G. Kramert.[2]

LORD KITCHENER'S DESPATCHES : *8th March* 1901.—Lieut. Evans.

8th July 1901.—Sgt. J. A. Anderson with 3 men, on railway patrol, surprised 50 Boers at Doornkop, killed 2, wounded several, and took 5 horses. Sgt. Grainger, with 5 men, kept off a strong party of Boers all night. Sgt.-Major M. C. Jameson, surprised by enemy, behaved with great steadiness, and extricated his patrol ; mentioned in A.O. Cpl. J. R. Shipley, in command of 7 men, was heavily attacked by enemy, repulsed them, and, though severely wounded, remained in charge.

8th August 1901.—Capt. A. W. Stockett, 1st Bn., for continuous good work in command of armoured train, and before that of corps of cyclists, and especially at Baatman's Siding, when he was largely instrumental in capture of De Wet's convoy.

8th March 1902.—1st Bn.—Pte. Creak, promoted corporal ; distinguished conduct defence of post at Brakpan, 5th February 1902, when 5 men repulsed 49 Boers. 3rd Bn.—Lieut. W. D. Oswald,[1] for rescue of native scout, January 31, enemy being close to him and pursuing for some miles. Cpl. E. C. Baker, promoted Sgt., Ptes. Murphy, J. M'Arthy, J. M'Knight, on 30th January, formed a lying-out post between two blockhouses in Vereeniging attacked

---

[1] Awarded D.S.O.   [2] Awarded D.C.M.

by 50 Boers, 2 wounded, refused to surrender, and eventually drove enemy off. 4th Bn.—Pte. W. Lowes, at Schoeman's Drift, December 30, returned under close fire to rescue a wounded comrade. Army promotion: To be Hon. Capt., Qrmr. and Hon. Lieut. G. Taylor, R.E., Adjutant Railway Pioneer Regiment.

23rd *June* 1902.—Capts. W. Roe, A. E. Page, Lieut. J. C. Rouse, Regtl. Sgt.-Major Reid, R.E.; Regtl. Qrmr.-Sgt. D. R. Stuart,[1] Sgt. E. P. Simmons, H. A. Lawrence, Sgt. G. Salter, R.E.; Pte. H. A. Lawrence.

SCOTT'S RAILWAY GUARDS.

(CAPE COLONY IRREGULAR CORPS.)

THIS corps, strength about 500, under Lieut.-Colonel R. G. Scott, V.C., D.S.O., did work on the Orange River-Kimberley line not unlike what the Railway Pioneer Regiment did on the Central Railway. Although the Kimberley railway was not in the centre of the theatre of operations, still the west of the Orange River Colony, and that portion of Cape Colony bordering on it, was infested by roving bands bent on destruction; and Scott's Railway Guards had often skirmishes involving losses, and had much dangerous patrol work to undertake. On 15th June 1901 the corps engaged the enemy at Hartebeestfontein, in the Western Transvaal, and captured some prisoners, stock, and ammunition. On 20th August Lieutenant A. V. Harvey and 1 man were killed and several wounded at Devondale. At Lillifontein on 19th October they had again several casualties, and at the various posts where

[1] Awarded D.C.M.

the corps were stationed—Devondale, Brussels, Content, &c.—they often had a few losses.

The Mentions gained were as follows :—

LORD KITCHENER'S DESPATCH : 23rd *June* 1902.—Capts. R. Brand and M. W. M'Loughlin,[1] Qrmr.-Sgt. Worrall, Tpr. Van Der Merwe.[2]

PRINCE OF WALES'S LIGHT HORSE.

IN the despatch of 8th March 1901 Lord Kitchener dealt with the entry of De Wet into Cape Colony in the beginning of February, the pursuit by British columns, and his subsequent expulsion. Lord Kitchener mentioned that the 1st King's Dragoon Guards, newly arrived from England, the Prince of Wales's Light Horse, then recently raised at Cape Town, and "G" Battery R.H.A., had been put under Colonel Bethune, and had assembled at Naauwpoort. The Prince of Wales's Light Horse was engaged near Colesberg about 12th February. The 3rd Dragoon Guards afterwards joined the column.

When De Wet moved west from the Colesberg district, Bethune's force also crossed the De Aar line, and the pursuit was continued through Britstown, and afterwards in a northerly direction to the Hopetown district. In this pursuit all De Wet's waggons, his guns, and most of his ammunition were taken. The hard riding involved a terrible strain on the pursuing columns, horses falling daily by the score. The newly

[1] Awarded D.S.O.   [2] Awarded D.C.M.

raised and newly arrived troops naturally felt the strain very severely, but all stuck to their work well.

The despatch of 8th May mentioned that Colonel Bethune's brigade "left Orange River on 1st March, and two days later attacked and dispersed a body of about 1000 Boers at Open Baar. The brigade moved north-east, and reached the Modder River, near Abraham's Kraal, on the 8th. On this date the Boers attacked an empty convoy returning from Colonel Bethune's column to Bloemfontein. The escort held its own, and being reinforced by a detachment of the Prince of Wales's Light Horse, drove off the enemy."

Colonel Bethune's Brigade now moved to the northeast of the Orange River Colony, where, under the general direction of Major-General Elliot, they and numerous other columns took part in many operations (see despatches of 8th July and subsequent dates). During March and April the corps suffered casualties on several occasions. On 31st March Lieut. C. F. Berry was killed. The despatch of 8th July shows the Prince of Wales's Light Horse to have been 500 strong shortly before that date. The corps was afterwards taken to Cape Colony, where they had a good deal of skirmishing, and on 14th November suffered casualties near Brande Kraal and Vogelfontein, including Captain E. T. Chittinden wounded.

Captain F. B. Hughes was mentioned in the despatch of 8th December 1901 for dash and gallantry.

MIDLAND MOUNTED RIFLES.

(CAPE COLONY IRREGULAR CORPS.)

THIS regiment came into being in the second phase of the war for the purpose of assisting to expel the invaders from the Colony. In April and May 1901 they were often in action, and were said to have done very well on two occasions in the latter month, particularly at Zwagershoek. At Doornhoek, on the 13th, they had Lieutenant P. E. H. Coombs and several men wounded.

The first reference in despatches to the corps by name was unfortunately associated with a mishap. In the despatch of 8th July 1901, dealing with the operations against Kritzinger's, Lotter's, and other commandos, Lord Kitchener said: "On the 21st of June a party of 60 Midland Mounted Rifles—a local corps—was surrounded and captured by Kritzinger between Cradock and Graaf Reinet; 9 men were killed and 2 officers and 10 men wounded." According to the published casualty lists the number of killed and wounded was slightly larger. Captain H. J. Spandow died of his wounds; Lieutenant A. P. Robertson was severely wounded. It is satisfactory that the detachment made a very good fight, and that there was no surrender until the losses became out of all proportion to the end to be gained in holding out.

The Midland Mounted Rifles were to get their chance in due time. The despatch of 8th September 1901 deals with the capture of Lotter's commando by Colonel Scobell on 5th September (see Cape Mounted Rifles).

In the despatch Lord Kitchener said: "It must also be mentioned that three days previously Lotter's commando had been checked by a party of Midland Mounted Rifles, who killed seven and wounded six of their number, and prevented the Boers escaping by a pass which the patrol was then holding."

The corps continued to do much useful work in the central districts of Cape Colony.

The Mentions gained were—

LORD KITCHENER'S DESPATCHES: 8*th* October 1901. — Lce.-Cpl. R. M'Knight; Pte. H. E. Spiers, for good work in capturing 16 armed Boers, 24th September.

8*th December* 1901.—Lieut. F. B. Doe, gallant defence, September 2nd, which prevented Lotter breaking south.

This last occasion seemed to be worthy of a larger number of Mentions.

FRONTIER LIGHT HORSE.

(CAPE COLONY IRREGULAR CORPS.)

THIS corps, called at first District Mounted Rifles, 3 squadrons strong, were commanded by Lieutenant-Colonel E. O. Hutchinson. They operated in Cape Colony during the second phase of the war, and were in numerous little engagements and many pursuits, and frequently suffered casualties, as in the Maraisburg district in August and September 1901, at Wilgekloof in February 1902—Lieutenant F. Legard being wounded on the 1st of that month,—and about Somerset East and Jamestown districts in March and April.

The Mentions gained were—

LORD KITCHENER'S DESPATCH: 1st *June* 1902.—Lieuts. G. Brabant[1] and L. Francis, "on March 11th, at Libertas, Cape Colony, led a small body of men in rear of a position held by 250 of enemy, and getting close up unperceived killed Commandant Odendaal and two Boers, wounded two others, and forced enemy to retire with loss of 21 horses." Qrmr.-Sgt. J. Welch[2]; Sgts. G. Metcalfe and C. R. Roberts for gallantry on same occasion.

23rd *June* 1902.—Lieut.-Col. E. O. Hutchinson.

COLONIAL LIGHT HORSE.

(CAPE COLONY IRREGULAR CORPS.)

THIS regiment, about 4 squadrons strong, was organised in 1901, the command being given to Major A. B. Baker, D.S.O. The regiment saw a good deal of service in Cape Colony at a time when glory was very hard to harvest, but they did useful work in worrying and running down small commandos, and they seem to have kept out of serious mishaps. They were still engaged with scattered bodies of the enemy when peace was declared, and had sharp fighting thirty-six miles east of Fraserburg on 3rd June 1902, actually four days after the declaration. The commandos had apparently not taken the news seriously, if these had reached the neighbourhood. On this last occasion Squadron Sergeant-Major Carter and 3 men were killed, and Lieutenant F. L. Whalley and 1 man were wounded.

[1] Awarded D.S.O.   [2] Awarded D.C.M.

WARREN'S MOUNTED INFANTRY.

THIS corps, about 3 squadrons strong, was raised in December 1900, and was commanded by Lieutenant-Colonel F. J. Warren, who had already seen service in other Colonial regiments.

Warren's M.I. were in the western district of Cape Colony in April 1901, and the despatch of 8th July 1901 shows that in May and following months 2 squadrons were attached to the column commanded by Colonel Henniker, afterwards by Colonel Doran, the principal work of which was to pursue scattered commandos. Sometimes a few prisoners were taken, but the corps do not seem to have been in any satisfactory stand-up fight.

Captain Bates was wounded at Oorlogspruit on 8th June, Lieutenant J. T. Jansen and Sergeant Pearson were killed at Platt Drift on 15th June, and there were some other slight casualties at different times. The whole of the war service of the corps was in Cape Colony.

CAPE COLONY CYCLIST CORPS.

THIS corps was raised at the end of December 1900, and in the first week of January 1901, when the enemy were penetrating to within easy distance of Cape Town, they were sent to occupy Pickaneer's Kloof. They just managed to arrive in time. Although fiercely attacked on the 28th, and losing 4 killed and 23 wounded, including Captain Rose, they held on to the positions commanding the pass. This was a most promising beginning, and during the next seven months the corps did much excellent work. By the middle of February the corps was 500 strong, their commander being Major Owen Lewis. They were much split up, sections being attached to many columns, both in Cape Colony and the Orange River Colony. The fine work of those with De Lisle and Bethune, when they were in Western Cape Colony and afterwards in the north-east of the Orange River Colony, was several times spoken of. In a telegram from Calvinia, dated 8th February 1901, the Press Association correspondent who was accompanying Colonel De Lisle said: "Very valuable assistance was given to our force by a section of the Cape Town Cyclist Corps under Captain Rose last week. We were cut off from all telegraphic communication, and Colonel De Lisle relied on them exclusively for the purpose of despatch-riding, a duty which they performed admirably." And again on the 24th he said: "The comprehensive manner in which the country has been scouted by Colonel De Lisle is largely due to the mobility and enterprise of the Cyclist Corps, who have done excellent work as scouts and despatch-riders."

The corps had casualties at various times. In July 1901, near Beaufort Station, 1 man was killed and Lieutenant Brunton and 1 man were wounded.

Major Owen Lewis was mentioned in Lord Kitchener's despatch of 23rd June 1902, and got the D.S.O.

COLONIAL DEFENCE FORCE, AND OTHER LOCALLY RAISED TROOPS.

DURING the second phase—that is, after Lord Roberts had given over the command to Lord Kitchener, and while the enemy were reinvading Cape Colony and were making serious efforts to get at the lines of communication passing through the Colony—an immense number of small forces were formed, some to protect a district from invasion, others to guard towns and villages. Although these troops were most inadequately trained and had few officers of any experience, the most of them behaved well when the enemy appeared, and many did really excellent service. Within the limits of this volume it would be impossible, as it would be fruitless, to recount the numberless skirmishes in which one or other of those locally raised bodies took part; suffice it to say that they had at times to bear sharp casualties, as for example in March 1901, near Tarkastad, where the Colonial Defence Force had Captain John Rennie and 1 man killed and Lieutenants A. Troppell and A. W. Pringle and 8 men wounded. The New England Mounted Rifles suffered on many occasions during 1901 in their endeavour to keep their district clear; and on 23rd September, near Laurieston, 1 man was killed and Lieutenant J. Geddes and 4 men were wounded. On 21st November 1901 a body coming under the generic title, South African Irregular Forces, when clearing the enemy from the native districts about Tembuland, lost Captain Drummond Elliot killed, Captain H. P. Everett and Lieu-

Colonial Defence Force and other Local Troops

tenants A. Baxter and A. Burmister wounded. The Sutherland district troops were often engaged, and suffered casualties on many occasions. On 29th May 1902, almost the last day of the war, the Jansenville District Mounted Troops were fortunate enough to capture Malan, one of the enterprising commando leaders who for a long time caused no little concern to Cape Colony.

Some of the Mentions gained by the Defence Forces were as follows :—

LORD ROBERTS' DESPATCHES : *2nd April* 1901. — Tembuland Mounted Rifle Corps, Capt. G. F. Smith ; Transkei Territories, Sir H. E. Elliot, awarded C.B. ; Lieut.-Cols. J. G. Leary, W. E. Stamford, awarded C.B. ; Capts. O. M. Blakeway, E. J. Hargreaves, W. W. Smith ; East Griqualand Mounted Rifle Volunteers, Lieut.-Col. F. W. Armstrong ; Capts. E. E. Dower, A. S. Leary, J. S. King ; Transkei Mounted Rifles, Major S. J. Henley, Surg.-Capt. C. P. B. Wall.

4th September 1901.—Knysna Rangers, Major W. Scott.

LORD KITCHENER'S DESPATCH : *8th July* 1901.—Koffyfontein (Orange River Colony) Defence Force, Cpl. H. J. Jellard, promoted Sgt. on October 11th, 1900, for exposing himself to heavy fire at sixty yards' range when getting on to a *débris* heap to connect a wire from a battery to a mine, and also for holding an advanced position with one native.

8th December 1901.—Adelaide District Mounted Troops, Capt. Welsh, for coolness and good leading, operations in Cape Colony, September. Bedford District Mounted Troops, Capt. E. J. T. Pringle for same. Colonial Defence Force, Capt. H. S. S. Harden for his defence of Sutherland, September 7th. Sutherland District Mounted Troops, Cpl. Sales, promoted Sgt., and Lce.-Cpl. Jouste, promoted Cpl., on September 7th, on patrol, on meeting enemy advancing to attack village, by their coolness alarmed the garrison, and got all their men to safety. Tarkastad Mounted Troops, Major H. T. Nickalls, 17th Lancers, attached, good service near Vaal Vlei, October 8th.

8th March 1902.—Piquetberg District Mounted Troops, Cpl. F. James, promoted Sgt., in defence of Piquetberg, November 7th, volunteered to carry ammunition to blockhouses at great personal risk from both sides. South African Mounted Irregular Forces, Capt. Ross for good services in operations north of Middelburg, Transvaal, in February.

23rd June 1902.—South African Mounted Irregular Forces, Major C. A. Tremeer,[1] Capts. C. Parker, P. T. Blakemore ; Cape Colony Defence Force,

---
[1] Awarded D.S.O.

Major Nourse, Capt. Nettleton; Warrington Town Guard, M. Van der Hooven; Willowmore Town Guard, Lieut. H. Rees; Barkly West Town Guard, Sgt. E. Mansfield; Prince Albert's District Mounted Troops, L. B. Liddell; Fraserburg District Mounted Troops, Sgt. W. Evans. Lieut.-Col. Southey, described as Cape Local Forces, got the C.B. Lieut. M. C. Foxcroft,[1] described as of the South African Mounted Irregular Forces, got the D.S.O.; and Sgts. C. Muller and J. Steevens,[2] and Cpls. C. Davies and G. Davidson,[2] similarly described, were awarded the D.C.M.

ORPEN'S HORSE.

THIS corps, 300 strong, was raised by Major Orpen early in 1900 in the Hopetown neighbourhood for service on the Lower Orange River and in the extreme west of Cape Colony. They were of great use, when the enemy was making serious efforts to stir up rebellion in that outlying district, as a protection to the loyal inhabitants; while as assisting to restrain the waverers from joining the rebels, the presence of the corps was invaluable.

A glance at any map of South Africa shows that the railway from Cape Town to Kimberley runs roughly in a north-easterly direction, and that the British possessions were, before the annexation of the Transvaal and the Orange Free State, much greater in area on the north-west than on the south-east of the line. When the Orange Free State, finding Britain unprepared, attempted an invasion of Cape Colony in October and November 1899, it was only natural that they should should choose to cross the Orange on the east of the railway. By doing so they struck more directly towards Cape Town and the other ports, and

[1] Awarded D.S.O.   [2] Awarded D.C.M.

they entered a district where the provisioning of their army was possible. Sympathisers they had in all districts, and in the first months of 1900 unrest and incipient rebellion showed themselves in the region west of Victoria West, De Aar, and Orange River Station.

When Lord Roberts was launching his movement to relieve Kimberley he had to take measures against the rebels. In the despatch of 15th March 1900, he said that in the "Prieska-Britstown and Carnarvon districts of Cape Colony, west of the railway, between De Aar and Orange River, I regret to report that signs of organised disaffection have been apparent during the past fortnight." Two columns were got ready, one including three companies of mounted infantry and 400 of the City Imperial Volunteers; another under Major-General Settle, which assembled at Hopetown, embraced about 80 of Orpen's Horse, one company of mounted infantry, a field battery, and half a battalion of infantry. Lord Kitchener was sent down from Paardeberg to direct the operations. After a little fighting these were successful, and the district, for a time, was fairly quiet and clear of the enemy, but disaffection soon broke out again. The enemy's bands scattered in one neighbourhood to reappear in another. A portion of Orpen's Horse were engaged about 11th March 1900 and inflicted some loss on the enemy. The corps had one casualty.

Orpen's Horse remained at Upington as garrison of that place, and as the balance of the regiment came up from Hopetown they, along with the Cheshire Yeomanry and the Royal Australian Battery, held Kenhardt, Draghoender, and Dopas Poort. In his telegram of 17th April 1900 Lord Roberts said: "Settle reports from Kenhardt on 14th that 200

Transvaalers made determined attack on Dopas Poort, held by a party of Orpen's Horse; our loss 2 killed and 9 wounded. Enemy's must have been heavy, as they applied for doctors and ambulance." Two other deaths from wounds on this occasion were afterwards reported. This was the regiment's first serious fight. General Settle complimented the corps on the way in which the detachment of about 40 had driven off an attack by very superior numbers. These were estimated at between 300 and 400. Near Kheis, 160 miles west of De Aar, Colonel Adye on 28th May inflicted some punishment on the enemy; while in Griqualand, north of the river, Sir Charles Warren beat his opponents in several stiff fights (see Duke of Edinburgh's Volunteers). For some months after May sympathy with the Boers was less active, but when the enemy reinvaded the north-east of Cape Colony in December 1900 every effort was made to relight the flame of rebellion west of the railway. Commandos under Hertzog and others penetrated to Calvinia, Clanwilliam, and Piquetberg. In January 1901 several columns were employed to drive these forces north, but the task was difficult in the extreme. The region is of vast extent, much of it the reverse of fertile, and although sparsely populated, very many of the farmers were anxious to assist the enemy with food, forage, or information. Roads were few, and for regular troops moving with the usual convoy, the district was one in which they could do little harm to mobile bands. In the despatch of 8th May 1901 Lord Kitchener remarked that unrest was showing in the extreme north-west, close to the frontier of German Namaqualand. In May 1902 the enemy were still moving about immediately to the north of

Calvinia, and were actually besieging the town of Ookiep close to the German frontier.

From the beginning of 1901 to the close of the war the local forces did much good work; indeed to them belongs the credit of preventing the enemy gaining complete control of this wide area.

The men of Orpen's Horse were only enlisted for six months, but they cheerfully served twelve. At the end of the year 200 took their discharge, and Major Orpen with the remainder joined the column of Major Jeudwine at Van Wyk's Vlei. Orpen's men were in action on various occasions, and were, along with the other mounted troops of the column, Nesbitt's Horse, and some Border Scouts, successful in capturing prisoners at various places. At Ganabosch in the Calvinia district, on 25th June 1901, a detachment was ambushed, when 3 men were killed and several wounded. On the same day Conroy was severely defeated (see Border Scouts, under whose heading some further particulars are given of the work of troops in this difficult country).

Major Orpen was mentioned by Lord Roberts and got the C.M.G.

BORDER SCOUTS.

THE Border Scouts were raised at Upington in May 1900 as a local defence force, and in September all the white troops in the district were withdrawn to Prieska. The men were all half-castes, chiefly descendants of Boer farmers and native women; many of them were well-to-do farmers having large herds, others were hunters in the Kalahari Desert. All could ride and shoot. Their knowledge of the country and excellent eyesight made them invaluable as scouts. In November 1900 the regiment was increased to 300; in January 1901 to 500; and shortly afterwards to 8 squadrons —total, all ranks, 786. The north-western district of Cape Colony, which the regiment patrolled, extended from Oomdries Vlei on the south to Rietfontein on the north, a distance of 400 miles; and from Prieska on the east to Ookiep on the west, about 350 miles. Kenhardt and Upington, two towns about the centre of this vast area, were garrisoned and entrenched. These towns are seventy-two miles apart over heavy sandy roads, and on one occasion in June 1901, when a Boer force threatened Upington, 2 squadrons of the regiment covered the distance in sixteen and a half hours, and after a short halt moved out on the 25th to meet the enemy, 250 strong, under Conroy, who, after a fight lasting all day, was completely defeated. The Border Scouts captured all Conroy's waggons, spare horses, ammunition, and some prisoners. Lieutenant Beresford of the regiment was killed, and 2 men wounded; 3 Boers were buried in the morning. On 8th July there was further fighting, when the Scouts lost 3 men killed, and Captain C. Tabuteau and 3 men wounded. The enemy now fled into Griqualand West, and the north-west district remained quiet for many months. A troop of the Border Scouts were long stationed at Prieska for scouting and despatch-riding.

The distance between Upington and De Aar is just over 300 miles, from which railway junction all supplies had to be drawn—a big undertaking when the convoy required an escort of 300 or 400 men to bring it safely through; and the convoy was of little use when it arrived, as the escort had consumed half the stuff on the road out, and wellnigh the other half was required by the escort when taking back the empty waggons. The officer commanding the Border Scouts frequently requested to be permitted to live on the country, in the same way as the Boers did, and thus do away with convoys and transport, but this was not allowed.

In April 1901, 300 of the regiment were ordered to join Major Jeudwine's column at Van Wyk's Vlei. These 3 squadrons remained on column for seven months, for the last three of which they were under Colonel Capper. During the whole time they did most of the scouting for the main body, and a day seldom passed without the advance or flanking scouts being fired on by the enemy, who, however, fled as the column advanced. Some very hard and trying marching was done, but the rebels generally kept a day or two's march in advance, and owing to its transport the column could not move as fast as the enemy. The 6th Battalion Lancashire Fusiliers was in this column, and in their war record it is noted, to illustrate the difficult nature of the country, that on 28th May only six miles were covered in nine hours' marching. Occasionally the waggons were left behind, and the mounted men—1 squadron of Orpen's Horse, 1 of Nesbitt's, and 3 of the Scouts—would, by a long night-march, try to surround the enemy. Twice Maritz was all but surrounded in very hilly country, but on each occasion he and his men escaped with the loss of a few men and all his spare horses.

At Ganabosch the column fought the combined commandos of Maritz and Louw; the enemy held some high ridges until dark, and then fled. In November 1901 the Border Scouts were ordered to return to the north-western district, as several commandos had moved north. On this trek they had a running fight with Van Reenan's commando, but owing to the horses being in a miserable condition only two prisoners were captured. They arrived in Upington in December, after having been as far south as Piquetberg Road Station. On one occasion they had been snowed up for three days in the hills near Sutherland.

The regiment received no pay during the time it was on column, and Major Birkbeck (4th Scottish Rifles), the commander, found on his return to Upington that all communication between that place and De Aar had been cut for several months. The wire was down for miles, and post-carts had been captured by the enemy, while there was hardly enough food for the garrison for one month, apart from the civilian population; lastly, there were not twenty pounds of money in the town. Meat rations became the order of the day, and remained so until the corn ripened at Keimeos, on the banks of the Orange, thirty miles from Upington. At this time there were about 600 rebels under arms in the district, while several commandos were being pushed into it by the columns in the south. On one occasion at this time 60 Border Scouts, under Captain Bracy Ramsbotham, D.S.O., did a good piece of work. They had gone out to get sheep, and, hearing of the enemy, they succeeded in ambushing a party of 80 Boers under Conroy. The enemy fled, almost after the first volley, being completely surprised. They left 15 dead and 8 severely wounded.

The regiment not having drawn any pay for many months, and the authorities stating it was impossible to get money safely through, Major Birkbeck decided to make his own money. A block stamp was cut out of wood to represent a jackal, as that animal's skin was worn on the men's hats. Underneath was written, "Issued by Paymaster Border Scouts, pay to Bearer"; then signature, John Birkbeck, Major, O.C.B.S. The notes were issued for £5, £2, 10s., and 2s. on cloth, and as few of the men could read, ink of a different colour was used for each value. Cloth, like everything else, began to run out, so that in the end blinds, bedsheets, and table-cloths were commandeered and torn up to make into money. £45,000 worth was issued and in circulation. It was the current coin of the district, the Post Office and Savings' Bank accepting it. The Civil Commissioner used it, while the traders took it or gave it as change. The notes were not redeemed until after peace was declared. Many were cashed far from the district; for example, the Standard Bank alone cashed many hundreds at Cape Town, and a few were presented even in Natal.

In January 1902 General Smuts came into the district to organise the Boer forces: he had the commandos of Maritz, Latagan, Conroy, and Louw. The Border Scouts were now divided as follows: 350 at De Aar for convoy duty, 50 at Prieska, 150 at Kenhardt, and a like number at Upington. The only other troops at these last two towns were Native Town Guards, each 100 strong, armed with very old rifles, mostly useless. Conroy seized this opportunity to reap the harvest at Keimeos, for the ripening of which

Upington had been wearying. News came that he was cutting the wheat and building trenches on the kopjes. He had with him about 100 men. The same evening Major Birkbeck marched for Keimeos with 100 of the Scouts mounted on half-starved horses. He arrived at Keimeos while it was still dark; dividing his force, he crept up the kopjes occupied by the enemy. At the first sign of dawn Captain Tabuteau shot a Boer who stood up within a yard of where he himself was hiding, and in a few seconds it was found that Boers and Border Scouts were lying mixed up amongst the rocks. No one could move an inch. Unable to move, both parties lay still all day, and when it was dusk orders were shouted to the Scouts to fix bayonets and be ready to charge: a previous signal had been arranged and a place to reassemble fixed. The latter signal having been given after dark, and the Scouts having reassembled, some men were sent into the village of Keimeos: they found that the Boers had fled. Captain Tabuteau remained out with 50 men, the others returning to Upington; 3 Boers were buried on the following morning. The Border Scouts lost 2 mortally wounded, and 20 others slightly wounded. The regiment now brought in and stored at Upington 1500 sacks of grain—a task which could not have been accomplished but for the marvellous scouting which prevented all interference with the working-parties or enabled them to beat off the attacks. Much has been heard lately of the qualities needed in scouts. A British officer who served with this regiment says that the men could always tell whether distant dust was made by ostriches, springbok, locusts, or mounted men, and never made a mistake in their judgment. If a party of horsemen had passed over the road they could roughly estimate the number, and could tell how many horses were ridden and how many led. They travelled by night as easily as by day, always going straight across country and never on the track. Not a waggon of any sort accompanied the regiment, the blanket being under the saddle and an overcoat strapped in front. They carried no cooking-pots nor food, as when on trek they only used meat. Spare ammunition was carried on horses.

The regiment's record is one of which they had every reason to be proud. They lost 1 officer killed and 1 wounded, 19 non-commissioned officers and men killed and over 100 wounded, but not a single man ever surrendered, although many times an unwounded man lay by a wounded comrade till dark. Not a single despatch rider was caught, although several got in only on wounded horses or on foot. These despatch riders had to cross from Kenhardt to Upington and Prieska once or twice a-week, often on starved horses.

Curiously enough, no man of the regiment died of disease.

The Mentions gained were—

LORD KITCHENER'S DESPATCHES: 8th July 1901.—Capt. J. B. Ramsbotham[1] and Lieut. Beresford behaved gallantly in repulse of Boer attack on patrol near Kenhardt, Cape Colony, May 17, 1901. Capt. J. B. Ramsbotham and Lieut. H. H. Hodges, near Kenhardt, Cape Colony, June 25, for good leading in attack on Boer position. Sgt.-Major Bowers, Sgts. Whitfield and Adamson, gallant conduct at Naroegas, Kenhardt, May 17; mentioned in Army Orders.

8th August 1901.—Cpl. Carl Darries,[2] promoted Sgt. On July 8, a small party of scouts being engaged with very superior force of the enemy, by his coolness and good shooting prevented the party from being surrounded, and saved the life of his officer by killing two Boers who were shooting at him at close range.

23rd June 1902.—Capts. E. F. M'Sheehy, C. Tabuteau; Sgt.-Major G. Panizza[2]; Sgts. Muller,[2] R. van der Colff.

---

[1] Awarded D.S.O.   [2] Awarded D.C.M.

WESTERN PROVINCE MOUNTED RIFLES.

(CAPE COLONY IRREGULAR CORPS.)

WHEN the second invasion of Cape Colony took place in December 1900 several new bodies of volunteers or irregulars were raised at Cape Town, among others this corps. They reached a strength of over 500. As soon as a squadron was ready it took the field, because the enemy in the first week of January 1901 had reached within a day's ride of Cape Town. During January and February the corps was constantly in action. In a telegram from Clanwilliam, dated 31st January, the Press Association correspondent remarked that a detachment under Lieut. Hellawell had driven 150 Boers from the Pakhuis Pass.

Throughout 1901 and 1902 the corps did an immense amount of arduous work in the extreme south-west of the Colony. They were often far from support and in a district much favoured by the enemy, and one almost impossible for regular troops. The corps had endless little engagements, frequently involving sharp casualties, and if they had a good many patrols captured this may be attributed to their being more than usually split up into little detachments at the request of the officer who commanded the district. A part of the corps were for a time in Colonel Capper's column. A patrol on 4th August 1901 made a smart capture of 7 prisoners, 70 horses, and 1000 rounds of ammunition.

The corps were for a time commanded by Major R. C. Master of the King's Royal Rifle Corps, and afterwards by Captain C. H. Rankin, 7th Hussars.

One of the most notable things done in the western district was the successful defence of Tontelbosch Kolk, the Boer force in the neighbourhood being stated by Lord Kitchener to be about 1000 strong. The garrison, which was partly composed of men of this corps, made use of their cover most expertly, and during the siege the W.P.M.R. only lost 2 killed and 3 wounded.

The Mentions gained were—

Despatch of 8th March 1902.—Capt. R. M. Bertram, for his very gallant defence of Tontelbosch Kolk, Cape Colony, from November 25 to December 3. Sgt. W. G. Somerset, Lce.-Cpl. S. van Breda (killed), Sgt. T. Bromley, particularly distinguished themselves in same defence. Cpl. W. Paton, promoted Sgt., in defence of Piquetberg, Nov. 7, commanded an exposed blockhouse and held it for twenty-four hours under continuous heavy fire; of his 7 men 3 were wounded.

Despatch of 23rd June 1902.—Capt. C. Kirkwood.

NAMAQUALAND BORDER SCOUTS.

(CAPE COLONY IRREGULAR CORPS.)

THIS corps, about 360 strong, was almost wholly recruited from half-castes. In the words of a British officer who, although not belonging to them, saw much of their work, " they were an excellent force, which did a great deal of hard patrol work under Colonel White, and had several stiff brushes with the enemy. They were conspicuous for consistently refusing to surrender when surrounded, as patrols were at times. They would keep up a fight till dark, and although half of them were killed the survivors of the party would escape. They made wonderful marches without water in their desert country." The work of the regiment was very similar to that of the Border Scouts. The corps was employed in their own district in 1901 and 1902, and had the good fortune to be part of the garrison of Ookiep when that town was besieged in April 1902. The force which held the town made a most excellent defence, and were complimented by Lord Kitchener. Lieut. Watkinson was wounded at Ookiep on 13th April.

In March 1902 a detachment at Garies had fighting on various occasions. Lieut. Darter was killed on the 18th and Squadron-Quartermaster Bidmead on the following day.

The Mentions gained were as follows :—

LORD KITCHENER'S DESPATCH : 23rd June 1902.—Capt. H. G. Maddison ; Lieut. Rich ; Sgt. G. Muller ; Qrmr.-Sgt. L. S. Panizza ; Pte. B. Links.

BUSHMANLAND BORDERERS.

THIS was, when first raised in 1901, a small corps about 100 strong, nearly all half-castes, who proved themselves excellent scouts and plucky fighters. They were stationed at Tontelbosch Kolk, and were the main part of the garrison when that place was attacked in November and December 1901. The enemy was strong and vigorous, and pressed their attack hard because they wanted the arms and ammunition in the place, but the spirit of the defence was all that could be desired, and the post was held until reinforcements approached.

In 1902 the corps was raised to 600 strong, and Lieut. Soames got the rank of Major. Their work all through was very much akin to that of the Border Scouts, to which reference is made.

The Mentions gained were—

LORD KITCHENER'S DESPATCHES : 8*th March* 1902.—Lieuts. R. N. Woolf, A. Soames,[1] T. W. K. Stephens, for good service in defence of Tontelbosch Kolk, November 25 to December 3. Cpl. Cloete particularly distinguished himself in same defence.

1*st June* 1902.—Tpr. Jan Scheepers,[2] promoted Cpl., for gallantry in Calvinia district, 5th February ; when called on to surrender at close range he opened fire, killing 2 Boers and wounding 1, thereby enabling his dismounted comrade to escape on foot.

23*rd June* 1902.—Lieut. H. E. Langfield ; Sgt. W. Shawe.

KITCHENER'S FIGHTING SCOUTS.

THE corps was raised in December 1900, being recruited in Cape Colony and Natal. As soon as they could be mounted they were sent into the field, and it is to the credit of the force and its leaders that they made no mistake.

It will be remembered that Hertzog and other leaders had penetrated to the south-west of Cape Colony. In his telegram of 3rd February 1901 Lord Kitchener said : " The commandos in Cape Colony are being hustled. Kitchener's Fighting Scouts attacked one hundred Boers at Doornbridge. Boers retired, leaving one killed. Horses, carts, ammunition, and tools were taken. We had two men

[1] Awarded D.S.O.   [2] Awarded D.C.M.

wounded." In the despatch of 8th March 1901 Lord Kitchener dealt with the efforts made to clear the Colony in the preceding December, January, and February. Speaking of events in the western parts of the Colony, his Lordship said: " While the pursuit from De Aar and Britstown was maintained by columns under Lieut.-Colonels Bethune (16th Lancers), Thorneycroft, and De Lisle, troops of local levies were hurried up to occupy centres of disaffection in the Ceres, Worcester, and Piquetberg district; at the same time Lieut.-Colonel Colenbrander's newly formed regiment of Kitchener's Fighting Scouts were railed to Matjesfontein, whence they moved out to hold the passes leading south from Sutherland. My object was to keep the enemy north of the Roggeveld Mountains, and to prevent any junction between Hertzog and Kritzinger in the Prince Albert or Worcester districts. This being achieved, it appeared to me useless to follow out into the far west an enemy at all times disinclined to fight and ever ready to scatter." On the 9th January Hertzog's commando withdrew north towards Calvinia. "A general advance northwards was commenced by the columns under Lieut.-Colonels De Lisle, Scobell (Scots Greys), and Colenbrander (commanding Kitchener's Fighting Scouts). These quite succeeded in driving the enemy out of Calvinia and Van Rhynsdorp, and pursued him as far north as Carnarvon." The regiment was taken to the central district of Cape Colony, where they had a very hard time. The pursuit of the enemy was not a task free from danger, and K.F.S. had one strong patrol captured near Richmond on 27th February 1901. Lieutenant A. E. Benson and 6 men were killed, Lieutenant Naughton and 12 men wounded, and some taken prisoners, "after a prolonged fight," the official telegram said. On 8th March Captain John Boyd was killed.

The corps had been fortunate in getting in Colonel Colenbrander a leader widely known and thoroughly respected as a fighting man in South Africa, and among the other officers were some who had already distinguished themselves by good work in other corps: it was thus soon possible to have a second regiment.

In the despatch of 8th July 1901, appendix, both regiments are referred to. It is there stated that Lieut.-Colonel Wilson's regiment in May was 417 strong, and Lieut.-Colonel Grenfell's 364, and both were then employed in the Pietersburg district, far north of Pretoria. In the despatch of 8th May 1901 Lord Kitchener, after detailing General Plumer's operations in that district, said that a commando had been reported at Klipdam, 15 miles north of Pietersburg, which was said to be under General Beyers. "Lieut.-Colonel Grenfell, whose regiment, K.F.S., had been sent by rail to Pietersburg, was, therefore, directed to clear up the situation. Starting on the night of the 26th April, Lieut.-Colonel Grenfell discovered the enemy's laager at Klipdam, and attacked it at dawn on the 27th with complete success, with the loss of only one man wounded. Seven Boers were killed, 41 were captured, besides which he obtained possession of the enemy's camp with 26 horses, 10 mules, many waggons and carts, and 76,000 rounds of ammunition. Information having been obtained that the enemy's last Long Tom was at Berg Plaats, about 20 miles east of Pietersburg, on the road to Haenertsburg, I desired Colonel Grenfell to make every effort to capture the gun. He moved at once, and at daylight on the 30th occupied Doornhoek, thence pushing on to Berg Plaats.

On his approach the enemy opened fire at over 10,000 yards' range, but after 16 rounds they blew up the gun, while Colonel Grenfell's men were still about 3000 yards distant, and retreated in a north-east direction. Colonel Grenfell captured 10 prisoners and 35 rounds of Long Tom ammunition, our only casualties being two men wounded. As the result of a careful search on the farm, Berg Vlei, adjoining Berg Plaats, 100,000 rounds of Martini-Henry ammunition were discovered and destroyed. With Berg Vlei as a centre Colonel Grenfell continued to operate for several days with success, and a detachment of the 12th Bn. M.I., under Major Thomson, was able, under cover of a thick fog, to effect the capture of Commandant Marais and 40 of his men. Other prisoners were brought in by Lieut.-Colonels Colenbrander and Wilson of K.F.S., and on his return to Pietersburg, on the 6th May, Colonel Grenfell reported that altogether he had accounted for 7 Boers killed, 129 prisoners, and 50 voluntary surrenders: 240,000 rounds of ammunition were destroyed."

In May Grenfell commanded an expedition to Louis Trichard, 100 miles north-east of Pietersburg. His force was 600 men of K.F.S., the 12th M.I. Regulars, 2 guns, and four companies of the Wiltshire Regiment. The column left Pietersburg, and two days later Colenbrander with the advanced force occupied Louis Trichard. About the 20th Colenbrander, " by a wellplanned night march, surprised a laager on the Klip Spruit. Field-Cornet Venter with 72 Burghers, 68 rifles, 18 waggons," and a large amount of ammunition and many cattle, were captured. On the 25th May Grenfell received the surrender of Commandant Van Rensburg and about 150 men. Shortly after this

Colenbrander, in the Buffels district, had some skirmishes, "killing seven and capturing a maxim. A detachment under Major Knott overtook a commando under Barend Viljoen and captured 79 prisoners." Lord Kitchener said, in his despatch of 8th July 1901, that this expedition did much to secure the pacification of the Northern Transvaal. While Grenfell was on this expedition, Wilson, with a wing of the K.F.S., two guns, and two companies 2nd Gordon Highlanders, was, in conjunction with Major M'Micking's column, doing most excellent work in the Nylstroom district. On 19th May 79 Burghers and 100 rifles, 33,000 rounds, 66 waggons, some dynamite, &c., were taken. On the 21st Wilson attacked another position and took 18 prisoners, 48 rifles, &c. On 2nd June a detached force drove the enemy on Wilson, who, after a stubborn fight, took 40 prisoners, 70 rifles, 8000 cattle, besides ammunition and dynamite (see despatch of 8th July). Of course all this could not be accomplished without loss. On 1st and 2nd June the regiment had 7 killed and 20 wounded.

On 1st July, at Hopewell, Grenfell surprised another laager, killing 1 and capturing 93 prisoners, 100 horses, much stock, ammunition, &c.

During August and September 1901 many other expeditions were undertaken by the corps, but the results of these were meagre compared to the splendid successes previously obtained, and to those obtained in October, November, and December. In the despatch of 8th November Lord Kitchener said: "In the Northern Transvaal Colonel Colenbrander, K.F.S., has traversed the Water Berg between Warmbaths and Magalapye on the Rhodesian Railway, a district hitherto unvisited by our troops." Leaving Warmbaths on 6th October, Colenbrander visited many "Boer supply depots, carefully located beforehand, and during the march captured 45 prisoners of war, 67 rifles, nearly 4000 rounds of ammunition, and a very large number of waggons and cattle." In the same month the column of Colonel Dawkins, formerly Grenfell's, did excellent work, capturing 97 prisoners.

In the despatch of 8th December 1901 Lord Kitchener said that Colenbrander, on his return march to Warmbaths, captured 54 prisoners and much stock. About the end of November Colenbrander and Dawkins were out again. On the 27th 200 of K.F.S. pushed out through the Zand River Poort. The enemy retreated; for two days "the pursuit was not relaxed, and on the 29th Colonel Colenbrander, with half of K.F.S., pressed on ahead of the remainder of the column upon Badenhorst's traces, and following them closely till the morning of 3rd December, Colonel Colenbrander, after a long and exhausting chase through an almost waterless region, came suddenly upon the enemy and captured 15 prisoners, with all the waggons of the commando." The remainder of the Scouts were successful "in killing 3 and capturing 17 Burghers, while 60 stragglers, driven into the hills near Sterkfontein, were cleverly secured by the 12th Mounted Infantry of Colonel Dawkins' column. The total results of these well-planned and carefully executed operations were 104 prisoners," many waggons, cattle, &c.

The two columns did good work all through December. On the 13th Colenbrander drove Badenhorst and 22 of his Burghers into the arms of Dawkins, and ten days later K.F.S. captured 60 prisoners at Jericho on the Crocodile. Again it may be remarked that all these splendid results could not be achieved without some losses, but these were marvellously small. On the 20th December 3 men were killed and Lieutenant J. Sampson and 6 men were wounded at Zoutpans Drift. On the 26th Colenbrander set out for Rustenburg, arriving there on 1st January 1902. "A skilful march through Magato Nek on the night of 4th January enabled him to capture a laager and 29 prisoners after an engagement at dawn, in which 5 of the enemy were killed." In his telegram regarding this affair, Lord Kitchener said: "This surprise was highly creditable to Colonel Colenbrander, who with a very small force effected it within a few miles of a superior force of the enemy." On this occasion there was one casualty. Lord Kitchener also mentioned in his despatch of 8th January 1902 that Colenbrander on 9th January came upon the native chief Linchwe and 2000 of his people searching for stock stolen by the Boer leader General Kemp. "Colenbrander directed the chief to return to the Pilandsberg, which order he obeyed forthwith, much to the relief of the families scattered throughout the district." Colenbrander, with the 1st K.F.S., continued to operate in the Western Transvaal during January, February, and part of March 1902. In the despatch of 8th February 1902 Lord Kitchener remarked that "in the Northern Transvaal operations at any distance from the railway have necessarily been temporarily suspended by the season of horse-sickness. The departure of Colonel Colenbrander's column for the south for this reason appears to have given General Beyers breathing-time, and sufficient leisure for the initiation of a plan which aimed at an attack on Pietersburg in conjunction with the simultaneous removal of a number of Burghers who had been residing voluntarily and as neutrals in the refugee camp at that place." The removal of some of the latter was effected, but otherwise the attack was repulsed, the Town Guard supporting the troops with great steadiness. In the despatch of 8th April it is stated that Beyers moved from Malips Poort, south-east of Pietersburg, about 13th March, and invested Fort Edward, a small fortified post near Louis Trichard. A column of 200 mounted men and 300 of the Northampton Regiment moved out to relieve the place, but was opposed, and on 24th March fell back. Colenbrander's column, 1st K.F.S., was therefore brought up from Krugersdorp. On the 27th he moved out from Pietersburg. On the 28th " he undertook a long night march from Dwars River, which terminated at daybreak on the 29th in the complete surprise of the enemy, who fled in an easterly direction, with the loss of 3 killed and 4 captured." This is a notable instance of irregulars succeeding brilliantly where regulars failed.

A portion of the 1st K.F.S. were with Colonel Keir's column, which, along with Colonel Cookson's column, was heavily attacked at Boschbult, 31st March 1902 (see 2nd Regiment Canadian Mounted Rifles). The detachment of K.F.S. had 1 man killed and 8 wounded.

In his final despatch, that of 1st June 1902, para. 3, Lord Kitchener said that " in the Northern Transvaal Lieut.-Colonel Colenbrander has carried out some successful operations against General Beyers, who, on 5th April, was in camp on the southern slopes of the hills close to Malips Poort." Colenbrander, who had returned from the relief of Fort Edward on the 5th, aimed at the surrounding of the enemy. " Two parties of 400 men each were sent out on the 6th under General Celliers, National Scouts, and Captain M'Queen, Steinaecker's Horse, to block the two roads open to the Boers to the south-east and south-west. A third party under Captain Lyle, 1st K.F.S., moved on the night of the 6th along the top of the hills to the west of the Poort to block all possible exits in that direction; whilst Colonel Colenbrander himself, with the 2nd Bn. Inniskilling Fusiliers and the remainder of his mounted men, left Pietersburg on the night of the 7th to make a direct attack on the Poort itself. The attack was delivered on the morning of the 8th, and after severe fighting extending over two days, in which, I regret to say, Lieut.-Colonel A. J. Murray, commanding 2nd Inniskilling Fusiliers, was dangerously wounded, resulted in the flight of the Boers in a south-easterly direction." Unfortunately Captain M'Queen had failed "to reach the exact position assigned to him, and this enabled General Beyers and the majority of his followers to make good their escape towards Haenertsburg," but the Boers left their laager, waggons, and camp equipment. Nine were killed, 11 wounded, and 108 unwounded prisoners were taken. "Colenbrander's subsequent pursuit of General Beyers in the direction of Oud Agatha after this highly successful engagement was unfortunately marred by a mishap to a small mounted force under Captain Blaine, 1st K.F.S., who, pushing on too eagerly into most difficult country, fell into a cleverly arranged ambuscade from which he only extricated his men with a loss of 6 killed, 1 officer and 11 men wounded, and 30 taken prisoners."

Operations were suspended for a time during a stage of the peace negotiations, but between 5th and 10th May Colenbrander's force was able to account for 1 Boer killed, 21 wounded, and 101 armed prisoners. On 10th May hostilities in the district practically ceased.

In August 1901 Colonel Wilson, with the 2nd K.F.S., was railed to the Orange River Colony, and in the despatches of October, November, and December 1901 there are frequent references to the work of Wilson's column. In their new sphere they had endless marching and constant fighting, and always made good use of their opportunities. The column had the good fortune to be working under and often with Colonel Rimington (see despatch of 8th October 1901, para. 7). On 4th October Wilson, marching from Kroonstad to Heilbron, was attacked near the Rhenoster River, but drove off the enemy. The regiment lost 4 killed and 6 wounded, including Lieutenants F. G. Schnadhorst and E. E. Jones, both severely wounded. Lieutenant Schnadhorst died of his wounds three weeks later.

On 14th November the columns of Colonel Byng, South African Light Horse, and Wilson, 2nd K.F.S., were very resolutely attacked. After two hours' fighting the attack was successfully repulsed by "Byng's rear-guard, which was well and skilfully handled by Lieut.-Colonel Wilson of K.F.S., and the enemy retired, leaving 8 dead on the field." The telegraphic despatch stated that the rear-guard was composed of K.F.S., who had all the losses, namely, 3 killed, including Lieutenant Hughes, and 8 wounded, including Lieutenants Prince Radziwill, A. E. Smith, and C. C. Allsopp. Captain J. B. Gedge was dangerously wounded about this time.

During December 1901 and January and February 1902 the 2nd K.F.S. took part in many big driving movements in the north of the Orange River Colony. In his telegram of 27th January 1902 Lord Kitchener said: "Colonel Wilson, K.F.S., moved out on Thursday night from Frankfort and surrounded a small laager at Damplatz, capturing 20 prisoners, including Field-Cornet Strydom. During the return march he was

Kitchener's Fighting Scouts

attacked by a superior force under Alberts, who was driven off after severe fighting, leaving 5 dead. All Wilson's prisoners, except three, escaped." Kitchener's Fighting Scouts lost 8 killed and 7 wounded. In the despatch of 8th February, dealing with events in that district, Lord Kitchener said that the columns of Keir and Wilson and Damant's Horse "have acted vigorously whenever opportunity offered against the enemy's bands under Commandants Alberts and Ross, which continued to frequent the valley of the Vaal to the north of Frankfort." In the beginning of March Wilson's column was, with other troops, taken to the Western Transvaal, where, it will be remembered, Lord Methuen had met with disaster. The 2nd K.F.S. were placed under General Walter Kitchener, and were present at the fiercely fought action of Boschbult on 31st March 1902, when they lost 1 killed and 7 wounded. They took part in the final great drives, under General Ian Hamilton, towards the Mafeking railway and back to Klerksdorp.

Kitchener's Fighting Scouts took the field when the war was far advanced, but during the whole of the second phase of the campaign they did splendid work. Judged by the losses inflicted on the enemy, no corps could point to a finer record, and they are an outstanding example of what can be made in a very short time of Colonial material, provided that officers suitable for irregulars are found. A regular regiment can pull through a campaign although it has in its commissioned ranks a fair proportion of those not unknown types—the inconsiderate scolder and the finicking old maid whose idea of taking responsibility stops short at the enforcement among the rank and file of well-shaved chins and very clean equipment. In an irregular corps there is no place for such people, and their presence is a sure source of trouble and failure. Officers must be had with great tact and commonsense, not unduly magnifying their position, and fearless of all consequences when they act conscientiously on their own initiative.

Having been taken to Pretoria after the declaration of peace, Kitchener's Fighting Scouts had, along with the Imperial Light Horse, Johannesburg Mounted Rifles, and Scottish Horse, the honour of marching past Lord Kitchener, who spoke highly of the work which had been done.

The Mentions gained by Kitchener's Fighting Scouts were as follows :—

Despatch of 8th December 1901.—Capt. E. St M. Hutchinson, Lt. L. S. C. Lister, Lt. L. C. Hughes (killed), for conspicuous gallantry in action near Heilbron, 14th November. Sgt. W. Marsburg,[1] 1st K.F.S., for continual good work with scouts of Col. Colenbrander's column.

8th March 1902. — Capt. W. Hurrell, 1st K.F.S., at Zoutpans Drift, December 21st, with 30 men charged an equal number of enemy in a difficult position and captured 22, including Commandant Nagal. Lt. J. Sampson, Sgt. G. Pirrie (died of wounds), for very valuable service in holding a ridge against much superior force of the enemy for over half an hour at Zoutpans Drift, December 30th. Cpl. E. P. Berlyn, promoted Sgt., at same place bandaged an officer under very heavy fire and then carried him under cover, being twice wounded in doing so, last time severely, and then continued to give directions as to other wounded men. Sgt. W. Marsburg,[1] 1st K.F.S., at Jericho, December 28th, when only accompanied by native scouts, rushed 7 Boers and captured them, thereby preventing them from giving the alarm to main body, which was subsequently taken. Sgt.-Majors R. B. Sheridon, Johnson-Scott, Sgt. C. Peters, for good service in north-western Transvaal, November and December 1901.

8th April 1902.—Lt.-Col. A. E. Wilson[2]; Lt.-Col. J. W. Colenbrander, got the C.B.

1st June 1902. — 1st K.F.S. — Capt. H. C. Lyle[2] and Armourer-Sgt. A. P. Pillan, good service in operations east of Pietersburg, 25th March to 21st April 1902. 2nd K.F.S. — Lt. J. S. Kelly, Sgt.-Major D. R. Bettington, Farrier-Sgt. W. Welsh, Sgt. E. Hanson, Tpr. De Wet, for good service in action at Boschbult, 31st March 1902.

---

[1] Awarded D.C.M. [2] Awarded D.S.O.

23rd June 1902.—1st Regiment—Capt. D. E. Henderson; Lt. E. Armstrong; Regl. Sgt.-Major J. H. Zeeder[1]; Qrmr.-Sgt. W. M. Croft; Pte. D. C. Scott. 2nd Regiment—Capts. J. B. Gedye,[2] O. W. Staten; Lt. J. N. Brown; Regl. Sgt.-Major D. Gormley; Squad. Sgt.-Major R. E. James; Tprs. C. Olsson,[1] R. De Vere.

JOHANNESBURG MOUNTED RIFLES.

THIS corps was founded on 12th December 1900, and soon two battalions were recruited. They had the good luck to get as commanding officer Lieut.-Colonel H. K. Stewart, Reserve of Officers, and under him did much valuable service. The greater portion of the corps was in the early part of 1901 stationed in the Springs district, where they always had the enemy near them and used worthily the opportunities they got. They had casualties at Springs on 6th January 1901 and on several other occasions during the three following months. In March and April two companies were in Colonel Colville's column, based on the Standerton line, and were said to 'have done good work particularly in an affair at Roberts' Drift. Both battalions afterwards did much column work. Early in 1901 part of the corps was sent to the Zululand border, a district in which they saw much arduous service. Towards the end of April 600 were with Colonel Stewart in a column working from about Volksrust. Colonel Stewart had also under him Gough's Mounted Infantry, 600; the Commander-in-Chief's Bodyguard, 1000; the 74th Battery Royal

[1] Awarded D.C.M.   [2] Awarded D.S.O.

Field Artillery, and a pom-pom. In July 1901 the two battalions were put together, and under Colonel Stewart operated as a column, which did much trekking and skirmishing generally in the east of the Transvaal and about the Zululand border. A Standerton telegram of 5th August mentioned that by a night raid on Amersfoort the J.M.R. had captured a laager and 20 prisoners.

Much of the work of the corps and of the columns which worked in conjunction with Colonel Stewart's is described in 'Two Years at the Front with the Mounted Infantry,' being the diary of Lieutenant B. Moeller, who had gone out with the City Imperial Volunteers, and who was afterwards mortally wounded at Holland, in the Eastern Transvaal, on 18th December 1901.

In September 1901 Colonel Stewart, with his own corps and Gough's Mounted Infantry, was operating to the north of the Natal Border. Gough, who, as stated in Lord Kitchener's despatch of 8th October 1901, was in advance, decided on 17th September to push on towards the Blood River in order to gain touch with the enemy about Scheeper's Nek. Gough, thinking he had about 300 of the enemy in front of him, galloped his force to seize a commanding ridge, but the enemy were at least 1000 strong, and the three companies of Mounted Infantry and two guns of the 69th Battery Royal Field Artillery were surrounded, and after a fierce fight, in which Gough's force suffered very severe casualties, were forced to surrender. Colonel Stewart, having to protect the baggage of both bodies, fell back on De Jager's Drift, thus at same time covering Dundee. In his despatch Lord

Kitchener said: "Lieutenant-Colonel Stewart, in falling back when he did, showed great judgment and a sound appreciation of the situation in a position of considerable difficulty." The Boers had collected in the Vryheid district in great strength to attempt a re-invasion of Natal, and on 26th September made most determined attacks on Forts Itala and Prospect, which were repulsed. Major Gough had on many occasions proved himself a fine soldier and most capable leader of mounted infantry.

Towards the close of 1901 and during the first quarter of 1902 the Johannesburg Mounted Rifles were chiefly employed in the Ermelo district of the Transvaal. In May 1902 they crossed the Vaal and had some skirmishes in the Frankfort district of the Orange River Colony. Down to the close of the campaign they did service which proved them a most useful and well-led body.

On 17th June, after peace had been declared, the Johannesburg Mounted Rifles, Imperial Light Horse, Kitchener's Fighting Scouts, and the Scottish Horse had the honour of marching past and being inspected by the Commander-in-Chief in Johannesburg. Lord Kitchener referred to the fine service of these splendid irregular regiments, and indicated that there was a prospect of permanent volunteer regiments being formed which would be successors to the work, traditions, and organisation of each of them.

The Mentions gained by the corps were :—

LORD KITCHENER's DESPATCHES : 8th July 1901.—Lieut. S. A. Anderson and Capt. D. W. Talbot, for good service in ambushing some Boers near Springs, 17th January. Lieut. C. G. Greetham, at Edenkop, Eastern Transvaal, 30th June, twice went out under heavy fire to bring in his brother, who was stunned by fall of his horse; Lieut. Greetham had gained mention by Lord Roberts while serving as troop sergeant-major of the Kimberley Mounted Corps.

8th October 1901.—Lieuts. Nicol[1] and C. Wells, for dash and judgment in attack on position at Waterval, 10th September.

8th April 1902.—Capt. J. Mossop.[1]

23rd June 1902.—Capts. R. Wishart,[1] J. Laing,[1] F. C. Beaumann; Cpl. A. Matthews; Pte. G. Smith.[2] Col. Stewart, the commander, was awarded the C.M.G.

THE RAND RIFLES.

THIS corps was raised towards the close of 1900, and was generally employed on the defences of Johannesburg and of posts in the surrounding district. They saw some skirmishing and some sharp attacks on posts, but they were not in any big engagement, and had few opportunities of gaining distinction. The corps remained on service till the end of the war.

The following Mention was gained:—

LORD KITCHENER'S DESPATCH: 8th March 1902.—Pte. P. N. Maskell, promoted Cpl. by Commander-in-Chief for distinguished conduct in defence of post at Brakpan, February 5, when 5 men repulsed 49 Boers.

JOHANNESBURG POLICE.

THIS body was generally stationed in and on the outskirts of the town, but as the enemy frequently visited the neighbourhood, the Police had, as will be

[1] Awarded D.S.O.   [2] Awarded D.C.M.

seen from the Mentions, occasions on which they proved their value as soldiers.

The Mentions gained were :—

LORD KITCHENER'S DESPATCH: 8*th August* 1901.—Capt. H. Samson, during attack on Florida, July 5, was conspicuous for his conduct of the defence. First-class Sgt. W. Parke, in command of 33 Police at Roodepoort when that place was attacked, July 5, after repulsing attack, led volunteers, who cleared village, and was severely wounded in doing so. Tpr. E. Hampton, sentry at entrance to village of Florida, when, on same date, 25 Boers galloped at him, held his position, and by his steady fire checked enemy till support arrived, when he had only three rounds left: his defence saved post.

STEINAECKER'S HORSE.

THIS corps was raised in June 1900 by Major F. Von Steinaecker to operate in Zululand and on the Swaziland border of the Transvaal. Their leader had served as a lieutenant in the Prussian Army, but had subsequently been, for nearly twenty years, in South and South-West Africa. Before raising his "Horse" he had done one of the most daring exploits performed in the course of the war.

In November 1899 Steinaecker had enlisted as a private in the Colonial Scouts, a Natal-raised corps. He was soon promoted squadron quartermaster-sergeant, but in December he left the Scouts to command a small party serving under the Intelligence Department. The Colonial Scouts were disbanded in March 1900, and in that month Steinaecker, now a lieutenant,[1] selected six men, of whom Scouts Duncan, Lawson, Gray, and Carmichael served with him for many

[1] Natal Volunteer Record, Durban, 1900, and private sources.

months, Lawson finishing as a captain, and being present at the disbandment of the corps in February 1903. With this small party Steinaecker left Eshowe on 3rd April 1900, and rode or walked through Zululand and Swaziland, a distance of 500 miles. Their horses having died of horse-sickness, the party were on foot when the Transvaal border was reached. On their journey they had picked up a British settler, Holgate, afterwards a captain in this corps. He knew the country thoroughly, and as a guide in the last stages was invaluable. The party intended to attempt the blowing up of the great bridge at Komati Poort, but found it too strongly guarded. Steinaecker and three men now struck through the bush, swam the Komati river "when the crocodiles were off their feed," travelled all the night of 16th June, and on the 17th, after dark, placed nearly 100 lb. of dynamite between the masonry and girders of a bridge at Malelane, forty miles up the line, and destroyed it. The fact that the Boers afterwards restored the bridge does not detract from the credit due to Steinaecker and his gallant men for their splendid piece of daring, which, strangely enough, was never recognised in despatches.

Having returned to Natal, Lieutenant Steinaecker now recruited for his "Horse"; and after having them equipped, he and his corps embarked on a warship and were landed through the surf at Kosi Bay, in the north corner of Zululand, not, however, without the loss of a boatload of arms and saddlery, the boat upsetting on the dangerous bar. Steinaecker's force now made their way to the Transvaal border, south of the Delagoa Railway. On 20th July 1900 he and a party of his men were successful in capturing Commandant Van Dam and another leader.

When the armies of Lord Roberts and General Buller reached the eastern confines of the Transvaal, Steinaecker's Horse, now recruited up to 450 men, moved farther out into the very wild and unhealthy country which lies west of the Portuguese border. From Komati as a centre they gradually extended their raids to the north and south for great distances, thereby denying to the enemy the use of the eastern lowlands for rest and recuperation. They also guarded closely the long eastern border against Boer despatch riders and ammunition runners. In time the corps completely occupied and pacified the whole low veldt to the Olifant's river, holding over a dozen permanent posts scattered over a large province.

The corps had now become one of the most complete and self-contained units in the country. They had their own intelligence, transport, workshops, &c., and were able for over a year to work the Selati railway with their own men.

In their eminently unhealthy district, Steinaecker's men had much most arduous and very dangerous guerilla campaigning; but being a corps specially recruited for such tasks, and having an admirable leader, they escaped serious casualties for a long time.

In Lord Roberts' telegram of 14th November 1900 he said: "On the 8th inst. a party of Steinaecker's Horse, raised for service in the Komati Poort district, captured 16 Boers trying to cross from Portuguese territory at Nomahash, a place by which the Boers have been trying to get ammunition brought into the Transvaal." A day or two later 5 more were taken. At this time there were several encounters with despatch riders, which almost uniformly ended in favour of the patrols of the corps.

In July 1901 the corps met their first piece of bad luck. On the 22nd a party of about 100, many of whom were without horses, returned from a successful foray, bringing in some prisoners, stock, and a party of surrendered Burghers to Bremersdorp in Swaziland, a post which had been held by the corps for six months. They were followed by a force of Boers under Generals Oppermann, Smuts, and Grobelaar which many times outnumbered them. The detachment evacuated the town, hoping to get clear away; but on the 23rd they were caught up by the enemy, and after a running fight, in which they lost 4 killed and a greater number wounded and captured, were forced to abandon their baggage.[1] Captain Greenhill-Gardyne was said to have conducted the retirement most ably. A party of the Yorkshire Regiment (Green Howards) made a very fine march from Komati Poort to assist, but did not arrive in time.

Shortly after this Major Steinaecker surprised a laager and took 18 prisoners, and from this time onwards the corps had on many occasions severe fighting in localities where help was very far distant. On 7th August 1901 a post of 25 men on the Sabie river was attacked by a strong force of Boers. The post had been newly established, and the fortifications were not complete. The enemy, who numbered about 300, attacked vigorously and lost heavily. Commandant or General Moll was wounded in the attack, and was afterwards captured by a patrol of the corps. The defenders had Captain H. Farmer Francis killed, several wounded, and the remainder captured. Captain Francis had served with the Imperial Light Horse throughout the siege of Ladysmith, and thereafter in the relief of

[1] See Lord Kitchener's telegram of 26th July 1901.

Mafeking. His brother, also in the I.L.H., was killed outside Mafeking.

At the end of August Captain Gardyne, in command of a small party, captured 11 Boers, some waggons, and much stock, 150 miles north of Komati Poort.

In February 1902 Captain Holgate, the scout of the bridge destruction party, with 16 men, surprised and captured 18 of the enemy on the Swaziland border.

Early in 1902 an extra squadron of Steinaecker's Horse was raised for service in the Pietersburg low veldt, in which district they did a lot of fighting under Colonel Colenbrander (see Kitchener's Fighting Scouts). On 16th April this squadron were heavily engaged, and lost 5 men killed and Lieutenant Robertson and 11 men wounded.

Lieutenant and Paymaster J. Hartley, who had been attached to Lord Methuen's column in the Western Transvaal, was killed in the disaster to that General's column on 7th March 1902 (see Cape Police).

After the conclusion of the war Steinaecker's Horse, in somewhat reduced strength, remained in occupation of the eastern border until February 1903, when the South African Constabulary took over a number of the officers and men, and the others were disbanded.

In 'Temple Bar' for July and August 1901 there are two admirably written articles, headed "A Byeway of the Boer War," by an officer of the 1st Gordon Highlanders—"A.D.G.G."—who was long attached to Steinaecker's, which give an excellent picture of the hard but most exciting—and to any lover of adventures most interesting—life led by Steinaecker's Horse. Their district was one in which few white men could live, as is proved by the fact that every regular regiment which had the misfortune to be stationed near

Komati Poort lost more than 50 per cent of its strength through fever. The regulars were generally accommodated in tents or huts, but Steinaecker's men had often to lie out for weeks at a time in districts so wild that lions were a most real danger,—as in the Sabie river valley,—and more than one poor fellow was seized and carried off almost from the camp fire, while one was taken by crocodiles. Many of the corps did not see the railway for months on end, while some of the wounded had actually to be carried over 150 miles before reaching any sort of hospital.

The Mentions gained by Steinaecker's Horse were as follows :—

LORD KITCHENER'S DESPATCHES : 8*th August* 1901.—Lieut. J. A. Baillie,[1] on July 4th, having heard that two despatch riders had crossed the Portuguese Border into Swaziland, followed them with one man by moonlight, and after a hand-to-hand fight killed them both and took despatches. Lce.-Cpl. W. S. Hains [2] (Harris in Gazette), who accompanied Lieut. Baillie, was also mentioned, and was promoted Sgt. by the Commander-in-Chief.

8*th March* 1902.—Tprs. D. E. Wilson and F. Hennessy, for most plucky rescue of the body of a comrade which had been carried off by a crocodile whilst bathing in Usutu River, 30th November.

8*th April* 1902.—Major F. V. Steinaecker.[1]

1*st June* 1902.—Lieut. W. P. Robertson for good service east of Pietersburg, 25th March to 21st April 1902. Tpr. W. W. Griffin, killed whilst trying to take a wounded comrade to cover.

23*rd June* 1902.—Capt. H. F. Francis (killed in action); Lieuts. J. M. Dallamore, D. Buchanan. Capt. A. Greenhill-Gardyne, Gordon Highlanders, Adjutant attached (got Brevet-Major).

Major von Steinaecker commenced the war as a private. His steps are worth noting—Squadron Quartermaster-Sergeant, Lieutenant, Captain, Major, D.S.O., Hon. Lieut.-Col. in army.

---

[1] Awarded D.S.O.   [2] Awarded D.C.M.

MENNE'S SCOUTS—MORLEY'S SCOUTS.

THESE corps did excellent and often very daring work in the Transvaal, chiefly in the neighbourhood of the Natal and Delagoa Railways during the second phase of the war. Night expeditions were numerous, and as the force employed was generally very slender, the true qualities of scouts had to be exhibited: each of these corps proved worthy of the appellation. "Linesman," in his now famous 'Words by an Eyewitness' (Blackwood: 1901), gives a very graphic picture of a night expedition and fight in the darkness, the actors in which on the British side were Menne's Scouts. They were raised and commanded by Major T. Menne, who had seen service in the first six months of the war with the Natal Colonial Scouts in Zululand, and afterwards with Bethune's Mounted Infantry, and thus had gained great experience in the field. The nucleus of the corps was his own—"G"—squadron of the Colonial Scouts. Menne's Scouts did much to protect the all-important railway communication between Natal and Pretoria, as well as to keep the Commander-in-Chief informed of the movements and strength of the enemy in the south and south-east of the Transvaal. The special work of the corps was sometimes particularly dangerous. In the beginning of May 1901 they lost Lieutenant Hemmingway and 2 men killed and several wounded. On 13th September at Platrand they had 2 men killed and Lieutenant H. B. Bradford and 1 man wounded. In November Menne's Scouts did the mounted work for the Leicestershire Regiment while the latter built the

Ermelo-Standerton blockhouse line. The corps was disbanded at Pietermaritzburg on 1st January 1902.

Morley's Scouts worked in the Eastern Transvaal, and, as will be seen from the following quotation, they had at least one very exciting experience. Lord Kitchener in his despatch of 8th September 1901, para. 13, dealing with operations in the Eastern Transvaal, said: "On 17th August a force of the South African Constabulary and Morley's Scouts which had been patrolling under Captain Wood, S.A.C., in front of the Constabulary posts to the south of Bronkhorst Spruit Station, unexpectedly came upon and attacked a greatly superior Boer force which was halted at Middelburg, 23 miles south of the railway. The enemy, who were subsequently reported to have numbered 800, were completely surprised by the sudden rush of our men. Twenty-three Boers were killed, 11 were taken prisoners, a large number were wounded, and all their horses stampeded. Our success, however, was rather short-lived. Discovering that the force by which they had been attacked was a small one, the enemy rallied, assumed the offensive, and drove our men back after a hand-to-hand fight in the direction of Bronkhorst Spruit. In the retirement the Boers were able to recover the 11 prisoners who had been taken from them and to capture 14 of our men, including Captain Morley of Morley's Scouts, who was dangerously wounded. Our other casualties were 1 man killed and 5 men wounded."

Menne's Scouts won the following Mentions by Lord Kitchener :—

Despatch of 8th August 1901.—Capt. F. C. Barker, for a successful raid at Joubert's Nek, July 29th, resulting in capture of laager and 7 men killed and 25 wounded Boers. Lieut. A. B. Lubbock, at Joubert's Nek, July

15th, assisted Sgt. Cima to save a native scout whose horse had been killed, Boers at time being within 150 yards and firing heavily. Sgt. J. C. Cima, at Joubert's Nek, 15th July, in retirement of a patrol, native scout having been dismounted, rode back under heavy fire, leading Boer being within 70 yards, and brought native away with him, thereby saving his life.

8th October 1901.—Tprs. Peterkin and Glasborrow (killed). At Platrand, September 13th, Glasborrow went back to assist a dismounted comrade, and was mortally wounded. Peterkin then returned under heavy fire and attended to him.

THE HEIDELBERG VOLUNTEERS AND SCOUTS.

THIS corps, which was largely composed of surrendered Boers, was employed on the Standerton line, their duties being chiefly to protect the line and the possessions of surrendered Burghers in the neighbourhood. But they did more active work, and on 24th May 1901 were credited with a smart capture of a laager, when they secured 9 armed prisoners and much stock. Major Vallentin was wounded on this occasion. On 24th July a party of the scouts fell into an ambush, and 4 were killed.

The following Mention was gained :—

LORD KITCHENER'S DESPATCH : *8th August* 1901.—Guide Gorman, near Heidelberg, July 24th, remained behind with Major Vallentin to cover the retirement of 4 dismounted men of Burgher Corps who would have been shot had they fallen into enemy's hands.

BUSH VELDT CARBINEERS.

THIS corps did useful work in the difficult country north of Pietersburg in 1901, and saw a lot of fighting, but it gained an unfortunate notoriety by the conviction of some of its members on charges that they had committed acts not in accordance with the rules of civilised warfare. Undoubtedly a corps such as this, acting beyond the immediate control of higher authorities and far from support, was placed in a very unenviable position. The enemies they had to deal with were not always members of regular commandos, but often leaderless gangs of ruffians not unacquainted with nefarious practices and incapable of appreciating anything but the most arbitrary justice. Mr Green,[1] who was chaplain to the Australian Bushmen, a corps that operated much in the Pietersburg district, speaks in terms of praise of the Bush Veldt Carbineers. He says that they were chiefly English refugees of that district. They acted as scouts for General Plumer, and did well. On one occasion they captured the convoy of a train-wrecking gang and 11 prisoners. These latter would not disclose where their mines were laid, so they were promptly put on a trolley; an explosion did take place, but none were killed. The corps had casualties on various occasions. Captain P. F. Hunt and Sergeant F. Elands were killed on 6th August 1901, and 1 man on the 10th.

The one Mention gained by the corps shows excellently the class of work they had :—

Despatch of 8th August 1901.—Sgt. Forbes, on own initiative, on hearing of presence of Boers marched 80 miles, surprised and captured the party.

---

[1] 'Story of the Australian Bushmen.' Sydney, 1903.

PIETERSBURG LIGHT HORSE.

LIKE the preceding, this corps was employed in the extreme north of the Transvaal—officially designated as "the wildest part" of that country. They had sharp fighting at Spelonkin on 23rd March 1902, when Sergeant-Major Evans was killed.

The Mentions gained were :—

LORD KITCHENER'S DESPATCHES : 1st *June* 1902.—Capt. S. Midgely[1] for good service in operations east of Pietersburg, 25th March to 21st April 1902.

23rd *June* 1902.—Sgt. J. R. Gray,[2] Cpl. J. Ballen.

BEDDY'S SCOUTS.

THIS corps was raised for service in the extreme north of the Transvaal, the same wild district in which the Bush Veldt Carbineers had worked until disbanded. Beddy's Scouts made sundry small captures of prisoners during the period January to April 1902. At Spelonkin on 23rd March 1902 their post was attacked, but held out; Captain Beddy and several men were wounded. On 16th April they had fighting at Haenertsburg, and suffered some losses. Captain W. Beddy was mentioned in Lord Kitchener's final despatch, under the heading, "Intelligence Department."

[1] Awarded D.S.O.   [2] Awarded D.C.M.

THE SCOTTISH HORSE.

MAJOR the Marquis of Tullibardine, M.V.O., D.S.O., in the written statement furnished by him to the War Commission and in his evidence [1] gives an admirably clear yet modest account of the organisation, composition, and work of the two regiments of the Scottish Horse, each of which earned great distinction by exceptionally fine work.

In November 1900 Lord Kitchener sanctioned the raising of a regiment to be known as the Scottish Horse. Lord Tullibardine soon started recruiting from Scotsmen, or men of Scottish descent, in South Africa, chiefly in Natal; and on 4th February 1901 he took the field with three squadrons. To these other squadrons were soon added. The Volunteer Service Companies of Scottish regiments furnished no less than 200 men. To these their leader gave the highest possible praise. "One hundred of them were the best body of men in every way that I saw in South Africa. This particular squadron had a reputation which extended far beyond the column with which it was trekking."

Recruiting was not confined to South Africa. Great Britain and the other Colonies were appealed to, and the Caledonian Societies in London and over the seas did grand work. The Highland Society of London sent out 386 officers and men, who sailed in February and March 1901; and the Marquis's father, the Duke of Atholl, personally raised 831 men before the war was over. The Society in Melbourne took up the matter with enthusiasm, and "about 300 men joined me on

[1] Minutes of Evidence, vol. ii. p. 446.

8th March. These were a splendid draft, very fine riders, and all Victorians." Later on more men joined from Australia, recruiting having been attended with success. The first regiment was soon six squadrons strong, and a second of five squadrons also took the field. In no way did Lord Tullibardine show his organising power to greater advantage than in the setting up of depots for his force for both men and horses. A central headquarters depot for both regiments, with a convalescent camp for sick men and overworked horses, was at Johannesburg, and there were advance depots for each regiment near the railway in the district in which each might be trekking. At these advance depots were remount establishments. Thus sick men could go to the regimental camp, and so not get lost in the great army hospitals. Horses needing a rest could be sent in to the rest-camp at the depot, and come out as well as ever. In selecting his officers his lordship showed the same wisdom, and in that all-important respect no corps was more fortunately situated. The commander, second in command, and adjutant of each regiment were all regulars of experience. "From first to last I had 157 officers: 14 were killed or died; 7 were invalided; 11 were removed or resigned at my request; 107 served to the end of the war, and the remainder resigned for private reasons. The officers were—Supplied from regular army, 22; appointed in South Africa outside the regiment, 78; through the ranks of the regiment, 46; and at home, 11." At another part Lord Tullibardine said: "Some of the most reliable officers I had were appointed through the ranks. They were of all classes, and were promoted principally on their merits." This coming from an officer of the Royal Horse Guards who had seen much active service, apart from South Africa, is surely a sufficient reply to the old-fashioned people who insist with tiresome reiteration that an officer must be selected for his pedigree.

Only a very brief account of the services of the corps can be given here. What follows is almost entirely taken from Lord Tullibardine's evidence and the official despatches.

1st Regiment.

This regiment was commanded at first by Lord Tullibardine, then by Major Blair, King's Own Scottish Borderers, after him by Lieut.-Colonel C. E. Duff, 8th Hussars, and finally by Lieut.-Colonel H. P. Leader, 6th Dragoon Guards. It served in the Western Transvaal in a column commanded (1) by Colonel Flint, (2) by Colonel Shekleton, (3) by Brigadier-General Cunningham, (4) by Brigadier-General Dixon, and (5) by Colonel Kekewich. They had a few casualties, but saw no very serious fighting till the action at Vlakfontein on 29th May 1901. When the fight commenced the Scottish Horse were detached, but they rejoined Brigadier Dixon in time to assist the infantry in driving off one of the fiercest attacks made during the war. The charge successfully made by a portion of the Sherwood Foresters in order to recapture the guns was a piece of work certainly unsurpassable in gallantry and dash. Brigadier-General Dixon having been appointed to another command, Colonel Kekewich took over the column. "Under this officer's magnificent leading the column then became one of the most useful in the country, being only equalled by Colonel Benson's for numbers of prisoners taken. The regiment improved rapidly. The next serious fight was when Delarey surprised the camp at Moedwill on September 30th 1901. The Scottish Horse casualties were 3 officers and 17 men killed, 12 officers and 41 men wounded. The regiment, owing to the greater part being away on command, were very weak that night, and behaved splendidly." No fewer than 7 officers and 3 non-commissioned officers and men of the regiment gained mention on this occasion. At Moedwill the officers' casualties were—Captain H. A. F. Watson, Lieutenant T. J. Irvine (killed), Lieutenant H. N. C. Erskine-Flower (died of wounds on 22nd November), Lieut.-Colonel C. E. Duff, Major A. Blair, Captains P. M. Rattray and P. N. Field, Surgeon-Captain W. S. Kidd; Lieutenants N. C. G. Cameron, W. Loring, J. Stuart Wortley, W. Jardine, Edwards, Prior, D. Rattray.

"Soon after this [Moedwill action] Lieut.-Colonel Leader, 6th Dragoon Guards (Carbineers), took over the command from Lieut.-Colonel Duff, who took over the command of his own regiment, the 8th Hussars. To Colonel Leader is due the high state of efficiency of the regiment at the end of the war." The regiment continued its good work in the Western Transvaal.

Between May and September the regiment had been almost constantly in contact with the enemy. They had 1 man killed and Lieutenant Duncan Stewart and 1 man wounded on 6th July. On 8th August, at Elandsdrift, 1 man was killed and Surgeon J. M. Bernstein and several men were wounded. At Witpoort on 13th December, Captain H. G. Field was severely wounded, and on this occasion 5 men were wounded. Among the next losses the regiment had to mourn was the death of Captain P. N. Field, who was killed at Doornlaagte on 2nd March 1902. This splendid officer had in September 1899 enlisted in the Natal

Mounted Rifles, had gone through the siege of Ladysmith, joined the Scottish Horse as a lieutenant in December 1900, been twice wounded, once captured, mentioned in despatches, invalided home in December 1901 after Moedwill, insisted on embarking again in February, and was killed as soon as he got to the front. His record is one of which not only his corps but every Volunteer or irregular must be proud.

In the early months of 1902 the regiment was constantly on the trek and fighting. At Gruisfontein, on February 5th, 1902, the whole of Sarel Albert's commando was captured. As to this action, Lord Kitchener, in his despatch of 8th February, said: "During Major Leader's advance he came upon and captured a Boer picket, from which he ascertained that General Delarey had already moved his camp, but that Commandant Sarel Albert's laager was for that night at Gruisfontein, which he reached just before daybreak. Our men charged the enemy's laager with great dash, the Scottish Horse taking the main share of the attack, and as most of the Boer horses had been stampeded by the fire of Major Leader's pom-pom, the gallantry of the attacking force was rewarded by an unusually large measure of success; 7 Boers were killed, 132 prisoners taken, 11 of whom were wounded, together with 130 rifles, 2800 rounds of ammunition, and a large number of horses, mules, cattle, and waggons were taken. Our casualties were 2 officers (Captain Ian R. M'Kenzie and Lieutenant W. Tanner) and 6 men wounded, all belonging to the Scottish Horse." In his telegram of 5th February Lord Kitchener said: "Leader reports that the Scottish Horse behaved with great gallantry."

The regiment was in the column of Colonel Kekewich and the brigade of General Walter Kitchener in the last great drives in the Western Transvaal. In the drive which started from the Klerksdorp blockhouse line on 23rd March, and came back to that line on the 24th, the troops covered 80 miles in twenty-four hours. To the 1st Scottish Horse chiefly belonged the credit for the capture of three 15 - pounder guns and two pom-poms.

The regiment bore an honourable part in another big fight at Rooival on 11th April 1902. It is described in Lord Kitchener's despatch of 1st June 1902, a quotation from which has been given under the Imperial Light Horse, who were present in the latter part of the action. Lord Tullibardine claimed for the Scottish Horse, apparently with good ground, the capture of some guns in the pursuit after a gallop of 20 miles. The official telegram certainly said that Kekewich had captured 2 guns, 1 pom-pom, 1 ammunition-cart, and 10 waggons. The regiment had 1 killed and 8 wounded in this engagement.

2ND REGIMENT.

"The second regiment started in Colonel Benson's column in the Eastern Transvaal, under Major Murray, Black Watch, and, thanks to Colonel Benson's good guidance, speedily became one of the best corps in the country, and never degenerated, even after his death. Their first serious skirmish was at Roodekrantz, on April 30th, 1901, when one man was killed, 4 officers and one man wounded. Their next (on 3rd July 1901) at Eland's Hoek [Kloof in the despatches, see Mentions], when three men were killed and nine wounded."[1] The officers wounded at Roodekrantz were Captains M. W. H. Linday and A. M. Creagh, and Lieutenants Oscar Hamilton and C. S. Long-Innes.

The despatches report Colonel Benson's operations in some detail, and the Scottish Horse are invariably mentioned in terms of credit. On 9th and 10th July 1901, near Dullstroom, north of the Delagoa Bay Railway, they are said to have pursued the enemy in a northerly direction, and to have captured some waggons. On the 11th the regiment was detached on a wide detour, during which they successfully located and captured 6 prisoners, 40 horses, and 24 vehicles belonging to Viljoen's commando, which were hidden in a kloof in the Tautesberg.[2] On 15th July, at Wagen Drift, Lieutenants O. W. Kelly and M'Letchie and 4 men were wounded. In August, September, and October Benson operated south of the Delagoa Railway, and was most successful in rushing laagers after long night marches, taking a large number of armed Boers and immense quantities of cattle and transport. For their fine work Lord Kitchener bestowed on the column and its gifted leader the highest praise. But to few soldiers is it given to know nothing but unqualified success.

It will be remembered that at the end of September 1901 a great concentration of Boers was reported in the Vryheid district. After making most determined but unsuccessful attacks on Forts Itala and Prospect, the enemy was driven from the south-east corner of the Transvaal. General Botha knew that Benson's column,

[1] Lord Tullibardine's statement.
[2] Despatch of 8th August 1901.

which had become a standing cause of terror to his subordinates, was operating alone in the Bethel district. Into that district the Boer commandant moved, determined to concentrate and strike hard. On the 30th October, at 4.30 A.M., Colonel Benson moved from Quaggalaagte northwards towards Brugspruit. He was soon opposed on his front and flanks and rear, but the attacks on front and flanks were not so serious as those on rear. At the crossing of a drift the enemy had a good opportunity of doing serious damage, but did not press home; the guns and waggons were got over, and the trek was continued in a torrent of rain. The soft ground caused serious trouble, and two waggons, which were bogged, had to be left. The accounts of what followed vary considerably. The despatch [1] states that—

"At about 9 A.M. the advance guard, on approaching the farm Bakenlaagte [more usually spelt Brakenlaagte], where Colonel Benson intended to halt, found the ground was held by the enemy, who after a short resistance was dislodged, and the column moved gradually into camp covered by the rear-guard, composed of two companies of mounted infantry, two squadrons 2nd Scottish Horse, two guns 84th Field Battery Royal Artillery, a pom-pom, and one company of the 2nd Battalion the Buffs [see p. 293], the whole under the command of Major Anley, 3rd Mounted Infantry.

"The guns, with the company of the Buffs and 50 mounted infantry, took up a position on an irregular ridge running generally east and west some 2500 yards south of the camp. Small posts of mounted infantry were well out on either flank, and the remainder, with

[1] Lord Kitchener's despatch of 8th November 1901.

the Scottish Horse, occupying some hillocks another 1000 yards to the south of the ridge, where the guns were in position, formed a screen to the whole. As the front of the column was cleared, the numbers of the enemy hovering round the flanks and the rear-guard increased. It was now past noon, the rain continued, and a strong wind was blowing from the south-west. The country was open, an expanse of vast rolling downs without any very marked features, giving a far-reaching command of view, while the deep hollows afforded cover for the approach of an enemy who knew the ground and avoided heights.

"As soon as the column and baggage had been brought into camp, and all arrangements made for the defence, Colonel Benson ordered the screen of Mounted Infantry and Scottish Horse to fall back on the remainder of the rear-guard at Gun Hill. When about to carry this out between 12 and 1 P.M., Major Anley, who was in command, reported that the enemy was advancing in greatly increasing numbers, and was already close to his position, which he could no longer hold. He at once retired on Gun Hill, sending a company of Mounted Infantry to some small kopjes well to the left. The movement had hardly commenced when a strong Boer force appeared over the rise, immediately to the left of the position just vacated by the screen, and, wheeling sharp to its left, pushed in the Scottish Horse and Mounted Infantry. Our men passed over the ridge to the northern slope, while the Boers formed up in a large area of dead ground, which lay immediately under and in front of its western extremity: here they dismounted and rapidly worked their way into a good position within close range of the guns on the crest. The company of the Buffs, which formed the original escort, posted well to the front of the guns on the south side of the ridge, was captured by the enemy as he rode practically into our position almost in touch with our men. [See p. 293.]

"In spite of the gallant efforts of the Mounted Infantry Company of the Yorkshire Light Infantry and a squadron of the Scottish Horse, which promptly formed up on the flanks of the guns, our troops were unable to offer any serious resistance, and the ridge, with the exception of the extreme western end, which was held by a party of the Mounted Infantry until dark, gradually fell into the enemy's hands.

"As soon as Colonel Benson had become aware of the nature of the attack he had ordered up two more companies of the Buffs to reinforce the rear-guard on the ridge, but these did not succeed in reaching any position whence their fire could be effectually brought to bear. [See p. 293.]

"It is now known that the sudden change in the enemy's tactics was brought about by the arrival of a reinforcement of 600 or 800 men under Commandant General Louis Botha, which came on the field from the direction of Ermelo shortly before noon. Their subsequent attack, which was delivered simultaneously both on the camp and rear-guard, was greatly aided by the heavy rain and mist which concealed the enemy's movements, as the storm burst in the faces of our troops. The attack on the camp was easily driven off, but no further reinforcements could be sent to the ridge, nor were the guns in camp able to materially assist the defence of those with the rear-guard.

"Both Colonel Benson and Colonel Guinness fell by the guns on the ridge, the former being wounded in three places. The fight was continued until dusk, and when our ambulance moved out after dark to collect the wounded, the guns were removed by the enemy."

In his statement before referred to Lord Tullibardine said : "The next fight was the big one at Brakenlaagte, when Colonel Benson and Major Murray were both killed. The men did magnificently trying to save the guns. Only 96 [actually fewer] were engaged at this point, and they stuck it out until only 6 were left unhit. Their casualties were 5 officers and 28 men killed, and 4 officers and 36 men wounded; total, 73 killed and wounded out of 96 engaged, all the officers engaged being hit. I do not think I ever heard of better or more determined fighting, and although we lost the guns the camp was saved by the delay, and the men really did cover themselves with glory." Major F. D. Murray and Captains M. W. H. Lindsay and A. Inglis, Lieutenants C. Woodman and J. B. Kelly were killed. Captain A. C. Murray and Lieutenants W. Campbell, T. Firns, A. T. Wardrop were wounded. Subsequently Lord Tullibardine informed the writer that the actual total of the officers and men of the corps engaged was 93. One officer and 13 men formed the covering troop when the rear-guard retired to Gun Hill. That troop was cut off. Seventy-three reached Gun Hill; of these only 6 were unhit at the close of the day, and many were hit several times.

Naturally every corps thinks well of its doings, and officers and men of the Scottish Horse have spoken proudly of what the regiment did. It is a satisfaction to them to know that officers of other corps have spoken and written in a similar strain. If more is needed, the Casualty List, which, after all, is the best test, proves that the mounted infantry, notably that of the Yorkshire Light Infantry and the King's Royal Rifle Corps, along with the Scottish Horse, particularly "L" Squadron, did all that men could do to hold the ridges and save the guns at Brakenlaagte.

No minor engagement of the war has engrossed greater attention than Brakenlaagte, and about no other has there been more written. The death of Colonel Benson, whose work as a column commander was unsurpassed by that of any other leader, gave it a tragic interest, but other causes contributed, and among these a degree of uncertainty as to the conduct of the troops. The infantry of a mounted or mobile column in South Africa was the part of the force which had little to do, when night attacks on the enemy's outposts or laagers were made, beyond marching to the point ordered; but if the column were seriously attacked, it behoved the infantry to hold their ground to the last man, "cost what it may," in the words of the red book. When the present writer published his 'Our Regiments in South Africa, 1900-1902,' he was taken to task for stating, as his opinion, that the conduct of the infantry at Brakenlaagte did seem to have fallen short of the heroic. Since then he has been able to obtain information which has satisfied him that the despatch, on which his previous account and criticism were based, is misleading on some points. From the despatch one would infer that there were two parties of Buffs concerned in the rear-guard action. There were actually three. These were—

1. The rear-guard company, actually 50 strong. They do not seem to have been on the ridge, but

to have been cut off and captured some 2500 yards south of the ridge. This company was supporting the mounted screen, which, forced to retire, galloped through the company, thus masking any fire of which the company was capable; for it had little ammunition left. Close behind the mounted screen came the enemy, smothering the company by sheer weight of numbers, and making resistance an impossibility. The casualties of the company were few.

2. A party of 30 men, belonging to the left flank guard of the convoy, who had been temporarily detained with Colonel Guinness' guns. The guns galloped back to the ridge or hill half a mile off, leaving this small party of infantry to follow. The detachment, while still moving back, was caught in the Boer charge, but made what stand they could, losing 19 killed and wounded.

3. Two companies. The despatch speaks of Colonel Benson ordering up two more companies of the Buffs to reinforce on the ridge. These had been escorting the convoy. The officer commanding them, hearing heavy firing in rear, had halted them near the ridge on his own initiative, but had been ordered by Colonel Benson to rejoin the convoy. Just as these companies were nearing camp, where the waggons had already arrived, they received a message to go back to the ridge. They at once turned about and advanced to the ridge. When they reached it the fighting was practically over; but they maintained the struggle for a time, and endeavoured to remove the guns. The Boers are said to have admitted that this advance, in which the companies lost 25 per cent of their strength, put an end to their aggressive movement. The distance from the ridge to the camp was 2000 yards.

The Scottish Horse

After October the 2nd Scottish Horse continued to operate in the Eastern Transvaal in the column of Colonel Mackenzie. There was often severe fighting, and on 20th December 1901 Major Jennings Bramley (19th Hussars), who had succeeded Major Murray in the command of the 2nd Scottish Horse, and Lieutenant John Dow were killed at Lake Banagher. In February the regiment made some smart captures of influential Boers about Carolina.

Having been brought to Pretoria after the declaration of peace, the Scottish Horse, along with the Imperial Light Horse, Johannesburg Mounted Rifles, and Kitchener's Fighting Scouts, marched past Lord Kitchener on 17th June, and the Commander-in-Chief intimated that arrangements might be made under which these corps would be placed on a permanent basis.

The Honours and Mentions gained by the corps are noted below. An attempt has been made to distinguish the regiments (1st and 2nd).

Lt. W. J. English, 2nd Regiment, was awarded the Victoria Cross. "This officer, with five men, was holding the right of a position at Vlakfontein [referred to already as Elandshoek] on July 3, 1901, during an attack by the Boers. Two of his men were killed and two wounded, but the position was still held, largely owing to Lt. English's personal pluck. When the ammunition ran short he went over to the next party and obtained more. To do this he had to cross some 15 yards of open ground under a heavy fire at a range of from 20 to 30 yards."—(Gazette, 4th October 1901.)

DESPATCH OF 8th July 1901.—Capt. P. N. Field, 1st, for conspicuous gallantry on several occasions, and notably on 29th May 1901 at Vlakfontein, when he went back at considerable personal risk to extricate two men who could not retire owing to fire. Sgt. J. C. Gange, 2nd, on Houtbosch Kop on 13th June 1901, a party of the regiment being under fire of Boers and of our men, voluntarily crossed a most difficult kloof under heavy fire from both sides to stop the firing of our own men, thereby saving many lives; also on June 15 crossed the Crocodile River under fire and burnt some Boer waggons and stores on opposite bank. Sgt. D. M'Ilwraith, 1st, on 4th April 1901, when scouts and cyclists were hard pressed, he, with one other man, covered the retirement of the whole party, and by his behaviour prevented the whole party from being rushed. Tprs. Gibbons, Ruddy, M. Shadwell, L. N. Smith, all 1st, as scouts have several times passed with messages through the Boer lines, and through country filled with the enemy.

8th August.—Lt. O. W. Kelly,[1] 2nd, shot through stomach at Laatse (Wagen) Drift, 15th July 1901, when with advanced patrol, but, having located some of the enemy, crawled back under heavy fire to inform the officer commanding. Staff Sgt.-Major J. Sharpe, 2nd, for his coolness and good command when opposed to very superior force of enemy at Mauchberg, 14th July 1901, and Elandshoek, 3rd July. Lce.-Cpl. A. Redpath, 2nd, on same occasion, called on to surrender and refused and tried to get away, wounded and again summoned to surrender, but continued to retire, and again wounded, still persisted, and got into camp with his rifle and bandolier; promoted Cpl. by the Commander-in-Chief. Sgt. W. L. Whiteman, Sgt. R. Fraser, Tpr. T. Fraser (promoted Cpl. by Commander-in-Chief), Sgt. T. Firns, all 2nd, at Elandskloof, 3rd July 1901, for gallantry and good conduct in an attack by 60 Boers on an extended position held by 26 men, of whom 3 were killed and 9 wounded. The attack was repulsed. Cpl. F. T. Kecrouse, 2nd, at Laatse Drift, 15th July 1901, galloped out under fire to fetch in a man whose horse had fallen and dragged him, and succeeded. Pte. F. W. Wilkinson, on same occasion, for gallantry in action and good example.

8th October 1901.—Capts. P. N. Field and Ian R. Mackenzie[1] and Lieut. W. Jardine, all 1st, for work done by them in clearing kloofs in Megaliesberg in September; Lt. Jardine, also for gallantry at Moedwill. Capts. R. H. Dick-Cunyngham (Lieut. 21st Lancers), P. M. Rattray,[1] Lieuts. J. H. Symonds, A. Rattray, N. C. G. Cameron (wounded), W. Loring, J. Stuart Wortley (wounded), all 1st, for gallantry, Moedwill, 30th September 1901. Surgeon-Capt. W. S. Kidd, wounded early in same action but continued at his duties many hours. Tpr. Richardson (promoted Cpl. by Commander-in-Chief), Sgt. Mainwaring, both 1st, for specially good service in the dangerous and difficult work of searching kloofs in the Megaliesberg, 5th September 1901. The three following gained mention for work at Moedwill: Farrier-Sgt. Kirkpatrick, 1st, conspicuous by leading and rallying the men at Moedwill; Tpr. G. Webster (promoted Cpl. by Commander-in-Chief), advanced with three comrades and when all were wounded continued alone, called on to surrender, refused, and continued to fight till reinforced, when he advanced again; Sgt. C. E. L'Anson, for continuing to serve and carry up ammunition though himself wounded.

8th December 1901.—Lieuts. C. E. Rice and W. A. King, 1st, for good service in capture of a laager at Beeste Kraal, 30th October 1901. Lieut. D. Robertson, 2nd, for distinguished good service in Colonel Benson's action at Brakenlaagte, 30th October 1901. Tpr. N. Grierson, 2nd (severely

---

[1] D.S.O.

wounded, promoted Cpl. by Commander-in-Chief), for gallantry, same occasion, crawling up to guns and offering to carry messages to the camp. Sgt.-Major Sharpe, 2nd, good service, same occasion.

8th March 1902.—The following are all of the 1st Battalion. Major H. P. Leader (Carbineers), for his capture of Sarel Alberts and his laager at Gruisfontein, 5th February 1902. Lieuts. W. Lawless, H. Selby, J. C. Wallace, for gallantry and good behaviour on same occasion. Staff Sgt.-Major J. Sharpe,[1] coolness and gallantry in directing the men under him in hand-to-hand fighting, same occasion. Tprs. J. S. Robb and M'Callum, promoted Cpls. (M'Callum was a son of the Governor of Natal), Tpr. C. Barclay, Staff Sgt.-Major F. Neal and Sgt. G. Gunning, all for gallantry, same occasion.

1st June 1902.—Capt. C. E. Rice, 1st, gallantry in action against Delarey, 24th March 1902. Major A. Blair, D.S.O., and Cpl. W. Parker (promoted Sgt.), 1st, good service at Brakspruit, 11th April 1902. Sgt. A. Martin, conspicuous good service, same occasion.

FINAL DESPATCH.—The Marquis of Tullibardine. 1st Regiment, Lieuts. W. F. Fison, S. H. Lewis, Squad. Sgt.-Major G. H. Manley, 13th Hussars, Squad. Qrmr.-Sgt., afterwards Lieut., E. A. Legge,[1] 18th Hussars, Farrier Qrmr.-Sgt. W. Fraser, Royal Horse Guards, Sgt.-Major M'Ilwraith, Farrier-Sgt. R. H. Tellam, Scout T. Tooms. 2nd Regiment, Lieuts. J. M. Baker, J. L. Jack, 2nd V.B. Argyll and Sutherland Highlanders, Qrmr. and Hon. Lieut. Murray, 3rd Dragoon Guards, Regimental Sgt.-Majors H. E. Varley,[1] 6th Dragoon Guards, W. G. Austin, 19th Hussars, Squad. Sgt.-Major E. Luther, Cpl. F. Helmkemp.

---

[1] Awarded D.C.M.

The Canadian Contingents.

THE ROYAL CANADIAN REGIMENT OF INFANTRY.

ON 3rd October 1899 it was announced in Canada that in the event of a war between Great Britain and the Boer States the Canadian Government would offer a contingent. On the same date Mr Chamberlain telegraphed to the Dominion Government that the Imperial Government accepted the offer. He stated that the force should be in units or companies of 125, the senior officer to be of a rank not higher than Major, and that infantry would be preferred. The two conditions mentioned were for the purpose of allowing the companies to be attached to battalions of the regular army. Before the campaign commenced and for some time afterwards the War Office had a prejudice, quite unfounded as it turned out, against allowing volunteers or irregulars to be embodied or mobilised as distinct battalions or regiments, on the ground, doubtless, that they imagined that only regular troops under regular officers could stand on their own legs. The history of the war proves how very far from the truth this view was. The two obnoxious conditions were withdrawn, at the request of the Canadian Government, and steps were at once taken to raise a regiment of infantry. Its title was the 2nd (Special Service) Battalion of the

Royal Canadian Regiment of Infantry. The 2nd was to distinguish it from, and yet connect it with, the battalion of the Royal Canadian Regiment of Infantry which formed part of the permanent military force of the Dominion. On 30th October 1899 the battalion, 1039 strong, under Colonel W. D. Otter, sailed from Quebec on the *Sardinian*, and on the 29th November the ship arrived at Cape Town. On 1st December the regiment entrained for De Aar, where for a few days they formed part of the garrison along with the 2nd Battalion Duke of Cornwall's Light Infantry. The battalion soon again got a move nearer the enemy, first to Orange River, and on the 9th and 10th December to Belmont—the locality of Lord Methuen's first battle. The next two months were mainly spent on the lines of communication between Orange River Bridge and Modder River. The work was of the kind usual to such service: making defence posts more perfect, repairing the lines, making and enlarging sidings, as well as outpost and patrol work. On 31st December 1899 "C" Company was chosen to be part of a force under Colonel Pilcher, consisting of about two companies Queensland Mounted Infantry, a section of Royal Horse Artillery, about 50 men of the Munster Fusilier Mounted Infantry, two companies of the Cornwall Light Infantry, and the company of the Royal Canadians, under Lieutenant Barker. The object of the expedition was to capture or break up a rebel laager near Douglas. For a great part of the way the Cornwalls and Canadians rode in waggons, the remainder of the force being mounted. About 9.45 A.M. on the 1st of January 1900 the enemy were found. The Canadians were on the right flank of the attack, and, like all the troops engaged, did excellently. Forty-two prisoners and the whole of the camp and its supplies were captured.

The two months spent on the lines were of the greatest value to the regiment. They were beside regular soldiers, they had military work, and the different ranks got to know one another. Without such knowledge *esprit de corps* cannot exist. When Lord Roberts was ready to start from the Modder he formed the 19th Brigade from the 2nd Battalion Duke of Cornwall's Light Infantry and the 2nd Battalion Shropshire Light Infantry, the 1st Battalion Gordon Highlanders, and the Royal Canadians. The first two named, like the last, had been on the lines. The Gordons had already fought at Magersfontein with Lord Methuen. The brigadier was Major-General Smith-Dorrien. The brigade formed part of the IXth Division under Major-General H. E. Colvile, the other brigade of the division being the Highland, so that the Canadians were in the best of company.

On the 13th a march of 15 miles from Gras Pan to Ramdam was done; on the 14th one of 12 to Waterval Drift on the Riet River. The Canadians gave valuable assistance in hauling the naval guns across the drift. Here the battalion was inspected and complimented by Lord Roberts. On the 14th and 15th the division moved north-east, Lord Roberts' intention being, apparently, to move it on Kimberley, skirting the left flank of Cronje's position at Magersfontein, as French with the cavalry had done. But on the 16th it was known that Cronje had left his fortress and was marching rapidly to the east. A force of mounted infantry, Kelly-Kenny's VIth Divi-

The Royal Canadian Regiment of Infantry

sion and Colvile's IXth Division, were at once hurried in pursuit, and French was ordered to leave Kimberley and head Cronje. The cavalry leader had been fighting all the 16th, but starting with Broadwood's Brigade on the 17th he was able to head the Boer waggons at Koedoesrand Drift on the Modder about mid-day, "G" and "P" batteries dropping some shells into the Boer column. French had, of course, to conceal the smallness of his force, and fortunately the enemy were too exhausted to make any great effort to ascertain or test his strength. That night Cronje might possibly have moved away, but he did not: next morning the VIth and IXth Divisions were ready to close with him. The Boer laager was on the north bank; French was on the same bank, but farther east; the British infantry were on the south bank. The river was flooded on the morning of the 18th, and it was 9 o'clock before General Colvile could get the 19th Brigade across the river to attack from the west and north-west. Kelly-Kenny's men were attacking from the south and south-east, Hannay's Mounted Infantry from the east, while the Highland Brigade, under General Hector MacDonald, were doing all that men could do to push in from the south-west. After crossing the Canadians were next the river, the Shropshire Light Infantry on their left, with the Gordons still farther to their left. The Cornwalls were in reserve. The Canadians were opposed by a force of Boers hidden and entrenched in the scrub by the river. Colonel Otter extended his regiment for the attack, "A" and "C" companies being the first firing line, but soon all the supports were pushed in. Major Buchan commanded the firing line. Nothing could have exceeded the gallantry of officers or men, and by all accounts all possible skill was exhibited, but the Boer fire was too powerful. Individuals got within 400 yards, but the line as a whole stuck outside that distance. During the forenoon some companies of the Black Watch and Seaforths also crossed the river and fought alongside the Canadians, but at no point of the huge crescent which the British formed could the troops get actually into the trenches. In the afternoon Lord Kitchener, who, according to various accounts, including that of the German staff, was somewhat impetuous and ill-timed in his orders, asked Colvile to make a more determined assault. The only troops available were the Cornwalls. Under Colonel Aldworth they, assisted by the other regiments, again charged the scrub, but without success. Colonel Aldworth was killed, and the battalion lost severely. On the 19th it was found the enemy had diminished his perimeter, withdrawing from the scrub he had held so tenaciously all the 18th. On the 16th to 18th the Canadians lost Captain H. M. Arnold (died of wounds), about 20 men killed, and Lieuts. J. C. Mason and Armstrong and about 70 men wounded.

Lord Roberts arrived on the 19th, and with that unfailing good judgment which he showed on every occasion decided that further assault was uncalled for. He ordered his force to sit down and bombard the enemy, advancing by spade work. On the night of the 21st the Shropshires made what General Colvile calls a fine advance, establishing themselves within 550 yards of the enemy, but further progress was found impossible without starting a new set of trenches.[1]

[1] 'The Work of the IXth Division,' by Sir H. E. Colvile. Arnold, London : 1901.

On the 22nd Lord Roberts wired to Lord Minto: "The Canadian Regiment has done admirable service since its arrival in South Africa. I deeply regret the heavy loss it suffered on the 18th, and beg that you will assure the people of Canada how much we all here admire the conspicuous gallantry displayed by our Canadian comrades on that occasion."

On the 26th General Colvile got Lord Roberts' sanction to try a fresh advance that night, and as it was the turn of the Canadians to occupy the trench it was theirs to do the rest. "A" Company was sent across the river to hold a post on the right of the advance. "B" Company was to hold the original or then existing trench. The remaining 6 companies under Lieut.-Colonel Buchan, at one pace interval between men, were to advance in two lines at 15 paces distance between the lines. When discovered the front rank was to lie down and fire, while a half company of the Royal Engineers and the rear rank dug. A party of Gordons with fixed bayonets were to support if necessary, but not to fire. The Shropshires, 2500 yards to the left, were to fire on the Boer trenches when the advance was discovered. The line, moving with wonderful silence, had got about 65 to 80 yards from the enemy's trenches when they were discovered, and the Boer fire broke out. The front rank lay down and returned the fire so well that the enemy shot wildly. The spademen worked like heroes, and when daylight came the Boers found a new trench practically commanding their own at 80 yards. Lord Roberts in his telegraphic despatch said: "At 3 A.M. to-day a most dashing advance was made by the Canadian Regiment and some Engineers, supported by the 1st Gordon Highlanders and 2nd Shropshire, resulting in our gaining a point some 600 yards nearer to the enemy, and within about 80 yards of his trenches, where our men entrenched themselves and maintained their positions till morning,—a gallant deed worthy of our Colonial comrades, and which I am glad to say was attended with comparatively small loss. This apparently clinched matters, for at daylight to-day a letter signed by General Cronje, in which he stated that he surrendered unconditionally, was brought to the outposts under a flag of truce." Without indulging in comparisons it seems to be admitted that the work of " G " and " H " Companies under Captains Macdonell and Stairs was superlatively fine; although it may be, as General Colvile points out, that the ground favoured these two companies.

This very telling incident put beyond all question the splendid military value of the Canadian Contingent. Their losses on the morning of the 27th were 8 non-commissioned officers and men killed, 1 officer, Major Pelletier, and 29 non-commissioned officers and men wounded.

During the remainder of the advance to Bloemfontein the IXth Division had comparatively little fighting to do.

When Lord Roberts commenced his northern advance the Division was broken up and the 19th Brigade was put under General Sir Ian Hamilton, as part of his army of the right flank.

At Yster Nek or Israel's Poort on the 25th April the enemy were found occupying a strong position. The Canadians and Grahamstown Volunteers (Marshall's Horse) advanced to about 800 yards, lay down under a heavy fire, and held the enemy in front while other troops worked round the flank. In the evening the

The Royal Canadian Regiment of Infantry 305

Boers fled. The Canadians and Marshall's Horse were praised by Major-General Smith-Dorrien and by Lord Roberts in his telegram of 27th April. The losses of the Canadians were few in number, but unfortunately Colonel Otter was wounded in the throat while steadying the fire-line at a critical point.

The regiment was present in the numerous other engagements which fell to the lot of Ian Hamilton's army on the way to Heilbron, and after he had crossed the front of Lord Roberts' army. At Doornkop or Florida, on 29th May, when the 1st Gordons added to their glorious reputation, the Canadians were in support and had some losses.

After Pretoria was occupied the regiment did not see a great deal of fighting. For a time they were garrison at Springs. In his telegram of 29th June Lord Roberts said that Springs was attacked on the morning of the 28th, and that the Canadian Regiment, which garrisoned the place, beat off the enemy. After De Wet broke out of the Wittebergen or Brandwater Basin, about 16th July, they were moved down the line to take part in an attempt to surround De Wet. Thereafter in August under General Hart they took part in the pursuit of that ever elusive foe, and did some very trying marches on the north side of the Vaal.

The brigade having been broken up at Krugersdorp, the Canadian regiment was taken back to the east of Pretoria. On 26th September Lord Roberts telegraphed, "17 officers and 319 men of the Royal Canadian Regiment left Pretoria this morning *en route* to Canada." But in his telegram of 25th October in regard to the ceremony of proclaiming the annexation of the Transvaal, Lord Roberts was able to say, "The Colonies were represented by the Royal Canadian Regiment, the New Zealand Mounted Infantry, the Bodyguard, Roberts' Horse, and various details." It was satisfactory that a substantial portion of the regiment were still in South Africa when the interesting ceremony took place.

CANADIAN MOUNTED RIFLES AND ROYAL CANADIAN DRAGOONS.

ON 7th November 1899 the Dominion offered a second contingent, but the War Office did not accept this offer until after the defeats of Magersfontein and Colenso. Preparations, however, had been going on, and when the acceptance arrived, the Canadian Government announced that its second contribution would be two battalions of Mounted Rifles,[1] 2 squadrons each, and three batteries field artillery, 6 guns each. The 1st Battalion M.R. was mainly officered from the permanent cavalry, and the second from the North-West Mounted Police. Of the artillery the officers, to the extent of a half, came from the permanent artillery. These troops sailed in three different vessels, and arrived at South Africa in February and March 1900.

Early in March the 2nd M.R. and "D" and "E"

[1] The title of the 1st Battalion M.R. was on 27th August 1900 changed to Royal Canadian Dragoons, and the 2nd M.R. became the Canadian Mounted Rifles, 1st Regiment.

Batteries became a portion of the Carnarvon Field Force under Sir C. Parsons which undertook an expedition into the Carnarvon-Douglas district, where rebels were giving much trouble. This service did not involve severe fighting, but the force covered 700 miles under conditions more severe than any subsequently met with.[1] The rebellion was for the time put down and the force came into De Aar in April, and the same month the two battalions of M.R. were ordered to Bloemfontein, where they joined the main army and formed part of Major-General Hutton's force of Colonial Mounted Infantry, which, under the direction of General French, swung out far on the left in the advance to Pretoria. Before that advance commenced the 1st C.M.R. had been engaged on 22nd, 23rd, and 24th April 1900 at Leeuwkop, south-east of Bloemfontein, and were said to have done well. The 2nd Battalion got back to De Aar on 14th April, and reached Bloemfontein on the 29th, just in time to take part in the advance to Pretoria.

In Lord Roberts' despatch of 21st May 1900 an account is given of the operations between his leaving Bloemfontein, 3rd May, and taking Kroonstad, 12th May. At para. 15, referring to the crossing of the Vet River, which was held by the enemy in force, his lordship says: "Just before dark the mounted infantry executed a turning movement, crossing the river six miles west of the railway bridge, which, like other bridges over the river along our line of advance, had been previously destroyed by the enemy. In this affair the Canadian, New South Wales, and New Zealand Mounted Infantry, and the Queensland

[1] Sessional paper 35th Department of Militia of Dominion, containing reports by commanders of Mounted Rifles and Artillery.

Mounted Rifles, vied with each other in their efforts to close with the enemy. We captured one maxim gun and twenty-six prisoners, our losses being slight." In these operations two companies of the Canadian M.R. under Lieutenants Borden and Turner crossed the river at a part where there was no ford, and established themselves on the north bank. The New South Wales men, supported by New Zealanders and Queenslanders, seized and crossed the main drift, and drove back the Boer rear-guard by a vigorous attack. After dark Captain Macdonald and one squadron C.M.R. rode through the Boer outpost lines and cut a telegraph wire to the north.

The crossing of the Zand was also opposed, and Hutton's 1st Mounted Infantry Brigade again had hard riding to do a wide turning movement.

In his telegram of 18th May Lord Roberts said: "Hutton's Mounted Infantry yesterday surprised and captured, about 30 miles north-west of Kroonstad, Commandant Botha and 23 Boers. No casualties on our side." There were other frequent references to the very fine work of Major-General Hutton and his Colonial Mounted Infantry.

The Vaal was crossed with little opposition, but the enemy took up a series of very strong positions to oppose the left flank of the British. French and Hutton had hard fighting 26th to 30th May, and the infantry had to be called upon to clear the kopjes at Doornkop. The Canadian M.R. had slight casualties on various occasions between 27th and 30th May. After Pretoria was occupied Hutton's men were chiefly posted north and east of the capital and frequently had fighting. They were heavily engaged on the British left at Diamond Hill, 11th and 12th June.

The casualty list showed that Captain A. C. Macdonald and 3 men of the 2nd C.M.R. were wounded.

On 18th June Lieutenant Young of the 1st Battalion M.R., with 12 Canadians and 3 Rimington's Guides, was sent out to reconnoitre. The small party took 40 prisoners, and having noticed marks of gun wheels, they boldly followed these up. The two guns were found; some oxen were captured and yoked to the guns, and although fired upon, the party were successful in returning to camp with their prisoners, the guns, and oxen. The small detachment received great credit, and Lieutenant Young and Sergeants Purdon and Ryan were specially mentioned by Lord Roberts.

From 15th June to 15th July the 2nd C.M.R. were employed, and saw some fighting, in the Orange River Colony, where, with other troops, they shared the all-important task of guarding the line, chiefly between Vereeniging and Kroonstad, at a time when the enemy was making great efforts to hamper Lord Roberts by cutting the communications. On 15th June Lieutenant L. Blanchard died at Kroonstad of wounds received. On the 22nd Lieutenant W. M. Ingles was wounded, and 2 men killed and 3 wounded, in an attack on a post at Honingspruit. Other posts were attacked on the same day, and at Katabosch 2 men were killed and several wounded. The defenders of these posts behaved with the greatest gallantry, and their conduct was praised by Lord Roberts in a telegram to Lord Minto. On 15th July the 2nd C.M.R. rejoined Hutton's Brigade and with him took part in the eastern advance.

On 6th and 7th July Colonel Mahon was attacked south-east of Irene, and Major-General Hutton had to reinforce him. The enemy, about 3000 strong with six guns, fought with determination, but were driven off.

Between the 6th and 11th part of Hutton's line was "practically surrounded and worried by enemy for six days."[1] In these engagements the 1st C.M.R. had Adjutant Nelles and 6 men wounded. Within a day or two Hutton was again attacked, and again repulsed the enemy. On this occasion Lieutenant Young, who had so distinguished himself three weeks before, was wounded. On the 11th Hutton made a "successful advance."

In Lord Roberts' telegram of 17th July he said: "Yesterday the enemy made a determined attack on the left of Pole Carew's position and along our left flank commanded by Hutton. The posts held by the Royal Irish Fusiliers under Major Munn, New Zealand Mounted Infantry under Captain Vaughan, and Canadian M.R. under Colonel Alderson were most gallantly defended." Among the casualties were—"1st Canadian M.R., Lieutenants H. Borden and J. Burch, killed." In his telegram of the 18th Lord Roberts said, "The two young Canadian officers mentioned in my telegram of yesterday were killed while gallantly leading their men in a counter-attack on the enemy's flank at a critical juncture of their assault on our position. Lieutenant Borden, only son of the Minister of Militia of Canada, had been twice before brought to my notice in despatches for gallant and intrepid conduct." The news of Lieutenant Borden's death caused a widespread feeling of sorrow in the Dominion. Both the 1st and 2nd Battalions were with Hutton in the fighting of 16th July.

On 17th July Colonel Reeves, commanding 2nd Royal Irish Fusiliers, wrote most highly complimenting the 1st C.M.R. for their gallantry "in going so nobly

[1] Reports by commanders already referred to.

and fearlessly to the succour of our beleaguered detachment at Witpoort yesterday."

On 24th July Lord Roberts' army took another step farther east, reaching Bronkhorst Spruit. Alderson's Brigade, including the Canadians, were far out on the right, and were in contact with the retiring enemy all day. The pursuit was continued on the 25th, the night of which was memorable for its wildness. So terrible was the driving rain and cold wind that very many transport animals died. Middelburg was occupied on the 27th. In August the advance was resumed, and the Canadian M.R. again had important duties. On 5th September a detachment of 105 men of the 2nd M.R. was guarding the line between Pan and Wonderfontein. They were attacked by the enemy with two guns and a pom-pom. Before the arrival of assistance, the party had succeeded in driving off the Boers. Major Sanders, Lieutenant Moodie, and 2 men were wounded, and 6 men taken prisoners. Lord Roberts, in his telegram of 5th September, characterised the repulse of the attack as a very creditable performance.

General Hutton's Brigade having been broken up, he issued a farewell order which was most flattering to the regulars and to all the Colonials who had served under him. He spoke of their "steadiness under fire, gallantry in the field, and uniform good conduct in camp." General Hutton also wrote to Colonel Lessard as to the fine work of the regiment, and added: "Nothing can be more certain than the impossibility of raising militia cavalry to the standard of regular cavalry; but it has been demonstrated and clearly proved that, organised as mounted rifles, our Colonies can put into the field a force of the utmost value. I devoutly hope that this fact will be brought home, not only to every man in the Dominion Militia Cavalry, but also to the Canadian people and Canadian public opinion. . . . It has been a constant pleasure to me to note how excellently your regiment has profited by its opportunities, and what real good service it has performed."

In October and November 1900 Colonel Lessard, with both battalions of the M.R. and two guns "D" Battery Canadian Artillery, were in a force operating under Major-General Smith-Dorrien from Belfast. On 2nd November the General moved out in two columns to attack a Boer encampment near Van Wyk's Vlei; but on account of a very severe rainstorm the attack had to be abandoned, and on the way back to Belfast the enemy assumed the offensive with the greatest vigour, coming up to within fifty yards of the flank and rear-guards. The Canadians particularly distinguished themselves. In his telegram of 5th November Lord Roberts said: "Smith-Dorrien reports that Major Sanders and Captain Chalmers of the Canadian M.R. behaved with great gallantry in the rear-guard action on November 2. The former rode under heavy and close fire to bring in a sergeant who had lost his horse. As the two were riding back together on Sanders' horse it was killed. Sanders was wounded. Chalmers went to his assistance. Sanders implored him to leave him. This Chalmers would not do, and the gallant fellow was, I grieve to say, killed."

On 6th November at 3.30 A.M. Smith-Dorrien again set out. About 8 o'clock fighting commenced; the enemy were driven back, but took up a very strong position on the Komati River. "Here they made a determined stand, and it was not till 4 P.M. that a wide turning movement brought the 1st Battalion Suffolk Regiment and the Royal Canadian Dragoons (1st C.M.R.) on the Boers' flank, and forced them to withdraw across the river towards Carolina. . . . On the following day Smith-Dorrien started to march in an easterly direction. Observing this, several hundred Boers at once galloped back to seize their position of the previous day, but were forestalled by Lieutenant-Colonel Evans and the Royal Canadian Dragoons and a section of the 84th Battery R.F.A., who, by going at full speed for two miles, succeeded in seizing the key of the position and in holding about 300 of the enemy in the bed of the river, while the 5-in. guns did good execution among masses of the Boers in the open. As it now became evident that the enemy had received large reinforcements after the engagement of the previous day, Smith-Dorrien directed Lieutenant-Colonel Spens, commanding the advance-guard, to secure the high ground near Van Wyk's Vlei, which was done by the 5th Lancers. Colonel Lessard, with the Royal Canadian Artillery under Lieutenant Morrison, with great gallantry covered the rear of the force against the enemy's close attack. About 2 P.M. some 200 Boers suddenly charged our rear-guard, and without dismounting fired wildly, coming to within seventy yards of the dismounted Dragoons. Not succeeding in this attempt on our rear-guard, the Boers then threatened us on both flanks in large numbers. Our guns were, however, so ably handled that they prevented them coming to close quarters and caused them to retire. Our casualties were 2 killed and 12 wounded, including Lieutenants Elmsley, Turner, and Cockburn, all of the Canadians. The Boers suffered very heavy losses. Amongst the killed were Commandant H. Prinsloo and

General Fourie, and amongst the wounded General John Grobelaar."[1] In his telegram of 8th November as to this affair, Lord Roberts most highly praised the conduct of the Canadians. Sergeant D. Builder, returned as wounded, died of his wounds within a few days. Lieutenant H. C. Z. Cockburn, Lieutenant R. E. W. Turner, and Sergeant E. Holland, all Canadians, were each awarded the Victoria Cross. Lieutenant Cockburn, at a critical moment, with a handful of men held off the Boers to allow the guns to get away. To do so he had to sacrifice himself and his party, all of whom were killed, wounded, or taken prisoners. Later in the day, when the Boers again threatened seriously to capture the guns, Lieutenant Turner, although twice previously wounded, dismounted and deployed his men at close quarters, and drove off the Boers, thus saving the guns. Sergeant Holland did splendid work with his Colt gun, and kept the Boers off the 12-pounders by its fire at close range. When he saw that the enemy were too near to allow him to escape with the carriage, he calmly lifted the gun off and galloped away with it under his arm.

That one small corps gained three Victoria Crosses in one engagement is a most worthy cause for pride, and the announcement did send a thrill through the Dominion.

On 20th November 1900 General Smith-Dorrien issued a complimentary order on the occasion of the Royal Canadian Dragoons and C.M.R. leaving his force. He used these words: " He can merely say he would choose no other mounted troops in the world if he had his choice." Brigadier-General Alderson also wrote in a letter to Colonel Lessard: " The more I get

[1] Lord Roberts' despatch of 15th November 1900.

to know the 1st C.M.R. (I must call them by the name I know them best by) the better I like them. . . . We in the regular army are brought up with cut-and-dried ideas and red tape, and I should like to say how much I appreciate the ready way in which those of your people who have not been so brought up have fallen in with my ways."

The regiment had marched more than 1700 miles and had fought on 44 days.

CANADIAN SCOUTS.

TOWARDS the close of 1900 and throughout 1901 Canada was represented at the front by a corps known as the Canadian Scouts, commanded by Major Howard. In December 1900 they were with General Alderson west of Pretoria, and immediately gained the confidence of their leaders, and were given the difficult task of scouting in front of the brigade. In January, February, and March 1901 they trekked with General Alderson through the Eastern Transvaal, his column being one of those which General French led to the Swazi border in a great sweeping movement, when practically all the enemy's artillery was captured. In Lieutenant Moeller's 'Two Years at the Front,' page 153, he says: "26th January 1901—Object of trek. We formed part of a big movement south to Ermelo to drive Boers east. We are one of six columns. Our force consists of the 14th Mounted Infantry (regulars), 400 men, Major Heigham; 13th Mounted Infantry (regulars), 300 men, Major Pratt; Canadian Scouts, 50 men, Major Howard; Canadian pom-pom, Lieutenant Hilton; Colonel Jenner, D.S.O., Colt guns, 6; 'J' Battery, 6 guns; 'G' Battery, 2 guns, Captain Sykes; battalion King's Own Yorkshire Light Infantry, 800—all under General Alderson." As appears from Lieutenant Moeller's Diary, the Canadian Scouts were constantly in the very front, and of course they had to pay the price; indeed on the following day, 27th January, he records that 2 scouts were killed. These were Sergeant-Major D. J. M'Gregor and Sergeant D. B. Hammond. Sergeant W. S. Gordon was wounded. All three had served with 'C' Battery Canadian Artillery. On the 28th Lieutenant Moeller remarks: "The Canadian Scouts are first-rate, and my men are doing well. 29th—A somewhat exciting incident occurred. Davidson, one of the Canadians, about 2500 yards ahead, was suddenly confronted with four Boers, one of whom demanded his surrender. He replied by shooting the man and killing him on the spot; the other three legged it." Under the 31st he says: "My skipper, King, captain in Canadian Dragoons, and a colonel, is a sterling good fellow and a first-rate soldier; all the Colonials indeed are splendid and real good fighters; most interesting too. Major Gat-Howard, who is in command of them, is a Yankee, and went all through the American War. He has seen much service with Red Indians, and is a typical scout leader." On 4th February Sergeant-Major J. A. Patterson was killed, and Sergeants H. Bredin, A. B. Cradock, and E. W. Muncey were wounded. The first two had served with the Mounted Rifles and Muncey with the Canadian Artillery. Under February 5th Moeller says: "To-day I got the billet I like, support to the Canadian Scouts.

February 8th — I met Callaghan,[1] officer, Canadian Scouts; Davis, Canadian Scout, and really a Red Indian; and another, who rode forty miles through the Boers with despatches from Kitchener, viâ French and Alderson, to Smith-Dorrien. They had a marvellous ride; one had to bury the despatches and dodge the Boers. Davis, the Redskin, was taken prisoner, but escaped by shooting several Boers with his revolver. At night Callaghan dug up the despatches and got them in safe. It reads like 'Fenimore Cooper.' I have no time to write details, but it was a wonderfully exciting ride. February 17th, Derby—Stood to arms at 3 A.M.; orders to go out at 6 A.M. east, then proceed south-east towards Swaziland border to round up 200 or 300 Boers shut up in the hills with their waggons. The force consisted of 14th Mounted Infantry (Captain Brass), 13th Mounted Infantry (Major Pratt), 4 guns 'J' Battery (Captain Sykes), 2 Colt guns, Canadian Scouts (Captain Ross)—all under Major Gat-Howard, Royal Canadians. Singular that a British force should be commanded by a semi-American officer. There is a cold drizzling rain, and it is very misty. We started at 8.30 A.M. I was support to scouts and advanced guard. Trekked eight miles east and southeast, and halted in the hills owing to the rain and thick white mist. Dick's force is also moving, as well as Campbell and Smith-Dorrien. Objective of all, to round up these Boers and waggons. Waited till 3 P.M. Still misty. Suddenly the scouts moved forward at a trot, and I followed on their heels. It is an extraordinarily difficult country, with its hills, valleys,

---

[1] Mr Callaghan's thirst for adventure and dangerous enterprise was not satiated in South Africa. In the Russo-Japanese war he obtained employment with the Japs as an officer in command of a body of scouts.

and deep gorges. Heard rifle-fire and Mausers going off, so pushed forward, dismounted my men and again pushed forward; found Canadians holding a rocky ridge immediately in front of a huge kopje, which was steep and covered with bush. In the valley were four Boer waggons; pushed on and joined them. I am sorry to say Major Howard and his orderly were found killed, and a native scout shot. Poor Major Howard no doubt met his death by going too far ahead alone. He spotted the waggons, went to them, and got shot. A little later I heard that he actually surrendered and the Boers shot him afterwards. He was hit in three places—arm, jaw, and stomach—all expanding cartridges. His orderly had a terrible wound through the back and stomach. Well, we burnt all the waggons, put the two dead men in sheets, and sent for an ambulance. I only saw the major in the morning, and he gave me all instructions about following his scouts up. He was fifty-five yesterday; a splendid scout and soldier, his one and only fault being his daring, if it can be called a fault. Beattie, the General's A.D.C., was the first to find them. He had his horse shot, and had a narrow escape as well, as they were potting at him at 200 and 300 yards. Major Pratt took the command, and sent back word that we were to retire as soon as we could, as it was getting dark, besides being more misty. The fact is that Major Howard and his orderly were foully murdered after surrendering and laying down their arms."[1] On 16th February the Scouts had Sergeant F. C. A. Douglas mortally wounded, and Sergeant G. L. Abbott and Sergeant Carter wounded; on the 18th Major Howard and Sergeant Northway,

[1] Of course this was only a hastily formed opinion. If Lieut. Moeller had lived to revise his proofs he might have modified it.

who had served with the Mounted Rifles, killed. As will have been seen, the casualties among the senior non-commissioned officers on this trek were most severe, and out of all proportion to the losses of the column, which were otherwise almost none. The fact was that the Canadian Scouts had undertaken extremely dangerous work, and had done it so thoroughly that their self-sacrifice saved all their comrades.

Major Ross got the command of the Scouts on Major Howard's death, and they continued to do splendidly under their new leader.

The extracts given above are the words, not written for publication, of a British officer of great insight and intelligence, and no better proof could be wanted of the value of the Canadian Scouts. Lieutenant Moeller was himself to fall in the same Eastern Transvaal on 18th December 1901. His Diary is one of the most valuable war books yet published.

The Canadian Scouts were with Colonel Hackett-Thompson's column in the Megaliesberg for part of the year 1901. In July they joined a column then being organised at Heilbron under Colonel Rimington, and in the war record of that leader's regiment, the Inniskilling Dragoons, there are many references to the fine work of the Canadian Scouts. The column did an immense lot of driving work in the north-east of the Orange River Colony. Under the 3rd New South Wales Mounted Rifles some extracts from the Inniskillings' record are given. These show the nature and great value of the work done by Rimington's force. In February 1902 the Scouts suffered casualties in the Orange River Colony on various occasions; 5 were wounded on the 9th. In April they were taken to the Transvaal and did more heavy work there. On 3rd May 1 was killed and Lieutenant J. M'Dougall and 3 men were wounded in the Balmoral district. In Lord Kitchener's despatch of 8th April 1902 he referred to the great drives in which Rimington's column took a most prominent share. After mentioning the captures, Lord Kitchener said: "In addition to this Major Ross of the Canadian Scouts, belonging to Rimington's column, had discovered in a cave near Tafel Kop a large Boer depot containing 300,000 rounds of small-arm ammunition, mostly Martini-Henry, also 10,000 Lee-Metford, some Krupp and 15-pounder shells and fuzes, 600 pom-pom shells, 200 lb. of powder, one maxim gun complete," &c.

2ND REGIMENT CANADIAN MOUNTED RIFLES.

On 25th November 1901 it was announced that the Imperial Government had accepted the offer, made by Canada, of a force of 600 mounted men. Recruiting at once commenced, and on 14th January 1902 470 men sailed on the *Manhattan*, the remainder embarking on the *Victorian* about the 28th, making a contingent of six squadrons. A field hospital accompanied the contingent. The total strength sent was nearly 900.

On arrival in South Africa the regiment, which was commanded by Colonel Evans, was taken to the Western Transvaal, where Lord Methuen had met with serious reverses shortly before, and they were employed under Major-General Walter Kitchener and Lieut.-General Ian Hamilton. On 31st March 1902 Major-General

2nd Regiment Canadian Mounted Rifles

Kitchener had sent forward two columns, those of Colonel Keir and Colonel Cookson, with the latter of whom were the newly arrived Canadian M.R., Damant's Horse, and two squadrons of Yeomanry. At Brakspruit Colonel Cookson, after being engaged with the enemy, decided to halt, entrench, and close up his baggage. In his despatch of 8th April 1902 Lord Kitchener said: "At 1.20 P.M. the enemy opened fire with three guns and a pom-pom, and then under cover of their artillery attempted to rush the eastern side of the camp." After very heavy fighting the enemy withdrew. Lord Kitchener adds: "The heaviest loss in this engagement fell upon the Canadian Mounted Rifles, who, in this, their first fight of importance since landing, displayed the utmost bravery and determination. Lieutenant Bruce Carruthers of the regiment especially distinguished himself. Being in command of a detachment of the rear-guard, when coming into camp he remained out in a position of observation, in which he eventually found himself isolated and surrounded by a large body of the enemy. Rejecting all idea of surrender, however, his small patrol of 21 men fought stubbornly on to the end, no less than six of their number, including Lieutenant Carruthers, being killed and 12 wounded. There have been few finer instances of heroism in the whole course of the campaign. The Boers who took part in this unsuccessful attack upon Colonel Cookson's camp were estimated to have numbered 1800 men, and were under the command of Generals Delarey and Kemp." In this action, generally referred to in the despatches and elsewhere as that of Boschbult, the Canadians lost Lieutenant Carruthers and 11 men killed, and Captain F. S. M. Howard and Lieutenants R. H. Ryan, G. B. Mackay, R. F. Markham, and A. T. London, and 42 men wounded. Major Evans wired to the Minister of Militia of Canada: "The regiment and field hospital have undergone severe test, and have acquitted themselves most creditably. I regret the heavy losses." Lord Roberts telegraphed his congratulations to the Governor - General as well as to South Africa.

The regiment took part in the last great drives between the Klerksdorp blockhouse line and the railway running from Kimberley and Vryburg to Mafeking. In these drives many prisoners were taken.

In addition to the contingents already mentioned, it should be borne in mind that Canada sent, in March and April 1901, 1238 officers and men to South Africa for the South African Constabulary (see evidence of Major-General O'Grady-Haly before the War Commission). Many of these had belonged to the Royal Canadian Regiment of Infantry or to the first contingent of mounted men. Further, on 18th March, Mr Chamberlain having intimated that assistance to the extent of 2000 men would be accepted, Canada in response despatched, in the beginning of May 1902, another immense force—namely, the 3rd, 4th, 5th, and 6th regiments of Mounted Rifles, each 509 strong. These arrived in South Africa just after peace was declared. Probably the fact that they were on the sea did help towards the attainment of the desired end.

CANADIAN ARTILLERY.

CANADA furnished three batteries of artillery, "C," "D," and "E," of six guns each.[1]

"C" arrived at the Cape about the end of March 1900, and, while still encamped at Stellenbosch, on 14th April they received orders to march back to Cape Town. Starting in the evening, the 33 miles were covered in a night, and by 12 noon on the 15th they had re-embarked on the *Columbian*, *en route* for Mafeking *viâ* Beira and Bulawayo. After a week at sea the battery landed at Beira, and there entrained for Marandellas. Thence to Bulawayo the *personnel* travelled on coaches, and the guns were hauled by mules, changed at posting depots, between 60 and 100 miles being covered each day. From Bulawayo to Ootsi the journey was accomplished by train, the latter town being reached on the 12th May, in seven days from Marandellas. By forced marches the battery covered the remaining 70 miles and joined Colonel Plumer on the 15th. On that date Plumer, from the north, and Mahon, from the south, joined hands, and on the 16th (see Imperial Light Horse) the combined force fought the stiffly contested action west of Mafeking which opened the gates of the town and raised a siege which had engrossed the attention of the British Empire for seven months. The officers of "C" Battery were Major Hudson, Captain Panet, and Lieutenants King and Leslie.

Colonel Mahon in his report said that the battery,

[1] See p. 351 of 'War Commission,' Major-General O'Grady-Haly's evidence.

by a series of forced marches, reached him on the morning of the fighting, and rendered very valuable assistance; and Colonel Baden-Powell, speaking of this, said they had joined "with incredible rapidity." To the Canadian Government the latter officer sent a telegram: "Mafeking relieved to-day, and most grateful for invaluable assistance of Canadian Artillery, which made record march from Beira to help us."[1]

The battery operated with Colonel Plumer after the relief while he was looking after the repair of the railway from the north, and towards the end of May was part of the force which he led to Zeerust, and thence farther east. They were in action on the following occasions: Olifant's Nek, 19th-25th July; Haman's Kraal, 20th August; Pienaar's River, 21st; Warmbad, 22nd; Nylstroom, 24th; Warmbad, 3rd-10th September; Jericho, 24th October; Twee River, 1st November; and at three places in the Zeerust district on the 4th, 6th, and 8th of that month.

"D" and "E" Batteries arrived at Cape Town on the *Laurentian* on 17th February 1900, and in the beginning of March were sent north to form part of a column which Lord Roberts arranged should operate from Victoria West under Colonel Sir C. Parsons. The district west of the railway was at the time very seriously disaffected, and quite unsafe for loyal farmers. It was therefore necessary to overawe the rebels. The column, which included the 2nd Canadian M.R., some West Australian and New Zealand M.R., and some Imperial Yeomanry, marched through the Kenhardt district, doing about 700 miles in six weeks. There was practically no fighting, but much hardship. It

[1] 'The Canadian Contingents,' by W. S. Evans, 1901.

was expected that a want of water would be a serious trouble, but for weeks the rain poured heavily, often making the rivers barely passable. About the middle of April the column was back on the railway near De Aar. The training during these six weeks of actual war service, although without serious fighting, was invaluable to every unit in the column.

In May Sir Charles Warren was again operating west of the railway against rebels, the area of his work being north of that gone over by Sir C. Parsons. On the night of 29th May Sir C. Warren's force, which included "E" Battery, was most fiercely attacked at Faber's Put near Campbell (see Duke of Edinburgh's Volunteers). After a trying fight the enemy were driven off. Sir C. Warren praised his troops very highly, and among those specially mentioned in his despatch of 29th June 1900 were the names of Major Ogilvie and Captain Mackie of "E" Battery. The battery had 1 killed and 8 wounded. After the engagement Warren operated northwards, and came into the line at Kimberley towards the end of June 1900. "E" Battery was then split up into sections to defend or work from posts on the Kimberley-Mafeking Railway.

"D" Battery remained on the Kimberley-De Aar line till July 1900, when they were entrained for Bloemfontein, and after a short time in that neighbourhood were railed to Pretoria. Here they joined Hickman's mounted column, which, with the infantry brigade of General Cunningham, was to operate under Ian Hamilton. The battery saw much hard marching and fighting in the Transvaal.[1] For example, in the march to Lydenburg "D" Battery had six days'

[1] Lord Roberts' despatch of 10th October 1900, para. 33.

fighting, and in October and November they were in action on twenty-two days, chiefly under General Smith-Dorrien.[1] As has already been mentioned under the Mounted Rifles, "D" Battery had two guns in the force of Brigadier-General Smith-Dorrien in the very severe fighting on 2nd and 6th November 1900.

About 80 of the *personnel* of the Canadian Artillery remained in South Africa until June 1901, serving eighteen months.

Apart from the V.C.'s already noted, the Mentions gained by the Canadian contingents, exclusive of Lord Strathcona's Corps, were as follows :—

LORD ROBERTS' DESPATCHES : 31*st March* 1900.—Major S. Dennison,[2] Royal Canadian Regiment, aide-de-camp ; Lieut.-Col. W. D. Otter,[3] Major L. Buchan,[2] Major O. C. C. Pelletier ; Capt. H. B. Stairs ; Capt. and Adjt. A. H. Macdonell ; Sgt. Utton ; Ptes. J. Kennedy, H. Andrews, J. H. Dickson, C. W. Duncafe, F. C. Page.

2*nd April* 1901. — Royal Canadian Dragoons — Lieut.-Cols. T. D. B. Evans,[3] F. L. Lessard[2] ; Lieut. R. E. W. Turner[4] ; Ptes. W. A. Knisley,[5] L. W. R. Molloy.[5] Artillery—Col. C. W. Drury[3] ; Majors Houdin,[2] G. Ogilvie ; Surgeon-Major A. N. Worthington ; Capt. H. A. Panet[4] ; Lieut. L. E. W. Irving[4] ; Battery Sgt.-Major W. H. Grimlett[5] ; Gunner Laidlaw.[5] Royal Canadian Regiment—Col. W. D. Otter[3] ; Lieut.-Col. L. Buchan[2] ; Major Dennison[2] ; Captain A. H. Macdonell[4] ; Lieut. J. H. J. Ogilvie,[4] adjt. ; Ptes. J. Kennedy,[5] J. Landen,[5] Crooke, R. R. Thomson. Mounted Infantry—Tpr. Waite.[5] Mounted Rifles—Capt. A. C. Macdonald[4] ; Lieuts. H. Davidson, A. L. Howard, W. M. Inglis, F. Young.; Regl. Sgt.-Major Church ; Sgt. R. H. Ryan ; Cpls. T. Callaghan,[5] T. R. Miles,[5] F. W. Whitlow ; Tpr. Crawley[5] ; Ptes. T. Kerr (killed), S. E. Morrison, Hammond, Miles.

In Lord Roberts' supplementary despatch of 1st March 1902 he announced that one of the four scarves worked by her late Majesty for presentation to private soldiers of the Colonies had been allotted to Private (since promoted lieutenant) Richard Roland Thompson, Royal Canadian Regiment.

SIR C. WARREN'S DESPATCH : 30*th May* 1900.—Col. Hughes, Major Ogilvie, Surgeon-Major Worthington. In this despatch Capt. Mackie,

---

[1] Sessional Papers, Department of Militia and Defence of Canada.
[2] Awarded C.M.G.   [3] Awarded C.B.
[4] Awarded D.S.O.   [5] Awarded D.C.M.

Canadian Artillery 327

Royal Canadian Artillery, was also mentioned under the heading "Warren's Scouts," a small body which Capt. Mackie at that time commanded.

LORD ROBERTS' DESPATCH: *4th September* 1901.—Royal Canadian Regiment — Major R. Cartwright,[1] Capt. Stairs, Lt. J. G. Mason.[2] Royal Canadian Dragoons—Majors Williams and Forester. Mounted Rifles—Major G. E. Sanders,[2] Lt. H. L. Borden (killed). Artillery—Lt. E. W. B. Morrison.[2]

LORD KITCHENER'S DESPATCHES: *8th May* 1901. — Lts. Borden and Chalmers (both killed), brought to notice for gallantry in action and stubborn fighting. Major A. L. Howard,[2] Scouts, repeatedly brought to notice for gallantry. Mounted Rifles—Cpl. Morden, killed on outpost duty whilst with five men holding off a large body of enemy. Sgt. Builder, killed whilst bringing in guns near Belfast.

8th December 1901.—Scouts—Tpr. George, at Zusterhoek, 21st October, returned for wounded man under close fire and brought him out to safety; second time brought to notice within three months. Sgt.-Major Wilkins, same action, excellent work with pom-poms under heavy fire; previously mentioned. Sgt.-Major Forrest, for good work with Colt Gun Section under heavy fire, same action.

8th March 1902.—Scouts—Pte. D. MacIntyre, promoted Cpl., conspicuous dash on several occasions. Capt. T. H. A. Williams, conspicuous good service, December and January.

LORD ROBERTS' DESPATCH: *1st March* 1902.—Mounted Rifles—Tpr. E. F. Waldie. Canadian Regiment—Surgeon Lieut.-Col. Fiset,[2] M.D., Capt. H. E. Burstall.

LORD KITCHENER'S DESPATCHES: *1st June* 1902.—Scouts—Cpl. E. C. Pearce, promoted Sgt., for gallantry, 4th April. Mounted Rifles—Surgeon-Major J. A. Devine,[2] for good service at Boschbult, 31st March 1902. Lt. Bruce Carruthers, in command of a detached party, fought till all were either killed or wounded. Cpl. J. A. Wilkinson, promoted Sgt., Lce.-Cpl. J. C. Bond, Pte. G. Beth, promoted Cpls., part of above party specially noticeable in rallying the troop. Pte. P. H. Kelly, promoted Cpl., for specially good work as hospital orderly under heavy fire. Sgt. J. C. Perry (killed), good service at Boschbult. Pte. C. N. Evans (killed), after being mortally wounded fired two bandoliers of ammunition and then broke his rifle to prevent it falling into enemy's hands. Sgt. H. A. Lee, twice tried to carry despatch through enemy's lines under heavy and close fire.

23rd June.—Lieut.-Col. T. D. B. Evans, C.B., Capt. T. H. Callaghan, Lts. R. H. Ryan, F. Church, Adjt., Squadron Sgt.-Major Docherty, Staff-Sgt. D. Forster-Bliss,[3] R. G. Dale.[3] Scouts—Major Ross, D.S.O., Capts. Macmillan,[2] Williams, Sgt.-Major Stallwood,[3] Regimental Qrmr.-Sgt. Sanders, Pte. A. Chesworth. Sister Miss G. Pope, the Royal Red Cross.

---

[1] Awarded C.M.G.   [2] Awarded D.S.O.   [3] Awarded D.C.M.

LORD STRATHCONA'S CORPS.

On 11th January 1900 Lord Strathcona offered "to equip and land at Cape Town, at his own expense, 500 Rough-riders from the Canadian North-West, as a special service corps of Mounted Rifles. Two days later his offer was accepted by the Secretary of State for War."[1]

On 16th March the force embarked 28 officers, 512 of other ranks, with 599 horses, 3 maxims, 1 pom-pom, 500 rounds per rifle and 50,000 rounds for each maxim. A more munificent offer has seldom been made by a subject to his country.

The regiment landed at Cape Town on 10th April. Unfortunately nearly 200 horses had been lost at sea, an unusually large proportion. After about five weeks impatiently spent near Cape Town, the force again re-embarked for Natal; two squadrons were put off at Durban and one, "B," was taken to Kosi Bay as part of an expedition into Swaziland, but this did not come off; perhaps the enemy was found to have heard of it. "B" squadron came back to Durban. In June the corps was taken by rail to Newcastle and joined General Buller's army, being put into the 3rd Mounted Brigade under Lord Dundonald, and attached for the time to General Clery's Division. On 1st July they had, near Waterval on the Natal-Pretoria Railway, the first of many skirmishes, and suffered their first losses in action. That week they were engaged on several occasions, having altogether about 15 casualties. In one of these little actions Sergeant A. H. L. Richardson

[1] Evans' 'Canadian Contingents,' p. 153.

gained the Victoria Cross. "On 5th July at Wolve Spruit, about 15 miles north of Standerton, a party of Lord Strathcona's Corps, only 38 in number, came into contact, and was engaged at close quarters, with a force of 80 of the enemy. When the order to retire had been given Sgt. Richardson rode back under a very heavy cross-fire and picked up a trooper whose horse had been shot and who was wounded in two places, and rode with him out of fire. At the time when this act of gallantry was performed Sgt. Richardson was within 300 yards of the enemy, and was himself riding a wounded horse."

General Buller did the regiment honour by asking them to provide 150 men as escort to himself to Heidelberg, on his way to Pretoria to meet Lord Roberts.

As a result of the conference between these leaders General Buller shortly commenced preparations for moving northwards across the Eastern Transvaal, so as to meet and co-operate with Lord Roberts' army in the neighbourhood of Belfast. Lord Dundonald's Brigade, the South African Light Horse, and Strathcona's Corps, were part of the force taken by General Buller, and right well did both regiments serve their General all through the advance to Belfast and Bergendal, and afterwards into the mountains of the Lydenburg district (see South African Light Horse).

Having returned to the Delagoa Railway line about the 7th October, the regiment were here told to make over their horses, and they entrained for Pretoria. The regiment parted regretfully from General Buller, a leader in whom they had learned to repose every trust, and who was ever ready to appreciate the good services they heartily gave. When he bade them farewell General Buller said that, having served in the north-west of Canada, he looked upon the corps as old friends, and he gave them and the South African Light Horse the highest praise. In his final despatch General Buller said: "Lord Strathcona's Corps joined the force in June, and from the moment of their arrival they served with marked success. I can hardly speak too highly of the value Strathcona's Horse have been to the Natal Field Force." As to Colonel Steele, he said: "Has great influence with all ranks in his regiment; having a thorough knowledge of frontier work, his services have been most valuable."

On 20th October horses were again served out to the regiment, and they were sent to reinforce General Barton near Frederickstad. On 10th November when acting as advance-guard they earned the commendation of that excellent leader. In a letter to Colonel Steele General Barton said: "I cannot speak too highly of the practical and effective manner in which the duty assigned to your splendid corps was carried out by yourself and all under your command yesterday. I have specially mentioned this in my report." The regiment had, among other good deeds, effected the capture of 600 cattle and 1200 sheep.

In his despatch of 8th March 1901 Lord Kitchener mentioned that when, in November 1900, he learned that De Wet was to attempt to invade Cape Colony, a big lot of troops was railed from the Transvaal to the south of Bloemfontein, and among these he included Strathcona's Corps. They were put under General C. Knox, and took part in the hard and exciting work which a "pursuit of De Wet" always entailed. This work lasted throughout December. On 20th January 1901 the regiment re-embarked for Canada, viâ Eng-

Lord Strathcona's Corps

land; and on 15th February they had the great honour to receive a Colour from King Edward, who also presented them with their medals.

The Honours and Mentions gained by the corps were as follows :—

Sgt. A. H. L. Richardson gained the Victoria Cross in the circumstances before mentioned.

GENERAL BULLER'S DESPATCH : *9th November* 1900.—Lieut.-Col. Steele, in terms already given ; Major A. M. Jarvis, Major R. Belcher, Capt. and Adjt. E. F. Mackie and Lt. R. H. B. Magee have done excellent service throughout, and proved themselves most useful soldiers in every duty they were called upon to perform. The following have been brought to my notice as having specially distinguished themselves : Regl. Sgt.-Major J. Hynes, Sgt. H. W. Nelles, Armr.-Sgt. J. R. Brigham, Cpl. A. K. M'Lellan, Ptes. C. W. Rooke, G. Gamsby, W. F. Graham, A. C. Garner. The following is a list of those who have performed special acts of bravery, or have been selected for and successfully carried out arduous reconnaissances or dangerous duties : Major A. E. Snyder, Capts. G. W. Cameron, F. L. Cartwright, Lts. F. Harper, J. A. Benyon, P. Fall, J. F. Macdonald, J. E. Leckie, T. E. Pooley, A. E. Christie, Surg.-Lt. C. B. Keenan, Lt. W. Parker (Qrmr.), Lt. I. R. Snider (Transport Officer), Lt. E. J. Steele (Paymaster), Lt. A. M'Millan (Veterinary Officer), Lt. A. H. L. Kyle (attached), Civil Surgeon A. E. Houseman, Squad. Sgt.-Major Richards, Sgt.-Trumpeter J. Farmer, Sgt. R. H. Moir, Farrier-Sgt. A. Gillies,[1] Sgts. J. S. Lambert, G. Clarke, C. A. W. Whitehead, S. A. Kelly,[1] P. G. Routh,[1] Cpls. E. H. Clarke, Alex. Norquay, W. M. Lafferty, F. Mulligan, C. R. M'Donald, R. N. Crogan, Read, Ptes. J. E. V. Carpenter, C. E. Kindrew, R. Hammond, H. D. Saxby, A. W. Stewart, J. T. Waite, J. Devine, S. A. White, R. Dearing, T. M. L. Pym.

LORD ROBERTS' DESPATCH : *2nd April* 1901.—Lieut.-Col. S. B. Steele,[2] Majors A. Belcher,[3] A. M. Jarvis,[3] Capts. G. W. Cameron,[4] F. L. Cartwright,[4] E. F. Mackie[4] (Adjt.), Lts. A. E. Christie,[4] J. E. Leckie,[4] Surg.-Lt. C. B. Keenan,[4] M.D., Regl. Sgt.-Major J. Hynes,[1] Squad. Sgt.-Major J. Richards,[1] Sgts. W. H. Nelles,[1] J. M. B. Skirving.

LORD KITCHENER'S DESPATCH : *8th March* 1901.—Lt. I. R. Snider.

LORD ROBERTS' DESPATCH : *1st March* 1902.—Tpr., afterwards Lt., S. T. St G. Carey.

---

[1] Awarded D.C.M. [2] Awarded C.B. [3] Awarded C.M.G. [4] Awarded D.S.O.

LUMSDEN'S HORSE.

THIS corps, consisting of two squadrons and a maxim gun detachment, represented Britain's great Dependency in the South African War. It was commanded by Lieutenant-Colonel D. M. Lumsden, of the Assam Valley Volunteers; while Lieutenant-Colonel Eden C. Showers, Commandant of the Surma Valley Light Horse, went as second in command with the rank of Major. "A" Company sailed from Calcutta on 26th February 1900, and "B" Company on 3rd March. "A" Company landed at Cape Town and "B" at East London, and both joined the army of Lord Roberts at Bloemfontein in April. On the 21st Lumsden's Horse marched out of camp to join General Tucker's Division, which had been holding the hills won at the battle of Karee Siding, 29th March. They were attached to a mounted infantry corps commanded by Colonel Ross, which consisted of Lumsden's Horse 240, Loch's Horse 220, West Riding and Oxford Light Infantry M.I. 220, and the 8th Battalion Regular M.I. 420.

On 29th April Ross received orders to make a demonstration against the Boer right, to draw them out, if possible, and allow Maxwell's Brigade to seize their position. Henry's Mounted Infantry were to co-operate. Lumsden's Horse occupied various spurs about 1500 yards from the Boer position; but the enemy moved out and took the offensive with vigour. Major Showers, who was exposing himself with rash bravery, was killed early in the action. So strong and determined was the enemy that Lumsden's men were ordered to retire. Lieutenant Crane, who with his section had been detached from Lieutenant-Colonel Lumsden's command, did not receive this order. He and his men held on to the position which they were holding, and were cut off and captured. The casualties of the two squadrons in this their first engagement were most severe. Major Showers and 5 men were killed, and Lieutenant Crane and 5 non-commissioned officers and men were wounded. After the engagement, General Tucker complimented Lumsden's Horse, but "rebuked" them for an exhibition of bravery which, he thought, bordered on rashness and the unnecessary courting of danger.

On 3rd May Lord Roberts commenced his advance to Pretoria. During this movement Lumsden's Horse scouted and skirmished in front of the right centre of the great army. At the Zand River on the 10th, at Viljoen's Drift on the Vaal on the 26th, and near Elandsfontein on the 29th, Ross's Mounted Infantry, including Lumsden's, did well, and their work was much praised by various correspondents. During the advance, and particularly after the Vaal was crossed, Lumsden's men had several casualties.

After the occupation of Pretoria, Lumsden's Horse were employed about Irene and at Springs, where they had the usual hard outpost work and some skirmishing. On 22nd July they marched into Pretoria and joined a force under Colonel Hickman, with whom they did some patrol work. About this time Lumsden's Horse left Colonel Ross, who issued an order in which he bestowed on them the highest possible compliments.

About the beginning of August the corps, now under Brigadier-General Mahon and General Ian Hamilton, started on a march to Rustenburg, thence to the country north of Pretoria, and back to the capital, which was reached about the end of August. At Zilikat's Nek there was stiff fighting, in which the Berkshire Regiment did very well.

Mahon was now ordered to make a forced march to Carolina. He arrived there on 6th September in order to co-operate with French in the march to Barberton—a splendid effort on the part of all ranks. It has been already touched on under the Imperial Light Horse.

Lumsden's Horse next took part in the march from Machododorp to Heidelberg along with the other troops of Generals French and Mahon. After some very severe fighting Heidelberg was reached on 26th October, and the corps then marched to Pretoria.

On 23rd November Lumsden's Horse left Pretoria for India. Lord Roberts telegraphed to the Viceroy expressing his "appreciation of their excellent services," and said : "It has been a pride and a pleasure to me to have under my command a volunteer contingent which has so well upheld the honour of the Indian Empire."

In the compilation of the foregoing notes, use has been made of 'The History of Lumsden's Horse,' Longmans, Green, & Co., 1903.

The Mentions gained by the corps were as follows :—

LORD ROBERTS' DESPATCHES : 2nd April 1901.—Col. D. M. Lumsden (awarded C.B.) ; Major H. Chamney (awarded C.M.G.) ; Capt. J. B. Rutherford[1] ; Lieut. H. O. Pugh.[1]

4th September 1901.—Capts. J. H. B. Beresford (Indian Staff Corps), L. H. Noblett (Royal Irish Rifles), F. Clifford, B. W. Holmes, C. L. Sidey ; Lieut. C. E. Crane ; Surg.-Capt. S. A. Powell, M.D. ; Coy. Sgt.-Major C. M. G. Marsham[2] ; Sgts. E. R. Dale, G. E. R. Llewellyn ; Cpls. P. Jones,[2] G. Peddie, C. E. Turner ; Tprs. J. A. Graham,[2] P. C. Preston,[2] H. N. Betts,[2] W. E. Dexter,[2] J. Graves, D. S. Fraser, H. R. Parkes.

1st March 1902.—Capt. N. C. Taylor, Indian Staff Corps.

LORD KITCHENER'S DESPATCH : 8th March 1901.—Tprs. Kelly, Granville, P. Jones. Capts. N. C. Taylor, Beresford, and Noblett got Brevet Majority.

---

[1] Awarded D.S.O. [2] Awarded D.C.M.

CEYLON MOUNTED INFANTRY.

EARLY in January 1900 the Legislative Council of Ceylon unanimously agreed to send a contingent of 125 mounted infantry raised from white men in the Colony. This offer was accepted, and the squadron sailed on 2nd February, having been equipped with the greatest possible despatch.

The Ceylon M.I. joined Lord Roberts while he was advancing on Bloemfontein, in time to be present at the engagement of Poplar Grove. On 6th March Lord Roberts wired to Ceylon: "I have just ridden out to meet Ceylon Mounted Infantry and welcome them to this force. They look most workmanlike, and are a valuable addition to Her Majesty the Queen's Army in South Africa." In the despatch of 15th March 1900 Lord Roberts noted that, along with the 5th and 7th Regiments of Regular Mounted Infantry and the 1st City of Grahamstown Volunteers, they formed the 4th Brigade of Mounted Infantry under Colonel Ridley.

The squadron was one of those praised by Lord Roberts in the despatch of 31st March 1900 for good work on the way to Bloemfontein. With Ian Hamilton and Ridley the corps took part in the advance to Pretoria, and was present at the battle of Diamond Hill, 11th and 12th June. Thereafter they were in the movement on Heidelberg under Ian Hamilton, crossed to the south of the Vaal with Hunter and Ridley, and under the latter took part in the first pursuit of De Wet to the Reitzburg Hills and into the Transvaal.

The squadron was afterwards operating in the Orange River Colony. Having been taken back to the Transvaal, they were present with General Clements in the action of Nooitgedacht, 13th December 1900, when his force suffered very severe loss. The Ceylon M.I. had 1 killed and 3 wounded. They sailed for home after about a year's service.

A second contingent, 103 strong, sailed from Ceylon on 23rd April 1902, but peace was declared before they took the field.

The Mentions gained were :—

LORD ROBERTS' DESPATCH : *2nd April* 1901.—Major Murray Menzies, Lieut. Thomas (killed). Major Menzies was subsequently granted the honorary rank of Lieut-Col. in the Army.

SIR R. BULLER'S DESPATCH : *19th June* 1900.—Under Thorneycroft's M.I. occurs the sentence, "Lieut. R. Villiers, who joined the regiment as a private, having been in the Ceylon M.I., has done specially good work throughout."

New Zealand Contingents.

The contingents furnished by New Zealand, according to the evidence of Sir A. Percy Douglas, Bart.,[1] and Lieut.-Col. A. P. Penton, R.A.,[2] given before the War Commission, were as follows:—

Description.	Strength. All Ranks.	Horses.	Date of sailing.
1. Two Companies Mounted Rifles	215	250	21st Oct. 1899.
2. Two do. do.	215	300	20th Jan. 1900.
One Hotchkiss Gun detachment	39	...	do.
3. Two Companies Mounted Rifles	273	277	17th Feb. 1900.
4. Battalion do.	500	660	24/31 Mar. 1900.
5. Do. do.	523	523	31st Mar. 1900.
Also Reserves	70	...	...
6. Battalion Mounted Rifles	578	580	30th Jan. 1901.
7. Do. do.	597	650	26th Mar. 1901 (actually sailed 10 days later).
8. Two Battalions Mounted Rifles	2268	2251	end of 1901 and beginning of 1902.
9. Do. do.			
10. Do. do.	1100	1000	

The total of the officers, men, and horses sent from the Colony is stated in the official publication, Australia and New Zealand,[3] as 342 officers, 6171 men, and 6662 horses.

As in the case of the contributions from Australia, each New Zealand contingent, except those numbered 8, 9, and 10 above, were in the field for more than

---

[1] Minutes of Evidence, vol. i. p. 424.   [2] Ibid., vol. i. p. 359.
[3] Sydney, 1904, p. 440.

a year. Some officers and men remained in South Africa after their respective corps had left, and joined the succeeding contingents.

THE 1ST, 2ND, AND 3RD N.Z. CONTINGENTS.

On landing at Cape Town the first two companies, under Major Robin, were entrained for De Aar, and thence they moved to the Arundel district, where, on 2nd December, they joined General French, who was then endeavouring to stem the Boer invasion in the central or Colesberg district. In the official telegram of 8th December it was noted that on the 7th the New Zealanders had occupied a ridge at Arundel, and covered the detrainment of other troops. Thus they were at the earliest moment placed in a position of responsibility, and they were soon to distinguish themselves. In the official telegram of 19th December it was stated that during a retirement the New Zealanders "were most steady under hot fire at short range."

In his despatch of 2nd February 1900, General French describes the efforts he made in December and January to drive or worry the enemy out of the very strong positions the latter had taken up about Arundel and Colesberg, and he used the words—"I wish particularly to bring to notice the excellent conduct and bearing of the New Zealand M.R., commanded by Major A. W. Robin, on one of these occasions. On 18th December I took them out with a battery of Horse Artillery to reconnoitre round the enemy's left flank, and determined to dislodge him from a farm called Jasfontein, lying on his left rear. The guns shelled the farm, and the New Zealand M.R. then gained possession of it. But the enemy very suddenly brought up strong reinforcements and pressed on us with his artillery. Our artillery had been left some way behind to avoid this latter fire, and I had to send back some distance for its support, during which time we were exposed to a heavy musketry fire from the surrounding hills. The conduct of the New Zealanders was admirable in thus maintaining a difficult position till the artillery caused the enemy to retire."

Regular troops with years of training could not have gained a more appreciative and complimentary reference, and coming as it did from General French, the most incorrigible detractor of irregulars or volunteers will not venture to say it was idle praise, such as is every day lavished by inspecting officers in peace time.

On the night of 31st December and on 1st January 1900 the New Zealand Mounted Rifles were again hotly engaged. General French had arranged that the Berkshire Regiment should assault a hill known as M'Cracken's Hill. At 3.45 A.M. the assault was successfully made and a strong position captured. Colonel Porter of the 6th Dragoon Guards was, before daybreak, to move out from Rensburg, his force being two guns R.H.A., two squadrons 6th Dragoon Guards, and one company New Zealand Mounted Rifles. Porter was to move to Porter's Hill, which was garrisoned by one squadron 6th Dragoon Guards and one company New Zealand Mounted Rifles, and from that point he was to co-operate. The words of the despatch are: "This he did at daybreak, with great effect at Porter's Hill and along the southern face of the position. The New Zealand M.R. made a most gallant attempt to effect a footing in the south-western corner, but were obliged to retire before greatly superior numbers."

General French described operations on 9th and 11th January 1900 in which the New Zealanders were engaged, and he gave an account as follows of a very severe fight on 15th January: "On the 15th January an attack was made by the enemy on my advanced post at Slinger's Farm. This is a high and rather steep hill, surrounded by a good deal of dead ground. The first was held by one company Yorkshire Regiment, and one company New Zealand Mounted Rifles, and was in charge of Captain Orr, Yorkshire Regiment. For some time during the morning of the 15th the enemy engaged in heavy and continuous firing at long ranges from the whole of his position opposite this post. At about 10 A.M. a movement was developed, which appeared to indicate an attack on the east side of the hill, where there was some cover, and the ground favoured it. Whilst this threat was in progress the firing from the enemy's main position was continued with great vigour. When the attention of our troops was chiefly engaged in watching for this attack on the east, it was suddenly reported that a large body of the enemy had established themselves at the foot of the western slope, which was very steep, and were creeping up the hill, taking all advantage of cover from rocks, &c. When the Boers found that their real attack was thus apparent, they opened a hot fire from their position on the western slope. Captain Orr at once fell badly wounded, and the Sergt.-Major was killed. The enemy came on briskly, and the moment was critical. Capt. Madocks, Royal

Artillery, attached to the New Zealand M.R., saw the critical situation of the Yorkshires, and that they were practically without a leader: with the greatest promptitude he took a few of his men to the west side of the hill, and rallied the troops holding it. He caused them to line their entrenchments and stem the enemy's advance, which had now become very bold, several of our men having fallen from their fire. Captain Madocks then jumped up, gave the order to fix bayonets, and charged down the hill, upon which the leading Boers immediately turned and ran down the hill, followed by many others, who had been under cover of rocks, &c., unseen. Our troops poured many well-directed volleys on the retreating enemy, who left 21 men dead at the foot of one hill, and it is estimated that their loss in wounded could not be less than 50. The greatest credit is due to Captain Madocks and his New Zealanders for their prompt action."

'The Times' History, vol. iii. p. 140, gives a very detailed account of this action, and bestows the highest praise on Captain Madocks and on those who, facing the very heavy fire on the crest, took part in the final charge on the enemy, who, according to 'The Times'' account, had established themselves in a sangar of the Yorkshires. The names of those who leapt the wall first, as mentioned by the historian, are Sergeant Gourlay, Madocks, Trooper Connell, and Lieutenant Hughes. The number of dead Boers found is stated at 29.

The foregoing extracts prove that the New Zealand Mounted Rifles had done splendidly about Colesberg, and Major Robin and his men were chosen to accompany General French and the Regular Cavalry to

Modder River, where, in the beginning of February 1900, Lord Roberts was concentrating a great force —first, to relieve Kimberley, and second, to march on Bloemfontein. The contingent was split up at Kimberley. One squadron was present at the battles of Paardeberg, Poplar Grove, and Driefontein. After Paardeberg they formed part of the 1st Brigade of Mounted Infantry under Brigadier-General Alderson, the other units being the 1st and 3rd regiments of Regular Mounted Infantry, Roberts' Horse, and Rimington's Guides.[1]

When the New Zealanders marched into Bloemfontein on 13th March, their strength was officially stated at 5 officers, 60 men, and 72 horses. The remainder of the contingent came in later.

Major A. W. Robin was mentioned in Lord Roberts' despatch of 31st March for his good work since 11th February, the date when the movement on Kimberley commenced.

Alderson's Brigade was present at Sannah's Post, east of Bloemfontein, on 31st March when Broadwood's force was ambushed (see Roberts' Horse). The New Zealanders formed part of the little body of Mounted Infantry which did so much to assist in bringing "Q" Battery into shelter. The detachment was the portion of the rear-guard to hold on upon the east side of the Koorn Spruit, and were the last to cross after having nobly covered the retirement. The New Zealanders lost about 17, taken prisoners.

About 20th December 1899—that is, a few days after the defeat at Colenso—it was announced that the Australian Colonies and New Zealand were to send further contingents—that from New Zealand being two

[1] Despatch of 15th March.

The 1st, 2nd, and 3rd N.Z. Contingents

squadrons of Mounted Rifles, which sailed on 20th January 1900 on the *Waiwera*, and landed at Cape Town on 25th February. This 2nd contingent, under Major Montagu Cradock, entrained at Cape Town for the north on February 27. They were detrained at Victoria West, and, together with the 2nd Canadian Mounted Rifles and a Canadian battery of field artillery, formed the advanced guard, under Major Cradock, of the Carnarvon Field Force, under Colonel Parsons, which was one of the three columns Lord Roberts mentioned in his despatch of 15th March 1900 as taking part in the expedition to put down the organised disaffection in the Prieska-Carnarvon district.

As already stated (see p. 307), the troops of the Carnarvon Field Force endured much hardship. On one occasion Major Cradock's men did 50 miles in twenty-four hours, but after all failed to get into contact with the enemy. Two New Zealand troopers, T. G. Anderson and T. Hempton, died of enteric during this expedition; and Lieutenant John Findlay and Corporal J. F. Neal, both of the 2nd New Zealand Mounted Rifles, had a narrow escape from drowning, but were gallantly rescued by Sergeant G. H. Street and Private W. Cassidy of the New Zealand Mounted Rifles and a trooper of the Canadians. Cassidy was for his fearlessness presented with the Royal Humane Society Medal. He received the award from the hands of Lord Roberts at Pretoria on 25th October, the day the annexation of the Transvaal was proclaimed. The advanced guard reached Kenhardt on 1st April and occupied it without opposition, being then 100 miles ahead of the main body. They captured a few rebels, many rifles, and 1900 rounds of ammunition. After three days' occupation they were relieved by a column under Major Burke, being part of a parallel force under General Settle, and were then marched back to Victoria West with all speed, and were there entrained to Norvals Pont. The contingent marched from Norvals Pont, and arrived at Bloemfontein on 29th April.

The Colonial Mounted Infantry under Hutton took a very prominent part in the advance from Bloemfontein (see Canadian Mounted Rifles). At the engagement of Brandfort, 3rd May, the 2nd New Zealand Mounted Rifles were directed to attack the town, and they captured it simultaneously with a successful attack by some of Rimington's Guides on the heights near it. Towards the end of April the 1st contingent had been operating east and south-east of Bloemfontein with General French; on 4th May they joined Hutton's force, and were put into the 3rd corps of Mounted Infantry under Colonel Pilcher, which was composed as follows: 1st and 2nd New Zealand Mounted Rifles, 1st and 2nd Queensland Mounted Infantry — Colonel Ricardo; 3rd Battalion Regular Mounted Infantry—Major Anley. This 3rd corps of Mounted Infantry took part in every engagement fought by French and Hutton on the way to Pretoria, often in the advanced guard. At Kroonstad, on 15th May, Pilcher was sent on a very lengthy circular march in the Bothaville direction. His column covered 200 miles; they captured 30 prisoners on the 19th.

The 3rd contingent, two squadrons of Mounted Rifles — frequently called the New Zealand Roughriders—commanded by Major Jowsey, sailed on 17th February 1900, and were landed at East London. It had been intended that they should go to Beira, but apparently their services were required in the Orange Free State in consequence of the activity of the Boer leaders in the south and east of that country. The contingent was engaged in the operations for the relief of Wepener and the clearing of the country east of the railway. Major Jowsey and his men joined Colonel Pilcher at Kroonstad on 20th May. After the Vaal was crossed there was heavy fighting on the left flank, in which the troops distinguished themselves. On 26th May the New Zealanders, under Robins and Cradock, dashed forward during an engagement, and, passing through some other troops, attacked a ridge and routed a Boer force, killing 5 and taking 7 prisoners. They suffered some casualties.

Before the surrender of Pretoria, French with the 1st and 4th Cavalry Brigades and Hutton with his Mounted Infantry were sent to the north of the capital, and at Waterval released over 3000 prisoners on 6th June: Lord Roberts had entered Pretoria on the 5th. After the enemy had evacuated Pretoria and had retired to the east, French and Hutton worked towards the north-east of the enemy's position, the centre of which, at Pienaars Poort, was of great natural strength. It was necessary to drive back the Boers, and with that object Lord Roberts fought the battle of Diamond Hill, 11th and 12th June 1900. French's cavalry and Hutton's Mounted Infantry—which still included the Canadians, New Zealanders, and Queensland men—were on the British left, and had very heavy fighting in most difficult country. The attempted turning movements were unsuccessful; but by very good work on the part of the infantry and artillery, notably the Sussex Regiment and the 82nd Battery, the enemy's centre was pierced on the 12th and a stiff battle was won.

On the 13th French and Hutton moved east to Doornkraal, but no enemy being found they returned to Kameelfontein, 12 miles north-east of Pretoria. During the next four weeks Hutton's troops, including the New Zealanders, were mainly employed holding posts to the east and south-east of Pretoria — work which entailed great watchfulness, because the enemy was at this time most enterprising. In the despatch of 10th October 1900, para. 24, Lord Roberts said: "Hutton, whose outposts were holding the Tigerpoort, Witpoort ridge, east of Irene, was attacked by 2000 Boers with 8 guns at daybreak on 16th July. On this occasion the detachment at Witpoort under Major Munn, 2nd Bn. Royal Irish Fusiliers, consisting of three companies of that regiment and 60 men of the New Zealand M.R. with two pom-poms, greatly distinguished themselves. By 3 P.M. the enemy fell back, and at dusk they were in full retreat eastward." The detachment of New Zealanders here mentioned belonged to the 2nd contingent, Lieutenant J. Findlay of that corps being severely wounded. On the same day a post held by a party of the 3rd New Zealanders was overwhelmed and captured, Captain J. Bourne and Lieutenant J. Cameron being taken prisoners.

At this time Lord Roberts was commencing his move from the confines of Pretoria to the eastern boundary of the Transvaal. Hutton's Mounted Infantry Division was split up. He himself, with Alderson's Brigade, which included the Canadians, moved eastward on the south of the Delagoa Railway, while Pilcher's Brigade or corps, which still included the New Zealanders, was put under the command of Mahon and General

Ian Hamilton, who with a strong force marched to the north-east of Pretoria, and thence eastward on the north of the railway. On the 25th July French and Hutton crossed the Wilge River, and Ian Hamilton occupied Balmoral. The enemy retreated in disorder through Middelburg, and Hutton occupied that place on the 27th. During this period the troops had to endure great hardships, the weather being very severe. The New Zealanders had a few casualties.

On 28th July Ian Hamilton, with Mahon's and Pilcher's troops, returned to Pretoria, as operations had to be undertaken west of the capital. On 1st August Hamilton led a fine force towards Rustenburg. The mounted troops, commanded by Mahon, included the Fife Light Horse, Dorset, Devon, and Sussex Yeomanry, Imperial Yeomanry Roughriders, 3rd Regular Mounted Infantry, and the 1st, 2nd, and 3rd New Zealanders. The latter were frequently engaged on this march, and on the 19th lost Lieutenant H. Bradburn of the 3rd and one trooper killed, and Captain Hutson of the 2nd and another trooper wounded. After relieving, or at least assisting, Baden-Powell at Rustenburg, Hamilton's force took part in a pursuit of De Wet, which was then in progress, into the Warmbaths district, whence they were recalled to Pretoria, which was reached on 28th August. During the four weeks 400 miles had been covered, and rations for man and horse had been far from plentiful. Colonel Pilcher now left the 3rd Mounted Infantry Brigade for a command in the Orange River Colony.

In August great events had been proceeding in the Eastern Transvaal. On the 15th General Buller, with part of the Natal army, had established touch with French. On the 27th the very strong Boer position at

Bergendal had been assaulted, successfully, by Buller's men, and the enemy had been driven to the Lydenburg hills and the Komati Poort district.

As ordered by Lord Roberts, Mahon marched from Pretoria eastwards towards the Belfast district. His force included "M" Battery R.H.A., the 3rd Mounted Infantry Regulars, some Queensland Mounted Infantry, and Queensland Bushmen, temporarily commanded by Colonel Cradock of the 2nd New Zealand; the 1st, 2nd, and 3rd New Zealanders, whose strength had fallen to 16 officers and 226 men, under Major Robin; the 79th Yeomanry, Imperial Light Horse, and Lumsden's Horse. After a forced march Mahon joined French at Carolina, south of the railway, to take part in the movement on Barberton (see Imperial Light Horse). Barberton was occupied on the 13th, after some wonderful marching and hill-climbing and no little stiff fighting. A part of the New Zealanders remained for some weeks at Barberton under General Spens; the remainder, under Colonel Cradock, returned to Pretoria, where, on 25th October, the 1st, 2nd, and 3rd contingents were present at the ceremony of proclaiming the annexation of the Transvaal. On the same evening some of the 1st contingent left Pretoria for Cape Town, and by the end of November practically all the 1st contingent had sailed for home.

On 26th October the New Zealanders, along with 500 other Colonials and four guns R.H.A., the whole under Colonel Cradock, took part in an expedition into the Schurveberg district, and, after returning to Pretoria, were again sent to the Rustenburg neighbourhood to endeavour to capture Steyn, who, it was thought, was thereabouts. On 20th November the column came back to Pretoria, and on the 22nd marched north-east to join General Paget, who on the 29th fought the very severely contested engagement known as Rhenoster Kop.

On the 28th the enemy had been attacked by General Plumer, and on the morning of the 29th General Paget found a strong force, said to number 4000 men, under General Viljoen, occupying a fine defensive position on a line of kopjes nearly seven miles long. The enemy was well supplied with pom-poms and machine-guns. Paget, who was expecting that a force under Colonel Campbell would co-operate from Balmoral, decided to attack without delay. Plumer's two mounted columns were ordered to attack the left of the enemy's positions, Colonel Lloyd with infantry, chiefly West Riding Regiment and Munster Fusiliers, attacking the centre and right. Cradock's column on the extreme left were the first to come into action, and for the next fourteen hours they were under very heavy fire. The West Australians, under Vialls, made a most determined advance over open ground to turn the enemy's right, but eventually they were prevented by the severity of the fire from either advancing or retiring. During the time Vialls was advancing, the 2nd and 3rd New Zealanders, under Captain Crawshaw, were fighting their way, under a terrible fire and over open ground, towards cover that was evidently very strongly held by the enemy. By sheer pluck and determination the New Zealanders managed to get within 300 yards of the position: there they were stopped, and only held their ground by a ceaseless and most accurate fire from a section of the 38th Battery R.F.A. under Lieutenant Craven. The fact that four guns of this battery fired during the day 866 rounds at fairly close range proves the severity of the fighting at Rhenoster Kop. Plumer's other column, under Hickman (see 4th Queensland Mounted Infantry), and Colonel Lloyd's infantry also got to positions almost as near the enemy as the New Zealanders, but nowhere was it found possible to get closer during daylight. By dusk Paget's force had about 100 casualties, including Colonel Lloyd of the West Riding Regiment and 13 men killed, and 10 officers and over 60 non-commissioned officers and men wounded. During the early part of the night desultory fire was kept up on both sides, and all the force, both officers and men, spent the night in digging trenches to make good the ground they had gained: however, in the darkness the Boers silently and quietly melted away. As soon as it was light enough to see, their position was found to be vacated. Signs were neither limited nor indistinct to show that the enemy had lost many killed.

In his telegram of 1st December 1900 Lord Kitchener remarked, "The troops behaved with great gallantry, especially the New Zealand Mounted Rifles, who showed exceptional bravery throughout the day." Out of a total of 6 officers they had 5 wounded—namely, Captain Crawshaw, 2nd contingent; Lieutenants Montgomerie and Somerville, 2nd; Tucker, 3rd; and Surgeon-Captain Godfrey, 3rd. Four non-commissioned officers and men of the New Zealanders were killed and 17 wounded.

Paget's force continued in this neighbourhood throughout December, making almost daily reconnaissances, and being constantly in touch with the enemy. Casualties were frequent. Two Queenslanders were killed one day, and Spencer of the 3rd New Zealand contingent was wounded on the 25th. On the 28th Paget set out on a march towards the north of Rustenburg, 140 miles away, to operate against Beyers. That district was reached on 3rd January 1901, and Paget continued to pursue Beyers' commandos till the 14th, when his force was recalled to Pretoria. This had been a very arduous three weeks, and sickness was rife. After a day or two at Pretoria the force marched to Balmoral, in which neighbourhood the 2nd and 3rd New Zealanders had a good deal of fighting, as on the 23rd, when a patrol of 120 New Zealand and Queensland men under Major Tunbridge was attacked by 400 Boers. The patrol made a fine stand, and drove off the enemy. Captain Crawshaw was again severely wounded, 2 men were killed and 5 wounded. In the despatch of 8th March 1901 Lord Kitchener spoke of the good work done by Paget and Plumer in this district, which tended to facilitate French's great sweep through the Eastern Transvaal.

About 7th February the troops under Paget and Plumer were called off from participation in French's eastern movement, and were railed to Naauwpoort, in Cape Colony, to take part in the operations against De Wet, who was threatening to invade that territory. They left Naauwpoort on the 10th, and were marched up north to intercept De Wet as he crossed the Orange River.

Paget entrusted Plumer with this expedition. His force consisted of the King's Dragoon Guards (who had just arrived from England) and one squadron of the Carbineers—about 500 men in all; Jeffreys' Corps (late Hickman's), mostly Colonials—some 750 men, with 4 guns and a pom-pom; Cradock's Corps—also about 750 strong. The latter included the New Zealanders. De Wet, with some 3000 men, crossed the river on night of 11th and morning of 12th, and Plumer was in grips with him by noon of the 12th. De Wet's men were in tremendous heart, and quite confident they had nothing to stop them marching straight to the Cape, looting every fat farm they came across on the way. However, from the time Plumer came in contact with them on the 12th he never left them alone for one moment until the 24th, when he—having engaged them almost every day, and having captured all their convoy, their ammunition, and their guns, to say nothing of well on to 200 prisoners — gave over the pursuit of their then disorganised crowd at Hopetown to others. Casualties on Plumer's side were, considering the fighting, very moderate, his chief loss being 24 casualties (including 2 New Zealanders, Heywood and Goldstone) on the day he turned the Boers out of the strong Wolvekuilen position. The Boers suffered much more heavily, and probably had 400 casualties between the 12th and 24th. (See also 4th Victorians.)

Plumer was entrained at Hopetown on the 26th for Springfontein, where he again took up the pursuit of De Wet, whose scattered forces had managed to recross the river back into the Orange Colony; but he never succeeded in inducing them to fight an engagement, and by the time he reached Brandfort they had split up and dwindled away to nothing. Plumer halted at Brandfort a day or two and then marched on to Winburg. After a stay of a day or two at this place, Plumer's forces were railed up to Pretoria, and from there commenced the advance on Pietersburg.

The 2nd and 3rd New Zealanders, about 300 war-worn veterans, returned home to New Zealand, under the command of Lieut.-Colonel Robin, from the halt at Winburg, sailing on 31st March, and Colonel Cradock was invalided home to England a few weeks later.

THE 4TH AND 5TH N.Z. CONTINGENTS.

In the beginning of February 1900 it was announced that New Zealand would send a fourth contingent, approximately three squadrons, but so great was the enthusiasm and so plentiful the supply of candidates that the contribution was increased to two full battalions of Mounted Rifles, known as the 4th and 5th New Zealand Contingents. They sailed at the end of March, and disembarked at Beira at the end of April. These two corps were, along with the 6th New South Wales Imperial Bushmen, intended to form the 2nd Brigade of the Rhodesian Field Force, which crossed Rhodesia and, under the leadership of General Carrington, entered the Transvaal from the north-west; but before Mafeking was reached the brigade was split up. The two New Zealand contingents took part in the attempt to relieve Colonel Hore at Elands River. (See Rhodesian Regiment.)

In Lord Roberts' telegram of 18th August he spoke of an engagement at Buffelshoek, in which Carrington and Lord Erroll drove back the enemy in the vicinity of Elands River on 16th August, the day on which Hore was relieved by Lord Kitchener from the south. Lord Roberts remarked, "The New Zealanders particularly distinguished themselves. Our casualties: killed, New Zealand M.I., Capt. Harvey and 2 men; wounded, 9 men." Captain J. A. Harvey was a squadron commander in the 4th contingent. Captain Fulton, Indian Staff Corps attached, and Lieutenant Collins, both of the 4th contingent, were wounded.

General Carrington left the seat of war about the end of August. After that both contingents saw much fighting under Lord Methuen, General Douglas, and other leaders in the Western Transvaal. Between 9th and 12th September both had casualties near Ottoshoop, in an engagement in which General Douglas took 40 prisoners. In Lord Roberts' telegram of 22nd October 1900, he said: " Lord Erroll occupied Buffelshoek from Ottoshoop on the 19th, without any casualties, owing to the good work done by the New Zealanders under Capt. Polson of the 5th Regiment Imperial Bushmen, New Zealand Contingent." In his telegram of 12th November 1900, speaking of Douglas's march from Zeerust district to Ventersdorp, the Commander-in-Chief said: " Douglas reports that the New South Wales Imperial Bushmen and New Zealanders did excellent work on the march." After this both battalions were operating in the Western Transvaal, chiefly about Ventersdorp and west of Krugersdorp, and they often saw fighting. The 4th had several casualties about 25th December, and Lieutenant Keddle of that corps was severely wounded on 12th January 1901 at Ventersdorp. The 5th was split up. During the first half of 1901 the greater portion of the regiment did column work under Brigadier-General Cunningham, and afterwards under his successor, Brigadier-General Dixon. In the War Record of the 1st Battalion Derbyshire Regiment occurs this sentence: " On 16th May 1901, to our great regret, we bade good-bye to the 5th New Zealand Contingent, as fine-looking and as useful a body of men as any in the field." Major Dennison, in his ' A Fight to a Finish,' mentions that a squadron of the 5th contingent was in a column based on the Kimberley-Vryburg railway, which operated in the south-west of the Transvaal and in the Orange River Colony towards the close of 1900 and in

1901. They had casualties on various occasions during the first three months of 1901. Major Dennison has nothing but praise for the New Zealanders. During part of 1900 and of 1901 Captain Polson's squadron of the 5th contingent was a component part of a "Composite Bushmen Regiment" which operated in various parts of the Transvaal under Colonel Von Donop, Royal Artillery.

In 1901 the 4th contingent did splendid work under various leaders, but it was while under General Babington that they got, and used to the full, more than one fine opportunity. In his telegram of 18th January 1901 Lord Kitchener said: "Colonel Grey, with New Zealanders and Bushmen, vigorously attacked the enemy 8 miles west of Ventersdorp, completely routing about 800 Boers. Four dead, 2 wounded, and 1 prisoner taken, many horses riderless, some rifles, &c. Our casualties, 1 man dangerously wounded." In Lord Kitchener's despatch of 8th May 1901, dealing with events in the Western Transvaal, he said: "Advancing northward from about Hartebeestfontein, early on 23rd March, General Babington pressed back the enemy and drove the main body north; Colonel Shekleton meanwhile operating against the enemy's right flank. Following up this success with mounted troops and guns only, General Babington, on the 24th, pushed on after the Boers, whose rear-guard was overtaken and driven in at Zwartlaagte. The enemy attempted to take up a second position a few miles farther north, to cover the withdrawal of the convoy, but Lieut.-Colonel Grey's New Zealanders and Bushmen overcoming all opposition, closed rapidly in on the convoy from both flanks. The enemy then abandoned guns and waggons and fled in confusion, pursued by

General Babington's troops. The captures included 140 prisoners, 2 15-pounder guns, 1 pom-pom, 6 maxims, 160 rifles," much ammunition, and many carts. "Twenty-two dead and 32 wounded Boers were found on the field. Our losses were 2 killed and 7 wounded." This action was by far the most successful engagement taking place in the Western Transvaal: it had a most disheartening effect on the enemy, and it was only when they found that the district was being denuded of troops to strengthen the driving columns in other parts that the Boers again commenced to show enterprise in a piece of country which was very favourable to their methods. Nothing could have been better than the conduct of the 4th New Zealand and the 6th (New South Wales) Imperial Bushmen in the action of 23rd-24th March, and both corps gained many mentions for exceptionally fine work on the part of individuals, as will be seen from the list of mentions.

The Appendix to the despatch of 8th July 1901 shows that in May the strength of the 4th New Zealand Mounted Rifles still in South Africa and on column work was 216 officers and men, with 280 horses.

When giving evidence before the War Commission Colonel Kekewich, the defender of Kimberley, was asked his opinion of the over-sea Colonials. He said: "I saw a good deal of the 6th Imperial Bushmen and the 4th and 5th New Zealanders, and these were all good fighting men who knew their job well."

At the end of May and beginning of June 1901 the 4th and 5th contingents sailed for home, and in recognition of their splendid work were allowed to take with them a captured gun and pom-pom.

THE 6TH N.Z. CONTINGENT.

The 6th contingent sailed from New Zealand on 30th January 1901. Throughout their war service they and the 5th Queensland Bushmen operated under General Plumer in almost every part of the seat of war, and the column distinguished itself by consistently good work. They could not have been more fortunate in their column commander. In the despatch of 8th May 1901 Lord Kitchener narrated the work of numerous columns in the North-eastern Transvaal in April, and said that he brought Plumer's troops from the Orange River Colony to Pretoria, and directed him to occupy Pietersburg in the north of the Transvaal, a district which, up to that time, had not been visited by British troops. General Plumer left Pretoria on 26th March and occupied Pietersburg on the morning of 8th April. During the advance 48 Boers were captured or surrendered. In Pietersburg other 46 Burghers surrendered; and the force took 1 gun and an immense quantity of ammunition. Between 14th and 28th April the results included 91 prisoners, 20 surrenders, 1 maxim, and more ammunition. On 24th April Captain Markham of the 6th was able to assist Lieutenant Reid of the 4th Imperial Bushmen in bringing off a fine capture. Correspondents about this time frequently referred to Captain Markham's good work. Plumer was now directed to march south to Eerste Fabriken, and he arrived there on 4th May. On the 14th the column again set out as one of several instructed to co-operate in clearing the country between the Delagoa and Natal railways. At Kromdrai, on

16th May, there was some stiff fighting, and on the 25th May a convoy was most severely attacked near Bethel, when some Colonials greatly distinguished themselves. Plumer arrived at Standerton at the end of May, and on 1st June started on another trek, this time to the extreme east of the Transvaal, making his way into the wild country, mountains, and almost impenetrable bush on the boundaries of Zululand and Swaziland. On this expedition many prisoners and horses were taken, but not without losses on the British side. Lieutenant F. J. Ryan was killed on 6th June, and there were other casualties in both corps about this time. On 28th June Plumer left Utrecht and marched north to Lake Chrissie, where he arrived on 7th July. In the despatch of 8th August, para. 5, Lord Kitchener noted that Plumer's column was in the second week of July taken by rail to Bloemfontein, whence on the 23rd they marched west to Modder River, almost on the tracks of Lord Roberts' army when he first invaded the Orange Free State, the direction being reversed. On this march some prisoners and stock were captured. On 4th August Plumer's men again moved out to take part in driving operations in the south-west of the Orange River Colony. On the 11th he returned with 32 prisoners and many cattle, and between the 15th and 30th he operated between the Modder and Orange Rivers, making more captures. He reached the Bloemfontein railway on 30th August and moved into the south-east of the Colony: here some very hard fighting and no little pursuing was done, the enemy being frequently found in strength. On 22nd September 1901 "a party of New Zealanders under Major Tucker (of the 6th contingent), belonging to Lt.-Col. Colvin's column (one of those under Plumer's direction), was engaged on the Elandsberg with 150 Boers under Field-Cornets Hugo and Bothma, both of whom, with several other prisoners, were captured." On 27th September there was stiff fighting at a drift on the Caledon, in which the Queenslanders suffered most of the casualties. The despatch of 8th October further narrated that in conjunction with operations south of Thabanchu "General Plumer despatched 200 New Zealanders under Major Andrew (of the Indian Staff Corps, attached 6th contingent) from Wepener to hold Mokari Drift on the Caledon. This party reached the drift on the 27th September, just in time to anticipate some 300 to 400 Boers who were about to cross the river to the south-east. In some sharp fighting which followed, the enemy, who were driven westward, left 6 dead and 7 wounded on the field."

In consequence of the enemy's activity in the south of the Transvaal, and the threatened reinvasion of Natal, Plumer's troops were, early in October 1901, railed to Volksrust, on the northern border of Natal. They marched from that station towards Wakkerstroom, and in that district they operated for several months.

In the despatch of 8th January 1902 Lord Kitchener dealt with the work of General Plumer's troops in the Eastern Transvaal, and said that "while watching the hilly district to the north of Wakkerstroom on 3rd January, a party of General Plumer's New Zealanders became hotly engaged with the enemy in the vicinity of Twyfelaar, when, despite the loss of the officer in command, who was wounded, and 20 (?) of their numbers, they effected the capture of 300 cattle and a waggon-load of ammunition." The casualties reported on the 3rd were Sergeant-Major Smith killed, Lieutenant Mitchell and Sergeant-Major Lewin and two men wounded.

"Another severe encounter between the Boers and General Plumer's troops took place on the following day (at Onverwachte), when about 50 of our mounted troops, under Major Vallentin, who were following up the commando which had been engaged with the New Zealanders, were suddenly attacked by several hundreds of the enemy. The Boers advanced at a gallop, with about 100 men in first line, and about 50 thrown back on each flank. The whole movement was covered by heavy fire from several hundred dismounted riflemen in the background; severe hand-to-hand fighting ensued, in which, I regret to say, Major Vallentin and 18 of his men were killed, and 5 officers and 28 men wounded, before the arrival of reinforcements, under Colonel Pultney, compelled the enemy to retire. The Boers, who were led on this occasion by General C. Botha on the one flank, and General J. D. Opperman on the other, fell back northwards, leaving 9 dead and 3 wounded in our hands. Amongst the former was General Opperman, who held chief command over a group of commandos, as well as the personal leadership of the Swaziland Commando."

Onverwachte was one of the most severely fought engagements of the second phase of the war. The writer has been told by a member of the 19th company Imperial Yeomanry, who was present, that they had been following up Boers all forenoon, and had halted, dismounted, and were at their midday meal, when they were surprised by the enemy, who had gathered behind a rise not far away. The chief losers were: the Hampshire Mounted Infantry, 7 killed and 5 wounded; 19th company Imperial Yeomanry, 1 officer and 1 man killed, 8 wounded ; 5th Queensland Bushmen, 12 men killed, 2 officers and 20 men wounded.

The column continued for some time to work in the Eastern Transvaal, and on several occasions made substantial captures.

THE 7TH N.Z. CONTINGENT.

The 7th New Zealand Mounted Rifles, along with the 6th Queensland Contingent, were, shortly after their arrival, put into the column of Lieutenant-Colonel Grey, afterwards of Colonel Garratt, which operated in the Eastern Transvaal, and also in the north-east of the Orange River Colony. In May 1901 the strength of the 7th was 489 officers and men, 504 horses, and 1 machine-gun. During May the column, then under Colonel Grey, worked in the Standerton district, "capturing many armed Burghers." During June there was constant skirmishing, and both corps suffered casualties on many occasions. At Blesbokspruit, on the 6th, the 7th lost 3 killed and 1 wounded. On 11th June Colonel Grey's troops had a sharp brush near Kaffir's Spruit, in the Ermelo district, in which they killed 1 and took 13 of the enemy (see despatch of 8th July). About the end of June Colonel Garratt took over the column, which moved to Springs, east of Johannesburg. From Springs Garratt advanced towards the south-east, and on 13th July surprised and captured a laager at Kopjiesfontein, on the right of the Vaal. On the 21st two Boer convoys were sighted, one on each side of the river ; both were ridden down and captured: "11 Boers were killed or wounded, 25 prisoners; 34 waggons, 31 carts, and 1240 cattle were captured." After a fight near Lindique Drift on the 22nd, Garratt's force co-operated in some driving operations under General Elliot, in the north-east of the Orange River Colony (see despatch of 8th August). About this time casualties were frequently suffered. Lieutenant Trotter and several men were wounded between 13th and 24th July.

In August Garratt's column made substantial captures at Bultfontein on the 12th, and on the 18th he detached 330 mounted troops under Lieutenant-Colonel the Hon. H. White, who at dawn on the 19th completely surprised Spannerberg's Laager, taking 25 prisoners, including Mr Steyn, Landdrost of Vredefort, 31 rifles, and much transport. Lord Kitchener noted that White's men covered 56 miles in 36 hours. At daylight on the 24th 3 Boers were killed, 8 taken prisoners, and again many waggons and Cape carts were captured. The enemy, numbering about 300, made a determined attempt to retake their convoy, but after five hours' fighting they were driven off. In this affair the 7th lost Lieutenant Leece and Sergeant-Major Love killed, and Lieutenant Whiteley and Sergeant-Major Lockett and one man wounded. On the 28th another night march was undertaken, and a laager attacked, when 13 prisoners, including General Delarey's nephew, Piet, were taken, besides rifles, ammunition, and horses. Garratt, on 5th September, entrained at Vereeniging *en route* for the Wakkerstroom district, in the extreme east of the Transvaal. His column continued to work in that district during the latter part of September, and throughout October and November. Casualties were not infrequent at this time. Between 17th and 21st October both corps had losses, including Captain Henry of the 7th New Zealand, wounded on the 21st. In the beginning of December Garratt marched to Newcastle, up Botha's Pass, and through the Drakensberg, in order to cover the making of block-houses in that corner of the Orange River Colony. This task having been completed, the column was, with that of Colonel Dunlop, put under the command of Colonel the Hon J. H. G. Byng, who with his own troops, chiefly the South African Light Horse, had been doing very fine work. On 2nd February 1902 Byng heard of a Boer convoy, and at once pursued (see South African Light Horse). "The New Zealanders and Queensland Imperial Bushmen at once charged the enemy's rearguard with the greatest dash and gallantry, while the S.A.L.H. rushed the centre with equal bravery." Three guns, 26 prisoners, including two captains and a field-cornet, 150 horses and mules, and 750 cattle were taken: 5 Boers were killed and 8 were wounded in this engagement. After this all the columns in the district made a big drive towards the railway, which ended on 8th February, when it was found that 300 prisoners had been taken. (See despatch of 8th February.)

In a few days another great concerted movement was undertaken. This time the column moved eastwards towards the Drakensberg. The troops, widely extended, swept forward during the day, searching all hiding-places; at night the vast length of line was entrenched. It was during this drive that the New Zealanders were to gain great glory, and, as a matter of course, pay the heavy price. The words in Lord Kitchener's despatch of 8th March 1902 are: "On the night of the 23rd a most determined and partially successful attempt to break out to the north was made by De Wet, Steyn, and some 700 of their followers, who had been driven east by Major-General Elliot's advance to the Wilge River into the net of our approaching columns. The attack was delivered under cover of darkness at Langverwacht, 18 miles south of Vrede, the point where, at the moment, the right of Colonel Byng's column was in touch with Colonel Rimington's left. Here again, as on the occasion of his previous escape, De Wet adopted the plan of advancing under cover of a large mob of cattle, which were rapidly driven up by natives to the point where the rush through was to be attempted. This expedient met, it is true, with a part of the desired success, for there is little doubt that De Wet, Ex-President Steyn, and a number of their men thus managed to break out of the toils. As a whole, however, the Boer force was very severely punished by the New Zealanders of Lieutenant-Colonel Garratt's column, who displayed great gallantry and resolution at a critical moment in resisting and in part repelling the attack. The conduct of the New Zealanders upon this occasion reflects the highest credit upon all ranks of the contingent, and upon the Colony to which it belongs. Nothing could have been finer than the behaviour of the men. The whole of the Boer cattle and vehicles were captured, and 31 of the enemy, together with over 160 horses, were killed at the point where the attempt to penetrate our line was made. Our own casualties were also severe, 2 officers and 18 men being killed, and 5 officers and 33 men wounded, the large majority of whom belonged to the New Zealand Contingent." In each of his telegrams of 25th and 28th February, Lord Kitchener referred to the very great gallantry of the 7th New Zealanders. In his wire of 1st March Lord Kitchener added, "All men worked day and night continuously, and, although tired, are in the best of spirits at satisfactory results obtained."

The officers killed were Lieutenants Harold, L. Dickinson, and William George Forsythe, and those wounded, Lieutenants James A. Colledge, Stapleton Cotton Gaulton, Charles O. Phair, W. H. Wilson, and Dennis A. Hickie, all of the 7th contingent. Twenty-two non-commissioned officers and men were killed and about 36 wounded. This loss it must be remembered fell almost entirely on the men in the outpost line, about 80.

The drive, which was the most fruitful of the many operations of that nature, resulted in 778 prisoners of war, 25,000 cattle, 2000 horses, 200 waggons, and 50,000 rounds of ammunition, and about 50 Boers killed.

During March 1902 Garratt's men took part in further drives in the Orange River Colony, and in April in a concerted movement of many columns from the Standerton line to the Delagoa railway and back. The latter, however, were not fruitful, few of the enemy being seen. On 22nd May the corps, reduced by a year's service from 650 to 370, sailed from Durban for home. On the journey to the coast they had the gratification of being addressed at Newcastle by their own Premier, Mr Seddon, whose efforts to assist the Empire had not been excelled by those of any other Briton—home or colonial.

THE 8TH, 9TH, AND 10TH N.Z. CONTINGENTS.

In December 1901 the Government of New Zealand offered further assistance, an offer which was at once accepted, and no time was lost in getting ready a very large contingent, nearly 1000 strong. It is worth noting that the Colonial Executive expressed the very reasonable desire that these battalions should not be split up and separated as some of the earlier ones had been.

The 8th contingent sailed in two portions: that from the north island on 29th January 1902, and that from the south island on 8th February, so that they saw comparatively short war service. The 9th contingent sailed on 12th March, two days after Lord Methuen's disaster had been announced. On the 15th the New Zealand Cabinet set an example to the British Empire by deciding to send a 10th contingent in April. It sailed on the 19th of that month, arriving on 27th May, four days before peace was declared.

The 8th had a cruel misfortune on 12th April 1902: through a railway accident at Machavie they lost 14 killed and slightly over that number injured.

The following quotation from the despatch of 1st June 1902 shows how hard service in the last days of the war was, especially for mounted men who had been for some weeks on the sea. It bears ample testimony to the good work of the newly arrived Australians and New Zealanders. Lord Kitchener, in referring to a great drive under General Sir Ian Hamilton, from about Klerksdorp to the Kimberley-Mafeking railway, said: "On 11th May the whole force closed in on the Vryburg railway, when it was found our captures included 367 prisoners of war, 326 horses, 95 mules, 175 waggons, 66 Cape carts, 3620 cattle, 106 trek oxen, and 7000 rounds of ammunition,—this loss to the enemy constituting a blow to his resources such as he had not previously experienced in the Western Transvaal. Most of the prisoners fell into the hands of Lieut.-Colonel De Lisle, who, with the 1st and 2nd Bns. of the Commonwealth Regiment, formed part of Colonel Thorneycroft's column. In reporting upon this extremely successful operation, General Sir Ian Hamilton desires to draw my attention to the enthusiasm and energy with which the troops met the exceptional hardships and work involved by lining out and entrenching themselves on four successive nights after long marches in a practically waterless country. On each of these nights every officer and man, after marching some 20 miles, had to spend the hours usually devoted to rest in entrenching, watching, and occasionally fighting. In this connection he draws special attention to the spade work done by the Commonwealth regiments—3rd New South Wales Bushmen, and the 8th New Zealand Regiment. Every night while the sweep was in progress these troops dug one redoubt to hold 20 men every 100 yards of their front of six miles. The redoubts were so solidly constructed that they would have afforded perfect cover from artillery fire, and the intervals between them were closed by waggons linked together with barbed wire. The commander of each group of columns had his own particular system, and it may be interesting to note that General Walter Kitchener's force held the line assigned to it by similar works, constructed to hold seven men each, and placed at intervals of 50 yards apart. The work done by the troops under Colonels Sir Henry Rawlinson, Kekewich, and Rochefort was equally satisfactory, barbed wire and obstacles being freely made use of to close the points at which the enemy would be most likely to break through."

On 4th June, four days after peace was concluded, the 9th contingent had the misfortune to lose Lieutenant Robert M'Keigh, killed, and Lieutenant Henry Rayne, wounded, near Vereeniging. Firing had been started under some misconception.

The 8th, 9th, and 10th contingents sailed for home in July 1902.

NEW ZEALAND BATTERY.

THE *personnel* of one of General Carrington's batteries was composed of New Zealanders under Major Powell. They formed part of the force which landed at Beira about the end of April 1900, crossed Rhodesia, and entered the Transvaal from Mafeking. As mentioned in Lord Roberts' telegram of 6th August, the battery was part of Carrington's force which made an endeavour to relieve Hore's garrison at Elands River (see 1st New South Wales Bushmen). Subsequently they did valuable service under General Carrington, Lord Methuen, and other leaders, chiefly at Zeerust and other posts in the Western Transvaal. Some of the *personnel* of the battery were in Lichtenburg when it was most fiercely attacked by Delarey on 3rd March 1901: 2 men were wounded during the attack. The guns of the battery were six 15-pounder Armstrong field-guns.

Mentions gained by New Zealanders

The Honours and Mentions gained by the New Zealanders were as follows:—

Farrier-Major W. J. Hardman, 4th New Zealand Contingent, gained the Victoria Cross on 28th January 1901 near Naauwpoort. This non-commissioned officer was with a section which was extended, and hotly engaged with a party of about 20 Boers. Just before the force commenced to retire Tpr. M'Crae was wounded and his horse killed; Farrier-Sergeant Hardman at once went, under a heavy fire, to his assistance, dismounted, and placed him on his own horse, and ran alongside until he had guided him to a place of safety.

GENERAL FRENCH'S DESPATCH: 2nd February 1900.—N.Z.M.I.: Major A. W. Robin, commanding, deserves special mention for the frequent occasions on which he and his men have performed signal service during these operations. Capt. Madocks and his company mentioned in body of despatch for work on 15th January.

LORD ROBERTS' DESPATCHES: 31st March 1900.—N.Z.M.I., with Cavalry Division for Relief of Kimberley, and advance to Bloemfontein, Major A. W. Robin.

2nd April 1901.—Lt. Seddon, Roughriders, one of Lord Roberts' Colonial A.D.C.'s, "performed duties loyally and well"; Lt.-Col. S. Newall[1] (5th Contingent); Majors M. Cradock[1] (2nd), A. W. Robin[1] (1st); Lts. J. G. Hughes[2] (1st), T. J. M. Todd[2] (2nd); Majors R. H. Davies[1] (4th), T. Jowsey[3] (3rd); Capts. C. T. Major[2] (4th), D. Polson[2] (5th); Lts. A. Bauchop (4th), S. R. Bradburne (3rd), G. H. R. Rolleston (4th); Sgt.-Majors W. J. Burn,[4] W. H. Fletcher[4] (5th); Sgt.-Major Harpur; Sgts. W. Cassidy[4] (2nd), E. Hazlett, Luck; Pioneer-Sgt. Harris; Cpls. Harler, Hogg; Tprs. Gallaway, Holroyd; Pte. W. B. Wade.[4]

4th September 1901.—Sgts. Bennett, Ebbs; Gunner Kelly, 1-pr. battery. Nursing Sister J. M. N. Williamson, who got the Royal Red Cross.

Lord Roberts, in despatch of 1st March 1902, announced that Pte. H. D. Coutts, N.Z.M.R., had been awarded one of the four woollen scarves knitted by Queen Victoria for distribution to the four most distinguished private soldiers in the forces of Canada, Australia, New Zealand, and South Africa.

LORD KITCHENER'S DESPATCHES: 8th March 1901.—N.Z.M.R.: Lt.-Col. Cradock (2nd); Capts. G. Crawshaw (2nd), E. W. C. Chaytor (3rd); Surgeon-Capt. S. C. Godfray (3rd); Lt. C. L. Somerville (2nd); Qrmr.-Sgt. Stephenson; Sgt. P. Tudor; Tprs. E. Hille, H. Harper, J. Stevens, H. Windgate.

8th May 1901, from General Babington's despatch as to capture of guns and convoy in Western Transvaal, 24th March.—4th New Zealand: Capts. G. H. Walker, D.S.O., and B. Arthur, for excellent services; Cpl. O'Dowd, promoted Sgt.; Ptes. Rumble and Drinan, promoted Cpls. Pte.

---

[1] Awarded C.B. [2] Awarded D.S.O.
[3] Awarded C.M.G. [4] Awarded D.C.M.

Rumble charged a gun, closely followed by Drinan and O'Dowd. They were met by a heavy fire from the gunners, Rumble's coat being shot through, and Drinan's hat. They took the gun. Pte. Thurlow (promoted Cpl.), conspicuous for his energy in turning round waggons of convoy under fire, and sending them to the rear. Pte. Wylie (promoted Cpl.) charged a gun by himself; it was defended by four of enemy, two of whom he killed and then captured the gun. Pte. D. Langham,[1] conduct in capture of guns. 5th N.Z. : Lce.-Cpl. Turnbull (promoted Cpl.), near Dwarsvlei, Krugersdorp, 23rd April, went with Major Brown, Border Regiment, into a dark cave and succeeded in getting out six armed Boers.

GENERAL PLUMER'S DESPATCHES : *6th April.*—6th N.Z.M.I. : Farrier-Sgt. G. Rouse[1] and Pte. A. Free[1] (promoted Cpl.), on April 5, near Pietpotgeitersrust, captured 12 armed Boers and 2 waggons with arms and ammunition.

8th July 1901.—N.Z.M.R. : Surgeon-Capt. E. J. O'Neill (6th), on June 16, under heavy fire, went three times to the wounded and succeeded in getting Lt. Ryan and three men. 4th. : Capt. A. Bauchop, at Spitz Kop, Feb. 11, for plucky action in rescuing a wounded man. Farrier-Major W. J. Hardman, near Cypherfontein, June 21, brought a wounded man out of fire on his horse, himself running beside him (mentioned in Army Orders). Farrier - Major Hardman got the Victoria Cross for another act of gallantry.

8th August 1901.—7th N.Z. Regt. : Lt. E. Hecklar, at Witkop, Transvaal, July 22, with two men, brought two dismounted men out of action under heavy fire, Sgt.-Major Callaway and Lce.-Cpl. Vicoe assisting in this.

8th October 1901.—7th N.Z. Regt. : Capt. C. Simpson greatly distinguished himself in night capture of Spannerberg's laager near Honingspruit, August 16. 6th N.Z.M.R. : Lt. P. L. Tudor, with only 12 men, crossed the Caledon on 16th Sept., and kept touch with 200 Boers for three days, and displayed great gallantry on 27th, holding position for three hours against 50 Boers. Major A. W. Andrew, Indian Staff Corps, in command during action at Mokari Drift, Caledon River, Sept. 27, and handled his troops very well. Capt. J. Findlay, East Kent, attached, and Capt. L. C. E. Knight, for excellent service in command of detached troops in Orange River Colony in September. Pte. J. E. Baigent,[1] one of a party which volunteered to carry despatches, ambushed and fired on at very close range, and the corporal's horse being shot, waited under heavy fire for him, and brought him away safely, Bastard's Drift, Orange River Colony, 27th September. 7th N.Z. : Sgt.-Major E. Lockett,[1] for most gallant rescue of a prisoner in the Hosberg, August 23. He was severely wounded, and lost an arm in consequence.

8th December 1901.—4th M.R. : Sgt. J. Walker, for capture, single-handed, of three armed Boers, in a farm near Standerton. 7th : Lt. J. D. G. Shera, for gallantry in attack on laager in Pongola Bosch, October 23. Sgt. J.

---

[1] Awarded D.C.M.

Davidson, Lce.-Cpl. W. Rutherford, for gallantry in bringing wounded men out of action under close fire, October 5.

8th March 1902.—7th: Major A. Bauchope;[1] Lts. P. T. Emerson, P. Overton, for good service in Colonel Byng's capture of laager at Fanny Home, February 2. Lt. D. A. Hickie,[2] for marked good service in action at Witkoppies on night of December 27. Farrier-Sgt. Quinn, for recovering stampeded horses which had gone through enemy's lines, under a hot and close fire, and closely pursued, December 27. Sgt. W. Kent,[3] at Holnek, December 21, when with 20 men, was charged by 50 Boers, dismounted his men and repulsed enemy by volleys.

8th April 1902.—N.Z.M.R.: Lt.-Col. T. W. Porter.

1st June 1902.—7th: Lce.-Cpl. Gregory, promoted corporal, for coolness and grasp of situation which enabled officer commanding regiment to make effective dispositions to repulse attack, 24th February 1902.

23rd June 1902.—New Zealand Forces: Nursing Sister D. Peiper; Col. R. H. Davies, C.B.; Majors F. W. Abbott,[2] E. Bartlett[2]; Capts. R. Stevenson,[2] C. L. Somerville, H. R. Potter, G. R. Johnstone; Lt. W. C. Morrison; Regl. Sgt.-Major G. C. Black[3]; Sgt.-Majors Pickett,[3] H. White[3]; Qrmr.-Sgt. G. Mitchell; Sgt. D. Smythe; Cpls. Cato, Burns, Beck; Lce.-Cpl. W. Thorp; Pte. J. Cassidy. Qrmr.-Sgt. Travers got the D.C.M.

---

[1] Awarded C.M.G.   [2] Awarded D.S.O.   [3] Awarded D.C.M.

New South Wales Contingents.

NEW SOUTH WALES LANCERS.

IN his evidence before the War Commission General Sir G. A. French said that the total contribution of this colony to the fighting strength in South Africa was 6945 officers and men and 6104 horses, with six 15-pounder guns. He also stated that the contingent of the N.S.W. Lancers, 70 all ranks, who had been at Aldershot for training, were the first over-sea Colonials to land in South Africa. They had sailed from Britain on 10th October 1899, actually before war was declared. They arrived on 2nd November. A draft of 5 officers, 1 warrant officer, 32 men, and 130 horses, sailed from New South Wales on 28th October to make up a complete squadron.

The Lancers, after their arrival at Cape Town, were sent to De Aar, but were shortly split up—one body, about 40, under Captain Cox, going to Colesberg, and another, about 30, under Lieutenant Osborne, to Orange River. The latter formed part of Lord Methuen's force when he advanced north from Orange River. This detachment was engaged at Belmont, 23rd November 1899; at Enslin on the 25th; at Modder River on the 28th; and at Magersfontein on 11th December.

In the last week of December Lieutenant Osborne and his detachment were taken from Lord Methuen and sent to join the remainder of the squadron, who had been doing good work under General Sir J. P. D. French in the Colesberg district. In a telegram of 19th January Lord Roberts said: "A patrol of the N.S.W. Lancers, halting at a drift for water, was taken by surprise. Two killed and fourteen missing." The incident happened on the 16th. Lieutenant Dowling of the 1st Australian Horse was in command; he was wounded. Corporal Kilpatrick of the Lancers was killed. The patrol made a very gallant fight, and six actually broke through, although the enemy were said to be 100 strong.

In his despatch of 2nd February 1900 General French mentions the squadron of Lancers as part of his force. They were put into a brigade consisting of the 6th Dragoon Guards, New Zealand M.R., and some Regular Mounted Infantry. The detachment with General French was the advance-guard of a force which reconnoitred towards Colesberg on 21st November, and were said to have behaved with steadiness. Thereafter they took their share in the very arduous work which fell to General French's force in the Colesberg district during December 1899 and January and February 1900.

When Lord Roberts was about to undertake the relief of Kimberley and the advance on Bloemfontein, the squadron of N.S.W. Lancers was taken to Modder River and put into the 1st Cavalry Brigade under Brigadier-General Porter. Lord Roberts' army commenced its advance on 11th February, and General French entered Kimberley with his cavalry and some mounted infantry on the 15th. An excellent account of the work of the 1st Brigade is to be found in the 'War Record of the Inniskilling Dragoons,' by Lieut.-Colonel Watkins-Yardley (Longmans, 1904), who at p. 43, speaking of the last halt to re-form and water before entering Kimberley, says : "There was but little subsequent resistance, but the march was long and thirsty, and the horses were badly done up. For instance, 'A' squadron Inniskilling Dragoons could only muster 42 horses on its arrival at Kimberley. There the N.S.W. Lancers under Major Lee were attached to it under Major Allenby, making the squadron up to 120 horses, and thereafter they remained with the regiment, rendering yeoman service until their return to New South Wales." From Modder River to Bloemfontein Major Allenby's men were constantly in the thickest, and always did well. Few cavalry leaders came out of the campaign with a better reputation than he did. On 12th March he led the advance-guard of the 1st Cavalry Brigade, and after a long march seized some hills a few miles south of Bloemfontein, which practically commanded the town. On the 13th the capital surrendered. The strength of the N.S.W. Lancers when they marched into Bloemfontein was 6 officers, 89 men, and 90 horses. On the 15th Major Allenby's men and some others escorted a convoy to Thabanchu *via* Sannah's Post, the scene of Broadwood's mishap on the 31st (see Roberts' Horse). The regiment now had much reconnoitring work to do, and on several occasions the Lancers had casualties. On the 29th March the 1st Cavalry Brigade, including the Australian Horse and the N.S.W. Lancers under Captain Cox, were engaged in the battle of Karee Siding, and their fine conduct was specially mentioned by various British correspondents who were present. On the 31st, the day of Sannah's Post, the brigade was sent out to help Broadwood, but was too late to be of any assistance in the way of recovering the lost guns or waggons: however, they were able to bring in the British wounded, who had been left in some buildings.

While the army was at Bloemfontein the Lancers received a reinforcing draft of nearly half a squadron, which had sailed about 16th February. The work of the cavalry had been such that, on 3rd April, the 1st Brigade had only 120 fit horses, "A" squadron of the Inniskillings only mustering 17. Throughout April many of the infantry battalions were able to get some rest, but the mounted men had to undertake long reconnoitring patrols and constant outpost work. Lord Roberts had, however, been reorganising his army, getting up stores and horses, and on 1st May he was ready to move again. Under that date Lieut.-Colonel Watkins-Yardley says (p. 57): "The New South Wales Lancers under Major Lee, who had hitherto been attached to 'A' squadron, were formed into a distinct squadron of the 6th Inniskilling Dragoons. They were proud to be considered a part of the Regiment: all officers will testify to their usefulness, the fine scouting and efficient work they rendered. Under splendid officers their coolness, self-reliance, and dash brought them out of difficulties where other troops might have suffered severely. . . . The Australian Horse were similarly attached to the Scots Greys."

It is impossible to embody here all the other references to the New South Wales Lancers; but up to the entry into Pretoria they did work of a very high order. On the 28th May they cleared the enemy from a farm at Olifant's Vlei. On 3rd June there was very severe fighting at Kalkheuvels Pass, when the squadron and "A" squadron of the Inniskillings averted what might very easily have developed into a panic, by rapidly dismounting and pouring in a heavy and well-directed fire on the enemy, who, posted in a strong position, had suddenly attacked the troops in front when passing through a difficult gorge. On 6th June, when the British prisoners were released, the enemy heavily attacked the relieving force when they had commenced to return. Allenby's men covered the retirement, and again did splendidly.

At Diamond Hill on 11th and 12th June the whole of the 1st Cavalry Brigade was very heavily engaged on the left, and only maintained their ground by exhibiting great determination. It will be remembered that the cavalry and mounted infantry on the right also found it difficult to make progress, and that the infantry had to attack and pierce the enemy's centre. From this time till the middle of July the squadron was much on outpost duty and in constant touch with the enemy. On 15th July two posts were attacked at dawn, and were only saved by the timely arrival of the Lancers and "B" squadron of the Inniskillings, who together drove back the enemy.

During the advance to Belfast, from there to Carolina, and thence to Barberton and Avoca, the Inniskillings and their Colonial comrades rendered splendid service, and Colonel Yardley makes many very flattering references to their work. As showing the complete confidence the leaders had in the squadron, it may be noted that when it became known that fifty-two locomotives were standing at Avoca, the men sent down to capture and guard this extremely valuable prize was a troop of N.S.W. Lancers under Lieutenant Nicholson. Colonel Yardley mentions his meeting, a few days later, with this officer, and relates how cleverly Nicholson had captured three prisoners: "Noticing small details is one of the arts of scouting, and in it our Colonial brothers excel. Lieut. Nicholson himself was a fine specimen. Though getting on in life, he was capable and worthy of a much higher command; but on the war breaking out he cheerfully undertook the duties of a subaltern." It was frequently remarked by regular officers that some of their brethren of the Colonial regiments were too old; but age alone brings caution and the "'cuteness" necessary to outwit a Boer: and to the mature years of a large proportion of their officers the immunity from mishaps and the general success of many Colonial contingents were undoubtedly due. Apart from this is the fact that volunteer corps, with many men of good position in the ranks, do not relish being "bossed" by very young officers.

The Lancers had some casualties about Carolina on 10th October 1900. They took part in General French's march from Machododorp to Heidelberg, 13th to 25th October 1900, and had a full share of the almost continuous fighting which took place throughout the fortnight. Speaking of 19th October, Colonel Yardley says: "Major Allenby, with the Inniskilling Dragoons, 2 guns and a pom-pom, fought a fine rearguard action, the Regiment bearing the brunt of the fighting. Capt. Stevenson Hamilton's squadron did good work, also the N.S.W. Lancers. The latter, which worked as a squadron of the Regiment, consistently rendered excellent service. They were a fine lot of men, and their officers — especially Major

Lee, Captain Cox, and Lt. Heron—were hard to beat anywhere."

The following extract is gratifying as showing that many of our late enemies were people of fine feeling: "October 15. A N.S.W. Lancer whom we left badly wounded at Carolina on our last occupation died a few days ago: the inhabitants reported that the enemy had buried him most reverently, numbers attending the funeral in tall hats and frock-coats. We found his grave beautifully decorated with flowers."

On 29th October Colonel Yardley says: "Major Lee with his squadron now left us on their return to New South Wales, greatly to our regret. Captain Cox, Second-in-Command, afterwards returned as Lieutenant-Colonel of the New South Wales Mounted Rifles, and rendered admirable service for twelve months under Colonel Rimington."

THE 1st AUSTRALIAN HORSE (NEW SOUTH WALES).

This corps was a portion of the second contingent of the Colony of New South Wales, the remainder of the contingent being Mounted Infantry.

The 1st Australian Horse sailed from Newcastle and Port Jackson on 14th November 1899 and 17th January 1900, both detachments being taken to Cape Colony.[1] On their arrival the first detachment was sent to General Sir J. P. D. French, who was then operating in the Colesberg district, and during part

---

[1] New South Wales Contingents to South Africa, Sydney, 1900.

of December 1899 and January 1900 the corps did much good work, and constantly saw hard fighting. On 16th January a patrol, made up of New South Wales Lancers and a few Australian Horse, was cut off, and in the endeavour to break through, Lieutenant W. V. Dowling of this corps was wounded and captured, and Sergeant-Major Griffin, also of this corps, and Corporal Kilpatrick of the Lancers, were killed. Lieutenant Dowling was found by Lord Roberts' troops in Bloemfontein when they entered that town on 13th March.

The squadron, as part of Colonel Porter's Brigade, accompanied General French to Modder River, and took part in the operations for the relief of Kimberley and in the advance of Lord Roberts' army to Bloemfontein. (See New South Wales Lancers.) The squadron had casualties at Poplar Grove and Driefontein.

When the 1st Australian Horse marched into Bloemfontein on 13th March their strength was 5 officers, 112 men, and 101 horses. They were now sent to the Glen position north of the town, where much heavy patrol work fell to them. On the 20th they lost 1 man killed and 8 wounded.

In March 1900 the squadron was attached permanently to the Royal Scots Greys,[1] and with that distinguished regiment fought at the battle of Karee Siding, 29th March; in several engagements southeast of Bloemfontein in April; in the advance to Pretoria, 3rd May to 6th June; and east of Pretoria in June, July, August, and September.

On 10th May, the day on which Lord Roberts crossed the Zand River, Lieutenant Wilkinson was,

[1] War Record of the Inniskilling Dragoons (6th), p. 57.

with some of the 6th Dragoons and Royal Scots Greys, fired on when approaching a kraal where a white flag was flying. The officer in command, Captain Elworthy, and several men were killed and others wounded, and Lieutenant Wilkinson and several men were taken prisoners. On this same day the squadron and two squadrons of the Greys had very heavy fighting. They had been pushed forward to seize a hill, and the enemy being in great force all round, they were wellnigh cut off. The hill had temporarily to be vacated, but on reinforcements and guns coming up the Boers retired.[1] Throughout the advance to Pretoria, particularly in the last days of May, after the Vaal was crossed, Porter's Brigade had frequently very heavy fighting, and progress was only made by all ranks showing great determination.

Along with the New South Wales Lancers the corps had the good fortune to be part of the force which released the prisoners at Waterval, north of Pretoria, on 6th June. This was not effected without difficulty. A strong force of Boers appeared as our troops were retiring; indeed the bulk of the brigade were far on their way, and the rearguard, about 400 strong, were pressed by 2000 of the enemy with artillery. Lieut.-Colonel Yardley of the Inniskillings in their War Record, p. 101, praised the men of his own regiment, the New South Wales Lancers, the Scots Greys, and 1st Australian Horse. He said: "I was much indebted to a small party of the Australian Horse who, at my request, remained to help hold an advanced post which, save

[1] Mr Goldmann's 'With French and the Cavalry,' p. 225.

for the shelter of a stone wall would not have been possible."

Along with the New South Wales Lancers the 1st Australian Horse were present under General French, in Porter's Brigade, on the extreme left, at Diamond Hill, on 11th and 12th June 1900. The brigade was strongly opposed in difficult country, and was unable to carry out a turning movement. So great had been the loss of horses that the squadron had only 2 officers and 8 men mounted in this battle.[1]

The corps took part in the advance from Pretoria to the Portuguese border. On 24th July Captain Ebsworth was killed—strangely enough, almost the only casualty in the army that day. "While standing by his horse and spying the enemy through his glass, a chance bullet, fired quite 2000 yards off, struck the glass and penetrated his brain." General French's further operations have been touched upon under the Imperial Light Horse and under the New South Wales Lancers. Part of the corps sailed for home in November 1900; the remainder continued to do good work down to March 1901. On the 31st of that month Captain Wilkinson and 32, all ranks, the remnant of the corps, sailed for home.

[1] Mr Paterson's account, printed in the War Record of the Inniskilling Dragoons, p. 116.

THE 1st NEW SOUTH WALES MOUNTED RIFLES AND MOUNTED INFANTRY.

One squadron of Mounted Rifles sailed from New South Wales in November 1899, and three squadrons of Mounted Infantry on 17th January 1900. Another squadron of Mounted Infantry was formed from the infantry unit, 125 men, which sailed on 3rd November 1899. It has to be kept in view that the 1st contingent from New South Wales, as from several other colonies, would have been much larger,—more had been offered,—but over-wise directors of military affairs at home wired on 3rd October 1899 desiring two units, about 125 men each, from each of the larger colonies, and one unit from each of the smaller. It has become the fashion to blame the civilians in the Cabinet or War Office for undue preparation and the studied discouragement of Colonial or Volunteer assistance generally. The blame, if any, seems to rest on one man alone, the Commander-in-Chief in 1899—that is, on the assumption that his title or office meant anything; and if it did not, he should not have held it a day.

The squadron of Mounted Rifles, commanded by Captain J. M. Antill, was, on arrival upon 6th December 1899, taken to Orange River, and during December and January did useful work in that neighbourhood, being sent to garrison Prieska for a time when there was good reason to believe many of the inhabitants in that district were disloyal. The squadron of infantry which was converted into mounted infantry was, during December and January, its period of foot service, working in the Enslin

1st N.S.W. Mounted Rifles and Mounted Infantry

neighbourhood along with the other units which composed the Australian Regiment of Infantry. Along with these other units it was taken to Naauwpoort, Central Cape Colony, in the end of January 1900, and was there served out with horses. Under Captain Legge, this squadron did good service in General Clements' operations, both in the retirement from the positions round Colesberg, in the fighting round Arundel, in the advance from Arundel to Colesberg and Norvals Pont, and on the march through the Orange Free State. (See 1st Victoria Mounted Rifles.) Lieutenant F. A. Dove was wounded on 26th February, and the squadron had losses on various occasions in this district.

The three squadrons of Mounted Infantry arrived in South Africa in time to take part, along with Antill's squadron of Mounted Rifles, in Lord Roberts' big operations for the relief of Kimberley and the capture of Bloemfontein. They were part of the brigade under Colonel Hannay which started from Orange River, marched to Ramdam, and following on the heels of General French's cavalry division, were the advance-guard of the great army after General French had branched off to Kimberley. When Cronje vacated his positions at Magersfontein and was discovered trekking eastward through the gap between General French's force and the main army, Colonel Hannay's Mounted Infantry was the first mounted force available for the pursuit. Colonel Hannay's men made every effort to drive in the Boer rear-guard, but as usual the latter was very skilfully commanded, successive positions being taken up and held to enable Cronje's convoy to get away. However, a good many waggons were either abandoned by the enemy through the animals being unable to proceed or were cut off by the Mounted Infantry. When the laager was discovered on the morning of the 18th Hannay's men again did excellent service, although both horses and men were utterly exhausted with the unceasing work of the previous seven days, during three of which they had had constant fighting. It will be remembered that General French had blocked Cronje's exits on the north and north-east. The infantry of the VIth and IXth Divisions were on the west and southern sides of the laager, while Hannay was ordered by Lord Kitchener to take his men past the laager and attack from the east. After several assaults had been driven back by the terrible fire from the Boers in the hollows about the river-bed, Hannay was ordered to make one more desperate attempt to get in from the east side. That such an effort could succeed could scarcely have occurred to any one who had seen the deadly accuracy of the Boer fire when they were attacked across level ground suitable for the low trajectory of the modern rifle. However, Hannay obeyed the command, and was killed in this last desperate charge undertaken at the imperious desire of Lord Kitchener.

After the surrender of Cronje the N.S.W. Mounted Infantry were in the 2nd Mounted Infantry Brigade commanded by Colonel P. W. J. Le Gallais, under whom they did most excellent work in the battles of Poplar Grove and Driefontein on the way to Bloemfontein. On 6th March, near Osfontein, the Mounted Infantry had Lieutenant Holborrow and 3 men wounded. At Driefontein the squadron of Mounted Rifles had 1 killed and 4 wounded. Captain J. M. Antill gained mention in the despatch of 31st March. The strength of the N.S.W. Mounted Infantry, including

Antill's squadron, when they marched into Bloemfontein on 13th March 1900, was officially stated at 22 officers, 408 men, and 345 horses.

The regiment, under the command of Colonel G. C. Knight, was said to have done good work at the battle of Karee Siding on 29th March, when General Tucker's infantry, French's cavalry, and Le Gallais' brigade of mounted infantry cleared the hills north of Bloemfontein and opened the road to Brandfort. In April the regiment was in some of the engagements southeast of Bloemfontein.

For the advance to Pretoria the regiment was put into the 2nd Mounted Infantry corps under De Lisle, part of Ian Hamilton's army, but in the earlier stages, on account of the cavalry having been unable to take their appointed place on the left flank until after the army had started north, the N.S.W. Mounted Infantry were detached from Hamilton and operated, under Hutton, with the other over-sea Colonials (see Canadian Mounted Rifles). After Kroonstad was left behind, De Lisle's corps, now including the N.S.W. Mounted Infantry, took a very prominent part in the operations which culminated in the surrender of Pretoria. In the despatch of 14th August, para. 22, Lord Roberts spoke of the Boers pressing the left flank and threatening the rear of his centre column, so he ordered Ian Hamilton, out on the left, to close in. "As soon as Ian Hamilton's troops came up and De Lisle's mounted infantry pushed well round the enemy's right flank, they fell back on Pretoria. . . . Shortly before dusk Lt.-Col. De Lisle, whose mounted infantry had followed up the enemy to within 2000 yards of Pretoria, sent an officer under a flag of truce to demand in my name the surrender of the town." The officer referred to was Lieutenant **Watson** of the N.S.W. Mounted Infantry. The town was surrendered on the following day.

The regiment frequently had casualties throughout May, as at the crossing of the Zand, where they lost 8 men. On the 21st Lieutenant A. J. M. Onslow was wounded.

The regiment was present, under De Lisle and Ian Hamilton, on the right, at the battle of Diamond Hill, 11th and 12th June 1900. Mr Paterson's excellent account of their very gallant work, reprinted in the War Record of the Inniskilling Dragoons, says: " Our mounted infantry, under Antill and Holmes, were ordered to advance over a lot of open country, and got possession of some kopjes outlying from the main hills. They made the advance in fine style, and got the hills on the first day without much trouble, although they were shelled as they went over." Next day they were ordered to drive the Boers off a steep rocky kopje on the extreme right. On the top of the hill Lieutenant Dragge was killed and Lieutenant W. R. Harrison mortally wounded. Captain Holmes and Sergeant-Majors Baker and Baring were wounded. In Lord Roberts' telegram of 15th June he referred to the good work done by De Lisle's men, and in that of the 16th he said that Botha's army had "retired, and that the rear-guard was surprised and thoroughly routed by Ian Hamilton's mounted infantry, chiefly West Australians and 6th Battalion" [regulars].

Towards the end of June Colonel De Lisle's mounted infantry were a part of the force which moved on Heidelberg, where the New South Wales men were engaged: thereafter part of the force re-crossed the Vaal, under Sir A. Hunter, to endeavour to close in on the Boers in the Brandwater Basin. De Wet having broken through on 15th July, Broadwood's cavalry and Ridley's mounted infantry, of which Colonel De Lisle's corps was part, were detached by Sir A. Hunter in pursuit (see Roberts' Horse). On the 19th there was a sharp fight at Palmietfontein, in which the N.S.W. Mounted Infantry lost 3 men killed and Lieutenant Lucas Tooth and several men wounded. De Wet took refuge in the Reitzburg Hills, but broke across the Vaal on 6th-7th August. De Lisle's mounted infantry and other troops followed, and continued the pursuit to the Megaliesberg, the New South Wales men suffering a few casualties on the way. After De Wet had got clear they assisted to relieve their fellow-Colonials under Hore at Elands River in August (see Rhodesian Regiment), one of the few casualties in the relieving force being Lieut.-Colonel De Lisle wounded. In the latter part of August and first half of September De Lisle's mounted infantry were operating under Clements in the Gatsrand and generally west of Pretoria. On 17th September they were railed to Rhenoster in the Orange River Colony, where they did a great deal of chasing and fighting. In an attempt to surround a Boer force at Elands Kop on 1st October, the contingent lost 2 men killed. They assisted to drive De Wet from the Reitzburg Hills to the north of the Vaal on 8th-9th October, and when he had re-crossed to the south they had an honourable share in the very successful actions at Rensburg and Parys Drifts, 27th October 1900, and Bothaville, 6th November 1900.

In his despatch of 15th November 1900, para. 14, when dealing with the Bothaville action, Lord Roberts said: "On the 3rd November Le Gallais was again in touch with De Wet's scouts east of Bothaville, and on the night of the 5th surprised the Boer force three miles south of that place, and was heavily engaged for five hours, when he was reinforced by Charles Knox with De Lisle's mounted infantry. This was a most successful engagement, reflecting great credit on Major-General Charles Knox and all serving with him, especially on the Australian and other mounted troops under Colonel Le Gallais and Lt.-Col. De Lisle, who must have felt themselves amply rewarded for the perseverance and energy they had displayed during the preceding weeks, which had been most harassing to all concerned." Lord Roberts then went on to detail the fruits of the victory: these included 6 field-guns, 1 pom-pom, 1 maxim, all the enemy's ammunition and waggons, and 100 prisoners; 25 dead and 30 wounded Boers were left on the field.

In his telegram of 3rd November 1900 Lord Roberts said: "One of the two guns taken from De Wet on the 27th October was a Krupp. It was captured by the New South Wales Mounted Infantry."

On 16th November 3 men of the Mounted Infantry were wounded at Rhenoster.

In Lord Roberts' telegram of 26th November 1900, he said: "De Lisle from Kroonstad reports that Colonel Fanshawe had a rear-guard action with about 60 Boers near Duinsfontein. One man of the N.S.W. Mounted Rifles was killed. Fanshawe reports that Capt. Watson performed a gallant act. Seeing Private Robinson, N.S.W. Mounted Rifles, fall, he turned back and carried him out on his own horse under a hot fire." Captain Watson was an officer of the N.S.W. Mounted Infantry. Most of the Mounted Rifles left South Africa before the end of 1900.

In Jan. and Feb. 1901 De Lisle, with some of the

N.S.W. Mounted Infantry and their old comrades the 6th Battalion Mounted Infantry (regulars), was doing very fine work in the Piquetberg-Clanwilliam district of Cape Colony,—work which greatly contributed to persuade the enemy of the hopelessness of any attempt to reach Cape Town or to get arms or ammunition from the sea-coast. The work of the N.S.W. men was over and over again most highly praised by the Press Association correspondent who accompanied the column on its march through very difficult country about the Roggeveld mountains. In order to turn a pass Captain Bennett led his men during darkness over a high mountain, climbing a very steep face for nearly 2000 feet. On another occasion the column did 72 miles in forty-eight hours in a district almost waterless. Writing on 25th January 1901, the Press Association correspondent remarked that the Intelligence officer of the column was Captain Legge, Colonel De Lisle's galloper was Captain Watson, while the Supply officer was Lieutenant Osborne—all N.S.W. officers. He said the work of all three was excellent, and the column the best fed he had been with. This latter fact may account for some of the praise. On the 19th February, the anniversary of the landing of the 2nd contingent, Colonel De Lisle addressed them. He could not have spoken in more flattering terms of them and their comrades the 1st Contingent N.S.W. Mounted Infantry.

On 31st March 1901 the last of the 1st and 2nd Contingents of N.S.W. Mounted Infantry sailed for home.

THE 1st NEW SOUTH WALES BUSHMEN
(3RD CONTINGENT).

IN January 1900 it was announced that the Imperial Government had accepted the offer of a corps, to be known as the Australian Bushmen, which would be furnished by the Australian colonies. This regiment, which was the quota of New South Wales, was about 530 strong, under the command of Lieut.-Colonel Airey, D.S.O. Four companies sailed on the *Atlantian* and one on the *Maplemore* on 1st March 1900. On arriving in South Africa the regiment was despatched by sea to Beira, and landed there on 14th April 1900. This was sometimes designed as the "Citizen's Bushmen Contingent," as contrasted with the "Imperial Bushmen Contingent," a later contribution.

The "Bushmen" who landed at Beira included the 4th and 5th New Zealanders, Colonel Airey's Regiment from New South Wales, and contingents from the other Australian colonies. Mr Green, chaplain of the regiment, in his 'Story of the Bushmen,' Sydney, 1903, says that it was announced that, apart from the New Zealanders, the other contingents would be divided as follows: 1st Regiment, New South Wales, Colonel Airey; 2nd Regiment, Victorians and West Australians, Major Vialls; 3rd Regiment, Queenslanders, Major Tunbridge. But the Victorian and West Australian Regiment was more generally designated the 3rd Bushmen. The different corps were very much split up and mixed up before they had gone far into the Transvaal; while a composite regiment was formed of one squadron from each of the 5th New Zealand, 3rd

The 1st New South Wales Bushmen

South Australians, 3rd Tasmanians, and "D" squadron of the 1st N.S.W. Bushmen. This composite regiment did excellent work under Lord Erroll and Lord Methuen. (See 3rd South Australians.)

To get to the Transvaal the Bushmen contingents had to cross a strip of Portuguese territory and the whole of Rhodesia. At Marandellas a camp was established in which the units could be collected and equipped, but the climate was unfavourable for horses, and many died. Their owners had to perform the long journey to Bulawayo on foot. In accomplishing as they did 300 miles in twenty days, these "foot-sloggers" did well. From Bulawayo to Mafeking the railway was used.

Having entered the Transvaal from the northwest corner, the N.S.W. Bushmen, apart from "D" squadron, in various detachments, crossed, viâ Zeerust, to the district about Rustenburg and then to that north of Pretoria, where for some months they did good service under Major-General Baden-Powell and Major-General Plumer. About 4th July Hanbury-Tracy was holding Rustenburg with a mixed force of 120 men. In his telegraphic despatch of 8th July 1900 Lord Roberts spoke of an attempt made on Rustenburg by Boers under Lemmer, "who were eventually driven off with the assistance of Colonel Holdsworth, 7th Hussars (attached to the British South Africa Police), who made a rapid march of 48 miles from the neighbourhood of Zeerust with Bushmen under Colonel Airey on hearing that Rustenburg was likely to be threatened." The enemy suffered heavy loss, and 5 prisoners were captured. Our casualties were—Bushmen, 2 killed, Captain Machattie and 3 men wounded." Three hundred of the Australian

Bushmen accompanied Holdsworth, and "C" squadron, Machattie's, did most of the fighting. At this time there was fighting daily in the north-west of the Transvaal. On 9th July Lieutenant Gells with "B" squadron of the N.S.W. Bushmen was engaged at Megato Pass. In his telegram of 16th July Lord Roberts said: "Baden-Powell reports that a patrol of Australian Bushmen encountered a party of Boers on the 13th and drove them back with loss. Sergeant Ryan (Ryrie?) wounded on shoulder." And on the 22nd July, at Koster's River between the Megato Pass and Elands River, there was very heavy fighting. In Lord Roberts' telegram of 24th July he said: "Baden-Powell reports from the Megato Pass on the 22nd that Colonels Airey and Lushington, with only 400 men, drove 1000 Boers from a strong position and scattered them with considerable loss." Mr Green, in 'The Story of the Bushmen,' gives some interesting details: he says that Baden-Powell had ordered Colonel Airey to go back to Elands River on the 22nd for a convoy. Airey's force was about 300 strong, made up in equal proportions of men from the New South Wales, Queensland, Victorian, and West Australian Bushmen. The Boers lay low while the advance-guard passed and then opened a heavy fire on the main body. The men instantly opened out a little and lay down in the grass, where they held on for eight hours. Captain C. W. Robertson was shot in the head while directing "B" squadron, N.S.W. Bushmen, and Lieutenant Eckford, who succeeded him, was wounded. Surgeon Lieut.-Colonel Ingoldsby and 2 officers of the Queenslanders were also wounded. Two English ladies resident in the neighbourhood, Miss Bach and Miss Macdonald, boldly entered the firing line and dressed wounds. Airey sent back for reinforcements, but the message was wrongly delivered or misunderstood. Miss Bach rode in as a second messenger, and 200 Australians under Colonel Lushington and Captain Fitzclarence, V.C. (Bechuanaland Protectorate Regiment), came out, and the enemy were driven off.

As Mr Green remarks, there are some "white flag" stories connected with this action. According to him a small party, an officer and 10 men, occupied an isolated position and could not leave it. As they were suffering casualties, apparently for no object, the officer put up a white flag. Colonel Airey hearing of this seemed to think his force were bound by this white flag. Major Vialls of the West Australians (who was already proving his splendid worth, and had earned his nickname, "Old Biltong"), and his men protested, "stamped and swore," and as the enemy evidently did not take the incident seriously and continued to fire, any idea of the force surrendering was soon abandoned. The losses of Airey's force were 6 killed and 22 wounded. Captain Robertson was an officer of the Royal Marine Light Infantry, who was on the Australian station when war broke out. Having volunteered for service with the New South Wales men, he was accepted, and proved himself a most gallant leader of mounted infantry.

About 100 men of the 1st N.S.W. Bushmen, chiefly from "A" squadron, under Captain Thomas and Lieutenants Zouch, Cope, Cornwall, and Bronowski, were in the garrison of Elands River, which made a splendid defence under Colonel Hore, 4th to 16th August (see Rhodesian Regiment). The detachment had about a dozen casualties, including Sergt.-Major J. A. Mitchell killed. After the relief of Colonel Hore's force the garrison were taken to Mafeking to refit. Thence they were railed *viâ* De Aar and the Orange River Colony to Pretoria, where Lord Roberts inspected and congratulated them on 1st October.

In October 1900 the 1st N.S.W. Bushmen, minus "D" squadron, were about Pienaars River, in which district they saw a good deal of skirmishing. One squadron, "A," was present at the battle of Rhenoster Kop, 29th November (see New Zealand 1st, 2nd, and 3rd Contingents). The detachment with Plumer saw further fighting in this district during December and January; as on 13th January, when the enemy attacked a convoy. In this affair Sergt.-Major Weir and one man were severely wounded. A part of the regiment, including "A" squadron, accompanied General Plumer to Cape Colony, and took part in the pursuit of De Wet in February 1901. They saw a great deal of fighting (see 4th Victorian Contingent), and had casualties on various occasions. While Plumer was in the south the other portion of the regiment did outpost work about Pienaars River and generally north-east of Pretoria.

In March it was announced that Plumer would lead an expedition to the Pietersburg district in the north of the Transvaal. The 1st, 2nd, and 3rd regiments of Australian Bushmen accompanied Plumer, excepting "D" squadron of the 1st, which was still in the Western Transvaal. The expedition was most ably managed, and was very successful, much loss being inflicted on the enemy at slight cost.

The doings of "D" squadron were much akin to those of the 6th Imperial Bushmen, to which reference is made (see also 3rd South Australians). The composite regiment did much good work. "D" squadron had losses on various occasions. They had several men wounded between Ottoshoop and Elands River on 5th and 6th August 1900, when Carrington attempted to relieve Hore, and were after that in very many actions in the Western Transvaal. In the first quarter of 1901 they had casualties on various occasions.

On 13th April it was announced that the Australian Bushmen would now return, their year of service being complete, and shortly afterwards they entrained for Cape Town.

6TH IMPERIAL BUSHMEN (4TH NEW SOUTH WALES CONTINGENT).

THE statement supplied by the Premier of New South Wales to the War Commission, Appendices to Evidence, p. 177, shows that the 6th Imperial Bushmen, which was raised in New South Wales, had a strength of 757 with 800 horses. It was under the command of Colonel the Hon. J. A. Kennett Mackay. They sailed from New South Wales on the *Armenian* on 23rd April 1900.

The corps landed at Beira, crossed Rhodesia, and operated in the north-west of the Transvaal. Under General Carrington they advanced to the relief of their noble Colonial brothers at Elands River and, having seen the enemy, took part in the very inglorious retreat. When the Elands River garrison, having been relieved, was marching to Mafeking, they found the 6th Imperial Bushmen at Zeerust, and the latter are said to have expressed themselves very freely at the humiliating *rôle* they had been forced to play. They had suffered some very trifling losses, but would gladly have borne much to have had the credit of relieving Hore. The Rev. J. Green, who was at Elands River (see Rhodesian Regiment), said the 6th were very sick at being in the "inglorious attempt to pull us out of the fire. . . . No one felt the humiliation like Lord Cecil"; and again, the evacuation of Zeerust was inexplicable. "Cecil broke down and wept like a child." The son of Britain's great Prime Minister had been one of the noble band who had held Mafeking for seven long months. He doubtless felt what a falling off in spirit was now come. Throughout August the regiment saw a good deal of skirmishing. On the 27th they had several casualties, including Sergeant-Major Messenger wounded. After General Carrington had gone home the regiment did excellent service under Lord Methuen and other leaders in the Western Transvaal, and their good work was frequently recognised. On 9th September the 6th had half a dozen men wounded. In Lord Roberts' telegram of 12th September, he said: "Methuen reports that Douglas was attacked yesterday morning when marching on the road from Ottoshoop to Lichtenburg. After some hours' fighting Douglas drove the enemy off and captured a quantity of grain and other stores. His casualties were — wounded, Capt. Bryce, Australian Bushmen, severely in shoulder, 2 men severely, 2 slightly"; and on 18th September he wired, "Methuen reports, Douglas came across a body of the enemy on the 12th near Lichtenburg. He captured 39 prisoners, 10 waggons, and some sheep and oxen.

His casualties were—Lt. R. J. White, 6th Imperial Bushmen, severely wounded and taken prisoner: a man of the regiment has died of wounds received on same occasion." At Lichtenburg on 28th September the regiment had 7 men wounded, 3 of whom died of their wounds. In Lord Roberts' telegram of 12th November 1900 he spoke of the "excellent work" of both the N.S.W. Bushmen and New Zealanders, then under General Douglas. The corps had several casualties about the 25th and 26th December, including Lieutenant D. F. Miller wounded.

During the first four months of 1901 the 6th Imperial Bushmen, or the greater portion of them, were with Lord Methuen and General Babington in the Western Transvaal (see 4th New Zealand contingent), and their work was most highly spoken of in despatches and by the correspondents. During February the corps was frequently engaged, and did many trying marches.

Major W. E. O'Brien, Lieutenants Thomson and Doyle, and many non-commissioned officers and men, gained mention on the 23rd and 24th March 1901, when General Babington and Colonel Grey had a most successful action with Delarey, in which they took 3 guns, 6 maxims, and many prisoners. It was very fortunate that the regiment got, and made such a fine use of, this grand opportunity, before their term of service came to an end. Some of the regiment were still in the field in June, and on the 4th of that month Lieutenant A. E. G. King was severely wounded in the north-west of the Transvaal. The appendix to the despatch of 8th July 1901 puts the strength of the 6th Imperial Bushmen with General Babington, in

May, at 193 : detachments were employed at other parts of the Transvaal at that time

Colonel Mackay and his contingent sailed for home on 26th June 1901.

2ND NEW SOUTH WALES MOUNTED RIFLES AND 3RD NEW SOUTH WALES BUSHMEN.

THE strength of the 2nd N.S.W. Mounted Rifles, Lieutenant-Colonel Lassetter commanding, was, on sailing, 709 all ranks.[1] They arrived in South Africa at the end of March 1901. The 2nd and 3rd N.S.W. Mounted Rifles formed the fifth contingent or contribution of the colony.

The 3rd N.S.W. Bushmen, Major the Hon. R. Carington commanding, was about 4 squadrons strong : they were split up after arrival.

Lord Kitchener in his despatch, 8th May 1901, para. 11, remarks that a fresh column of mounted Australian troops was, in April, organised at Klerksdorp in the Transvaal, under Lieutenant-Colonel E. C. Williams, to reinforce General Babington. The appendix to the despatch of 8th July 1901 shows that the column was, in May, composed of 2nd N.S.W. Mounted Rifles, 526 ; 3rd N.S.W. Bushmen, 229 ; 21st Battalion Mounted Infantry, 432 ; 78th Battery Royal Field Artillery, 2 guns ; Elswick Battery, 1 gun ; "A" Battery Royal Australian Artillery, 2 guns ; 2 sections of pom-poms ; 192 men of the 2nd

[1] Statement at p. 177, Appendix to War Commission Report.

Cheshire Regiment; Australian Medical Corps; and 7th company Royal Engineers.

Colonel Williams' column, in the beginning of May, took part in operations in the south-west of the Transvaal, and on the 10th had sharp fighting, when Lieutenant E. Lamb and 4 men were killed and 7 wounded. On the 15th Captain M'Lean, of the 2nd Mounted Rifles, was severely wounded at Koranafontein. "On the 24th, on the right bank of the Vaal, near Klerksdorp, this force had a successful action with Van Rensburg's Commando, in the course of which 24 prisoners, 6200 rounds of ammunition, and 30 oxwaggons were taken."[1] Thirty-five Burghers surrendered on the march back. Throughout June and July the column was in the Western Transvaal. In the end of June and first half of July, along with three other columns, all under General Fetherstonhaugh, Williams marched through the Megaliesberg to Zeerust and back to Klerksdorp. There were many sharp skirmishes, and a fair number of prisoners were taken.[2] Another long march to the western railway and back was next undertaken. On 19th August Williams, hearing that a Boer convoy was to the north of him, sent his waggons in another direction to deceive the enemy; "then with his Australians, New South Wales M.R., and Bushmen, made a rapid night march" towards the Boers. "After a gallop of 12 miles he was able to ride down and capture the whole convoy, with 18 prisoners, 65 waggons,"[3] and much stock. On this occasion the column covered 60 miles in twenty-seven hours. In September and October the

[1] Despatch of 8th July 1901, para. 7.
[2] Despatch of 8th August, para. 8.
[3] Despatch of 8th September, para. 11.

same kind of thing went on—the column always doing well and keeping out of mishaps. On 20th October 1901 Williams and his "600 Australians" (the Mounted Infantry and Cheshires had left the column) were railed from Klerksdorp to the Eastern Transvaal, and on the 26th drove in a Boer picket and took 50 prisoners and much stock. The next day the very difficult Witnek defile was forced. "The enemy held the pass in some strength, and brought a pom-pom into action. The energetic advance of our troops, however, eventually forced him to abandon his strong position, and he finally fled, leaving 5 dead on the ground."[1] In the pass, which is 6 miles long, a few prisoners were taken. Williams was now brought to the east of Pretoria, and moved first to Leeuwkop and then to Pienaars River Station. In November and December he was working south of Wonderfontein on the Delagoa line, and took part in the very successful operations of General Bruce Hamilton. On the 6th December Williams had stiff fighting at Weltevreden, killing 5 and capturing 12 of the enemy. Throughout December and four following months many night marches were undertaken, often with luck. On one occasion the force fought a successful action and marched 60 miles within forty-eight hours.[2] During these last months of the war the mobile columns had terribly hard work, and few of them came out better than that of Colonel E. C. Williams. On the whole, it escaped with wonderfully few casualties.

About the end of April 1902, immediately after a very successful movement, "the column was broken

[1] Despatch of 8th November, para. 2.
[2] Despatch of 8th January 1902.

up, the Over-Sea Colonials of whom it was composed having completed their period of service in South Africa."[1] In Lord Kitchener's despatch of 1st June 1902 (see 8th New Zealand Contingent), a corps, there designated 3rd New South Wales Bushmen, is mentioned, but doubtless the General meant to refer to one of the New South Wales battalions of Commonwealth Horse.

The bulk of the 2nd N.S.W. Mounted Rifles, under Lieut.-Colonel Lassetter, arrived at Sydney on 5th June while the Peace celebrations were in progress, and got a magnificent reception.

3RD NEW SOUTH WALES MOUNTED RIFLES.

THIS contingent arrived in South Africa in April 1901. Their strength on sailing was 1086 all ranks. They were commanded by Lieut.-Colonel C. W. Cox, who had served with the N.S.W. Lancers.

The 3rd N.S.W. Mounted Rifles joined the column of Colonel Rimington in May 1901. This was one of several columns which worked almost incessantly during the last thirteen months of the war in the north-east of the Orange River Colony, and by the splendid way in which they carried out their task under the faultless leadership of Rimington the column did a great deal towards bringing the war to an end. The district allotted to them was the stronghold of the Free Staters, and was well adapted to

[1] Despatch of 1st June 1902.

their style of warfare. Rundle's VIIIth Division had marched about in it since May 1900, and Sir Archibald Hunter had there taken 4000 prisoners in July of that year; but it was not until the mobile mounted columns were organised that any impression could be made on the enemy's vigour in this quarter.

On 21st July 1901 the column was at Heilbron: it then numbered a little over 2000, of which the N.S.W. Mounted Rifles contributed 800 and the 6th Inniskilling Dragoons 466. A history of the column's work is given in the War Record of the latter regiment, already quoted from under the N.S.W. Lancers. It would be quite impossible to detail here the numberless engagements, marches, and the enormous captures of prisoners, rifles, ammunition, and transport by which the column so ably contributed to wear out the enemy. A few examples from the Inniskilling's record to show what the work was must suffice.

It having been decided to attempt to surprise a laager with which it was reported De Wet then was,—

"At 7 P.M. on 14th September 1901 the surprise force, consisting, as usual, of the Inniskillings, N.S.W. Mounted Rifles, Canadian Scouts, and section R.H.A., under Colonel Rimington, started on a night march. After crossing the Klip River near Parys about 2 A.M., the column was obliged to halt on account of the intense darkness. The moon had gone·down and heavy rain set in. The troops lay by their horses in bitter cold and rain until dawn, and then pushed on fast and rounded up Brakoog. Ten Boers escaped. Pushing on to Anderkant and towards Sodas, a few Boers were caught, and our convoy was rejoined in the valley below Kat Kop. The night had been against the enterprise. About 46 miles had been covered and De Wet had not been taken, but the capture included 6 Boers, 6 rifles, 300 rounds of S.A. ammunition, 6 waggons, 9 Cape carts, 350 cattle, 11 mules, and 6 riding-horses." On 24th-25th September 60 miles were covered in thirty hours in a similar operation. These marches—generally starting at dusk —went on continuously, and, of course, the strain on all was very great. "On 10th October, in passing the eastern spurs of Leeuwkop, a N.S.W. Mounted Rifles sergeant-major was mortally wounded and 2 horses of the Inniskillings killed by snipers. The sergeant-major was buried next day under the Sugar Loaf Kopje on the march to Langspruit." About the middle of October an attempt was made to capture General Louis Botha, then living near Amsterdam, in the east of the Transvaal. Rimington's men were chosen to go, and, leaving the Standerton Railway with sixteen days' rations, they set out on their long march. They reached the farm at dawn on the 24th. The morning was misty, but cleared at 7 A.M. and revealed the column to some Boers, about one hundred. These opened fire and Botha galloped off. His papers were taken, and doubtless were of use to Lord Kitchener. To be selected for this enterprise was the highest compliment the Commander-in-Chief could have paid Rimington's column. On 2nd November they were back to Standerton, from which they worked south.

In December 1901 and the first four months of 1902 the N.S.W. Mounted Rifles took part in the great drives which it had been decided, on the suggestion of Colonel Rimington, was the only method by which the war could be ended. During these drives the amount of work done by men and horses was incredible. Lieut.-Colonel Watkins-Yardley notes that, on the occasion of a drive in February, the troops were on outpost for eleven consecutive nights. It is generally recognised that outpost duty for three consecutive nights is a most severe strain on all ranks.

On the occasion of the most important of these drives the enemy, on the night of 23rd February 1902, made a desperate and partially successful attempt to break the line in the Vrede district held by Colonel Garratt (see 7th New Zealand Contingent). In his telegram of 1st March 1902 Lord Kitchener said: "On that occasion, besides the New Zealanders, already mentioned, the 3rd New South Wales Mounted Rifles, under Colonel Cox, behaved extremely well, bringing heavy fire on the enemy. The cattle that fell into our hands showed the effective nature of that fire, a large proportion being wounded."

During these operations the contingent had never very serious casualties; but as a matter of course there were some losses, as on 28th January 1902 when Surgeon Seddon and one man were wounded.

On 28th April 1902 "The New South Wales Mounted Rifles, under Lieut.-Colonel Cox, entrained this day for Cape Town for embarkation back to Australia. They had put in a most valuable year's service with Colonel Rimington's column. Lieut.-Colonel Cox himself and many of the men had rendered conspicuous service in the earlier stages of the war with the New South Wales Lancers, when they were attached to and formed a squadron of the

Inniskilling Dragoons. The following extract from Force Orders by Colonel M. F. Rimington, C.B., was truly merited :—

"'KRAAL, *Monday, April* 28, 1902.

"'The Brigadier in saying good-bye to the Officers, N.C.O.'s, and men of 3rd New South Wales Mounted Rifles, desires to thank all ranks for their good work during the year they have served under his command. They have shown by their dash in attack, steadiness in action, and alert behaviour on outpost duties that they are thorough good soldiers, of whom the Empire may well be proud. Their cheerful conduct under privations and exposure is above praise. He wishes them God-speed, and good luck wherever they go. (Sgd.) G. K. ANSELL, Major, C.S.O.'"[1]

New South Wales furnished several reinforcing drafts to the contingents already mentioned, as well as three battalions of Mounted Rifles as the Colony's contribution to the Commonwealth troops. (See that heading.)

NEW SOUTH WALES ARTILLERY.

ON 11th October 1899 New South Wales offered to send, as part of the first contingent, a fully-equipped battery of six guns, but the War Office was foolish enough to refuse the offer. After Magersfontein the offer was renewed, and this time it was accepted.[2] No time was lost, and "A" Battery, Royal Australian

[1] Inniskilling Dragoons War Record, p. 328.
[2] 'Times' History, vol. iii. p. 34.

Artillery—strength, all ranks, 179—under the command of Colonel S. C. U. Smith, sailed on the *Warrigal* from Port Jackson on 30th December 1899, and landed in South Africa on 6th February 1900. On their arrival they were inspected by Lord Roberts, who expressed himself as most highly pleased with both men and horses.

During the greater portion of Lord Roberts' tenure of the command in South Africa, the battery operated in the western portion of Cape Colony, chiefly in the Prieska district, being part of the force which it was necessary to maintain there in order to overawe that section of the inhabitants who were in active sympathy with the enemy, and to prevent incursions from the Transvaal or Free State. The battery was mentioned in the despatch of 28th February 1900 as a portion of the force at the disposal of Lord Methuen for the protection of Kimberley and the Western Railway. Later in 1900 the battery, having been split up, was much scattered. One gun, under Captain Antill, did particularly valuable service in a column which operated in September 1900 and following months in the west of the Transvaal and Orange River Colony and in Griqualand.[1]

Colonel Smith was for a time commandant of the north-west portion of Cape Colony.

When Cape Colony was invaded, January and February 1901, a portion of the battery was acting under Colonel Crabbe, and took part in the arduous pursuit of De Wet. Lieutenant E. Christian's section was said by Colonel Crabbe to have been admirably handled,— " He is a very good gunner and horsemaster " (see Lord Kitchener's despatch of 8th May 1901).

[1] See 'A Fight to a Finish,' by Major Dennison, D.S.O. London, 1904.

During a great portion of 1901 four guns were with Colonel Rimington's column, which did splendid work in the north-east of the Orange River Colony (see 3rd New South Wales Mounted Rifles); and two guns were in the column of Colonel E. Williams, which also distinguished itself (see 2nd New South Wales Mounted Rifles).

In May 1901 part of the *personnel* of the battery's first contingent started for home; but it was not till 16th September, after nearly two years' absence, that the main portion of the battery reached Sydney. They received a magnificent reception.

In his telegram of 25th August 1901 Lord Kitchener said that it had been brought to his notice that on 6th June, near Reitz, in the Orange River Colony, Lieutenant Mair, of N.S.W. Artillery, and Privates Harvey and Blunt were shot down after they had surrendered. Fortunately such occurrences were uncommon. Our late enemies had not imbibed the brutal doctrines of the German Staff that the shooting of prisoners is, or at times may be, justifiable.

NEW SOUTH WALES MEDICAL STAFF.

THE splendid field hospital and bearer company furnished by New South Wales were organised and commanded by Colonel, now Surgeon-General, W. D. C. Williams, of that Colony. They arrived in South Africa in two portions: the first, 50 beds and half a bearer company—91 all ranks—was accepted about 11th October 1899, and sailed on the 28th; and the remainder was accepted in December of the same year, and sailed in January 1900.

The corps saw an immense deal of service. On arrival in South Africa, the first detachment went to the De Aar-Modder River line. Under Surgeon-Major Dodds they served with Colonel Pilcher in the expedition to Sunnyside about 1st January 1900 (see 1st Queensland Contingent), and in other operations in that neighbourhood; and they took part in the advance from Modder River to Bloemfontein. The second portion was in the operations for relieving Wepener, the cool work of Major Eames and Captain Green under shell-fire being much praised.

On the way to Pretoria the N.S.W. Field Hospital was attached to the army of General Ian Hamilton, who, it will be remembered, had constant fighting between 3rd May 1900 and 5th June. In July the hospital was with Hutton east of Pretoria, but a detachment was in the Orange River Colony for a time; and Captain H. R. Howse, of the Medical Staff Corps, won the Victoria Cross at Vredefort on 24th July. Captain Howse went out under a heavy cross-fire, picked up a wounded man, and carried him to a place of shelter.

After advancing from Pretoria to Belfast in July and August, one portion of the hospital and bearer company accompanied General Hutton in his memorable march over the Kaapsche Hoop Mountains in the Eastern Transvaal (see 1st Victoria Contingent); another portion accompanied General French in the equally arduous march to Barberton (see Imperial Light Horse).

In a telegram dated 20th September 1900 Lord Roberts mentioned that Captain Perkins, of the

N.S.W. Medical Staff, and some non-commissioned officers and men had been taken prisoners near Rustenburg, but they were soon afterwards released. The Boers, however, did not return the ambulances at the time, as they said they found in them some rifles. Probably these were curios which the men had been intending to take home. In December a detachment was with General Clements when he met with his reverse at Nooitgedacht on the 13th. 'The Standard' correspondent, in a letter describing this action, said that the Red Cross flag brought no protection, owing to the terrible cross-fire; and he mentioned that Captain Green and his bearers attended to the wounded in a hail of bullets which actually splintered some of the stretchers.

In the second phase of the war a detachment was for a considerable part of 1901 with Colonel Williams, who commanded a column composed of Australian troops (see 2nd New South Wales Mounted Rifles). A detachment—3 officers and 27 men—sailed for home on 31st March 1901.

During a great part of 1901 Colonel R. V. Kelly commanded a N.S.W. Hospital in the field, and when the Commonwealth troops were sent in 1902, New South Wales contributed to the Army Medical Corps a detachment of about 40, all ranks.

In the despatch of 31st March 1900, mentioning those who had distinguished themselves at Paardeberg, Poplar Grove, and Driefontein, Lord Roberts, in mentioning Major J. H. Fiaschi, N.S.W. Medical Staff Corps, said, "Is deserving of special mention on account of the assistance which he rendered to the sick and wounded, as well as on the efficient condition in which he has kept the ambulance under his command, the services of which, ever since its arrival, have been most valuable."

The Honours and Mentions gained were as follows :—

Captain H. R. Howse, of the New South Wales Medical Staff Corps, won the Victoria Cross on 24th July 1900, in the circumstances already mentioned.

LORD ROBERTS' DESPATCHES: 31st March 1900.—Mounted Infantry: Capt. J. M. Antill [1]; Cpl. English. Royal Australian Artillery: Lt.-Col. C. Umphelby, killed.; Lt.-Col. J. J. Byron, Aide-de-camp to Lord Roberts.[2] 2nd April 1901.—Mounted Rifles: Major J. M. Antill, M.I.; Lt.-Col. H. P. Airey,[2] D.S.O.; Capts. A. J. Bennett,[3] M. A. Hilliard,[3] W. Holmes,[3] A. A. M'Lean [3]; Lts. F. A. Dove,[3] F. C. Learmonth,[3] C. G. S. Lydiard, D. K. Tooth, W. W. R. Watson; Sgt.-Majors R. C. Holman,[4] F. Ligguns, Pallack, J. Wasson [4]; Lce.-Sgt. S. R. Antill; Pts. L. Hayward,[4] J. M'Cracken, W. Neeld, F. Rudd.[4] Imperial Bushmen: Col. Hon. J. A. Mackay [1] (6th); Capt. A. B. Baker [3] (1st); Lts. W. Butler, H. B. Christie [3] (1st), S. C. Cape [3] (1st), R. D. Doyle [3] (1st), T. M. Moore [3] (1st), R. E. Zouch (1st). Army Medical Corps: Col. W. D. C. Williams [1]; Major Fiaschi.[3] Bearer Company: Capts. T. A. Green,[3] R. E. Roth,[3] A. E. Perkins [3]; Sgts. G. Dart, T. Hender,[4] G. Rose; Cpl. C. Linfield; [4] Pts. G. Helmes,[4] P. Murphy.[4] Lt. G. J. Grieve, killed (at Paardeberg, when attached to the Black Watch: General Macdonald wrote that Lt. Grieve's name would find honourable mention and abiding record in the history of that famous Regiment). Australian Horse: Sgt.-Major H. Arnold.

4th Sept. 1901.—Mounted Infantry: Lt.-Col. J. W. M. Onslow. Medical Corps: Majors W. L. Eames,[1] Hon. A. MacCormisk; Lts. Newmarsh, Dick, Horsfall.[3] New South Wales Lancers: Major Lee; [3] Squadron Sgt.-Major G. E. Morris; [4] Sgt. Houston.[4] Bushmen's Contingent: Capts. K. Wray,[3] H. H. Browne; [3] Lt. P. W. Vaughan (1st Australian Horse); Sgt.-Major Hargreaves (1st Australian Horse); Pte., afterwards Lt., D. Drummond; [4] Nursing Sister E. Nixon, who got the Royal Red Cross.

LORD KITCHENER'S DESPATCHES: 8th March 1901.—New South Wales Medical Corps: Capt. T. A. Green.

8th May 1901.—6th Imperial Bushmen: Major W. E. O'Brien,[3] handled his men well in action of 23rd, and in pursuit of 24th; Lts. E. H. Thomas and R. Doyle,[3] and Corporal Moy,[4] for excellent services in capture of Delarey's guns on 24th March 1900; Cpl. W. Fyfe (promoted Sgt.), operations near Potchefstroom, as my head conductor, has done excellent work throughout, and on March 24th, when convoy was attacked, was of greatest assistance (from Col. Benson's Despatch). Sgt. Thomson (promoted 2nd

---

[1] Awarded C.B. [2] Awarded C.M.G.
[3] Awarded D.S.O. [4] Awarded D.C.M.

Mentions gained by N.S.W. Contingents

Lt.), seeing 80 of enemy about to occupy a wood, took 15 men and galloped to anticipate them, which he did. Had this wood been occupied, advance would have been impeded and checked for a time. Lce.-Cpl. M'Clymont (promoted Cpl.), noticing a Boer shooting at Lt. Hungerford from the pass, at close range charged and shot him. Cpl. Newlands (promoted Sgt.), seeing some Boers trying to get a gun limber away, charged them by himself, and engaged them till supported by more men, when limber was taken. Pte. Rhodenback (promoted Cpl.) was a scout on the extreme right of advance, and found 50 Boers in a gully : he opened fire and kept on firing till Boers retired. Pte. Fewkes (promoted Cpl.) charged a kopje under heavy fire, firing himself from his horse ; rest of troop followed and enemy fled. Pte. H. Selby took a man's horse to him under close fire, and remained with him whilst he resaddled his horse, in Gatsrand, April. 1st Australian Bushmen, from General Plumer's Despatch of March 23 : Sgt. Davenport,[1] during Boer attack on convoy near Rhenoster Kop, May 23, was twice severely wounded while fetching ammunition ; also did excellent service at Elands River ; Sgt.-Major Weir, on same occasion, dressed Sgt. Davenport's wounds under fire, and did good service generally.

8th July 1901.—6th Imperial Bushmen : Tpr. H. Ruddle (promoted Cpl.), on May 23, when convoy to Ventersdorp was attacked, volunteered to carry a message through enemy's lines from Ventersdorp to officer commanding convoy, and succeeded.

8th October 1901.—Bushmen : Lt. Quintal, greatly distinguished himself in night capture of Spannerbergs Laager, near Honingspruit, August 16. 3rd Mounted Infantry : Lt. W. Moffitt, gallant conduct on Vaal River, September 23.

8th December 1901.—3rd Bushmen : Major H. Hamilton Browne, D.S.O., for several instances of marked good service with 6th Regiment Imperial Bushmen.

8th March 1902.—Mounted Rifles : Capt. F. Lydiard, Lt. E. F. Airey (2nd) ; Lt. Fortescue (3rd), for conspicuous good service in December and January ; Sgt.-Major J. Wasson (2nd), in Ermelo district, December 1901, for dash and for holding a kopje with only four men, to cover the retirement of some wounded men.

LORD ROBERTS' FINAL DESPATCH : *1st March* 1902.—Medical Corps : Lt.-Col. R. V. Kelly.[2] Bushmen : Tprs. W. F. Hunt[1] (now Sgt.), T. Borlase,[1] J. Waddell (killed). Pte. Duffyer, Mounted Rifles, got one of the four scarves worked by her late Majesty for distribution among men of Colonial Contingent.

LORD KITCHENER'S DESPATCHES : *8th April* 1902.—Mounted Rifles : Lt.-Col. C. W. Cox.[2]

1st June 1902.—3rd Mounted Rifles : Warrant-Officer M'Coll, for prompt initiative and good work in action of 24th February 1902. Australian

---

[1] Awarded D.C.M.   [2] Awarded C.B.

Bushmen : Sgt.-Major Harden, conspicuous good service at Brakspruit, 11th April 1902 ; Cpl. H. B. Wall, same action (promoted Sgt.)

23rd June 1902.—Nursing Sister A. B. Pocock ; Lt.-Col. H. B. Lassetter [1] ; Majors C. G. S. Lydiard, A. J. Bennett, Hon. R. Carrington,[2] V. H. Edwards ; Capts. Soame, R. C. Holman,[2] T. M'Donald,[2] R. H. Herron, C. E. Middleton ; Lt. J. Dickson ; Regtl. Sgt.-Majors J. Wasson, J. W. Porter [3] ; Warrant-Officer J. M'Coll ; Sgt.-Majors P. J. Moy, J. Hardy ; Squadron Sgt.-Majors H. Pearce, C. T. Murphy, Webster, A. E. Digby ; Sgts. W. Maxwell,[3] J. D. Sutton, J. Macdonald, D. Felts ; Cpl. E. A. Evans ; Pte. G. L. Hobson.[3]

---

[1] Awarded C.B.   [2] Awarded D.S.O.   [3] Awarded D.C.M.

Victorian Contingents.

1ST AND 2ND VICTORIA MOUNTED RIFLES, AND MOUNTED INFANTRY.

SIR G. A. FRENCH informed the War Commission[1] that the total of the various contributions from Victoria was 3757, all ranks.

The 1st contingent sailed on the *Medic* on 20th October 1899. By desire of the War Office it was limited to one company of mounted rifles and one company of infantry: the latter was mounted in January 1900.

On arrival at Cape Town the 1st contingent was sent to De Aar. About the beginning of January the mounted squadron was with General Babington, assisting to protect the communications of Lord Methuen. On 8th January Babington, with the 9th and 12th Lancers, Victoria M.R., and "G" Battery, made a reconnaissance to Ramdam in the Orange River Colony; but although they took part in various expeditions of this kind, both to the east and west of the railway, the Victorians did little real fighting in this neighbourhood. The infantry unit, under Captain M'Inerney, formed part of the Australian Regiment, and during December

---

[1] Appendices, p. 174.

and January was stationed about Enslin and Belmont, and other points on the line between Orange and Modder Rivers. Towards the close of January it was decided to mount the whole regiment. They were taken to Naauwpoort, Central Cape Colony, and there received horses. The original mounted squadron, under Captain M'Leish, entrained at Belmont on 31st January, and also came on to Naauwpoort. In this district both squadrons did fine work under General Clements, at a time when good work was greatly needed. About 3rd February they were ordered to hold positions beyond Maeder's Farm, near Colesberg, on the extreme left of the line which the British were holding, and which was at that time nearly twenty-five miles long. A detachment was part of the garrison of "The Windmill Posts of Hobkirk's Farm and Bastard's Nek, two most risky posts." After General French and his cavalry had left the Colesberg district to undertake the relief of Kimberley the Boers became very aggressive, and on 10th February they fiercely attacked the positions held by the Victoria Mounted Rifles, who were driven from part of the ridges, losing 3 killed and several wounded.

On the 12th the fighting in this neighbourhood was most severe, especially on the right flank, where the Worcestershire Regiment and Tasmanians held the position, and on the left, where the Victorians, South Australians, and Inniskilling Dragoons were posted. These troops were hardly pressed, and lost heavily. Speaking of the attack on Pink Hill on the British left, 'The Times' historian, vol. iii. p. 466, says: "The position was now held by a company of Wiltshires and some 80 to 100 Victorians and South Australians, under Major Eddy, Victoria M.R., some 200 men in all. So rapid was the Boer advance that it threatened not only to annihilate the detachment on Pink Hill, but also to rush Windmill Camp and endanger the Coleskop and Kloof positions. But the force on Pink Hill made so determined a stand that it was not till 3 P.M. that the Boers secured the hill, too late in the day and too exhausted themselves to follow up their success. The main credit of the defence of Pink Hill belongs to the Australians, who, inspired by the splendid gallantry of their commander, hung on to the very last, most heroically covering the withdrawal of the infantry from Pink Hill and Windmill Camp. Their losses amounted to nearly 40 per cent of their strength. Of their officers, Eddy and two others were killed, the remaining two severely wounded. As an exhibition of resolute courage on the part of comparatively untrained troops, this performance of the Australians is well worthy of mention."

The account of this engagement given by Major Reay in 'With the Australian Regiment' is in terms practically similar to the foregoing. He states the garrison of the hill as 50 Victoria M.I., 25 Victoria M.R., 20 South Australians, 50 Inniskillings, 50 of the Wiltshires, while close at hand were 2 guns, 75 of the Victoria M.R., 80 of the Bedfordshire Regiment, and about 40 N.S.W. Mounted Infantry, Major Eddy of the Victorians being in chief command. Up to the moment of his death he was, quite regardless of the very heavy fire, moving about, placing and encouraging his men. General Clements highly praised the fine stand made by the Victorians and Wilts, the troops who were most heavily engaged, and issued a complimentary order placing " on record his appreciation of the spirit and determination of the troops in the operations 9th to 14th February. The powers and endurance of the troops were fully taxed, and they well sustained the strain." The stand which was made at Pink Hill enabled the artillery to get down their guns from the lofty Coles Kop.

In addition to their leader the Victorians lost Lieutenant Roberts, died of wounds, 6 non-commissioned officers and men killed, Captain M'Inerney, wounded and taken prisoner, Lieutenant Tremearne and about 20 men wounded. Many acts of gallantry on the part of individuals are mentioned in Major Reay's account of the fighting.

On the 13th the Boers did not renew the attack, but the numbers of the enemy in the Colesberg district were seen to be so overwhelmingly superior that General Clements decided on a midnight retirement from the positions in front of Rensburg to Arundel. During this movement, which commenced shortly before midnight on the 13th, the Victoria M.R. protected the right flank and formed the advance guard; Captain Moor's West Australians were the left flank guard; Inniskillings and South Australians the rear-guard. A company of New South Wales Mounted Infantry were escort to the ammunition column. For two days and two nights the fighting had been almost incessant, and the men had got practically no rest or sleep, but when on arrival at Arundel it was found that two companies of the Wiltshire Regiment had been left behind, many of the Australians volunteered to go back and assist the unfortunate infantrymen. Captain Lascelles, South Australians, took back a party, and assisted a detachment of the Bedfordshire Regiment to gain the camp; but the two companies of the Wiltshires had been cut off and surrounded by a large body of Boers, and after holding out for some time they were forced to surrender.

The 2nd contingent, strength 262, all ranks, under Colonel Price, sailed on the *Euryalus* on 13th January, and having arrived at Cape Town on 6th February, was on the 12th entrained, with the object of joining General Clements, but Colonel Price received a message to get out and hold Hanover Road, between De Aar and Naauwpoort, as the Boers were swarming down into the country behind Clements' left rear. With great smartness positions were selected, and put into a defensive state.

Lord Roberts commenced his advance from Modder River on 11th February, but it was quite fourteen days before that movement had any apparent effect on the vigour of the enemy in Central Cape Colony. On the 20th the Boers again attacked from all sides, Clements' position being almost surrounded, but the attacks were driven off and the whole of the ground held. On the 20th Clements brought up the 2nd Victorian contingent from Hanover Road, and he also got some additional artillery, notably two 5-inch guns, with which he was able to cope with the long-range cannon of the Boers. The 2nd Victorians were instructed to hold a position at Elandsfontein, ten miles west of Arundel. Clements now took the initiative, and made an endeavour to regain some of the ground he had lost. On the 22nd, 23rd, and 24th there was a great deal of fighting, but the British failed to drive the enemy from any of his main positions. Both contingents of the Victorians were engaged on these days. The plight of Cronje at Paardeberg, and the need of concentrating their troops to protect Bloemfontein, were at last influencing the Boer leaders in Cape Colony, and on the 27th a reconnaissance proved that the enemy were weakening their hold on the

Rensburg position, and on that day they were driven from the town. On the 28th Colesberg was occupied by the Australians. In the latter town the officers of the 1st and 2nd contingents of the Victorians had their first opportunity of meeting : the stress of affairs during the previous fortnight, with the incessant hard work and fighting, had prevented any communication between the two detachments. During the first days of March there was much skirmishing and scouting in all directions. The advance guard between 1st and 15th March was generally 4 guns, 4th Battery R.F.A., 1 squadron Inniskilling Dragoons, 100 Victoria M.R., Captain M'Leish, a squadron West Australians, and a company of Regular Mounted Infantry. On 3rd March a fine bit of reconnaissance and some bold fighting was done by 20 Victoria M.R., Lieutenant Thorne, and 30 Inniskillings, Lieutenant Paterson. On the 4th the 1st Victorian contingent and the West Australians had a sharp fight in which they drove off the enemy, whose losses were heavy: 8 were buried. On the 5th the 2nd contingent moved out to Reitfontein and there joined the Tasmanians. Clements now moved forward his troops towards Norvals Pont, where the railway bridge crosses the Orange River. On the 7th a party of officers and some men, including Captain M'Leish of the Victoria M.R., rode down to the south bank of the river, and were fired at by the enemy on the opposite side. By the 12th the artillery had been got into position, and the ground held by the Boers on the north bank was carefully searched. If the Boers had stood it would have been very difficult, if not impossible, for a force such as General Clements had to have fought their way across the river. Preparations were, however, made for the formation of a pontoon bridge: the railway bridge had been blown up. Before daylight on the 15th some companies of infantry from the Worcestershire, Bedfordshire, and Berkshire Regiments were ferried across the river: the enemy did not seek to prevent their landing on the opposite bank. By twelve o'clock in the day the pontoon bridge was completed, and the Inniskilling Dragoons, followed by M'Leish's company of the Victoria M.R. and Legge's company of the New South Wales Mounted Infantry, crossed. On the 16th General Clements continued his advance northwards. For the march to Bloemfontein he divided his force into three columns: the 2nd Victorians, "under the personal command of Colonel Price, had the honour of forming the mounted portion of the advance guard to the main column, and therefore led the way."[1] The Westralians and South Australians were in the right column, under Major Dauncey, and the remainder of the Australian Regiment, including the 1st Victorians, were in the left column, under Major Slee. The columns marched viâ Philippolis, Jagersfontein, Fauresmith, and Petrusburg to Bloemfontein, which was entered by General Clements' troops on 4th April.

Before advancing from Bloemfontein Lord Roberts reorganised the Mounted Infantry or Mounted Rifles as they were very often called; and the Victorians were put into Colonel Henry's Mounted Infantry, the Fourth corps, which worked as screen and scouts to the centre of Lord Roberts' great force in the advance to Pretoria. The Victorians took their share of the work. On 30th April, when Lord Roberts was clearing the ground for his advance northwards, Lieut. and Adjutant Lilley of

[1] Major Reay's 'With the Australian Regiment.'

the Victorians was severely wounded and taken prisoner, and they suffered other casualties. Lieut. Lilley was found in Brandfort when the troops entered the town four days later. Henry's men had much fighting on this march, particularly at and immediately after the crossing of the Vaal, and outside Pretoria. Their good work was referred to by Lord Roberts, and was most highly praised by various correspondents who were present.

After Pretoria was occupied the Victoria M.R. were employed on the outpost line to the east and north-east of the capital. They were present at the battle of Diamond Hill, 11th - 12th June. On 20th June it was announced that Captain M'Inerney had been appointed Her Majesty's Advocate in the New High Court at Pretoria: an honour to his corps as to himself. During the first half of July the contingents were often engaged and several times suffered loss. Henry's Mounted Infantry, including the Victoria M.R., South Australians, and Tasmanians, were in Lord Roberts' advance along the Delagoa Railway, first to Middelburg, which was occupied on 27th July, and starting thence on 21st August to the Portuguese border. They had fighting several times during the long march, particularly near Balmoral and in the neighbourhood of Belfast. All through this eastern advance the troops of Hutton and Henry did remarkably fine work.

General French with his regular cavalry and some Colonials having been directed to move on Carolina and Barberton far south of the direct line to Komati Poort. Hutton's Colonials, now including Brabant's Horse, Alderson's Canadians, and Henry's men were the only mounted troops in the last stage of the great eastern movement—that is, between 9th September and the

24th, the day on which Henry's men, including the Victoria M.R., entered Komati Poort. There immense quantities of rolling-stock, provisions, and war stores were found. The Victoria M.R. were present at the big review by General Pole-Carew at that place on 28th September. In October they were brought away from that unhealthy neighbourhood, and later to Pretoria, where, on the 15th of that month, Lord Roberts inspected and congratulated on their work the 1st contingents of the Victorians, South and West Australians, and Tasmanians. Before the end of November most of the men of the 1st contingents had entrained for Cape Town *en route* for home.

In Lord Kitchener's telegram of 6th December 1900 he mentioned that 28 men of the Victoria M.R. were part of the escort of a convoy which was attacked on the Rustenburg road on 3rd December: "The escort took up a position on some kopjes, and fought with great gallantry." The Boers succeeded in setting fire to one half of the waggons, but the other half was saved. So determined were the enemy, that some were killed by case-shot within fifty yards of the guns.

About the middle of January 1901 a party of this contingent, the 2nd, under Captain Umphelby, made a good capture of cattle from the enemy near Rustenburg. A detachment was present under Brigadier-General Cunningham in a severe engagement at Middelfontein on 24th January. They continued for some time to work in the district west of Pretoria.

On 31st March 1901 Captain Kirkby, with what remained of the 2nd contingent, sailed for home.

THE 3RD VICTORIAN CONTINGENT.

The 3rd contingent consisted of two squadrons of Mounted Infantry commanded by Major Dobbin. They were very frequently designated Victorian Bushmen, sometimes Australian Bushmen. The contingent arrived at Beira on the *Euryalus* on 12th April 1900, and formed part of the force which, under General Carrington, crossed Rhodesia and entered the Transvaal from Mafeking. A party of Victorian nursing sisters landed at Beira with the troops and accompanied them on the long journey to Mafeking.

The 3rd Victorians were associated with the 3rd West Australians, the two forming the 3rd, but sometimes called the 2nd, Regiment of Australian Bushmen. The 3rd Victorian contingent was split up, but the larger portion moved eastward from Mafeking and Zeerust with Plumer, under whom they acted, and did fine work during their term in the field.

A detachment of about 50, under Captain Ham, was dropped at Elands River, east of Zeerust, and formed a portion of the garrison which, under Colonel Hore, made a splendid defence from 4th to 16th August (see Rhodesian Regiment). About 60 of the contingent were in the force of Colonel Airey, one of those which attempted, but unsuccessfully, to push through to Hore. In Airey's engagement at Kosters River, 22nd July (see 1st New South Wales Bushmen), the Victorian detachment had 4 killed and 7 wounded. Ham's detachment was in September brought by rail from Mafeking to Pretoria and joined Plumer north of that town.

In Lord Roberts' telegram of 2nd November he mentioned that Paget and Plumer had had an engagement on the 1st to the south-west of the Megato Pass in the Megaliesberg. He said Plumer's mounted troops drove the Boers "from two strong positions over difficult country. The Yorkshire and Warwickshire Yeomanry, under Colonel Howard, carried one position by assault. The 3rd Imperial Bushmen, under Major Vialls, turned another position which caused the enemy to retreat precipitately." Major Vialls was an officer of the West Australians, but commanded the 3rd Bushmen. This detachment of Victorians saw an immense deal of hard fighting service under Generals Paget and Plumer. In August, September, and October they were constantly in touch with the enemy in the district north of Pretoria, and afterwards worked both north-west and north-east of the capital. They were in the hardly contested battle at Rhenoster Kop, 29th November 1900 (see 1st, 2nd, and 3rd New Zealand Contingents), in other engagements about Balmoral, and afterwards, in February 1901, in the pursuit of De Wet in Cape Colony, where they had various casualties (see 4th Victorian contingent); and again, after the middle of March, in the district north of Pretoria.

In his despatch of 8th May 1901 Lord Kitchener, dealing with General Plumer's operations in the Eastern Transvaal in April, said "a party of the enemy driven westward by General Beatson was pursued and overtaken by a detachment from General Plumer's force under Major Vialls, 3rd Victorian Bushmen." Twenty-seven prisoners and 1000 head of cattle were taken on this occasion. As has already been stated, Major Vialls had the 3rd Victorians under his command.

A small detachment of the 3rd were in the Western Transvaal along with the 4th from August 1900 onwards.

Practically all the 3rd Australian contingents sailed for home in May 1901.

Lieutenant J. M'L. Cameron, of the 3rd contingent, organised and commanded a body of specially picked and trained scouts whose good work was on several occasions referred to by correspondents and other writers.

THE 4TH VICTORIAN CONTINGENT.

This corps, consisting of a battalion—five companies —of mounted rifles, commanded by Lieut.-Colonel N. W. Kelly, was a portion of the second or "Imperial" Bushmen force which was contributed to by all the Australian colonies. This Victorian Contingent was often officially referred to as the Victorian Imperial Regiment, and sometimes as the Victorian Imperial Bushmen.

The regiment sailed from Melbourne on the *Victorian* upon 1st May 1900 and landed at Beira. For a time their work was much akin to that of the 6th New South Wales Imperial Bushmen, to which reference is made.

The 4th Victorians were split up at an early stage of their fighting career. Colonel Kelly, with one portion, long fought with Lord Methuen and other leaders in the Western Transvaal, where they took a prominent part in many actions. In his telegraphic despatch of 24th August 1900 Lord Roberts said that General Carrington had been engaged at Ottoshoop on the

22nd, when Lieutenant A. G. Gilpin and one man of the 4th Victorians were killed. From this time onwards they were constantly engaged, but for long escaped serious casualties. They served with columns based on Mafeking and Zeerust, and did an immense amount of arduous trekking. In an expedition through Griqualand West, in January and February 1901, there was some fighting, most of which fell to the New South Wales and Victorian Bushmen.

In his telegram of 21st February 1901 Lord Kitchener mentioned that Lord Methuen had marched into Klerksdorp, in the south-west of the Transvaal, and he said that " At Hartebeestfontein he was opposed by a force of 1400 Boers under Generals De Villiers and Lichtenburg. The Boers held a strong position obstinately, but were turned out after severe fighting, in which the 10th Yeomanry, Victorian Bushmen, and the Loyal North Lancashire Regiment distinguished themselves." The Victorians lost 3 killed, and 3 officers of the 4th contingent—Lieut.-Colonel Kelly and Lieutenants Parkin and Mann—and 8 men wounded.

The other portion of the 4th Victorians operated with General Plumer, and under him gained great distinction. Along with the greater part of Plumer's mounted troops they were taken to Cape Colony to assist in the endeavour to expel De Wet (see 1st, 2nd, and 3rd New Zealand). During the pursuit of his forces, and also after he and the greater portion of his men had been driven back across the Orange, the contingent saw a great deal of hard service in Cape Colony, and Major Clarke, D.S.O., who commanded this portion of the 4th, was selected for very high praise.

In Lord Kitchener's despatch of 8th March 1901 he dealt with the invasion of Cape Colony, and said: "On the 12th February a party of about 300 Boers approached Philipstown, but were completely baffled and driven off by the energetic defence made by detachments of Imperial Yeomanry and the Victorian Imperial Regiment, who were reinforced on the 13th by the arrival of Colonel Henniker's column from De Aar and mounted infantry from Hanover Road. Moving as fast as the bad state of the roads and the exhausted condition of their transport animals would allow, the main body of the enemy made for the De Aar-Orange River line. On the 14th De Wet was severely handled by Plumer at Wolvekuilen, being forced to abandon many of his waggons, and at daybreak on the 15th he crossed the railway about four miles north of Houtkraal, where he was engaged by Colonel Crabbe's column and the armoured train under Captain Nanton, R.E. The enemy made but little resistance, and pushed on towards the north-west. Large numbers of waggons and much ammunition now fell into our hands, the Boers being unable to urge their weary transport animals along at a sufficiently rapid pace owing to the sodden state of the ground." On the 13th Lieutenants F. W. Mason and F. G. Code, both of the 4th, and several men were wounded. On the 14th the Victorians had Lieutenants Frew and Gartside, both of the 3rd contingent, and about 17 men wounded. The West Australian Bushmen and New Zealand Mounted Infantry had also casualties in this action.

After the 15th the pursuit of De Wet continued with very great vigour; and in his telegram of 24th February Lord Kitchener was able to say, " Plumer reports Colonel Owen, with detachments of King's Dragoon Guards, Victorian Imperial Regiment, and

Imperial Light Horse, captured De Wet's 15-pounder and pom-pom on the 23rd. The enemy is in full retreat and dispersing: he is being vigorously pursued. De Wet's attempt to invade Cape Colony has evidently completely failed. . . . Plumer took 50 prisoners and some carts of ammunition with the 15-pounder." The Victorians alluded to in this telegram are evidently the 4th contingent, but, as will be seen from the casualties, the 3rd were with Plumer, as were also some New South Wales, New Zealand, and Queensland men, South and West Australians, and other Colonials. By general consensus of opinion among all correspondents then present in Cape Colony, it was to Plumer and his Colonials that the greatest share of credit must be given for the eventual expulsion of De Wet from the colony. The cleverness and energy of the leader were splendidly backed up by all ranks under him. No better example of this fine spirit could be found than in an incident referred to in the following words of Lord Kitchener's telegram of 4th March 1901: "Captain Dallimore (4th contingent) and 16 Victorian Rifles captured 33 Boers and 50 horses on Seacow River," in the Colesberg district. Captain Dallimore and his 16 men had been detached to reconnoitre. He located a party of Boers, but kept out of sight. After dark he drove off their horses, and at dawn he fired some volleys. The enemy, finding their horses gone, complied with a demand to surrender. Telegraphing on the 4th of March as to the capture of the guns, &c., on 23d February, the Press Association correspondent said: "Perhaps General Plumer distinguished himself more than the rest of the commanders in the recent operations. . . . During the whole of that fatiguing day the Victorians did splendid work. Captain Tivey (4th contingent) especially distinguished himself by his magnificent persistence and clever handling of his men." The correspondent of 'The Daily Mail,' Mr Edgar Wallace, who had nothing to gain by disparaging the work of the regulars, wrote : " So De Wet struck eastward, leaving the Victorians gloating over the two guns they captured, and the colonel of the King's Dragoon Guards wondering how in the world he got the credit for capturing them. I would like to say a word about the Victorians. Victoria is a colony which has produced some splendid soldiers, but no better nor finer troops have ever been put in the field than those men who form part of Colonel Henniker's column."

This body of Victorians did not go back to the north of the Transvaal with Plumer. They remained in Cape Colony, and during March, April, and May were engaged in hunting down scattered bands under Kritzinger, Scheepers, and Malan, and the despatch of 8th July 1901 shows that up to the end of May they were operating with Colonel Henniker in the central district of the colony.

As will be seen from the list of Mentions, the Victorian Imperial Regiment or Imperial Bushmen gained honour on many occasions in Cape Colony. The lack of really distinctive names, and the fact that the different contingents were so much split up and mixed up, makes any endeavour to trace the doings of any of the Australian contingents very difficult: even the official designation of a corps seems to have changed at times in an aimless fashion. The record of the Victorians suffers in this way perhaps more than that of any of the other Colonials.

The bulk of the 4th contingent, with some of the 3rd—together about 460,—sailed for home on the 26th June 1901.

THE 5TH VICTORIAN MOUNTED RIFLES.

This contingent, 1000 strong, sailed on 15th February 1901, and on the same day there embarked at Melbourne 250 Victorians as volunteers for the Scottish Horse (see that corps). Soon after landing the 5th contingent were taken to the Transvaal.

In May and June 1901 the 5th Victorian M.R were operating in the Eastern Transvaal under General Beatson. On 7th May they had sharp fighting at Rhenoster Kop, when Captain John Kelly and Lieutenant Johnston and 1 man were killed and 3 men wounded. On the 25th they had Lieutenant W. S. Wedd and several men wounded. On 12th June the corps met with a mishap—one of the very few incidents of that nature, we might say the only one, happening in connection with any of the oversea Colonials. The words of Lord Kitchener's despatch of 8th July relating to this affair are as follows: "On 6th June General Beatson again moved out to the junction of the Olifant's River and Steenkool Spruit to operate round that locality on his way to Bethel. While encamped at Van Dyck's Drift on the 10th, he detached a force of four companies Victorian Mounted Rifles, with two pom-poms, under Major Morris, to act against a small force of the enemy reported at Boschmanfontein. The detachment reached its destination and found the laager evacuated. On the 12th General Beatson sent instructions to Major Morris to combine with him at dawn on the 13th in an attack on another body of the enemy reported to be at Elandsfontein. The detachment bivouacked on the evening of the 12th at Wilmansrust. At about

7.30 P.M. a body of the enemy which, in the darkness, had evaded the outposts, crept up close to the bivouac, opened a heavy fire, stampeded the horses, and after a few minutes rushed the camp. The pom-poms were captured and removed. Two officers and 16 men were killed and 4 officers and 38 men wounded : a number of the men were made prisoners, but shortly afterwards released. General Beatson received information of this reverse at 1.30 A.M. on the 13th : leaving his baggage under the guard of his infantry, he set out at once with all available mounted men and arrived at Wilmansrust shortly after daybreak. The Boers, however, had moved off again immediately after the action and were out of reach. General Beatson therefore concentrated his force at Koornfontein. The column then moved east and came in touch with General Blood's troops at Hartebeestspruit, north of Ermelo, on the 19th. General Beatson's force proceeded to Middelburg, a few days later, to refit. The results of his operations from the 6th to 19th June were as follows : Boers killed and wounded 16, prisoners 23, rifles 160, ammunition 10,850 rounds, 58 waggons and carts, besides some stock."

It may be noted that the detached force, although consisting almost entirely of Victorians, was put by General Beatson under the command of Major Morris, an artillery officer. Captain Watson of the 7th Battery Royal Field Artillery, and Surgeon-Lieutenant Palmer of the Victorians, were the officers killed, and Captains Righetti and J. H. Patterson, and Lieutenants Dallimore and Henwood, were those wounded. It was subsequently intimated that Lieutenant S. Sherlock was also wounded.

The appendix to this despatch shows that Beatson's

column was composed of 5th Victorian M.R., 740; 9th Battery Royal Field Artillery, 4 guns; 2nd Duke of Cornwall's Light Infantry, 366; 2nd Seaforth Highlanders, 178; 26th company Royal Engineers, 20th Field Hospital, 26; and the 84th company Army Service Corps, 18.

It was reported that General Beatson said some ungenerous things about the Victorian M.R. It serves no purpose to rake up these disagreeable matters. Words which should never have been uttered may have been spoken in haste, but at all events the subsequent service of the corps showed that they were capable of, and did carry out, very fine work.

The despatch of 8th September mentions that, in consequence of a reported concentration of the enemy in the south-east of the Transvaal, several columns were, in August, thrown into that district,—among others that of Colonel Pulteney. The latter consisted of the Victorian M.R. brought round from Brugspruit, on the Delagoa line, a squadron of the 8th Hussars, the Dublin Fusiliers M.I., and 2 guns. On 8th August there was fighting, in which Lieutenant S. Selman and some men of the Victorians were wounded; and Lord Kitchener mentioned in his despatch that "on the 23rd August Lt.-Col. Pulteney had a sharp engagement with the enemy on the west side of the Schurveberg, in which the Victorian M.R. had 2 men killed and 5 wounded." Near Vryheid, on the 27th, Lieutenant S. R. Coulter was killed and 3 men were wounded.

The Victorian M.R. continued almost till the close of the war to march and fight in Pulteney's column in the south-east of the Transvaal and along the Zululand border. The corps suffered casualties on several occasions during that period, as on 5th November 1901, when Lieutenant H. Chrisp and 2 men were killed and 5 wounded. On this occasion Major Fraser had taken out 150 Victorian M.R. to surround a farm. The enemy was in strength, but 2 were killed and 12 captured : 70 horses were also secured. The conduct of this detachment was much praised. Lieutenant G. J. Bell and some men were wounded on 4th January 1902, and Lieutenant O'Reilly on 5th March. Speaking of the work of the troops in this district, Lord Kitchener expressed appreciation of the cheerful manner in which they underwent the hardships of incessant marching by day and night in extremely wet weather, and in perhaps the most difficult piece of country in South Africa. The columns did not see a tent on many occasions for seven and eight weeks at a time. Pulteney's column had endless skirmishing, and always came out of all difficulties with distinction. They did not get the opportunities of making large captures which fell to some other forces, but they contributed to the defeat of all Botha's attempts to reinvade Natal.

On 3rd April 1902 the corps embarked at Durban for home.

The first Victorian quota of the Commonwealth Horse, numbering 360 officers and men, sailed on the *St Andrew* on 12th February 1902. On arrival they were present at some of the closing scenes in the Western Transvaal. The colony's section of the second Commonwealth contingent sailed on the *Templemore* on 27th March, and that of the third Commonwealth Horse, over 400, on 19th May. Victoria contributed about 300 recruits to the Scottish Horse (see that regiment).

Mentions gained by Victorian Contingents

The following Honours and Mentions were gained by the Victorian Contingents:—

Lt. L. C. Maygar, 5th V.M.R., gained the Victoria Cross under the following circumstances: "At Geelhoutboom, November 23rd 1901, Lieut. Maygar galloped out and ordered the men of a detached post, which was being outflanked, to retire. The horse of one of them being shot under him when the enemy were within 200 yards, Lieut. Maygar dismounted and lifted him on to his own horse, which bolted into boggy ground, causing both of them to dismount. On extricating the horse, and finding that it could not carry them both, Lieut. Maygar again put him on its back and told him to gallop to cover at once, he himself proceeding on foot. All this took place under a very heavy fire."

LORD ROBERTS' DESPATCH: *2nd April* 1901.—Mounted Rifles: Col. T. Price;[1] Majors Eddy (killed), D. M'Leish;[2] Lts. M. T. Kirby,[3] J. L. Lilley;[3] Adjt. T. S. Staughton[3]; Sgts. H. H. Bell, P. J. Dalimore; Ptes. H. J. Cooke,[4] R. J. Gardiner,[4] E. Starkey.[4] Mounted Infantry: Col. J. C. Hoad.[2] Impl. Bushmen: Lieut.-Col. N. W. Kelly.[1]

LORD KITCHENER'S DESPATCHES: *8th March* 1901.—Impl. Bushmen, 4th contingent: Lieut.-Col. N. W. Kelly; Capts. E. Tivey, J. Dallimore[3] (contingent not stated); Lce.-Cpl. R. M'Rae; Ptes. W. Sheehan, J. Clay, J. Green, P. O'Brien (promoted corporals); Cpl. Elliot; Ptes. A. M. Burke, D. E. Wallace.

8th May 1901.—Victorian Imperial Regiment (4th contingent): Capt. A. H. Sturdee, medical officer at Middelwater, Cape Colony, on April 22nd rode half a mile under fire to a donga near enemy's position, in which were some wounded men who needed medical aid,—Lce.-Cpl. J. W. Willing assisting on same occasion. 5th V.M.R.: Lt. and Adjt. H. A. Anderson has shown a fine dash on several occasions under fire, and by his coolness and determination extricated a patrol from a very difficult situation near Rhenoster Kop on May 7th 1901. Lt. J. H. Paterson, medical officer, on same occasion proceeded, under fire, to within 70 yards of enemy in order to assist wounded, and remained under close fire for over two hours; and though constantly shot at, continued to attend wounded, and remained behind with them when the patrol withdrew, though he was without Red Cross brassard.

From Colonel Henniker's Despatch on operations in Zuurberg, C.C., in March 1901.—Victorian Imperial Bushmen, 4th contingent: I cannot speak too highly of the excellent way in which Major Clarke[3] has always carried out his orders, and the manner in which his officers and men back him up. In the announcement of the award of D.S.O. to Major Clarke, it was said to be "for able command of operations against De Wet."

---

[1] Awarded C.B.
[2] Awarded C.M.G.
[3] Awarded D.S.O.
[4] Awarded D.C.M.

From Lord Methuen's Despatch of 16th March as to attack on Wolmaranstad, 6th March.—Victorian Imperial Bushmen: Lce.-Cpl. A. N. Gregg, promoted Sgt., rode twice across open and bullet-swept ground to look for missing man, found him, and brought him back safely. Seems specially deserving of praise. Cpl. Walker, Staff-Sgt. A. S. Mackenzie, Tprs. J. J. Butler, Jamieson, and Duncan took back spare horses to bring out men whose horses had bolted.

From Colonel Henniker's Special Despatch of April 1st.—V.I.B.: Sgt. D. Sandford, Lce.-Cpl. Legerwood, Tpr. J. Browning, at Zuurberg, C.C., March 31, in returning from reconnoitring, and pressed by enemy, a man's horse fell and pinned him to the ground; these three men went back under fire, released him, and brought him in.

8th July 1901.—Vet.-Lt. S. Sherlock, on June 7th, at Wilmansrust, when doctor was killed, took charge of 40 wounded, and by his skill and attention much alleviated suffering and danger; an excellent officer in his own department. Vict. Imperial Regiment: Cpl. Hewitt (promoted Sgt.), under a heavy fire, in response to a call for volunteers, with Q.M.-Sgt. Johnstone, entered a farm and brought out four armed Boers. May 13th, in Cape Colony, Tpr. Hipland (promoted Cpl.), on same occasion, though wounded, rode back to cover retreat of another man, Q.M.-Sgt. Johnstone,[1] same occasion, twice brought to notice, mentioned in Army Orders. V.M.R.: Pte. H. A. Wilson (promoted Cpl.), along with Private G. Davidson, Kitchener's Horse, as a scout has on many occasions shown exceptional skill and nerve. At time Delarey and Beyers were in Megaliesberg, voluntarily and alone on several occasions took most important messages through Boer lines.

8th August 1901.—V.I. Regt.: Cpl. Pike, promoted Sgt. at Grootreitvlei, C.C., May 13, same occasion as Q.M.-Sgt. Johnstone (see above).

1st June 1902.—5th V.M.R.: Sgt.-Major Keeble, for gallant capture of Boers single-handed at Rhenoster Kop in May 1901.

26th June 1902.—Nursing Sisters M. Rawson (got Royal Red Cross) and Isobel Ivey. Major M. O'Farrell;[2] Capts. G. G. F. Chomley, A. J. Christie; Lts. G. J. Bell,[2] T. S. L. O'Reilly, H. Kessell; Regl. Sgt.-Major R. S. Goode (1st Dragoon Guards);[1] Coy. Sgt.-Major J. W. Keeble;[1] Sgts. J. Kilbeg, A. Watt; Lce.-Cpl. W. Hutchins; Pte. J. Birch.

---

[1] Awarded D.C.M.   [2] Awarded D.S.O.

Queensland Contingents.

1ST AND 2ND CONTINGENTS.

To Queensland belongs the credit of being the first colony to make an offer of assistance to the mother country in connection with the South African War. On 11th July 1899, three months before the Boer ultimatum was sent, the Queensland Government despatched to Mr Chamberlain an offer of 250 mounted men, with machine-guns. The credit for this foresight belongs to Lieut.-Colonel J. Sanderson-Lyster, late 71st, Highland Light Infantry, who, as chief staff-officer in Queensland, made the suggestion to the commandant, Major-General H. Gunter. The latter interviewed the Premier, the Hon. J. R. Dickson, since deceased, and he at once acted on the suggestion.

The total contribution from the colony was 143 officers, 2756 men, and 3085 horses.[1] The first contingent was two companies of mounted infantry, 262 strong, all ranks, and was mainly composed of men of the Queensland Militia Regiment of Mounted Infantry. They were commanded by Lieut.-Colonel P. R. Ricardo. The contingent sailed on the *Cornwall* on 1st November 1899, and were, on arrival upon 11th December,

[1] 'Australia and New Zealand,' Sydney, 1904.

sent to the De Aar-Modder River line in order to protect the communications of Lord Methuen. They remained in this district until Lord Roberts commenced his advance into the Free State on 11th February 1900.

On 1st January 1900, 200 Queenslanders, under Lieut.-Colonel Ricardo and Captains Chauvel and Pinnock, were part of a force which Colonel Pilcher led out from Belmont towards Douglas,—an expedition which was entirely successful. Colonel Pilcher took extraordinary care to prevent any news of his march leaking out, and owing to this care he was able to surprise the enemy, capturing their laager and 40 prisoners. The work of the Queenslanders was greatly praised. They had a difficult task to perform, and the most highly-trained troops could not have done it more satisfactorily. When it was known that the column was in the vicinity of the laager, Colonel Pilcher's main endeavour was to throw some of his troops round the enemy's flanks. The Queenslanders got round on one flank unseen, and before they were discovered had gained a position which put the Boers at disadvantage. Privates M'Leod and Jones were killed,— the first Australian soldiers to die by Boer bullets. Lieutenant Aidie and Private Rose were dangerously wounded. There were a few other casualties. Rose was said to have been struck while returning to help Lieutenant Aidie.

In the beginning of February preparations were being made for the relief of Kimberley and the advance on Bloemfontein, and the Queensland Mounted Infantry were destined to take part in these stirring operations. In the appendix to his despatch of 16th February, Lord Roberts gives a statement of the troops available. He

The 1st and 2nd Queensland Contingents 437

puts the Queensland Mounted Infantry as two hundred and seventy-five strong.

In the rush to Kimberley and during the fighting on the north side of the town on 16th February 1900, the Queenslanders were under Pilcher, along with the 3rd Mounted Infantry (Regulars) and a squadron of New Zealanders. They succeeded in capturing a part of the Boer position, and were left out on outpost at Macfarlane's Siding during the night of the 16th, but before morning the enemy had decamped, getting away their convoy and guns. When French got the message announcing that Cronje had left Magersfontein he pushed on, first, Broadwood's Cavalry and then his other troops to Koedoesrand and Paardeberg drifts on the Modder to endeavour to head-off Cronje; and in this he was successful (see Canadian Regiment).

The 2nd contingent, about 162 all ranks, commanded by Lieut.-Colonel K. Hutchison, left Brisbane on 13th January 1900, and arrived at Cape Town in February. They were at once hurried to the front, and a portion were able to take part in the advance after Cronje's surrender. After Paardeberg the Queenslanders (called in the despatch the 1st and 2nd Queensland Mounted Infantry) were put into the 3rd Brigade of Mounted Infantry, the commander of the brigade being Lieut.-Colonel C. G. Martyr. The remainder of the brigade were regulars. The brigade had several times very stiff work on the way to Bloemfontein, and bore its share of the fighting with credit. In the despatch of 31st March 1900, giving the names of those who had distinguished themselves in the advance, Captains Reid and Browne of the Queensland 1st Contingent were mentioned. The strength of the Queenslanders who marched into Bloemfontein on 13th

March 1900 was officially stated at 16 officers, 312 men, and 369 horses.

At Sannahs Post, 31st March 1900, when Broadwood's force was ambushed (see Roberts' Horse), the troops of Colonel Martyr were about Boesman's Kop, on the west side of the spruit, and they fought hard to relieve the pressure on Broadwood. The Queenslanders, who were under Colonel Ricardo, lost 2 killed, 3 wounded, and 5 taken prisoners.

In the advance to Pretoria the Queenslanders, now about 400 strong, were in the 3rd Mounted Infantry Corps under Pilcher, the other regiments in Pilcher's corps being the 3rd Mounted Infantry (Regulars) and the 1st and 2nd New Zealand Mounted Rifles. Pilcher's corps were part of the Mounted Infantry Brigade which distinguished itself during the next few months under General Hutton and other leaders. They operated on the left in the advance from Bloemfontein northwards, and frequently earned praise from the Commander-in-Chief (see Canadian Mounted Rifles and New Zealand Mounted Rifles). At the crossing of the Vet the Queenslanders had several casualties, and again, after the Vaal was crossed, they had some sharp brushes with the enemy and suffered some losses. In Lord Roberts' telegram of 2nd June 1900 he remarked: "Very few guns were left in the Johannesburg forts, only one 6·3 muzzle-loading howitzer, made at Woolwich in 1878, and two 65 mm. Krupps. On May 30 the Queenslanders captured a Creusot gun and waggon, 11 waggons of military stores and ammunition."

After the occupation of Pretoria the Queensland Mounted Infantry, along with the other Mounted Colonials, under Hutton, operated to the east of the capital. They were present at the battle of Diamond

The 1st and 2nd Queensland Contingents 439

Hill, 11th to 13th June, and afterwards had much outpost work, generally in that direction.

In the beginning of August 1900 Colonel B. Mahon left Pretoria with a column containing the Imperial Light Horse, Lumsden's Horse, New Zealanders, 1st and 2nd Queensland Mounted Infantry, and the 4th Queensland Imperial Bushmen, which had landed at Cape Town in June, and some Yeomanry. The column operated towards Rustenburg in conjunction with Ian Hamilton, then by the north of Pretoria back to the capital. Lieutenant G. Newton of the 4th Queensland Imperial Bushmen was wounded on 12th August. Mahon left Pretoria again on 30th August and made a forced march to Wonderfontein, and after assisting a post, held by 125 Canadians, who had been pressed, Mahon struck south and joined General French at Carolina (see Imperial Light Horse). After a wonderful march through most rugged country, and after no little fighting, in which the Colonials did well, Barberton was captured on 13th September. Mr Goldmann, in his 'With General French and the Cavalry,' gives a good account of the fine work accomplished by Generals French and Mahon and their troops.

When Mahon left Pretoria on 30th August the Queensland Mounted Infantry, now much reduced in numbers, and one squadron of the 4th Queensland Imperial Bushmen, commanded by Captain F. L. Jones, accompanied him. The remainder of the 4th joined General Ridley's mounted column. The Queenslanders who had been with Mahon returned to Pretoria in October.

In the beginning of November the Press Association correspondent at Pretoria wired: "A portion of the Queensland Mounted Infantry left here this morning *en route* for Australia. Like the rest of their fellow-Australians, they have done magnificent work during the campaign, and their skill and daring have been generally admired in the army."

The 2nd contingent were now employed in the central portion of the Transvaal, chiefly north of Pretoria and on the Delagoa Railway. A portion of the 2nd contingent was in the Belfast district, on that line, in January and February 1901; and at Schwartz Kopjes on 13th February they were in a stiff brush, and suffered several casualties.

On 31st March 1901 Captains Harris and Thompson, with 3 other officers and 76 men of the 2nd contingent, sailed for home. Some time previous to that the remnant of the 1st contingent had been released from further service.

Captain Robert Gordon, D.S.O., of the 1st Queensland Mounted Infantry, who as a colonial officer had been attached to the 1st Battalion Gordon Highlanders in India, and with that battalion had served in the Tirah campaign, was, after the battle of Magersfontein, again attached to the 1st Gordons, and with them fought at Paardeberg. He was then appointed to command the M.I. company of the 1st Gordons, a portion of the famous 6th Mounted Infantry which, under De Lisle, was in many a hard-fought action. This command he retained until 18th January 1901, when he was wounded at Doorn River, Western Cape Colony. On this occasion the Gordons had Lieutenant Clowes and some men killed. As to De Lisle's work, see 1st and 2nd N.S.W. Mounted Infantry.

3RD QUEENSLAND CONTINGENT (3RD QUEENSLAND BUSHMEN).

This contingent, 320 mounted infantry, commanded by Major W. H. Tunbridge, sailed on the *Duke of Portland* upon 1st March 1900; arrived at the Cape on 3rd April, and was sent to Beira, where it arrived before the middle of April. The contingent was a portion of the Australian Bushmen Corps which in January 1900 it had been arranged to send to South Africa.

In his evidence before the War Commission General Plumer mentioned "that before the relief of Mafeking was effected in May 1900, he was joined by a Canadian battery and by some Queenslanders, part of the force which was landed at Beira." These Queenslanders were "D" Squadron of the 3rd contingent, Captain Kellie and Lieutenants Fowles, Harris, and Annat being among the officers. General Plumer spoke very highly of these troops, as of all the Australians and New Zealanders who served under him, and he had the most ample opportunities, throughout two years' campaigning, of putting the qualities of his men to all manner of severe tests.

After Mafeking was relieved, Captain Kellie's men moved eastward with Generals Baden-Powell and Plumer, viâ Ottoshoop and Zeerust to the Rustenburg district, where they were employed during July and August. In the fighting at Kosters River, 22nd July (see 1st New South Wales Bushmen), the Queensland detachment had Lieutenants Walsh and Leask and 6 men wounded. Lieutenant Leask died of his wounds at Pretoria on 20th August.

Captain H. C. W. Hamilton, who had been left sick in hospital at Marandellas, died there on 12th July 1900.

The larger portion of the 3rd contingent, under Major Tunbridge, also crossed Rhodesia and entered the Transvaal from about Mafeking, but they were not to see Kellie's squadron for a long time. The contingent, like other regiments of the Rhodesian Field Force, was thus much split up.

Mr Green, who was at Elands River during the investment, says in his 'Story of the Australian Bushmen' that on 19th July Major Tunbridge, with a detachment of his Queenslanders, brought a convoy into camp. It had been intended that Tunbridge and his men should join Baden-Powell about the Megato Pass; but in view of the great strength of the enemy in the neighbourhood, that was found to be impracticable. As things turned out, it was most fortunate that this squadron remained at Elands River, as Tunbridge and his men were a very valuable part of the garrison when the post was attacked on 5th August, and throughout the investment, 4th to 16th (see Rhodesian Regiment). During that period the Queenslanders lost Lieutenant Annat, killed — he had been previously wounded — and they had about 12 other casualties. The subsequent history of the 3rd Queensland Bushmen is very much akin to that of the 4th Queensland Contingent. Having been railed to Pretoria, where they were inspected and congratulated by Lord Roberts, the Elands River squadron joined the rest of the contingent, the column commander being Colonel Hickman, whose troops acted with General Plumer in numerous engagements in the country north and north-east of Pretoria, including the battle at Rhenoster Kop on 29th November. In December Colonel Jeffreys took over Hickman's column. A detachment under Major Tunbridge had a sharp fight on 23rd January 1901 near Balmoral (see New Zealand Mounted Rifles). On 3rd February Plumer's troops were railed to Cape Colony to endeavour to expel De Wet, who had crossed to the south of the Orange with a strong force. The work in the pursuit was most arduous, and, as will be seen from the Mentions, this contingent saw sharp fighting. Major Tunbridge distinguished himself in the action of 12th February 1901 (see 4th Victorian Imperial Bushmen and 3rd New Zealand).

The contingent accompanied Plumer in his chase after De Wet's commandos through the Orange River Colony to the Brandfort district, whence they were railed to the north of Pretoria. They then took part in the expedition to Pietersburg, and in May were relieved from further service in South Africa.

4TH QUEENSLAND CONTINGENT (4TH QUEENSLAND IMPERIAL BUSHMEN).

The 4th contingent, 392 strong, all ranks, under the command of Lieut.-Colonel A. Aytoun, Captain in the Argyll and Sutherland Highlanders, sailed from Brisbane upon 18th May 1900, on the *Manchester Port*. The ship touched at Beira and also at Port Elizabeth, but the contingent landed at Cape Town, and was taken to the north of the Orange River Colony. There they joined the mounted column of Colonel Hickman, which, after assisting to keep De Wet off the railway, was ordered to Pretoria, where it joined General Ian Hamilton's Division, and took part in the march to and occupation of Balmoral on the Delagoa railway. During this march the 4th Q.I.B. was transferred to Colonel Pilcher's mounted corps, Mahon being in command of all Ian Hamilton's mounted men. During the month of August Ian Hamilton's force marched to Rustenburg and back to Pretoria. On 31st August Captain Jones' company started with Mahon for the Eastern Transvaal, and with that leader took part in General French's memorable march to Barberton (see Imperial Light Horse). The headquarters of the 4th Q.I.B. joined Brigadier-General Ridley's mounted column, which, in conjunction with a force under General Clements, operated in the Central Transvaal. On 15th October the regiment moved into Pretoria, and on the 18th left to reinforce General Plumer, who was working to the north of the capital. They were now again in the corps of Colonel Hickman.

In his telegram of 22nd October 1900 Lord Roberts said: "Paget reports a successful surprise made by a small force under Lt.-Col. Lloyd, West Riding Regiment, and another by the Queensland Imperial Bushmen, under Lt.-Col. Aytoun (Argyll and Sutherland Highlanders), west of the Pienaars River. We had one casualty, Tr. Brickwood, Queensland M.I., severely wounded. Eighteen Boers were captured, and large numbers of sheep and cattle were taken." And in his telegram of 24th October Lord Roberts said: "On the 24th Colonel Aytoun, Queensland M.I., with a small force, captured two field cornets, Doonsen and De Beer, and 5 waggons. One man of Colonel Aytoun's was wounded." Again, on 12th November,

Lord Roberts wired: "Paget reports that a patrol of Queensland Bushmen, under Lts. Bell and Kemp, captured six of the enemy near Pienaars River yesterday,—two of the six are badly wounded."

Apart from these instances in which the Queenslanders were specially mentioned, the various Bushmen contingents under Baden-Powell, Paget, and Plumer had endless fighting during August, September, October, and November, and were very successful in making large captures from the enemy in the district north of Pretoria. While in this district the 4th had 4 men killed, and Lieutenant J. Higson (who afterwards died of his wounds) and 3 men wounded.

On 29th November Paget and Plumer fought a stiffly contested battle at Rhenoster Kop, north of the Delagoa Railway. The enemy were in great force, and strongly posted. The engagement has been referred to under the New Zealand Mounted Rifles. The 4th Queenslanders were said to have done well. They suffered several casualties. Lieut.-Colonel Aytoun having been sent to hospital on 20th November, Major W. Deacon took over the command.

The regiment, along with the greater part of Plumer's mounted men, was, in the beginning of February 1901, railed from the Transvaal to Naauwpoort in Cape Colony, and took part in the arduous but most exciting work which the pursuit of De Wet through and out of that colony entailed (see 3rd Contingent and 4th Victorians). Lieutenant Kellaway was wounded at Grasfontein on 2nd February, and the corps had several other casualties. Plumer's men got much credit for the fine way they held on to their elusive opponent. The regiment was afterwards with

General Plumer in the north of the Transvaal, and in the great sweep to the Piet Retief district.

The bulk of the contingent under Major Deacon sailed for home on 7th July 1901.

5TH QUEENSLAND CONTINGENT.

This contingent, 500 strong, with a cyclist section, was commanded by Lieut.-Colonel J. F. Flewell-Smith. They sailed on the *Templemore* on 6th March 1901, and arrived in South Africa in the beginning of April. They at once took the field.

The appendix to the despatch of 8th July 1901 shows that the 5th Q.I.B. (strength in May about 340, with 361 horses) took the place of the 4th in the column of General Plumer—a body which did very fine service in practically all parts of the seat of war. The work of Plumer's column during the time the 5th Queensland were with him has already been briefly sketched under the 6th New Zealand Contingent. The 5th Queensland took their full share of that work, and quite their full share of the captures. On 15th June Lieutenant Halse was severely wounded in the difficult country about Piet Retief. On 15th August 2 men were killed and several wounded at Kopjesfontein, in the Orange River Colony. In September the column was doing good work in the southeast of that country, and was constantly in touch with the enemy. At a drift on the Caledon River on 27th September there was a sharp fight, in which this contingent had Lieutenants A. E. Pooley and L. E.

Caskey and 2 men killed, and several wounded. Lieutenant Pooley had served as a sergeant with the 4th contingent.

The corps was present at the hard-fought engagement known as Onverwachte, in the south-east of the Transvaal, on 4th January 1902, when they suffered very severely,—about 12 being killed and 20 wounded, the latter including Captain H. R. Carter and Lieutenant Higginson, both severely wounded.

According to the Press Association correspondent with General Plumer, Lieutenant Joss of the 5th Queensland (Cyclist Corps) did a smart piece of work in the Warmbaths district soon after the corps took the field. When riding with despatches, and accompanied by only 10 men, he captured 9 Boers with 3 waggons.

Some details of the regiment were with a convoy which was fiercely attacked on the Bethel Road on 25th May 1901. The detachment lost 1 killed and 5 wounded.

6TH QUEENSLAND CONTINGENT.

Before the 5th contingent had embarked Queensland again gave proof of her splendid spirit by offering another regiment of mounted infantry. The offer was at once accepted, and the 6th contingent sailed on the *Victorian* on 5th April 1901, their strength being 4 squadrons. They were under the command of Lieut.-Colonel O. A. Tunbridge. In June the corps, so far as on column duty, numbered 307, all ranks, with about 300 horses.

The contingent was, along with the 7th New Zealand, throughout the greater part of 1901 and the first three months of 1902, in a column which was commanded by Lieut.-Colonel Grey, and afterwards by Lieut.-Colonel Garratt. A short account of the very excellent and telling work of that column has already been given under the 7th New Zealand Contingent.

The 6th Queensland bore their share of the work and of the casualties, but on the whole were, as regards losses, more lucky than their New Zealand comrades. Colonel Tunbridge was slightly wounded on 23rd July 1901 near Vereeniging. Lieutenant S. B. Boland and 1 man were wounded at Tabankulu on 1st December; and on the 6th of that month, near Wakkerstroom, 2 men were killed and Lieutenant J. Loynes and 8 men were wounded. In the very severe fighting on the night of 23rd February 1902, near Vrede, in the north-east of the Orange River Colony, when the New Zealanders suffered so severely, this contingent escaped with almost no loss. They sailed for home in June.

7TH AND 8TH QUEENSLAND CONTINGENTS.

These were two strong battalions of mounted infantry which formed part of the Commonwealth Horse (see that corps). The 7th contingent was commanded by Lieut.-Colonel J. Sanderson-Lyster, formerly of the 71st Highland Light Infantry. They arrived in time to take part in the closing scenes in the Western Transvaal. The 8th, commanded by Lieut.-Colonel H. Chauvel, who had served with distinction as Adjutant of the 1st contingent, arrived in South Africa too late to see fighting.

The following Mentions were gained by members of the Queensland contingents :—

LORD ROBERTS' DESPATCHES : 31st *March* 1900.—Q.M.I. : Capts. D. Reid [3] and R. Browne.[1]

2nd *April* 1901.—Q.M.I. : Lt.-Col. P. R. Ricardo,[1] Major W. T. Deacon,[1] R. S. Browne, H. G. Chauvel,[2] V. C. M. Selheim,[1] W. H. Tunbridge ; [1] Capts. A. T. Duka (medical officer, 3rd Q.M.I.),[3] R. Gordon,[3] D. E. Reid ; [3] Lt. T. W. Glasgow,[3] Sgt.-Major Cooney,[4] Cpl. Harris,[4] Lce.-Cpl. Trickett.[4] 4th Imperial Bushmen : Sgt.-Major J. Loynes, Qmr.-Sgt. W. F. L. Wright,[4] Coy. Sgt.-Major J. F. Gill, Cpl. Davidson,[4] Pte. Keogh,[4] Trumpeter A. E. Forbes ; [4] Ptes. C. G. Barnes, A. Clark, R. E. Hutchinson, F. W. Lucas.

4th *Sept.* 1901.—Lt.-Col. A. Aytoun, 4th Q.I.B. (Captain A. and S. Highlanders),[3] Coy. Sgt.-Major J. J. Walker,[4] Sgts. J. B. Ryan and G. Tancred, Cpl. J. C. Brosnan, Pte. W. J. Stevens—all of the Q.M.I.

LORD KITCHENER'S DESPATCHES : 8th *March* 1901.—4th Q.I.B. : Major W. T. Deacon.[1]

8th *May* 1901.—3rd Q.I.B. : Major W. H. Tunbridge, very good service engagement of 12th February 1901. Actg. Sgt. E. C. Shadforth, 4th Q.I.B. (promoted Sgt.) : on patrol near Boschkop, Cape Colony, Feb. 12, 1901, brought Pte. Sutter, whose horse had been shot, out of action under heavy fire. Pte. G. Alford, 4th Q.I.B. (promoted Cpl.) : at Driekuilen, C.C., Feb. 15, single-handed, took prisoners 3 armed and mounted Boers and a Kaffir. Pte. E. Culliford, 4th Q.I.B. (promoted Cpl.) : same place and date took prisoners 4 armed Boers. Pte. G. Holland, 4th Q.I.B. (promoted Cpl.) : same date and place took prisoners 3 armed men and 2 Kaffirs.

8th *July* 1901.—5th Q.I.B. : Lt. C. G. B. Reese and Sgt. H. Smith, special good service during Boer attack on convoy near Mooifontein, south of Bethel, 25th May 1901. Cpl. F. C. V. King and Pte. J. Marmont came from good cover and carried a wounded comrade to dressing station 700 yards under fire, June 16. Pte. G. J. Kells (promoted Cpl.) on same occasion crossed open ground three times under fire to carry messages. 6th Q.I.B. : Lt. D. C. Cameron, at Leeuwspruit, 16th June, seeing a trooper fall, went under heavy fire and brought him in. Sgt. T. Doyle, same action, seeing a man fall, returned and brought him in.

8th *March* 1901.—5th Q.I.B. : Lt. L. J. Caskey (killed) and Pte. G. H. White (killed), great gallantry at Caledon River, Orange River Colony, 27th Sept. 1901.

---

[1] Awarded C.B.   [2] Awarded C.M.G.
[3] Awarded D.S.O.   [4] Awarded D.C.M.

8th December 1901.—6th Q.I.B. : Lt. D. St G. Rich, gallantry in attack on laager, Pongola Bosch (Eastern Transvaal), 2nd Oct. 1901.

8th March 1902.—5th Q.I.B. : Major F. W. Toll, for resolute and capable way in which he led his regiment on four separate occasions in Nov., Dec., and Jan. 6th Q.I.B. : Lt. C. R. G. Vaughan, for good service in Col. Byng's capture of laager, Fanny's Home, Orange River Colony, 2nd Feb. 1902. 5th Q.I.B. : Lt. C. G. B. Rees, for good service and gallantry in action at Onverwachte on 4th Jan. 1902 ; Coy. Sgt.-Major F. Knyvett, Sgt. J. Power (killed), gallantry, same action.

8th April 1902.—Lt.-Col. O. A. Tunbridge, 6th contingent, got C.M.G.

23rd June 1902.—Queensland Contingent : Surg.-Capt. H. J. Hutchins.[1] 4th Q.I.B. : Capts. F. L. Jones, T. H. Dodds,[1] J. K. Berry. 4th Q.I.B. : Lts. S. B. Boland,[1] D. St G. Rich ; Reg. Sgt.-Majors J. G. Price, F. H. Trask ;[2] Qmr.-Sgt. T. H. Doyle, Coy. Sgt.-Major Knyvett,[2] Bugler W. N. Busby ; Ptes. F. Henrickson, H. E. Watt. Major J. J. Byron, a special service officer, got the C.M.G. Pte. E. Sweeney, 5th contingent, was awarded the D.C.M.

---

[1] Awarded D.S.O.   [2] Awarded D.C.M.

South Australian Contingents.

1st and 2nd CONTINGENTS.

ACCORDING to the official publication 'Australia and New Zealand,' Sydney, 1904, p. 440, the contribution of the colony to the army in South Africa was 78 officers, 1450 men, and 1524 horses.

The 1st contingent, which, by the desire of the War Office, was limited to one infantry unit, 127 all ranks, sailed on the *Medic* on 31st October 1899, and arrived at the Cape on 26th November. Captain F. H. Howland was commander, and Captain G. R. Lascelles, Royal Fusiliers, was adjutant. The contingent was on arrival sent to the De Aar-Modder River line of railway, and was employed occupying posts, first at Belmont, and after 10th December at Enslin, to protect the line. At the end of January the South Australians were, along with the remainder of the Australian regiment, converted into mounted infantry and taken to Naauwpoort, where they received horses and joined the force of General Clements, who was holding a long line opposite the Boers' positions at Colesberg. The contingent took a prominent part in the severe fighting which occurred in this district during the last three weeks of February 1900 (see

Victorian Mounted Rifles). Lieutenant J. Powell was killed on the 12th, the day on which the Boers, in very strong force, attacked the whole of Clements' extended line. Fortunately, the Worcestershire Regiment, on the extreme right, and the Victorians and other troops on the left, held the ground with admirable determination, although at both flanks the losses were heavy. Twenty of the South Australians, under Powell, were in the garrison of Pinkhill, the attack on which was most fierce and persistent.

The result of the action on the 12th was to convince General Clements that he must retire to Arundel. During the movement, which commenced at midnight, 13th and 14th, the South Australians formed the rearguard, a position of honour and great responsibility, seeing that General Clements' men had been without rest or sleep for nearly forty-eight hours. Notwithstanding these great exertions, Captain Lascelles, of the South Australians, on arriving in the neighbourhood of Arundel, went back with a mixed body of volunteers, mostly Australians, to endeavour to bring in or assist some infantry who had been left behind (see 1st and 2nd Victoria Mounted Rifles). Competent judges have said that the withdrawal of the force to Arundel was one of the best-managed operations undertaken during the campaign. On the 20th the Boers again attacked Clements, but were driven back. During the next eight days there was constant fighting, in which the South Australians took their share. On the 21st Trooper W. E. Smith was killed. On the 24th Captain Lascelles took out two squadrons of Prince Alfred's Guards (Cape Colonials) in order to ascertain whether the enemy was still holding his positions in strength. The little force got into a place

The 1st and 2nd South Australian Contingents 453

where they were subjected to an extremely heavy fire for three hours. Ultimately they withdrew with the loss of a few wounded and taken prisoners. Captain Lascelles and his men were complimented by General Clements. In the advance from Arundel on the 28th the South Australians again formed the rear-guard. When Clements was preparing to cross the Orange River the South Australians were sent forward on 8th March to the front at Norvals Pont, where they were in contact with the enemy until the 15th, when the force crossed. During the march through the Orange Free State the squadron was in the right column under Major Dauncey of the Inniskillings.

The 2nd contingent, 8 officers and 113 other ranks, commanded by Captain C. J. Reade, embarked on the *Surrey* on 26th January 1900, arrived at the Cape on 25th February, and at De Aar on 6th March. Here they at once marched off as a portion of a column designed to put down the rebellion about Prieska (see Orpen's Horse). Some very hard riding was done, but the squadron managed to bring back their horses in fair condition to De Aar. Here they entrained for Norvals Pont and marched thence to Bloemfontein, where they joined the 1st contingent and the main army. A party of Nursing Sisters from the colony also joined the army at this time.

In the advance from Bloemfontein to Pretoria, which commenced on 3rd May, the South Australians, commanded by Captain Reade, along with the Victorian M.R., Tasmanians, and a battalion of regular mounted infantry, formed the 4th Corps of Mounted Infantry under Colonel St G. C. Henry, which acted as the screen and scouts of the centre of Lord Roberts' army. Their task entailed much hard riding, and they had fighting on many occasions, particularly between the Vaal and Pretoria. The work of Henry's corps in these engagements was much praised. At Johannesburg the South Australians were first into the fort. Henry's corps was engaged at Diamond Hill 11th-13th June, and thereafter held posts east of Pretoria. On 21st July the South Australians had a rather warm skirmish. On the 28th they set off in the eastern advance, still as part of Colonel Henry's corps. The South Australians had severe fighting and some casualties about Belfast on 7th September; thereafter they marched to Komati Poort. Near that place they discovered some of the enemy's abandoned guns. They were in the big review at the Poort on 28th September. On 9th October the two contingents entrained for Pretoria. Soon after this the 1st contingent and 25 of the 2nd entrained for Cape Town, and arrived at Adelaide on 30th November. The remainder of the 2nd were attached to Alderson's column, which was one of those employed in February and March 1901 in a big sweep through the Eastern Transvaal. On 29th March they sailed for home.

THE 3RD SOUTH AUSTRALIAN (BUSHMEN) CONTINGENT.

The 3rd contingent, 100 strong, commanded by Captain S. Gran Hubbe, sailed on the *Maplemore* from Adelaide upon 7th March 1900, and landed at Beira on 11th April. They formed part of General Carrington's force which crossed Rhodesia and entered the Transvaal from about Mafeking.

The 3rd South Australian (Bushmen) Contingent

It was intended that the 2nd Regiment of the Rhodesian Field Force should consist of the 3rd South Australians, 3rd Tasmanians, and the 3rd Queenslanders; but before Mafeking was reached, on 24th June, the regiment was split up and was never brought together. Between 4th July and 9th August the squadron was patrolling the Marico and working towards Elands River district (see Rhodesian Regiment). On 6th August Lieutenant Collins was wounded. On the 9th the squadron retired to Mafeking with Carrington. On 13th August they had a skirmish. Next day they were in a sharp fight at Buffelshoek. On the 15th the squadron was put into a Composite Bushmen Regiment, along with "D" Squadron of the 1st New South Wales Bushmen, Captain Polson's squadron of the 5th New Zealand, and the 3rd Tasmanians. For a long time the regiment did excellent work in the Western Transvaal as part of Lord Methuen's force. At Buffelshoek on the 21st of that month the South Australians had sharp fighting and suffered casualties. For a second time they were in action at Ottoshoop, on 12th September, when Captain Gran Hubbe was killed, and the squadron suffered other losses. At Lichtenburg on the 26th of the same month they again had casualties. Lieutenant Collins having recovered, he was appointed to command the contingent with the rank of Captain.

Throughout the latter part of 1900 and the first quarter of 1901 the Composite Bushmen Regiment was in many engagements, chiefly in the Western Transvaal, but also in the north of the Orange River Colony. In several of these the enemy fought with considerable determination, and as a matter of course losses were frequent. For many months the Western Transvaal was dangerously denuded of troops, and consequently the strain on those who were there was severe. The most constant watchfulness was necessary, for the enemy was ever alert and was ably led. At Uitvalskop, on 3rd February 1901, the squadron lost 1 man killed and Lieutenant J. T. Dempsey and 5 men wounded; and in the very severely contested action near Hartebeestfontein, on 16th February, Captain Collins, for the second time, and 1 man were wounded. Altogether the squadron had 4 killed and 20 wounded.

In April the squadron left Lord Methuen's force for home, and he wrote to the Secretary of the South Australian Bushmen's Committee a letter, in which he " tendered his tribute of praise " for the splendid work performed by the squadron,—their cheerfulness in hardship, and good discipline. Among other things, his Lordship said, " I cannot conceive any body of men of whom a commander has greater reason to be proud."

THE 4TH SOUTH AUSTRALIAN (IMPERIAL BUSHMEN) CONTINGENT.

This corps, strength 230 all ranks, under the command of Lieut.-Colonel J. Rowell, C.B., sailed on the *Manhattan* on 1st May 1900, touched at Beira, were sent on to Durban, and landed at Port Elizabeth, Cape Colony, on 19th June 1900. They were very soon to see brisk fighting and to gain distinction.

About the middle of June Lord Roberts commenced operations to encircle the Boers who were in the Wittebergen or Brandwater Basin, a mountain stronghold in the north-east of the Orange River Colony.

Rundle, with the VIIIth Division, and Brabant, with the South African Colonial Division, were holding the line from Senekal eastward to the Basutoland border. Clements and Paget, a little farther west, were about Lindley, the south-west point of the Boer stronghold. These masses of men either could not or were not allowed to live on the country, hence huge convoys of supplies had to be sent from the railway. On 23rd June a very large convoy left Kroonstad for General Paget's force at Lindley. The escort was commanded by Colonel Brookfield, 14th Imperial Yeomanry, and consisted of 200 of that corps. 114 other Yeomanry, 400 Imperial Bushmen—namely, two squadrons 4th South Australians, Colonel Rowell; one squadron 4th West Australians, Major Rose; one squadron 4th Tasmanians, Captain R. C. Lewis; 27 Rimington's Guides; 93 Prince Alfred's Guards; 2 guns 17th Royal Field Artillery; 4 guns C.I.V. Battery; half battalion Yorkshire Light Infantry; and the 3rd East Kent (Buffs) Militia. The whole of the Australians were treated as one regiment under Colonel Rowell. To Colonel Brookfield the writer is indebted for many of the particulars now given.

On the morning of the 26th Theron's Scouts suddenly attacked the convoy near Elands Spruit, but they were driven off. In the afternoon, near Swartz Farm, Piet de Wet attacked. Colonel Rowell's men were ordered to dismount, and advancing with "great go," the enemy was again driven off. On the 27th the convoy marched sixteen miles, the escort being engaged practically all the day. Near Lindley the traction engines stuck in a spruit. Colonel Rowell's men were rear-guard, and were heavily pressed by the enemy, who endeavoured to cut off the Tasmanians who were rear-screen; but the City Imperial Volunteer Battery did good work, and Colonel Brookfield having sent a fresh squadron to Rowell's assistance, he was able to keep the Boers off the convoy. Next day Lindley was reached. The 4th South Australians had several casualties on the 26th and 27th.

It was only to be expected that the Yorkshire Light Infantry, who had done very fine work in Lord Methuen's earlier battles, would do all that soldiers could do; but Colonel Brookfield could not have been so confident about the Militia and Yeomanry and his absolutely untried Bushmen, who had not, before this, fired a shot in earnest. In a despatch to General Kelly-Kenny, commanding in the Orange River Colony, the chief of the staff said that Lord Roberts was of opinion that the march of the convoy had been "conducted with skill and foresight, that no precautions were neglected, and that the behaviour of the troops was creditable to all ranks. His Lordship is glad to observe that besides the regular troops employed, a Militia Battalion (3rd Buffs), the corps of Imperial Bushmen, the Imperial Yeomanry, and the City Imperial Volunteer Artillery, distinguished themselves on this occasion."

Colonel Brookfield and most of his troops now joined General Paget's command. On 3rd July Paget had a very stiff engagement with a strong force of the enemy. The action has been called "Barkin Kop," "Baken Kop," and "Leeuw Kop," and phases of it are well described by the authors of 'The H.A.C. (Honourable Artillery Company) in South Africa.' (Smith, Elder, & Co.: London, 1903.) In the course of the fighting the guns had been taken to a ridge, and during a pause in the action the escort had been removed to the rear. The Boers, with great skill and secrecy, delivered a sudden and fierce counter-attack, in which they gained temporary possession of the guns. The authors of 'The H.A.C. in South Africa' say: "Captain Budworth managed to reach his pony, and galloped back at once to call upon the Australians to return. That he succeeded in bringing them back, and promptly too, reflects the highest credit on him, and also, be it added, on the men he had to deal with. Who ordered their retirement it is impossible to ascertain; but it is just to say that when called upon to come back again they did so willingly: and it is common knowledge that it requires more courage, both moral and physical, for troops in retreat to rally and face fire than to sit tight and suffer it from the first." For some time there was great cause for anxiety, but "the period of imminent danger did not last long. It was over from the moment that, owing to the Australian fire, the Boers left the disabled guns and retreated."

Colonel Rowell having got a broken rib through his horse falling, he was unable to be present on the 3rd. Major Rose, of the West Australians, commanded the Bushmen, and he was wounded. The Tasmanian squadron having been kept on other duty near Lindley, only joined their comrades as the Boers were driven off. The South Australians had on the 3rd about a dozen casualties.

After further heavy fighting, Bethlehem was taken on 7th July. In his account of the taking of Bethlehem, the Press Association correspondent said: "Three hundred Bushmen, mostly South and West Australians, joined in the attack and behaved most gallantly." When De Wet broke through the cordon,

16th July, the contingent took part in his pursuit to the Reitzburg Hills. At Palmietfontein on the 19th there was a sharp engagement, and on the 24th at Stinkhoutboom the South Australians lost 3 killed and several wounded. On the 18th the 4th Tasmanians were detached from the regiment.

De Wet having crossed to the north of the Vaal, the 4th South Australians were taken to the Transvaal. In November they joined General Plumer (see 1st, 2nd, and 3rd New Zealand and 4th Queensland). The 4th Imperial Bushmen were now together again, and under that heading are given some features of the work they did when referred to in despatches by that name. The regiment was again commanded by Colonel Rowell. In February the South Australians had several casualties in Cape Colony during the pursuit of De Wet.

In March, April, and May 1901 the 4th South Australians distinguished themselves in the operations between Pretoria and Pietersburg; and when General Plumer, after the occupation of the latter town, was moving southwards, Captain F. W. Hurcombe gained notice for his bold and successful leading. Unfortunately, on an occasion when he was far in advance with only a few men, he fell among a party of the enemy concealed in a mealie field. It was said that before he would surrender Captain Hurcombe had to be knocked down by a clubbed rifle. During May the 4th South Australians had casualties on various occasions in the Eastern Transvaal. The contingent, still under Colonel Rowell, sailed for home on 7th July 1901.

THE 5TH AND 6TH SOUTH AUSTRALIAN CONTINGENTS.

The 5th contingent, 24 officers and 300 other ranks, landed at Port Elizabeth on 23rd March 1901; and the 6th, 11 officers and 127 other ranks, landed at Durban on 19th April. On arrival the 5th contingent was taken to the Kroonstad district, where they joined Colonel De Lisle. On 18th May the 6th joined the column at Vrede, and afterwards the 5th and 6th worked together as a regiment, Major Shea, Indian Staff Corps, being in command, with Majors Wilson and Hurcombe.

From May 1901 to March 1902 De Lisle's column did outstanding work in the north-eastern quarter of the Orange River Colony. On 6th June 1901 his troops gained great distinction by the capture of a large convoy, and by retaining practically all their captures, although the small mounted body which had effected them was most fiercely attacked by a strong force of Boers under De Wet and Delarey. Seldom in the course of the campaign was the fighting of a more determined character. The losses of the South Australians were 10 killed and 6 wounded, the large proportion of killed being accounted for by the fact that much of the firing was at ranges of less than 100 yards. The corps on this occasion gained several mentions.

The despatch of 8th August 1901 contains several references to the fine work of the 5th and 6th South Australians. In para. 4 Lord Kitchener mentions that Broadwood, on 29th July, made a night march on Bothaville, which resulted in his "driving a number of

Boers into the arms of Lt.-Col. De Lisle's South Australians, who captured 18 prisoners and 12 waggons": and on 2nd August " Major Shea, with 200 of Colonel De Lisle's South Australians, made a gallant attack on Smut's commando at Grootvallier Farm, near the Vet River. Wire-fencing, unseen in the darkness, prevented the complete success of the plan, and enabled the Boers to escape, despite the fact that the South Australians pressed forward on foot with fixed bayonets. Five Boers were left dead upon the ground, and 11 were captured, including Field-Cornet Wolmarans, of Potchefstroom. . . . On the 6th and 7th Colonel De Lisle was able to account for 40 prisoners, 147 waggons, 600 horses, and 2000 cattle."

In an order dated 2nd August 1901, Colonel De Lisle congratulated the regiment on " their successful night enterprises," and said that " the very dashing night attack at Grootvallier was worthy of the best traditions of the Australian troops in the war."

The South Australians who were with Colonel De Lisle saw, as did other troops who happened to be under any of the outstanding leaders, endless hard work and much severe fighting; but Colonel De Lisle never made a mistake, and could do a great deal on a comparatively small casualty list. Both contingents took part in the driving operations in the north-east of the Orange River Colony throughout January, February, and March 1902, the success of which did much to terminate hostilities. During these great drives the outpost work was so arduous that the general ordered the officers to take their turn on sentry.

The fact that the regiment during its service caught and broke in 867 veldt ponies proves the usefulness of the " Bushman."

Mentions gained by South Australian Contingents 463

The casualties of the regiment were 14 killed and 28 wounded. They trekked 3825 miles, and accounted for nearly 300 of the enemy. They were never three consecutive days in one place. The regiment sailed for home from Natal on 5th April 1902.

South Australia furnished her quota to the troops sent by Federated Australia in 1902 (see Commonwealth Horse). A squadron under Captain De Passey sailed on 20th February, and having landed at Durban, was employed near Laing's Nek, and thereafter was railed to the Western Transvaal, where, as part of the Australian Horse, it took part under De Lisle and Thorneycroft in some great drives. The second contribution was a squadron under Captain A. E. Collins, which sailed on 1st April 1902; while the third was two squadrons under Captain A. E. Cook, which sailed on 26th May.

The Mentions gained by the South Australian Contingents are as follows :—

LORD ROBERTS' DESPATCHES : *2nd April* 1901.—S.A. Bushmen : Col. J. M. Gordon,[1] Lt.-Col. J. Rowell[1] (4th contingent); Capts. A. E. Collins, 3rd,[2] Gran Hubbe, 3rd, J. H. Stapleton, 1st[2]; Lt. C. M. Ives, 3rd.[2] Mounted Rifles : Major C. J. Reade, 2nd[1]; Capt. J. F. Humphris, 2nd[2]; Sgts. Ive, Knapman ; Cpls. Currie, Fornby, V. M. Newland[3]; Lce.-Cpl. H. Balfour Ogilvy[3]; Ptes. H. W. Brown,[3] Cornish, Fetch.

4th September 1901.—South Australian Bushmen : Capt. A. E. M. Norton, 4th[2]; Lt. A. W. Leane, 4th ; Sgt. Spencer[3]; Cpls. Allnut,[3] Catchlowe (now Lt.); Tprs. Gardiner, Lennox, Mayfield, Stott, Thorne[3]; Nursing Sister M. S. Bidmead (got the Royal Red Cross).

LORD KITCHENER'S DESPATCHES : *8th March* 1901.—S.A. Impl. Bushmen, 4th contingent : ¡Capt. Wilson, 4th. Despatch of 8th May 1901. From General Plumer's Special Despatch on Lt. Reid's capture of Commandant

---

[1] Awarded C.B.   [2] D.S.O.   [3] D.C. Medal.

Schroeder and his laager and 40 men, near Commissie Drift, April 25. S.A. Impl. Bushmen : Sgt. Ward.

8th July 1901.—S. A. Bushmen : Capt. E. J. F. Langley, 5th contgt.,[1] conspicuous gallantry in fight for convoy near Reitz, June 6 (D.S.O. June 24) ; Sgt. L. Grewar, 5th, same occasion, by his courage and example greatly contributed to defeat of desperate attack (mentioned in A.O.)

8th August 1901.—S.A.M.I. (5th and 6th contgts.) : Capt. J. Watt,[1] and Lt. D. Macfarlane,[1] conspicuous for gallantry and fearless leading in night attack on Smut's laager, August 1 ; Capt. J. S. Shea, 15th Bengal Lancers, attached, also got D.S.O. for leading 200 S. Australians in night attack on Smut's laager of over 300 men, and, after hand-to-hand fighting, killing 7 and capturing 11 ; Tpr. T. Kermode promoted Cpl. same occasion. He was first man into the farm, and bayoneted the first man, and although wounded in three places continued to fight ; Tpr. P. Brandt (promoted Cpl.) for gallantry same occasion.

23rd June 1902. — S. Australians : Lts. F. B. Muir, J. H. Shearer, W. C. N. Waite ; Sgt. J. Rundle ; Lce.-Cpl. J. Berry [2] ; Cpl. R. Gully [2].

---

[1] Awarded D.S.O. [2] D.C. Medal.

The West Australian Contingents.

THE 1st AND 2nd CONTINGENTS.

THE total contribution from Western Australia was 63 officers, 1160 men, and 1044 horses.[1]

The 1st contingent, 130 all ranks, with two maxims, sailed on the *Medic* from Albany on 5th November 1899, and arrived at Cape Town on the 26th of the same month. On their arrival in South Africa they were, along with the remainder of the Australian Regiment of infantry, employed on the lines of communication between De Aar and Modder River (see 1st Victorians). In January 1900 they were converted into mounted infantry, and were about the beginning of February sent to join the forces under General Clements in the Colesberg district; and the good work which they did there was frequently mentioned by correspondents and other writers on the war. On 6th February the West Australians were under fire for the first time, and had their first casualty. A reconnaissance in difficult country being necessary, 80 Westralians under Major Moor, an officer of the Royal Artillery, commanding the contingent, and Lieutenant Parker, formed part of a force sent out towards Potfontein.

[1] Official publication, 'Australia and New Zealand,' Sydney, 1904, p. 440.

Moor's men came under a very heavy fire, but only one man was wounded. Major Moor himself narrowly escaped capture. He had given his horse to a dismounted Lancer, and was endeavouring to catch another horse: while doing so he was close to a party of Boers ensconced among rocks which some Lancers had just vacated. His subaltern noticed the peril of his senior, and galloping up took him up behind, and both got away. On the 9th Moor and 20 of his squadron were ordered to hold a kopje, which was placed as inside the heels of a horse-shoe. The Boers occupied the whole of the hills forming the shoe itself, and brought a very heavy fire to bear on Moor's position, but he held on till ordered to retire. Sergeant Hensman was mortally wounded, and Private Conway was killed while tending his non-commissioned officer. Six other men were wounded. Major Reay, in his 'With the Australian Regiment,' gives a detailed account of the engagement. He mentions that Private Kruger built a sangar round Hensman under a very heavy fire: his helmet was pierced by one bullet, his bandolier torn by another, while a third skinned his knuckles. Other non-commissioned officers and men distinguished themselves by running with messages across a bullet-swept zone. General Clements was very highly pleased with the conduct of the West Australians, and published the following order: "Operations at Slingersfontein, 9th February 1900.—The General Officer Commanding wishes to place on record his high appreciation of the courage and determination shown by a party of 20 men of the West Australians under Captain Moor in the above operations. By their determined stand against 300 or 400 men they entirely frustrated the enemy's attempt to turn the flank of the position."

In the fighting between the 10th and 13th February the West Australians were on the right of the line, near the Worcestershire Regiment, along with whom they took an honourable share in the very severe engagement on the 12th, when the Boers attacked Clements' positions, particularly on the two flanks (see Victorian Mounted Rifles), with the very greatest determination and in great strength. As has already been stated under the Victorian Contingents, the Boers did not renew their attack on the 13th, but General Clements decided that, in view of the overwhelming numbers of the enemy, it would be well to retire from the positions in front of Rensburg to Arundel. During this movement, which commenced about midnight 13th-14th, Major Moor's West Australians formed the left flank guard. During the next fortnight the outpost duty was very severe: the Boers being in great strength, Clements had to exercise every possible precaution. On the 20th the enemy renewed his attack, but the British were able to hold all their positions till fighting ceased. On this occasion the West Australians had been holding advanced outposts during the preceding night, and when the engagement commenced they could neither be fed, relieved, nor reinforced. Their position being well prepared they held it without loss, and claimed to have inflicted many casualties on their assailants. On the 22nd, 23rd, and 24th there was more fighting—General Clements making a bold but unsuccessful effort to drive back the enemy. A composite company of West and South Australians, officered by Major Moor, Lieutenants Darling and Campbell, West Australians, and Stapleton, South Australians, did good work, and got so far forward that they had difficulty in getting back. On the 27th it was found that the Boer leaders were withdrawing towards the Orange River. On the 28th Colesberg was occupied. On the 4th of March the West Australians, along with the 1st Victorian Contingent, were in a sharp engagement, in which they drove back the enemy, who left 8 dead.

Captain Forrest, in an excellent record of the work done by the Mounted Infantry Company of his battalion, published in the 'Oxfordshire Light Infantry in South Africa,' says, under date 27th February, "The company was attached to a force, under Major King-King, ordered to guard the right flank of the advance" (from Colesberg to Norvals Pont on the Orange River). "The force consisted, besides ourselves, of one section 'J' Battery, R.H.A., one company West Australians, and two companies Prince Alfred's Guards. The West Australians, under Major Moor, were a splendid body of men. They compared more than favourably with any other Colonials met with afterwards. When the column arrived at the Orange River, it was found that the three centre arches of the bridge had been destroyed by dynamite. The Boer position on the north bank having been shelled, volunteers who could row were then asked for, and the West Australians were able to send in, among others, the name of the champion sculler of Australia."

In the advance to Bloemfontein the West Australians were attached to the right column of General Clements' force. This column consisted of a squadron Inniskilling Dragoons, some guns R.F.A., the Mounted Infantry of the Oxford Light Infantry and West Riding Regiments, and the West Australians.

In Lord Roberts' despatch of 15th March 1900 he mentioned that there was organised disaffection in the Prieska district, and that various columns were dealing

1st and 2nd West Australian Contingents 469

with the rebels. Among the troops engaged was one company of West Australian Mounted Infantry. This was the 2nd contingent, commanded by Captain H. L. Pilkington, which had sailed from Freemantle on 3rd February. The rising was put down in March, but some West Australians continued to operate in the district during part of April. The 2nd contingent arrived at Bloemfontein in time to take part in the advance to Pretoria in May.

After their arrival at Bloemfontein the 1st West Australians were put into a Mounted Infantry Corps, commanded by Lieut.-Colonel De Lisle, and composed of themselves, the 6th Battalion Mounted Infantry (Regulars), and the New South Wales Mounted Infantry. This corps saw much fighting on the way to Pretoria. It had been announced that the 1st and 2nd West Australians would be put together, but this was not carried out. On their arrival at Bloemfontein, the 2nd contingent was attached to General Pole-Carew's XIth Division, with which they served from 1st May to the end of October 1900, with the exception of a period of a few weeks about the end of June and beginning of July, when they were detached to assist on the lines of communication in the Orange River Colony. The 2nd contingent were engaged at Brandfort, 3rd May; Vet River, 4th May; Zand River, 9th and 10th May; at the Vaal, 26th May; outside Johannesburg on the 28th, 29th, and 30th; at Six-Mile Spruit on 4th June; Silverton, 8th June; Diamond Hill, 11th and 12th June.

The despatches and unofficial accounts contained many references to the work of the West Australians. At the crossing of the Vet River about 30 of the 2nd contingent seized a kopje of much importance, and, although far from support, held on till next morning. Lord Roberts congratulated them on this piece of good service. In his telegram of 7th May he gave the West Australians the credit of discovering explosives on the railway and thus saving accidents. Again, in his wire of 28th May from Klip River, Lord Roberts said: "The enemy had prepared several positions where they intended to oppose us, but they abandoned one after another as we neared them. We pressed them so hard that they only just had time to get their five guns into the train and leave this station as some of the West Australian Mounted Infantry entered it." A party were also said to have gained credit by holding a drift, shortly before the surrender of Johannesburg, for eight hours against a very superior force of the enemy. Lieutenant L. D. H. Potter was wounded on 30th May.

Both contingents were heavily engaged at Diamond Hill. They had some casualties. De Lisle's men were said by Lord Roberts to have done well. In his telegram of the 16th Lord Roberts said: "Botha's army has retired, believed to Middelburg. His rear-guard was surprised and thoroughly routed by Ian Hamilton's Mounted Infantry, chiefly West Australians and 6th Battalion."

On 16th July a detachment of the 2nd West Australians at Pienaar's Poort, on the left of General Pole-Carew's position, east of Pretoria, successfully repulsed a Boer attack.

In his telegram of June 28th and despatch of October 10th, para. 15, Lord Roberts remarks: "On the 27th June the post on the railway near Roodeval Station was attacked, but the enemy was repulsed by a detachment of the Shropshire Light Infantry and the West Australian Mounted Infantry, with the aid of a

15-pounder gun on an armoured train." The party here mentioned was the 1st contingent.

Ridley's Mounted Infantry Brigade, including the 1st West Australians, formed part of the force which Sir Archibald Hunter led into the north-east of the Orange River Colony with the view of surrounding, if possible, the enemy under De Wet and Prinsloo in the Wittebergen or Brandwater Basin, as the district was more generally called. On the night of 15th July De Wet, with about 1600 men and some guns, escaped from Slabbert's Nek. Broadwood with the 2nd Cavalry Brigade and Ridley's Mounted Infantry were sent in pursuit. The Boers succeeded in reaching the railway and cutting the line. On 22nd July General Knox at Kroonstad wired to the General in Command at Cape Town as follows: "Following from General Broadwood, commanding 2nd Cavalry Brigade, sent by despatch rider to Honingspruit and wired from there to Kroonstad, begins—Have followed commando since July 16th, had sharp fight at Palmietfontein on July 19th. Prevented from pursuing laager by darkness: eight dead Boers found. Our casualties: killed, Major Moor, West Australian M.I., and 4 men; wounded, Lt. Stanley, 10th Hussars; Lt. Tooth, Australian Contingent, and 14 men." Major Moor's death was a heavy loss to the West Australians. His fine leadership had brought his corps into great prominence, when their small numbers are kept in mind. The West Australian losses at Palmietfontein, as afterwards announced, were, apart from Major Moor, 1 killed and 6 wounded. In the fighting at Stinkhoutboom on 24th July, the West Australians had 2 men killed and 3 severely wounded. After this De Wet took refuge in the Reitzburg hills on the south side of the Vaal, but about 7th August he crossed the river, evaded Lord Methuen's forces on the north bank, and made for the Northern Transvaal, crossing the Megaliesberg mountains by a pass which Lord Roberts had intended to have blocked, but from which the troops had been removed by an error. Lord Kitchener, with Broadwood's, Ridley's, and other columns, took up the pursuit, crossed the Vaal with all possible rapidity, and followed up at a great pace; but beyond releasing some 60 British prisoners and taking some waggons and one gun, the pursuit failed. Lord Kitchener was, however, able on 16th August to relieve Colonel Hore at Elands River (see Rhodesian Regiment). Mr Green, in his 'Story of the Australian Bushmen,' mentions that the first troops to ride into Elands River and receive the heartfelt thanks of the gallant garrison were De Lisle's West Australians, who were scouting in front of Lord Kitchener's force, —an honourable post, because six regiments of regular cavalry were in that force. De Lisle's corps reached Pretoria on 28th August, and was thereafter employed in the Central Transvaal.

The 2nd contingent took part, under Pole-Carew, in the advance from Pretoria to Komati Poort, starting about 23rd July. They had fighting in the Belfast district on 28th August and frequently thereafter. In his telegram of 13th September Lord Roberts remarked that the West Australians had been scouting in front of Pole-Carew's Division. At Waterval Onder, on 3rd September, Lieutenant Darling and 8 men were wounded. The West Australians were said to have been the first to discover much railway material and other valuable stores near the Poort. They were present at the big review held there on 28th September. After their stay in that unhealthy neighbourhood, they were employed about Machododorp, where they suffered some casualties throughout October.

On 15th October the 1st contingent was inspected by Lord Roberts in Pretoria, and were complimented on their work. In November most of the 1st contingent sailed for home.

In January and February 1901 the 2nd contingent was employed in Cape Colony, and assisted to drive out the invaders. At Klipplaat, on 5th February, Captain Olliver and several men were wounded. Captain Olliver had been sent in command of a small force, 12 men of the 7th Dragoon Guards, 12 West Australians, and 3 Cape Police, carrying despatches from Colonel Haig to another leader. The little body was surrounded by several hundreds of the enemy. They kept up a good fight from 11 A.M. till sundown, but were eventually all overpowered. Four of the Dragoons were killed and several were wounded.

On 31st March 1901 the last of the 2nd contingent, under Lieutenant Duffy, sailed for Australia.

THE 3RD WEST AUSTRALIAN (BUSHMEN) CONTINGENT.

This contingent, commanded by Major H. G. Vialls, Captain in the Reserve of Officers, was taken to Beira, where they landed in April 1900. They formed part of the force of Bushmen which, under General Carrington, crossed Rhodesia and entered the Transvaal from Mafeking. The contingent, small as it was, was split up, but they saw a great deal of fighting throughout

July, August, and September 1900 in the district between Mafeking on the west and Warmbad, north of Pretoria, on the east. At Kosters River, on 21st and 22nd July (see 1st N.S.W. Bushmen), there was a stiff engagement in which parties from the different Australian colonies bore the brunt. The West Australians, strength about 70, had Surgeon-Captain F. J. Ingoldsby and Lieutenant Davies and several men wounded. A few West Australians, acting under Captain Ham, 3rd Victorians, were in Colonel Hore's garrison which made a very fine defence at Elands River, 4th to 16th August (see Rhodesian Regiment). Another small detachment were with Carrington when he attempted to effect Hore's relief from the west; while the first troops to march into the place as the advance scouts of Lord Kitchener's force, which relieved the garrison from the south-east, were, as already stated, men of the 1st West Australians.

During the last four months of 1901 and the first few months of 1902, the 3rd contingent, as part of the 3rd Australian Bushmen, commanded by Major Vialls, saw much fighting in many parts of the seat of war, and under Vialls' fine leadership always did well. Some of the work of the 3rd Australian Bushmen is sketched under the 3rd Victorians, to which reference is made (see also 1st, 2nd, and 3rd New Zealanders).

Captain Hurst of the 3rd contingent remained in South Africa after his squadron had sailed. In the spring of 1902, while attached to "G" Battery Royal Horse Artillery, then converted into Mounted Rifles, he was severely wounded in the action of Boschbult, Western Transvaal, 31st March.

THE 4TH WEST AUSTRALIAN CONTINGENT (WEST AUSTRALIAN IMPERIAL BUSHMEN).

The 4th contingent, one squadron, commanded by Major J. Rose, sailed on the *Manhattan* on 7th May 1900, and after having touched at Beira and Durban, landed at Port Elizabeth on 19th June. They were at once taken to the Kroonstad district of the Orange River Colony, where, on 23rd June, they joined a force under Colonel Brookfield which was to see some very severe fighting in the ensuing three weeks. In the action of Barkin or Baken Kop, 3rd July, Major Rose was wounded. This action has already been referred to under the 4th South Australians, with whom this contingent did over a year's hard campaigning. These two contingents, along with the 4th Tasmanians, formed what was known as the 4th Imperial Bushmen, and some notes of the very fine work of the regiment are to be found under that heading. While the 4th Imperial Bushmen operated with Plumer in Cape Colony, and in the north of and east of the Transvaal, this squadron had casualties on various occasions.

5TH AND 6TH WEST AUSTRALIAN CONTINGENTS.

These contingents, approximately five squadrons strong, sailed early in March 1901. Major J. R. Royston, D.S.O., was appointed to command these contingents. He had begun the war as a Lieutenant in the Border Mounted Rifles—a Natal volunteer corps,

—and had gained distinction at the defence of Ladysmith. As will be seen from the Mentions, Major—soon Lieut.-Colonel—Royston added as commander of a regiment to the fine reputation he had made as a subaltern and captain.

The despatches of 1901 show that for a great part of that year the 5th and 6th West Australian Mounted Infantry—combined strength in June about 355 men and 380 horses—were in the column of Major-General F. W. Kitchener, who long worked in the Lydenburg district, and generally over the Eastern Transvaal.

In April 1901 General F. W. Kitchener's column, working from Lydenburg, took part in the operations of Sir Bindon Blood to the north of the Delagoa Railway and in the Middelburg district.[1] During April West Australians were several times engaged, and made some captures of prisoners and stock. On 13th May Major-General Kitchener's column crossed to the south of the railway and made for the Ermelo district, to take part in another sweeping movement towards the east under the direction of General Bindon Blood, and back towards the Ermelo-Bethel district. On 15th May there was severe fighting at Grobelaar Recht, in which the 5th had Lieutenant Forrest and Sergeant Ejards and 1 man killed and 5 men wounded, and the 6th 4 men killed and Lieutenant S. S. Reid and 3 men wounded. On the 16th there was again heavy fighting, in which Lieutenant F. W. Bell distinguished himself so greatly that he was recommended for and received the Victoria Cross. The circumstances are detailed under the Honours and Mentions gained. On 23rd June, at Renshoogte, there was again fighting, when Lieutenant S. S. Reid and 2 men were killed and 2 severely

[1] Despatch of 8th May 1901.

5th and 6th West Australian Contingents

wounded. During these operations a fair number of prisoners and some carts with ammunition were taken. In July Kitchener's column was back at Middelburg, and after refitting moved north of the railway and had some encounters in which more prisoners were taken. On 16th August 1 man of the 6th was killed, and Lieutenant W. H. Young of that contingent and 1 man were wounded.

A portion of these contingents were from August to October 1901 with Colonel Benson when he was doing very fine work in the Eastern Transvaal. One of the 6th was wounded in his engagement at Bakenlaagte, 30th October, when Benson was killed (see Scottish Horse).

Towards the close of 1901, and in the early months of 1902, both contingents were acting under General Bruce Hamilton in the Eastern Transvaal, and took part in many of that fine leader's most successful enterprises. They had a few casualties on various occasions. On 1st February 1902 the 5th had 2 men killed at Waterval River, and the 6th had 1 man wounded in the same action; and on the following day Lieutenant G. A. Morris was killed at Rolspruit. At Roodepoort, on 26th February, Sergeant P. J. Daly was severely wounded. While with Colonel Wing's column in February and March 1902 the West Australians undertook many arduous marches in the endeavour to get into contact with the enemy, but he had been so often worsted in the Eastern Transvaal, to keep out of sight had become his one desire.

West Australia furnished contributions to the Commonwealth Troops (see that heading). Only the first squadron were in time to take part in the closing drives.

The Honours and Mentions gained by the West Australians were as follows :—

Lieut. F. W. Bell, West Australian M.I. (5th and 6th contingents). At Brakpan, Eastern Transvaal, May 16, 1901, when retiring through a heavy fire after holding the right flank, Lieut. Bell noticed a man dismounted, and returned and took him up behind him. The horse not being equal to the weight, fell with them. Lieut. Bell then remained behind, and covered the man's retirement till he was out of danger.

LORD ROBERTS' DESPATCHES : *2nd April* 1901.—W.A.M.I. : Lieut.-Col. W. L. Pilkington,[1] 2nd contingent, Reserve of Officers ; Capts.[J. Harris, F. M. Parker[2] ; Lts. H. F. Darling,[2] J. C. De Castilla,[2] R. R. C. Vernon,[2] S. A. Olliver[2] ; Sgts. J. Barry, E. H. Draper, P. M. Edwards ; Cpl. W. H. Clarkson, Lce.-Cpl. J. Burley ; Ptes. R. Corkhill, H. Force, M. A. Spiers. Bushman's Corps : Major H. G. Vialls.[1]

4th September 1901.—Lieut. C. H. Ord.

1st March 1902.—Major H. G. Moor, Royal Artillery, commanding 1st contingent (killed in action). W.A. Medical Staff : Surgeon Lieut.-Col. F. J. Ingoldsby.

LORD KITCHENER'S DESPATCHES : *8th March* 1901.—Major Vialls.

8th May 1901.—From General Plumer's of 7th April.—W.A. Bushmen : Sgt. W. George, D.C.M., on April 6th, near De Berg Pass, Pietesberg (Pietersburg) district, when in advance with 8 scouts held his own on most difficult ground against 40 Boers. He displayed conspicuous personal bravery, as he has done to my personal knowledge on several previous occasions. Pte. F. Angel, D.C.M. (since dead), one of scouts above-mentioned, and was very severely wounded in going forward to assist another wounded man.

8th July 1901.—Lieut. F. W. Bell, awarded V.C. as before mentioned. Capt. J. Campbell for assisting Lieut. Bell. Lieut. S. S. Reid at same place and date remained with his men, though severely wounded early in fight. Lieut. A. A. Forrest (killed) and A. J. Brown, conspicuous gallantry on same occasion. (All foregoing brought to notice of Australian Government.) Surgeon-Capt. F. B. Reid showed absolute disregard of danger in performing his duties on same occasion.

8th December 1901.—W.A. 5th M.I. : Major J. R. Royston, for single-handed capture of 2 armed Boers, November 8, 1901, and for saving a man's life on same occasion.

8th March 1902.—W.A.M.I. : Lieut. P. J. Daly,[2] along with Lieut. Archer

---

[1] Awarded C.B.   [2] Awarded D.S.O.

Mentions gained by West Australian Contingents

Shee, 19th Hussars, gallantry in pursuit of a superior force of the enemy near Kromdrai on 28th February; both very severely wounded, but captured 7 of the enemy. Cpl. P. J. Daly (promoted Sgt.), for gallant services on three occasions with scouts when parties of Boers were taken. Lieut. E. S. Clifford, D.S.O., for conspicuous service in December and January. Lieut.-Col. J. R. Royston, D.S.O., Capt. A. J. B. Brown, 5th,[1] and Lieut. R. Clifton, 6th, for conspicuous good services, General Bruce Hamilton's operations in Eastern Transvaal, in December and January.

23rd June 1902—Capt. H. F. Darling, D.S.O., 5th; Lts. J. L. Ochiltree, 5th; A. E. Maley, 6th; Sgt. J. G. Dale[2]; Ptes. Forrest, A. P. Abbot,[2] G. Robinson.

---

[1] Awarded D.S.O.   [2] Awarded D.C.M.

Tasmanian Contingents.

FIRST, or CAMERON'S, TASMANIAN CONTINGENT.

THE small colony of Tasmania sent its quota of men to South Africa.

According to the official publication, 'Australia and New Zealand,' the total contribution from Tasmania was 35 officers, 827 men, and 725 horses. The 1st contingent, consisting of 80 infantry, sailed on the *Medic* on 28th October 1899, and landed at Cape Town on 26th November. They were commanded by Captain Cameron, who as an officer of the 9th Lancers had taken part in Lord Roberts' great march across Afghanistan: he had therefore most ample experience of war. The contingent were at first on the De Aar-Modder line, where, along with the other units composing the Australian Regiment, they garrisoned Enslin and other posts protecting the railway. Towards the close of January 1900 they were converted into mounted infantry, and were sent to Naauwpoort, Cape Colony, where they received horses and joined the force of General Clements, then holding a long line opposite the Boer position about Colesberg (see Victoria M.R.)

During the severe encounters, 9th to 13th February,

1st, or Cameron's, Tasmanian Contingent

the Tasmanians were on the British right. On the 9th the contingent saw serious fighting for the first time. During the previous day or two it had become evident that the enemy were making efforts to occupy certain positions which would facilitate the outflanking of the British right, and General Clements had decided that the strength of the enemy opposite Jasfontein, where the Tasmanians were posted, should be ascertained. Two small bodies went out, one under Captain Salmon, Victoria M.R., and Lieutenant G. E. Reid of the Tasmanians: this detachment consisted of about 30 men of different Australian contingents. The other body, under Captain Cameron, was composed of Tasmanians only. Both detachments took up positions some miles in front of Jasfontein, but the Boers, who were in great strength, succeeded in wedging in between the detachments, and then proceeded to encircle each. To avoid being totally surrounded it was decided that it was necessary to retire. The men had to gallop singly from the positions under a heavy fire at decisive range, but camp was regained without loss. The only casualty was a non-combatant. Mr Lambie, the Australian correspondent, who had accompanied the troops, was killed in the retirement, and Mr Hales of the 'Daily News,' who stayed with his friend, was taken prisoner: he was afterwards released. Some gallant pieces of work took place during the gallop back: Corporal Whitelaw returned for a dismounted comrade; and Private Pears, whose horse was killed, made his way back on foot by a circuitous route, killing three Boers who tried to take him. On the same day a detached post of six Tasmanians was cut off, two men, Gilham and Hutton, being killed.

The Tasmanians were in the hard-fought engagement of 12th February, and along with other troops under General Clements retired on the 14th to Arundel. On the 15th they were ordered to join the 2nd Victorian Contingent on the left rear, which was being seriously threatened; and thereafter they generally operated with that contingent in the movements and fighting down to the time of crossing the Orange River. On the 22nd, when General Clements was making a big effort to clear his left flank and front, the Tasmanians had a foremost place, getting, if anything, too far forward. Unfortunately their gallant leader, Major Cameron, was wounded and taken prisoner. It was reported at the time that, seeing one of his men without a horse, the Major ordered the man to mount his own animal, he intending to retire on foot; but he was cut off, wounded, and captured. Major Reay, author of 'With the Australian Regiment,' was told that the Boers said of Cameron that he was the bravest man they had come across. On the 28th the Tasmanians and Victorians were among the first troops to enter Colesberg, an objective which for over three months the British had been struggling hard to obtain. The Tasmanians, now under Lieutenant W. Brown, were about the 29th ordered to hold an outpost at Rietfontein. On 15th March they crossed the Orange with the other troops.

A draft of 45 Tasmanians, sometimes called the 2nd contingent, had landed at the Cape about the time Colesberg was occupied, but they proceeded to Bloemfontein by rail, and joined the squadron there.

During General Clements' march from Norvals Pont, on the Orange, to the capital of the Free State, the Tasmanians were generally attached to the centre

1st, or Cameron's, Tasmanian Contingent

column. There was no fighting on this march: indeed so peaceful was the turn of affairs at the time, that at Philippolis the squadron gave a concert. Small as the contingent was, it was split up, and did not march into Bloemfontein as one unit.

After their arrival at Bloemfontein about 4th April, the Tasmanians, who had received a reinforcing draft of 40 men, were, along with 1st and 2nd Victoria M.R. and the South Australians, put under Colonel Henry, whose mounted infantry were holding the outpost line north of Glen Station. They took part in many reconnoitring patrols before the advance to Pretoria began. Major Cameron had been found in Bloemfontein, and rejoined his corps before Lord Roberts' army started for the north. During the march to Pretoria, which commenced on 3rd May, Colonel Henry's men were generally the screen in front of the centre and left centre. They had very hard riding, often covering from 40 to 50 miles a-day, and took a prominent part in a number of skirmishes, and in some sharply-fought actions, as near Hout Nek on 30th April, at the crossing of the Vet on 6th May, at the crossing of the Zand River on 10th May, when Major Cameron was again wounded, and at the coal mines on the banks of the Vaal, and in the fighting outside Pretoria. After the occupation of Pretoria Colonel Henry's men were mostly stationed on the eastern front.

Colonel Henry's corps of Mounted Infantry, including the Victorian M.R., South Australians, and Tasmanians, were at the battle of Diamond Hill and in the eastern advance from Pretoria, and had fighting on occasions, particularly about Balmoral at end of July, and near Belfast on 7th September. After some very hard marching through the roughest of country, where scouting was difficult, Komati Poort was entered on 24th September. Henry's corps was present at the review there on the 28th. In October they were taken to Pretoria, where they were inspected by Lord Roberts, and in November the men of the 1st contingent sailed for home.

1st TASMANIAN BUSHMEN.

The 2nd contingent (3rd if the draft of 40 men is counted as a contingent) sailed from Hobart on the *Atlantian* upon 5th March 1900. This was half a squadron, commanded by Captain Riggall, and was generally known as the 1st Bushmen Contingent. Along with other Bushmen they landed at Beira in April, and having crossed Rhodesia towards Mafeking, took part in many operations in the Western Transvaal under Carrington, Lord Erroll, and Lord Methuen. They had several casualties near Ottoshoop on 6th August, when Carrington was endeavouring to assist Hore (see Rhodesian Regiment). This Tasmanian contingent formed a composite Bushmen Regiment along with "D" Squadron of the 1st New South Wales Bushmen, 1 squadron of the 5th New Zealanders, and the 3rd South Australians. The regiment saw much fighting, and some of their engagements have already been mentioned under these other squadrons.

THE 1st TASMANIAN IMPERIAL BUSHMEN
(FOURTH CONTINGENT).

This contingent, 5 officers and 117 men, with 130 horses, sailed on the *Manhattan* from Hobart on 26th April 1900. Captain R. C. Lewis commanded the contingent. The *Manhattan* touched at Beira and at Durban, but ultimately the troops on board, which included the 4th South Australians and 4th West Australians, were landed at Port Elizabeth on 19th June. The three contingents formed what was known as the 4th Imperial Bushmen—Colonel Rowell of the 4th South Australians commanding. Under the latter corps the work of the regiment up to 16th July has already been described. On the 26th June the Tasmanian squadron, acting as rear screen, was pressed by the enemy, who had got into good cover within 300 yards. The squadron had Trooper Firth very badly wounded, and about a dozen horses hit when retiring. The men were said to have behaved extremely well.

Between 18th July and the middle of November the Tasmanians were separated from the remainder of the regiment. Captain Lewis and his men joined General Paget, and after doing some work about the Bethlehem-Winburg district, they formed part of the escort which took the Boers prisoners from the Wittebergen to the railway. On 14th August the contingent entrained for Pretoria, and on the 16th they marched past Lord Roberts, who was very complimentary. On the afternoon of the same day the corps moved out to join General Paget, under whom they were, during the next three months, to see endless hard marching and some very stiff fighting. As Captain Lewis says in his excellent but very modest account,[1] "We were constantly under the fire of the enemy: pretty well every day brought its contribution of experience in the shape of small engagements."

On the 20th August the contingent was put into the mounted brigade of Colonel Hickman, under whom they acted till he left the column in December. That the squadron was most highly thought of by Colonel Hickman is best proved by the fact that he almost invariably asked them to act as advance-guard when he expected to find the enemy.

On 1st September 20 men of the squadron, under Lieutenant Guy Wylly, were out after cattle. They were caught in very bad country, and got back with great difficulty. Trooper G. H. Brown was killed, and 5 others were wounded, including Wylly. It was on this occasion that Lieutenant Wylly and Private Bisdee gained the V.C. (see Mentions). After this the services of Lewis's squadron were much the same as those of the 4th Queensland Imperial Bushmen, to which, and to the 4th Imperial Bushmen, reference is made.

In November the 4th South and 4th West Australians joined Hickman, and the regiment were together again.

At Rhenoster Kop, 29th November (see 3rd New Zealand), Lewis's men were escort to the guns.

In December Captain Lewis was invalided with enteric, and Lieutenant Sale took command: under him the squadron, much reduced in numbers, took a prominent part in the pursuit of De Wet through and out of Cape Colony. Lewis rejoined before the march to Pietersburg took place. After the town was

[1] 'On the Veldt.' Hobart, 1902.

occupied, 8th April 1901, the Tasmanians being the first to enter the place, Captain Sale with a small troop galloped to a ridge beyond. He was shot dead by a Boer concealed in long grass a few paces from him, and Lieutenant Walter, going to his assistance, was mortally wounded. The day was a sad one for the squadron.

On 25th April Sergeant Stocker gained great distinction for his share in the capture of 35 prisoners (see Mentions).

In May the squadron operated under Plumer through the Eastern Transvaal to Bethel and Piet Retief. On 7th July the contingent sailed for home.

5TH TASMANIAN CONTINGENT (2ND TASMANIAN IMPERIAL BUSHMEN).

This contingent, 2 squadrons, 260 all ranks, was commanded by Lieut.-Colonel Watchorn, V.D., with Captains T. A. Spencer and C. Henderson. They sailed from Hobart on 27th March 1901, and landed at Port Elizabeth on 21st April. Soon after landing the corps was in a sharp fight with Scheepers at Ganna Hoek, in Cape Colony, where Trooper Wharbeston, was killed. Trooper Brownell distinguished himself in this affair, and afterwards received a commission in the regular army. On 19th May the corps joined Scobell's column, one of the most successful. On 1st June they were put under Colonel Gorringe, whose force was formed into a "flying column" without wheeled transport (see Cape Police). On 13th February 1902

Colonel Doran took over the column, and the contingent served with him till 4th May. On 18th February they suffered several casualties.

The strain on men and horses was very great; but the column did most excellent work, and was frequently complimented by General French and Lord Kitchener. The various leaders under whom they served commended the contingent for their fearlessness, horsemastership, and cheerful endurance of the greatest hardship. On 13th August 1901 Sergeant-Major Young of the Cape Police, along with Quartermaster-Sergeant Lyne, Sergeant Coombes, and 8 other Tasmanians, charged a kopje where the enemy were strongly entrenched and captured Commandant Erasmus (see Mentions). Young got the V.C. for this affair. The contingent were at various times successful in capturing several influential Boer leaders. For twelve months their work went on absolutely without cessation, long marches often being undertaken by night, followed by actions with the commandos of Kritzinger, Scheepers, Myberg, and others. The whole of the war service of the contingent was done in Cape Colony. They sailed for home on 22nd May 1901, and as they arrived at Hobart on 17th June after peace had been declared, they landed amidst the greatest enthusiasm.

Tasmania furnished its quota to the Commonwealth regiments. One detachment, 63 strong, sailed from Hobart on 14th February 1902, and were in time to do some good but trying work in the last great drives. The next contribution, 121 strong, sailed at the end of March, and another, 120 strong, about 22nd May.

The Honours and Mentions gained by the Tasmanian contingents were as follows :—

Pte. J. H. Bisdee, Tasmanian Imperial Bushmen, won the Victoria Cross in the following circumstances : On September 1, 1900, " Pte. Bisdee was one of an advanced scouting party passing through a rocky defile near Warm Bad, Transvaal. The enemy, who were in ambuscade, opened a sudden fire at close range, and six out of the party of eight were hit, including two officers. The horse of one of the wounded officers broke away and bolted. Pte. Bisdee gave the officer his stirrup leather to help him out of action, but finding that the officer was too badly wounded to go on, he dismounted, placed him on his horse, mounted behind him, and conveyed him out of range. The act was performed under a very hot fire and in a very exposed place." Pte. Bisdee was later on promoted lieutenant. Lieut. Guy G. E. Wylly of the same corps also gained the Cross at the same place. Although wounded, "this officer, seeing that one of his men was badly wounded in the leg and that his horse was shot, went back to the man's assistance, made him take his (Lt. Wylly's) horse, and opened fire from behind a rock, to cover the retreat of the others, at the imminent risk of being cut off himself. Colonel T. E. Hickman, D.S.O., considered that the gallant conduct of Lt. Wylly saved Corporal Brown from being killed or captured, and that his subsequent action in firing to cover the retreat was instrumental in saving others of his men from death or capture." Lieut. Wylly afterwards got a commission in the South Lancashire Regiment, and was wounded on the night of 7th January 1901 when the Boers fiercely attacked the posts on the railway about Belfast.

LORD ROBERTS' DESPATCH : *2nd April* 1901.—Tasmanian Imperial Bushmen : Col. E. T. Wallack ; Capts. R. O. Lewis,[2] A. H. Riggall[2]; Lts. R. Anderson, R. Perkins[2]; Sgt. J. J. Gardiner ; Tprs. R. Chant, P. Clark,[3] R. Douglas, F. A. Groom,[3] A. G. Hillier, E. R. Jacson (killed). Mounted Infantry : Major C. Cameron[1]; Sgt.-Major J. Costello.[3]

LORD KITCHENER'S DESPATCH : *8th March* 1901.—Tasmanian Imperial Bushmen : Lieut. A. A. Sale ; Sgt. Kernsley. Mounted Infantry: Lieut. F. B. Adams (2nd contingent).

8th May 1901.—Extract from General Plumer's Special Despatch on Lieut. Reid's capture of Commandant Schroeder and his laager and 40 men near Commissic Drift, April 25 : "Tasmanian Imperial Bushmen : Sgt. Stocker[3] (promoted Lieutenant) succeeded in getting right behind the laager during night, thereby enabling Lt. Reid to surround it and rush it from all sides at once."

8th July 1901.—Tasmanian Imperial Bushmen : Tpr. E. L. D. Brownell (promoted Cpl.), on May 9th at Ganna Hoek, Cape Colony, showed distinguished bravery in fighting with only one man (Pte. J. E. Wharbeston,

---

[1] Awarded C.B.   [2] Awarded D.S.O.   [3] Awarded D.C.M.

same corps) 20 Boers, killing 2 Boers and 2 horses; finding he could not escape, and his comrade being mortally wounded, shot both horses to prevent them falling into the enemy's hands; taken prisoner and stripped; he was released, when he walked into camp and at once took an ambulance, remained out all night, and brought in Pte. Wharbeston.

8th December 1901. — 2nd Tasmanians (evidently 5th contingent): Qrmr.-Sgt. D. N. Lyne, Sgt. A. Coombes followed Sgt.-Major Young of the Cape Police on the occasion on which he captured Commandant Erasmus at Ruiter's Kraal, August 13. Sgt.-Major Young got the V.C.

8th April 1902. — Tasmanian Imperial Bushmen: Lieut.-Col. E. T. Watchorn (5th).

23rd June 1902.—Capt. F. B. Adams (5th); Lieut. A. N. Boyes; Lieut. and Adjt. J. M'Cormick (5th)[1]; Lieut. G. F. Richardson. Transport: Sgts. A. Coombes, G. Murphy, G. Kemsley[2]; Tpr. C. Cawthorn.

THE 4TH REGIMENT IMPERIAL BUSHMEN.

THIS was a composite corps containing—

> The 4th South Australian Contingent, Lieutenant-Colonel Rowell commanding. (See that Corps.)
> The 4th West Australian Contingent, Major J. Rose.
> The 4th Tasmanian Contingent, Captain R. C. Lewis, D.S.O.

The regiment was long with General Plumer in different parts of the seat of war, and did very good work, particularly in the operations north of Pretoria, and in the Eastern Transvaal. As stated in the despatch of 8th March 1901, when it was clear that De Wet was to attempt a serious invasion of Cape Colony, Lord Kitchener, about the end of January 1901, railed Plumer's troops from Brugspruit in the Eastern Transvaal to Cape Colony; and it was largely

---

[1] Awarded D.S.O.   [2] Awarded D.C.M.

due to them that De Wet was driven out of the Colony (see 4th Victorian Contingent). Both the South and West Australians suffered some casualties in the numerous rear-guard actions which the Boer commandos fought. After pursuing the remnant of these commandos northward, Plumer's men were again entrained at Brandfort for the district north of Pretoria, to take part in the expedition to Pietersburg. In Lord Kitchener's despatch of 8th May 1901 he says: "On the night of the 24th April a very gallant act was performed by Lt. Reid, Imperial Bushmen Corps, who had been detached from General Plumer's post at Commissie Drift, on the Olifants River, Transvaal. This officer, when in charge of a patrol of 20 Australians, located a Boer laager some 15 miles S.E. of the drift, which he surrounded, and boldly attacked at dawn. The enemy at once surrendered, Commandant Schroeder and 41 other prisoners, with a maxim, being taken." This is certainly one of the very finest exploits undertaken by any small body during the whole war, and shows a boldness and initiative that was far too often absent from the doings of the regulars. Lieutenant Reid ran the great risk involved in his action, but his fearlessness was rewarded with success; and further, he was serving under a General who was most quick to recognise pluck, skilfulness, and the all-important quality of willingness to take risk. Lieutenant Reid belonged to the South Australian Contingent.

On the Pietersburg trek, and after the occupation of that place, the 4th Imperial Bushmen contributed largely to the success of Major Vialls, who operated generally in advance of General Plumer's force, and took many prisoners and waggons, and one gun.

Some of the 4th Imperial Bushmen were in the escort to a convoy which "was heavily attacked by some 400 of the enemy on the Bethel Standerton Road on 25th May." The escort under Colonel Gallwey "fought with great gallantry, and completely foiled the enemy's repeated efforts to press into close quarters." — Lord Kitchener's Despatch of 8th July 1900, para. 8.

The following Mentions were gained under the heading 4th Imperial Bushmen :—

8th May 1901.—Lieut. H. A. Reid, for the exceedingly smart manner in which he effected the capture of a force double his number, together with a maxim gun. Sgt. F. J. Williams and Pte. T. H. Porter (promoted Cpl.) volunteered to carry despatches from General Plumer to General Beatson, a distance of 60 miles through enemy's country; they got there and returned safely, though fired on, burning a Boer field forge en route.

8th July 1901.—Tpr. G. De Rehyr, during attack on convoy near Bethel, May 25, carried a man out of action on his own horse, thereby incurring great risk. Sgt.-Major J. S. Brigman, Sgt. B. C. Philliphant, gallantry same occasion.

DOYLE'S SCOUTS.

THIS was a corps of specially selected men, raised by Captain R. D. Doyle, D.S.O., of the New South Wales forces. He had served in the 6th Imperial Bushmen and the 3rd Regiment of New South Wales Bushmen. The officers and men were not, however, restricted to those from New South Wales. The small corps did most excellent work in the latter stages of the war, and for its numbers gained a large proportion of Mentions. These were :—

LORD KITCHENER'S DESPATCH : 23*rd June* 1902. — Capt. R. D. Doyle, D.S.O.; Lts. W. V. Townley, D. D. Byrne ; Sgt.-Major Lambert ; Qrmr.-Sgt. Travers ; Sgt. A. A. Harris, Cpl. Waltisbuhl ; Tpr. Rush.

COMMONWEALTH TROOPS.

IN December 1901 it was arranged that Federated Australia would send more men to South Africa, and on the 30th Mr Barton announced that the 1st Federal Contingent would consist of nine units, contributed as follows: New South Wales and Victoria three each, Queensland one, West Australia one, South Australia and Tasmania each one-half. But these arrangements were somewhat altered.

According to the evidence given before the War Commission and the statements in the appendices, New South Wales furnished three battalions of Commonwealth Horse, there called the 1st, 2nd, and 5th Battalions, amounting altogether to 1169 officers and men, with 1300 horses.

The first lot of Commonwealth troops sailed in the latter half of February 1902. Their war service was thus short, and they had few opportunities of acquiring distinction, but they took part in the last great drives in the Western Transvaal under General Ian Hamilton, and their good work was specially referred to by Lord Kitchener in his despatch of 1st June 1902 (see 8th New Zealand Contingent).

The second lot of Commonwealth troops sailed from the various Australian ports between 1st and 10th April 1902, and on the 5th of that month it was announced that Australia would furnish a further contribution of 2000 men, being four regiments of 500 each. These were at once recruited, and sailed about the middle of May, but peace was declared before they arrived in South Africa. Some notes as to the contributions from the respective Colonies have been already given.

INTELLIGENCE DEPARTMENT.

THE value of local guides and of information provided by those who had local knowledge was emphasised in many of the despatches; and under the Natal Volunteers and Guides many names are given of officers, men, and civilians who risked much for the good of the army in Natal. Many names are also given under the various corps of "Scouts" of those who obtained Mention by Lord Roberts and Lord Kitchener. In addition to these, the following were commended under the headings given below:—

LORD ROBERTS' DESPATCHES: 31*st March* 1900.—Civil Guide: Mr Hogg.
2*nd April* 1901.—Corps of Guides: Lieut. H. F. C. Ross[1]; Tpr. Newton.[2]
8*th March* 1901.—Mr Carlyle (Carlisle), Intelligence Department.
8*th May* 1901.—Mr Carlisle assisted Major Browne to get six armed Boers out of a dark cave, 23rd April, near Krugersdorp.
8*th December* 1901.—Tprs. E. Maasdorp and R. Currie and Sgt. G. Brotherton assisting to capture Commandant Erasmus.

LORD KITCHENER'S DESPATCH: 23*rd June* 1902.—Intelligence Department: Capts. F. Smithermann, D.S.O.; A. N. Hughes,[1] J. Quayle-Dickson,[1] W. Beddy; Lts. C. R. De la Porte, G. S. Doyle; Messrs R. Haigh, F. Webber, E. Mooney. Field Intelligence Department (Guides): W. Hanger,[2] W. C. Carlisle,[2] A. J. Hunter,[2] J. C. Paton,[2] J. W. S. Dimock,[2] H. Loxton,[2] E. E. Schweizer,[2] J. Duke,[2] E. Thornhill,[2] W. H. Howard,[2] J. Agnew, W. Forbes, R. L. Estmont, J. J. Williams, G. L. Langridge, G. A. Cooper, C. S. Ladsberg, M. Bergh, R. Whipp, P. M'Master. Capt. D. Forbes, Field Intelligence, was awarded D.S.O.

---

[1] Awarded D.S.O.   [2] Awarded D.C.M.

INDEX.

Adelaide District Troops, 240.
Alleman's Nek, 56.
Artillery—
    Australian, 405.
    Canadian, 323.
    Cape Garrison, 134.
    Natal, 26.
    New South Wales, 405.
    New Zealand, 368.
    Prince Alfred's Cape, 139.
Ashburner's Light Horse, 224.
Australian Artillery, 405.
Australian Bushmen. See various Colonies.
Australian Horse, 378.

Bakenlaagte, 289.
Barberton, 15.
Barkly West Guard, 242.
Beaconsfield Town Guard, 186.
Bechuanaland Protectorate Regiment, 209.
Bechuanaland Rifle Volunteers, 217.
Beddy's Scouts, 281.
Bedford Troops, 240.
Bethune's Mounted Infantry, 62.
Border Horse, 122.
Border Mounted Rifles, 26.
Border Scouts, 245.
Boschbult, 158.
Botha's Pass, 56.
Bothaville, 387.
Brabant's Horse, 116.
British South Africa Police, 219.
Buffs, The (2nd Battalion), 293.
Bushmanland Borderers, 254.
Bushmen. Under various Australian Colonies.

Bush Veldt Carbineers, 280.

Canadian Artillery, 323.
Canadian Contingents, 298.
Canadian Dragoons, 306.
Canadian 1st Bn. Mounted Rifles, 306.
Canadian 2nd Bn. Mounted Rifles, 306.
Canadian 2nd Regiment Mounted Rifles, 320.
Canadian Royal Regiment of Infantry, 298.
Canadian Scouts, 315.
Canadian Later Contingents, 322.
Cape Colony Cyclists, 238.
Cape Garrison Artillery, 134.
Cape Medical Staff Corps, 138.
Cape Mounted Rifles, 100.
Cape Police, 89.
Cape Town Highlanders, 131.
Ceylon Mounted Infantry, 335.
City of Grahamston Volunteers, 143.
Colenso, 10, 33, 38, 50, 53, 86.
Colesberg, 414.
Colonial Defence Force, 240.
Colonial Light Horse, 237.
Colonial Scouts, 45.
Commander-in-Chief's Bodyguard, 225.
Commonwealth Troops, 493.
Cullinan's Horse, 224.

Damant's Horse, 150.
Dennison's Scouts, 222.
Diamond Fields Artillery, 186.
Diamond Fields Horse, 186.

Index

Diamond Hill, 376, 386.
District Mounted Rifles, 236.
Dordrecht, 102.
Doyle's Scouts, 492.
Driscoll's Scouts, 127.
Duke of Edinburgh's Own Volunteers, 135.
Durban Light Infantry, 26.

East Griqualand Volunteers, 240.
Eastern Province Horse, 178.
Elandslaagte, 3, 30.
Eland's River, 203.

Fraserburg District Troops, 242.
Frederickstad, 15.
French's Scouts, 183.
Frontier Light Horse, 236.
Frontier Mounted Rifles, 126.

Hartebeestfontein, 425.
Hart's Hill, 87.
Heidelberg Volunteers, 279.
Houtnek, 170.

Imperial Bushmen, 4th, 490.
Imperial Bushmen, 6th, 395. See also under Australian Colonies.
Imperial Light Horse, 1.
Imperial Light Infantry, 83.
India. See Lumsden's Horse, 332.
Intelligence Department, 494.

Jansenville District Troops, 241.
Johannesburg Mounted Rifles, 267.
Johannesburg Police, 270.

Kaffrarian Rifles, 112.
Karee Siding, 170.
Kimberley, Defence of, 186.
Kimberley Troops — Light Horse, Mounted Corps, Regiment, Town Guard, 186.
Kitchener's Fighting Scouts, 255.
Kitchener's Horse, 168.
Knysna Rangers, 240.
Koffyfontein Defence Force, 241.
Koffyfontein, Defence of, 196.
Koster's River, 392.
Kuruman, Defence of, 93.

Ladysmith, Defence of, 6, 32.
Langverwacht, 364.
Lindley, 457.

Loch's Horse, 184.
Lombard's Kop, 6, 32.
Lumsden's Horse, 332.
Lydenburg, 57.

Mafeking, Defence of, 209.
Mafeking, Relief of, 11, 200.
Marshall's Horse, 143.
Menne's Scouts, 277.
Midland Mounted Rifles, 235.
Moedwill, 285.
Montmorency's Scouts, 124.
Morley's Scouts, 277.
Murray's Horse, 45.

Namaqualand Border Scouts, 253.
Natal, Border Mounted Rifles, Bridge Guards, Carbineers, Medical Corps, Mounted Rifles, Police and Guides, Naval Volunteers, Royal Rifles, Umvoti Mounted Rifles, and Veterinary Corps, 26.
Natal Colonial Scouts, 45.
Natal Composite Regiment, 43.
Nesbitt's Horse, 175.
New England Mounted Rifles, 240.
New South Wales Artillery, 405.
New South Wales 1st Australian Horse, 378.
New South Wales 1st Bushmen, 390.
New South Wales 3rd Bushmen, 398.
New South Wales 6th Imperial Bushmen, 395.
New South Wales Lancers, 372.
New South Wales Medical Staff Corps, 407.
New South Wales 1st Mounted Rifles and Mounted Infantry, 382.
New South Wales 2nd Mounted Rifles, 398.
New South Wales 3rd Mounted Rifles, 401. See also Commonwealth Troops.
New Zealand Artillery, 368.
New Zealand 1st, 2nd, and 3rd Contingents, 337.
New Zealand 4th and 5th Contingents, 353.
New Zealand 6th Contingent, 357.
New Zealand 7th Contingent, 361.
New Zealand 8th, 9th, and 10th Contingents, 366.
Nooitgedacht, 173.

Index

Onverwachte, 360, 447.
Orpen's Horse, 242.

Paardeberg, 162, 300, 384.
Pietersburg Light Horse, 281.
Piquetberg District Troops, 241.
Prince Albert District Troops, 242.
Prince Alfred's Own Cape Artillery, 139.
Prince Alfred's Volunteer Guard, 139.
Prince of Wales's Light Horse, 233.

Queensland 1st and 2nd Contingents, 435.
Queensland 3rd Contingent, 441.
Queensland 4th Contingent, 443.
Queensland 5th Contingent, 446.
Queensland 6th Contingent, 447.
Queensland 7th and 8th Contingents (Commonwealth Troops), 448.
Queenstown Rifle Volunteers, 148.

Railway Pioneer Regiment, 226.
Rand Rifles, 270.
Rhenoster Kop, 349.
Rhodesian Regiment and Volunteers, 200.
Rietfontein, 5, 31.
Rimington's Guides, 150.
Roberts' Horse, 160.
Rooiral, 22, 287.

Sannah's Post, 163.
Scottish Horse, 282.
Scott's Railway Guards, 232.
South African Light Horse, 50.
South African Irregular Forces, 240.
South Australia 1st and 2nd Contingents, 451.
South Australia 3rd Contingent, 454.
South Australia 4th Contingent, 456.
South Australia 5th and 6th Contingents, 461.
South Australia 7th, 8th, and 9th Contingents (Commonwealth Troops), 463.
Spion Kop, 69, 83.
Steinaecker's Horse, 271.
Stormberg, 101.
Strathcona's Corps, 328.

Sutherland District Troops, 241.

Tafelkop, 156.
Talana Hill, 29.
Tarkastad Troops, 240.
Tasmania 1st and 2nd Contingents, 480.
Tasmania 1st Bushmen, 484.
Tasmania 4th Contingent, or 1st Imperial Bushmen, 485.
Tasmania 5th Contingent, or 2nd Imperial Bushmen, 487.
Tasmania 6th, 7th, and 8th Contingents (Commonwealth Troops), 488.
Tembuland Volunteers, 240.
Thorneycroft's Mounted Infantry, 68.
Transkei Territories Troops, 240.

Uitenhage Volunteer Rifles, 143.
Umvoti Mounted Rifles, 26.

Victoria 1st and 2nd Contingents, 413.
Victoria 3rd Contingent (Bushmen), 422.
Victoria 4th Contingent (Imperial Bushmen), 424.
Victoria 5th Contingent (Mounted Rifles), 429.
Victoria 6th, 7th, and 8th Contingents (Commonwealth Troops), 432.
Vlakfontein, 284.

Wagon Hill, 7, 35.
Warren's Mounted Infantry, 238.
Warren's Scouts, 136.
Warrington Town Guard, 240.
Warwick's Scouts, 182.
Wepener, 103.
West Australia 1st and 2nd Contingents, 465.
West Australia 3rd Contingent (Bushmen), 473.
West Australia 4th Contingent (Imperial Bushmen), 475.
West Australia 5th and 6th Contingents (Imperial Bushmen), 475. See also Commonwealth Troops.
Western Province Mounted Rifles, 252.
Willow Grange, 10, 39.
Willowmore Guard, 242.